The Complete Kitten
and Cat Book

The Complete Kitten and Cat Book

NORMAN H. JOHNSON, D.V.M.,
with SAUL GALIN

ROBERT HALE · LONDON

ISBN 0 7091 8357 7

Robert Hale Limited
Clerkenwell House
Clerkenwell Green
London, EC1R 0HT

Photoset by
Kelly Typesetting Limited
Bradford-on-Avon, Wiltshire
and printed in Great Britain by
Lowe & Brydone Ltd.,
Thetford, Norfolk

To cat-owners

AUTHORS' NOTE

We are indebted to the research of C. A. W. Guggisberg.

Contents

Illustrations

11

Birman
Two typical house cats
Bobcat, kittens
Bobcat, adult
Leopard (Afghanistan)
African lioness and cubs
Siberian tiger
Leopard cat
Puma or cougar or mountain lion, juvenile, with baby spots
Clouded leopard
Jaguar
Palestine jungle cat
Serval
Snow leopard
Cheetah
Burmese or Siamese jungle cat
Marbled cat
Black leopard (panther)
Flat-headed cat
Steppe cat, kitten
Caracal
Ocelot

ONE

You and Your Cat

You have just acquired a cat, or you plan to acquire one. Perhaps a friend or neighbour has an extra kitten (or cat) and you have decided to take it, or you have chosen to buy one from a store or breeder. If you buy one, chances are you will make a more considered choice. In any event, you should think about several factors.

Many of us, at one time or another, have lived with a cat, and we know what to expect. We recognize that a cat may be loving and affectionate as well as independent, that it may be companionable and playful as well as withdrawn. Cats as individuals and as breeds differ from one another. We tend to speak in generalities, and we say that dogs are companions, whereas cats provide a different kind of experience. But such generalities lose sight of one important fact: your own cat. It is an individual. It has had a unique experience as a kitten, and each cat reacts to the household in which it grows up and lives.

If your cat is an individual, then, what can you expect of it? A lot, of course, depends on what you are looking for. Have you defined your needs? Do you want a female for breeding-purposes? Do you even want a pedigree cat, or do you simply want a *cat*—a regular domestic house cat? Do you want a male? If so, do you know that about ninety-five per cent of them have to be neutered when they reach sexual maturity? Are you looking for companionship? Or do you really only want something vital and vibrant around your house or flat?

Before we go into some of these questions, let me say first that a cat living in your house should make a difference to you. Even the most independent of cats will make demands on you. And if you feel you do not want to be bothered, then a cat is not for you. Just as people, emotionally and psychologically, need the presence of a cat, so does the cat—maybe only intermittently—need the reciprocal presence of the owner. Cats need and require love, although perhaps not so continuously as do dogs. Also, they require thought and some care—food, water, change of litter and grooming (coat and claws). They are, as you may already know, very easy to take care of. They can become accustomed to their litter box as early as three weeks. They will continue to eat for the rest of their lives any diet they accept as kittens. And they never have to be walked outside, unless you choose to do so.

But a cat can be very unhappy in your house if you make a poor decision as to breed (or regular house cat) or sex or even age. Many people receive a kitten from a friend whose queen (the mother) has produced a half dozen fluffy balls. Yet once the pleasure of the kitten has worn off—and it might in only a few days or weeks, the new owner tires of his or her pet. The next stage is neglect. Such a kitten and cat will eventually sense it is unwanted, and its behaviour will reflect that feeling. Or else you wanted a male, and then felt uneasy with the male's aggressiveness, or else you were not sure you wanted to have your pet neutered. When the problems surrounding a pet become greater than the pleasure and reassurance you should feel from having the animal, then something has gone wrong.

There should be a circuit of pleasure between you and your pet. Each should suit the other. Are you a member of a family some of whose members dislike or feel uneasy about cats? That will make a difference if you decide on your own to acquire a cat and bring it into the house. Many people are simply afraid of cats. At many times in history cats have been considered emissaries from Satan, and the association of the cat with satanic forces remains with many people—a superstition, of course, but very real to the person who has the fear. A cat brought into such a hostile household will react and become emotionally twisted or undependable. It is not so independent that it can exist without some sense of acceptance. What this means is that the relationship between the owner and his or her cat is deep rather than superficial.

Whereas a healthy dog is an accepting and trusting animal, setting the relationship at an open level, the cat requires a different kind of expectation. You may feel friendly and warm, but your cat may withdraw. Its moods are unpredictable, and its temperament seems based on a mysterious core. That mystery is the element that drew you to the cat in the first place. Do not be surprised or disappointed if the cat displays an independent or impersonal nature—it moves to a different beat. The house cat, incidentally, can show the same temperament as the pedigree cats—they are all cats when it comes to temperament. They simply differ from one another as individuals, and some breeds tend to be developed for different reasons.

You definitely want a cat that is compatible with your style of life and your way of running your household. If your cat is basically healthy, you can count on perhaps fifteen years of life together, even longer. I find that one of the primary considerations is hair length: whether to own a short-hair or a long-hair. The long-coated cat will leave a lot of hair around a house, and for the fastidious housekeeper this could prove a vexing problem. Also, the long-hair needs somewhat more attention, since its coat must be brushed regularly so that the cat does not swallow too much hair while grooming itself. While a short-hair should be groomed, it tends more to take care of itself, since the demands of the coat are less.

If you have decided to buy a cat and are inclined toward a definite breed, then you have fifty or more to select from, with many colour varieties, as well as choice of hair length. If you acquire a house cat, the chances are it will be variations of grey and its coat will be on the shorter side. Most cats are house cats, not particular breeds. If a friend gives you a kitten or kittens, then your choice is made for you when you decide to accept the gift. Another consideration is the question of allergy, which afflicts some people when any kind of pet is brought into the house but is particularly intensified when a long-hair is introduced. A member of the family may be far less allergic to a short-hair.

In the event you need rodent control, nearly any cat will do, although I find that a regular house cat is most suitable.

Disposition is a real consideration in your plan to obtain a cat. The ordinary house cat has a fine temperament and you need look no further. But I also recommend that you read over the chapter on breeds toward the end of this book. There I list all the major breeds and their variations in the United States and Britain. They are divided into long-hairs, short-hairs and foreign types, so that once you have decided on coat-length you can seek out the kind of temperament (or colour) you want. Remember that each cat is an individual, but certain breeds are more playful, more companionable or more regal than others. Do you want playfulness? Companionship? Or do you prefer a cat that is very much its own self, independent, impersonal, impregnable? Or are you seeking a particular coat or eye colour or combination of elements?

For example, among long-hairs the Blue Persian makes a fine family pet, as do the Bicoloured (few extremes of temperament), the Birman, the Blue Cream (noted for its affectionate nature), the Colourpoint, or Himalayan (very attached), the Tabby (noted for its love of play and attention) and the Turkish. Among short-hairs, the following are fine within a family situation: the Bicoloured (affectionate), the British Blue, the Cream, the Siamese, the Tabby (Brown, Red and Silver varieties) and the Tortoise-shell. Among the so-called foreign breeds, the following: the Abyssinian, the Foreign Short-hair, the Havana (which enjoys attention and play), the Manx (if you want a tailless cat, a good conversation-piece) and the Rex (the Cornish and, especially, the Devon).

None of this is meant to suggest that the breeds I have omitted do not make good family pets. Most of them do, but certain breeds seem to mix better with the household than others. If you want greater independence, opt for the Siamese, the Russian Blue and the Korat among the short-hairs. If you would like a cat with one blue eye and one orange, then try the White (Long- or Short-hair); if you like orange eyes against a black coat, try the Black (Long- or Short-hair). You can also find blue eyes against a white coat; and, with the Siamese, blue eyes against a whole variety of coats.

If, however, you acquire a house cat, you have no opportunity to choose these traits. The cat is a haphazard arrangement of colours, of this and that, although in temperament and loyalty it may be everything that you want.

As I mention throughout this book, the choice between male and female involves some forethought. If you want to have a male, in nearly all instances you will need to have the cat neutered to avoid the urine odour. A mature male sprays, and the odour is very unpleasant. Unless you have separate living-quarters for the male—and plenty of distance between you and your neighbours because of the screeching, you will not be able to stand the male's crying out and spraying. If you have a female, the sexual need is periodical, but even here, unless you choose to breed from her, you may want to have her neutered. With the female, you have some choice—you can live with her unspayed.

WHERE TO GET A CAT AND WHAT TO LOOK FOR

If someone gives you a cat, then you have solved the problem of acquisition. Many cats change ownership that way, especially when kittens are born to a neighbour's or relative's cat. If you want to obtain a cat on your own, however, you should steer clear of bargain-basement stores. *Or else you should be very careful.* If you want a pedigree cat, then I highly recommend that you look in *Fur and Feather*, a periodical which publishes advertisements for all varieties of kittens, or else in your local paper (or the *Sunday Times*). You might even be on the lookout for cat shows in your area and inquire from breeders there, if you see what you want.

If you do buy at a store or a pet-shop, then check out a few items. See if the kitten has been inoculated against feline enteritis (panleukopenia), perhaps ask for a diet chart and, if the cat is a distinct breed, be certain to get its pedigree-papers. In selecting a kitten or larger cat, choose a healthy-looking one. Do not become carried away by a sad, withdrawn kitten—it may look beguiling, but it may also be sickly. Make sure the eyes are bright; they should have a keen lustre to them, an alert look. The coat should be vibrant, springy to the touch and free of all external parasites or scrubby areas. Check for bald areas. The ears should be clean and springy. Check out the stomach area to make sure there is no swelling; a swollen belly can mean worms or poor diet. Look under the tail to make certain everything is normal—no worms, diarrhoea or protuberances. The body should be well fleshed, especially around the ribs.

The best age at which to acquire a kitten is after it has been weaned and fully housebroken—at about twelve weeks. If it is too young and the mother is missing, you will have to feed it with an eyedropper or bottle. Kittens are easy to housetrain—many do it by themselves, but it is still easier if the job has already been done. After all, you are paying. At twelve weeks the average kitten will be not at all difficult to handle. Be sure to carry it home in a cat-basket. The first few hours are trying for the kitten, and a closed basket or cat-box will help ensure a safe and more pleasant journey. Once you are home, you can check what to do by consulting the appropriate pages in Chapter 2 of this book. I discuss the kitten at every stage until adulthood.

Some of the following may seem obvious to you, but many potential owners forget essential items. I will make a list of points, and you might read (or glance) through them.

1. Buy only in a place that is scrupulously sanitary. There should be a

fresh odour, clean water, sufficient space for the pets to move around in and a general sense of caring.

2. Decide ahead of time what sex you want.

3. Decide whether you want a house cat or a pedigree, a long-hair or a short-hair.

4. Make certain that you acquire a healthy kitten. Check eyes, ears, coat, belly, tail area, general look.

5. Check for external parasites—fleas, ticks, mange (red or bald spots).

6. Check for sight—with light, to see if the cat blinks; for hearing—with a bell or some other sudden noise.

7. If you buy an older kitten, check its inoculation record.

8. If someone is giving a kitten or cat away, avoid a sick or stunted one. Do not choose it simply because it looks shy and appealing. You may justly feel charitable, but you may have to get rid of the cat later.

9. Do you have a dog that cannot possibly accept a cat? Dogs and cats can mix well, but some dogs are so temperamental that they will not accept a cat. An older dog may be so set and jealous that it will resent any intrusion.

10. If you have a baby, it and the cat should become pals. (If you have a tiny infant, be certain the cat does not lie on top of it at night.)

11. If you buy a pure-bred cat, check its proof of pedigree.

12. If you accept a kitten or cat, or buy one, find out about its diet and feeding-schedule. You may vary such matters, of course, but do it gradually. A cat grows best and thrives on a routine.

13. **Important:** Although you probably will not do this, it is an excellent idea to have a veterinary surgeon check out any cat you acquire.

What equipment will you need? I assume the kitten has been weaned and is on its way to adulthood. For the very young or newborn kitten, turn to the chapter on the kitten, Chapter 2.

It is good to have a carrying-box from the beginning. If you do not already own one when you pick up the cat for the first time, then buy one soon after. At the start, you might carry a heavy towel, in the event the cat is frightened by its new situation and starts to claw or bite.

For the home, you will need a litter box and litter. Unless the cat is permitted to sleep anywhere in the house, you should also provide a bed. A box or carton filled with newspaper and an old blanket will do. It should be situated outside of draughts. All of this is replaceable material if the cat wets or dirties it.

As for the rest:

nail-clippers—your own are sufficient

a comb—open-toothed so you can get at matted hair—and *a brush*

a collar—with identification tag—if needed

a water-dish and *a food-dish*—two separate dishes

a scratching-post—to protect your furniture and woodwork from the growing kitten's claws

Add these items to the litter box, a sleeping-place, and a carrying-box or basket, and you are outfitted for the life of your cat. One trip to the pet-shop is all it should take.

Get to know your nearest veterinary surgeon. If a friend recommends one, so much the better.

THE DEEPER RELATIONSHIP

Since the first domesticated cat came into existence perhaps 5,500 years ago, in Egypt, its relationship to people has been magical. One of the most attractive elements of the cat is its sheer irrationality, its unpredictability, its temperament, which remain beyond analysis. Why do we, as owners, feel so drawn to an animal that defies logic and that remains unfathomable even after thousands of years of living with us?

I think a good part of the attraction people feel for a cat is based on the appeal of opposites. People think of themselves as sane, rational, logical, as belonging to the world of daylight and consciousness. They believe they see things as they really exist. They feel lucid, understanding, controlling their universe rather than being controlled by it. Since the Old Testament gave man dominion over animals, he likes to think he sets the rules. Man, in this respect, is persuaded that non-human things understand who is boss and, in most instances, are prepared to obey him. It does not matter that most of this reasoning is not supported by nature's plan for all living things; man insists on accepting himself as the master. Part of the attraction of the cat is that it upsets this sense of order, that it presents another kind of existence, suggesting mystery, myth, blackness, even unconsciousness.

Ownership of a dog is very different—a completely distinct experience from that of owning a cat. The dog agrees with man's sense of things. It will fit itself into whatever is required, and unless it is deranged, it will accept nearly anything that man dishes out—whether persecution or benevolence. The owner is the final authority. The dog will follow rules, it will be trained, it will obey, it will play games, and it will show affection for anyone the owner adds to his or her household. The dog is very comfortable with all this. It does not have to stretch itself to find comfort under the authority of the owner, even when the latter is harsh. A dog will remain loyal to the craziest of households, and it will usually be stable.

The cat, of course, provides another kind of experience. No question that it gives owners considerable happiness and satisfaction, because far more cats than dogs exist in the United States. Since cats do not require a licence, we cannot be certain how many there are, but from my thirty-five years of experience as vet I would estimate that cats in American homes outnumber dogs by almost two to one. And yet, with all my experience with cats, I find one irreducible fact: they are a mystery. And that mystery is what constitutes their attraction. Everything about them is mysterious: their history is obscure, their motives are uncertain, their will is unpredictable; they seem self-sufficient in a world where nearly everything else is dependent. The cat is aloof, silent, enigmatic, loving one moment and indifferent the next, coquettish, then fiery. It will appear to lack all energy and then show tremendous spurts of energy by speeding around a room and leaping on walls. From being open and friendly, it may pass into a non-committal or passive phase that lasts hours or days.

The cat may also be destructive—of curtains, furniture and even the owner's arms and legs. I have seen owners with lacerations on their limbs and even on their face from cats that are excitable and independent. The mystique of owning a cat runs deep. It is as fierce as some people's dislike of cats, what is referred to as ailurophobia (ailurophilia, love of cats, is the opposite). Such dislike or hatred runs deeper than, say, the fear that people have of a dog. Fear of dogs is almost always physical. A person may have been bitten as a child or may associate the dog with some other bad experience. People who hate cats react differently; their emotional reaction is well beyond physical fear, since the cat is small and rarely bites or claws strangers.

The fear is often in normal, outgoing people—and what they react to is the significance of the cat at a profound level. Their response is connected to the mythology of the cat, its function in history as something divine (a goddess for the ancient Egyptians), demonic (a devil for medieval Europe) or a saviour (for those who found the cat a destroyer of the rats that carried the plague). The cat is deeply involved with history, and at various times it has been either revered or reviled. Part of the reaction experienced by those who reject cats—as by those who love them—is attached to the deep way in which the animal has become part of our subconscious.

Both the fear and the deep attachment lie well beneath rationality. But just what is the cat? As one writer puts it, "It is loving and ferocious. It is a tender and loving parent but an implacable enemy. It is usually hardy, but fastidious about its comforts. It loves routine but will suddenly and completely change its habits. It is cautious and courageous, indolent and athletic." It may appear to lack direction, and then it will demonstrate tremendous concentration and patience while hunting. It is essentially a carnivore, but it has a wide-ranging taste for vegetables. No one knows how it acquired its taste for fish and milk. It can be an exhibitionist one moment and then demand privacy the next. It may depend on human beings for a time and then seek the wild. It appears highly intelligent but also very obstinate. In many ways, the cat remains the animal of the jungle and the wilds. As we shall see later, when I describe the wild cats, the domestic cat has evolved only in some ways, not in others. It is a jungle cat still in many of its routines, although it has become domesticated in others.

Many of these formulations, however, are too neat. Actually, the cat fits into all and into none. The cat, we can say, is a survivor, and its manner of adapting in order to survive helps to constitute its behaviour. It has learned to use its tight, compact form, its speed, its caution and patience, its courage, as ways of surviving, whether in the home or in the alley. It is as though the cat did not need people—and we know that it can live on its own ingeniously, staying alive for weeks by licking grease and drinking drain-water. Cats grow up cautious, courageous and independent. They are, of course, capable of showing love and affection, but this is not their primary drive.

Survival, on their terms, is. Although we can probably say that about all domestic animals—for example, the dog learned to survive by attaching itself to man and by showing love and affection, the cat's kind of survival-instinct is different. Its attraction for an owner is perhaps the very fact that it has found a way to come to terms with dependency, that it has made man accept it on *its* terms. That balance of charm and indifference defines its style, its manner of negotiating between jungle and domesticity.

It is almost impossible for owners to impose themselves on a cat or to show it who is master or mistress. It simply does not fit into that type of game. It may clown and play, but it usually dislikes public performances—and when it feels like stopping, nothing can make it continue. Cats insist on their privacy. Most cats are individualists, although they differ enormously as individuals. Some will adapt to the owners' whims and ingratiate themselves; some breeds more than others are like this (as you can see in the chapter on breeds). But do not expect it.

The vast majority are more like the cat in Rudyard Kipling's 'The Cat That Walked by Himself', in the *Just So Stories*. In this tale, our ancient mothers and fathers came to an understanding with the dog, the horse and the cow. The woman tricks them into becoming servants and doing what they are ordered to do. But the clever cat tricks the woman into giving it a place by the fire and a drink of warm milk. It will do what it feels has to be done but always reminds the woman that "Still I am the Cat that walks by himself." At the end of the story Kipling tells us that the cat is needed in the house, "but between times, and when the moon gets up and night comes, he is the cat that walks by himself and all places are alike to him".

Working for several decades with cats and their owners has taught me something about the connection between the two. People who need the approval of others to complete their own lives will generally not get along too well with cats. People who see themselves as aggressive, dominating, strong-willed, firm in their opinions and used to obedience and submission in others may not get along with cats. And people who fear that silence is a weapon against them and expect a band or cheerleader to greet them at the door when they arrive home will never get along with cats.

Who, then, is best suited? Those who can stand silence and some uncertainty and do not need regular doses of attention and affection would seem right. This covers a great many people: those who are happy in the presence of something domestic that is not completely tamed or understood. Such people can treat the cat as it should be treated, can let it be what it is, because it will be that anyway.

For all owners, however, the cat has meanings beyond the physical fact. It helps reduce selfishness and narcissism, for it is something to care for. It becomes an easy companion for the sick and the elderly. For the emotionally or psychologically disturbed, it is a connection with the living world. For the owner who seeks status, a rare breed is a conversation-piece. The cat can, for all, relieve loneliness and provide an anchor in the world outside oneself. For children, it is a ready friend and companion.

Montaigne, the French Renaissance philosopher and essayist, said about his cat, "I don't know if she is playing with me or I am playing with her." He accepted it at that. Perhaps he was playing with the distinction between a domesticated animal and a household pet. 'A domesticated animal' describes the dog—it becomes part of the domestic scene. On the other hand, a household pet is an animal, which may or may not be domesticated, taken into the household. The cat fits into this category. It moves in and out of domestication. The house cat reminds us that it is only one of thirty-eight species of the family *Felidae*, all of them mammals and carnivores. It has the characteristics of this family; in fact the poet Coleridge once commented that, while caressing his gentle cat, he felt "closest to the tiger". Behind every house cat stands that large family of jungle and wilderness cats, some of whom are fifty times the weight of the house cat. This fact attracts us. We like to think that, when we see our pet move lithely and stealthily, it is moving and sensing the world as do those dozens of cat varieties in the wild.

SOME HISTORY AND MYTHOLOGY

The distant ancestor of the cat appears to have been a weasel type of animal called miacis, a carnivore. This same miacis appears to be the ancestor of the dog, civet, raccoon, hyena and others. The cat very possibly comes down to us by way of some mating between the miacis and the civet, as long ago as 40 million years into prehistory. The intermediate stages between miacis and the cat as we know it were numerous, of course, involving millions of years and hundreds of evolutionary changes. Just how this took place remains a mystery, although it is thought that the domestic cat evolved from three intermediate types: the Kaffir, or African cat (*Felis lybica*), the related African wildcat (*Felis ocreata*) and the European wildcat (*Felis sylvestris*).

The entire structure of the cat, wild or domestic, has remained true to the type: designed for hunting and killing. The cat is a specialized creature, adapted for stalking prey and the eating of meat. The teeth of the wild cats enabled them to survive in the wilderness or jungle, giving them the opportunity to stab and cut. Their method is stealth, and their speed is great for short spurts, not for distances. Their ability to bound is connected to this—they must catch their prey after a short run and then leap on it. Their claws are designed for catching and holding, and their neck is heavy and muscular to take up the shock of contact. The canine teeth stab, and the other teeth serve as shears. The rest of the teeth are almost useless, like our wisdom-teeth. Although cats have the reputation of great climbers, the big cats (except for the leopard) hunted on the ground not in trees. From this, we can see how the cat—wild and domestic—has remained true to type.

Our information is incomplete, of course, but the cat—perhaps all thirty-seven varieties of the wild cat—developed in the period before man made his appearance. (I take up the various types of wild cat in a separate section, Chapter 9.) Cats appear in nearly every part of the world, whether as the great cats, the smaller wild cat or the domestic cat. Perhaps only Australia and a few other remote places were exempt from the cat migration, until house cats were brought there as pets.

The background of the house cat is intermixed with legend. One thing is clear, however: as soon as the cat became domesticated, it also became part of mythology. That is, it came to represent aspects of life that the Egyptians placed in their gods and heroic figures. The earliest period for the house cat is between 3500 and 3000 BC—about five thousand years ago—when it entered Egyptian homes and began to be deified. A portrait of Bastet, the feline goddess, can be dated from about 3000 BC.

Although the cat eventually came to be called Bastet, goddess of fertility, it went through many previous stages of worship. The Egyptian word for cat is 'mau', which in English means 'to see'. Very probably, the mythological aspect of the cat was connected to its ability to see in the dark, especially since the Egyptians feared the night and had built up many of their legends about blackness. The cat's capability in the dark, so that day and night were indistinguishable, impressed the Egyptians, who connected this ability with wonder, magic, myth. The cat would eventually be associated with the sun, as well as the moon. Even the eyes of the cat, with their widening and narrowing according to the amount of light, accommodated the legend.

This idea of the cat's connection to light and dark at first made it fit as a kind of moon-goddess, the protectress of the Egyptian during the night. Also, the cat was seen as a force associated with crops and tides, and thus with fertility itself; although not until around 1000 BC was this aspect really stressed. This association with fertility was gradual, and it connected the cat to Isis, goddess of fertility and wife of Osiris (called Ra by the Egyptians), the sun-god. According to some legends, the cat was the female offspring of a union of Isis and Osiris and was called Bastet. Through this union, Bastet (also known as Bast or Pasht) blended nearly all the important functions of the life-cycle: both fertility and virginity, love, maternity, control of the sun and the moon, restoration of the ill and protection of the dying and dead. We can see that the cat served a divine function in virtually every aspect of Egyptian life.

Of course, none of this could be maintained forever, although the intensity with which the belief was held can be found in the law that anyone who killed a cat was himself doomed. The death of a cat, from natural causes or injury, was followed by formal mourning by the entire family. Besides the divinity of the regular house cat, there was the extraordinary godliness of the temple cats. These were, like the vestal virgins of the ancient Romans, the holiest of the holy. When they were buried, it was with the ceremony of the interment of a pharaoh. The tomb was a sarcophagus—that is, a sacred container, and food and drink as well as costly goods were buried with the cat.

At the height of cat worship, in about 1000 BC, the Egyptians held the festival of Bubastis, named after a city near the Nile delta. This was a true pilgrimage, in which hundreds of thousands of people visited the city in mid-spring to worship Bastet. The nature of the pilgrimage and its connection with April and May would indicate that the cat was a harvest—or fertility-goddess and that the pilgrimage was a mixture of religious and agricultural worship. The fact that Bacchic orgies may have occurred at the same time reinforces our belief that the cat's powers were directly connected with fertility-rites.

The Egyptians, then, placed the cat and cat mythology at the exact centre of their lives. Although this lasted for hundreds of years, the worship of the cat began to wane when cats themselves became more plentiful and when they became needed for the mundane purpose of exterminating rodents. Thus, from a deity, the cat was returned to its place in nature.

The mythicizing of the cat took several turns. While cat-worship began to falter in Egypt, the Greeks had all along considered the animal a lesser deity, although still connected with the moon. Aesop identified cats with women, especially with Venus; but the Romans—a far more practical people—began to see the cat as a pleasant, small animal without larger magical powers, although still with some household powers. By the time of Jesus Christ, the cat was being introduced into northern Europe, probably by traders. We find the first mention of the word 'cat' in the fourth century AD. The cat became very valuable for rodent-control, a factor that became a matter of survival for the European population when the Black Death struck in the mid-fourteenth century. The plague resulted from rats brought back by the Crusaders from the Holy Land; the rats carried fleas, which in turn carried the plague and led to the loss of three-quarters of Europe's population.

The cat was, once again, needed, and needed badly, not as a deity but as a killer of rodents. But now something strange, but perhaps inevitable, in feline history occurred. The cat in medieval Europe came to be seen as the opposite of a deity, now as an emissary of Satan. The very mystery of the cat, which had captured the Egyptians' imagination, became the source of suspicion and fear. Its unfathomable habits, its slinking movements, its association with the moon, its connection with bad luck or ill fortune—all these factors identified it as having trafficked with the Devil himself. From the Christian point of view, the cat was the enemy, and the cat population was burned, crucified, murdered in orgiastic ceremonies of religious purgation. The ceremony of burning was particularly important, since fire allegedly burned out the devil harboured in the cat's body and soul.

Furthermore, cats were associated with witches, who used feline parts as ingredients in their various brews and stews. The connection of the cat with women (witches or not) further drove it into the camp of Eve, the female in Christian belief who was responsible for man's fall. Once the tide turned against the cat, it turned almost completely. Although European cats continued to produce and intermix with the cats brought back by the Crusaders from the East, they were also killed in huge numbers as destructive pagans. Their reputation was such that forbidden, outlawed organizations worshipped the Devil in the body of the black cat. Nevertheless, through it all, the persistence of the cats' mysterious powers remained despite religious persecution and the growth of more rational ideas. This is a constant: that the cat's mystery was honoured even when the cat was banished. The cat was still viewed as a protector of the hearth—as it was originally with the ancient Romans, and its presence at funerals was considered a good omen. The black cat was often seen as a good-luck totem, and the white as the forerunner of bad luck. Often, live cats would be interred in walls or fireplaces to ensure good fortune for the household. In the South of

France, certain 'magician cats' were believed to bring prosperity to the home.

Over the years, the identification of the cat with woman intensified. The cat's mystery was viewed as identical with the mystery of the female. The cat's sensibility was womanly, and the feline image and presence entered the arts by the way of many female writers who loved and kept cats.

Further, the cat remained a strong bulwark against rodents, especially in America when the colonies were invaded by what was facetiously called 'the Hanover rat' (the British kings were from Hanover, Germany).

Not until 1871, however, organized under the auspices of the cat fancier Harrison Weir, did the first formal cat show take place. This was followed by several others, and it led, of course, to the breeding of pedigreed cats for show purposes and for ownership. Many of the well-known breeds were developed at this time. The Siamese, as we know it in Britain and America, can be dated from this period, imported and shown at a London exhibition in 1896. Over the centuries, many famous people have publicized their cats, among them Montaigne and Petrarch, Cardinal Richelieu, Dr Samuel Johnson, Sir Walter Scott, T. S. Eliot and Winston Churchill.

With the modern development and breeding of cats, and with the vast increase in ownership, we no longer have the mythical or legendary cat. But even in a rational, secular world such as ours, the cat retains some of its past powers—not as a reality but as an idea. We like to think of it not as a goddess, of course, but as a representative of the unknown, of areas that lie beneath consciousness. We still speak of mystery. We attach some of our superstitions to cats—the black representing good luck, each cat as having nine lives, and other aspects. Unlike other pets, the cat always represents something besides itself. It points to inner worlds, to unfathomable depths, to a core of vitality that goes well beyond rational examination.

TWO

The Kitten from Birth to Maturity

A kitten is a cat under nine months of age, and you may have just acquired one, or several. The chances are good that your kitten is already a few weeks or months old. Very seldom does an owner acquire a kitten at birth, unless his own cat has had a litter. The kitten, like an infant, is kept with its mother until it can be weaned (at about eight weeks old). But suppose you want to raise your kittens from birth, or someone gives you a kitten whose mother has died or run off. Then you must start from the beginning, right here. If, however, your kitten is older, simply turn to its age-group in this chapter and follow it through its first year.

A kitten is probably the easiest of all pets to raise. If the mother is present, there is almost nothing for you to do after birth if everything goes well. And if the mother is not present, the kitten will normally be very adaptable anyway. Housetraining has few of the problems you associate with a dog, and growth does not involve the huge leaps in weight also associated with dogs. Your kitten will gain perhaps 8 to 10 pounds in its first twelve months, possibly less. Some breeds of dog may gain over 100 pounds in that same time, in some months gaining as much as 8 or 10 pounds.

The newborn kitten is extremely fragile. It takes several days for it to get used to the world in even the simplest way, and it starts out by weighing perhaps ¼ pound. For the first ten days, it cannot see; it can barely stand, although it can crawl. It has no idea what is out there, and it does not know where its next meal is coming from. Everything is a buzz of confusion. This is equally true of the tiger cub, born at 2 to 3 pounds, which will become a 300-pound jungle cat. In this respect, your kitten is simply a smaller version of the larger cat, and at birth not even that much smaller. Not until it is three to four weeks old does it have complete sight and hearing.

Many queens (mother cats) will choose a nest a week or so before their kittens are born. There is nothing wrong with that, since the nesting instinct of the queen is very strong. Let her choose a spot if you want, or you define the place—necessary if you have only limited space in a flat or a small house. Make sure the spot you pick is clean. And it should be draught-free. The danger to small things comes from draughts—chills, upper-respiratory infections and so on. When you pick a spot—or if your cat picks a spot, test the area well to see that it is free of draughts and then put low sides around the sleeping-area. The temperature should be kept warm—in the range of 75 to 80 degrees. Too much warmth is not a problem, whereas too little can be.

The area should be large enough to accommodate several kittens. Also, be sure to allow some space for growth. Kittens do not grow at a great rate, but they do need space to move around in as they get older.

Do not be surprised, however, if after all your trouble with making a nest, your cat decides to move to one of her own devising. This is quite normal behaviour, and you should expect it. If she does that, then simply be sure that the nest she has arranged for herself meets with your approval—that it is draught-free, safe for the kittens and sufficiently protected against the kittens' getting away and underfoot once they can crawl or walk.

Since a kitten has little control over its bladder and bowels, you should line the carton or general area with removable material. At first, the queen—if she is available—will take care of those needs, cleaning the kittens after their birth, but this will occur only at the very beginning. In a short time the job becomes too much. And then the problem becomes yours. The best thing is several thicknesses of newspaper, which can be disposed of as soon as they are soiled. In addition, provide something soft—an old blanket, some large, clean rags, even some straw. Many owners have found that children's blankets work well for the nest, or old torn sheets. This will give the kitten (or kittens) a home, and as it begins to move around, it can shape the material to fit its body.

Be sure that whatever you use is clean. Kittens, like infants, are suscept-ible to all kinds of ailments because their resistance is low. It will prove easier for you if you can provide washable material that can be re-used.

Prepare the shelter before you get your kitten, no matter what its age. If you have a pregnant cat, you will want to prepare the shelter several days before she queens. You then need room for the mother as well as for the entire litter. Keep in mind that you will need space for the mother and perhaps four kittens. If you have an orphan kitten, then of course the required space is considerably less.

A single kitten can do well in a wooden crate, or even a small barrel, as long as plenty of air circulates. Prevent the barrel from rolling by wedging it between a couple of chairs. If you use wire as a gate, be sure it is of the heavy-duty variety, or else it may work loose or its loose ends may damage the kitten when it becomes curious.

The newborn kitten will not know what is going on, but the older kitten will react to its surroundings, and it is a good idea to let it hear people moving around. It has, after all, been separated from its mother and litter-mates; it may feel lonely or anxious. It is not as yet sure where to centre its affections. While cats on the whole seem sure of themselves and without any real need to attach themselves to people, nevertheless the young kitten has many of the feelings infants have—insecurity, loneliness and anxiety. This is true of the entire cat family—a newborn tiger cub will hang on to a human 'mother' for very life itself. The kitten may not have such feelings in the complex way the infant does, but nevertheless they are present.

These words are directed at the owner who has placed the kitten in a separate room. Many owners prefer to keep the kitten in the same room with them. Be sure that the kitten stays away from any open windows. A direct draught may give you only a stiff neck, but it may make a kitten very ill.

If the kitten is acquired in the summer, it is possible to keep it outdoors, *but not* if it is under three months old. The weather should be mild, and at night, if the evenings become chilly, bring the kitten inside.

Keep the kitten in some kind of enclosure when it is outside. The box should be off the ground so that no moisture gets in. Also, it should be covered with soft, warm bedding material and be draught-free. Sudden shifts in temperature from warm to cold can give the young kitten trouble: upper-respiratory ailments and ear-aches, for example.

Just as you prepared the kitten's sleeping-quarters before you brought it home, or before the queening, so you should have on hand several other pieces of equipment. A litter box is absolutely necessary. Cats train themselves very easily and then keep themselves meticulously clean. A few sessions with a litter box and the young kitten will rarely make a mistake after that. You also need a pan for food, large enough for the grown cat to get its muzzle into, and a water-pan.

You will need a brush, a wide-toothed comb and perhaps a collar and leash or lead if you plan to walk your kitten, as many people do. If that is your plan, then train your kitten from the beginning, and it will respond easily. In addition it will need some toys, especially when those early needle teeth begin to come in. All these items are standard equipment, and any pet-shop carries them. If you do buy toys for your kitten or cat, remember that a kitten will be eager to try its teeth on anything, especially as it teethes, and a soft rubber ball or toy may turn into fragments. The pieces are indigestible, and they may be swallowed. Get something hard and tough. A piece of leather or hard rubber is excellent. Some toys may have toxic paint, which the kitten will lick off, so buy only those toys made especially for cats or dogs.

If you obtained your kitten from a cattery or pet-shop, or from a previous owner, continue to feed it what it is accustomed to eating. If you wish to change over to some other recommended foods, do so gradually. This chapter tells you about several systems of feeding, any one of which will enable your kitten to grow to healthy maturity. But remember that a sudden change in foods, no matter how nourishing you believe the new ones to be, can upset the kitten's delicate system. Continuity is best.

Before you make any of these preparations, it is always a good idea to locate a veterinary surgeon whom you trust and respect. You may have little need of him or her once your cat is grown, but you should have one available. One of the best ways is to get information from a friend who owns a cat or dog, much the same way we find out about a family doctor or a specialist. You may ask to see the vet and inspect his office. Do not necessarily be impressed if he has all the newest equipment, although there is nothing against him if he has. *The most important thing to check is cleanliness.* Another point to respond to: does he or she seem to like animals, and does he treat your pet with consideration?

SOME POINTERS ON THE NEW KITTEN

If you bring home a very young kitten by car, do not be surprised if the motion of the vehicle upsets it. It may be a combination of the car and the strangeness of the situation that upsets the kitten. The best thing is to spread a sheet around the area where it is sitting. Keep a towel nearby.

If the kitten is sick, keep a brush handy, a brush with long bristles for a long-hair, one with short bristles for a short-hair—but if the kitten is very young, it will not make much difference. Also, some kind of mild solvent may prove useful; apply some with a rag and wipe off the soiled spot. Do not bathe the young kitten, not until it is at least six months old or even one year old. And if you feel you must bathe it, make sure the room is free from draughts and shifts in temperature.

Your new kitten may be a great joy and pleasure. The kitten itself, however, does not know what an excellent owner you will make. And if it is only a few days or weeks old, it knows nothing. Even if it is a few months old, it needs time to become accustomed to its new surroundings, to new voices and to what you expect of it. You should, therefore, take some precautions that will ensure the safety and happiness of your new acquisition and the fulfilment of your own needs.

1. A new pet creates great excitement, especially if there are young children in the house. Yet you should try to hold down unnecessary excitement. Even though cats are self-contained, the new kitten requires some equilibrium.

2. Once the cat attains its size and matures, it can handle nearly every situation. But until that time you must keep children within bounds. Encourage them to look and touch, but do not allow them to lift or poke the kitten; certainly no exploratory examinations into ears or elsewhere.

3. Avoid picking up the young kitten too much. If you must, do it securely. Put one hand firmly under the kitten's chest, the other under its hindquarters, and lift. *Do not* pick up a kitten by the scruff of the neck. This is precarious and slippery, and it may well cause pain.

4. Do not take a kitten out in cold weather. Avoid exposure to sharp shifts in temperature. Also, do not bathe the kitten until it is at least six months old, preferably a year old, if at all.

5. Do not feed bones to the young kitten—and not to the grown cat either. The kitten has non-permanent teeth by four to five weeks, and its full complement of permanent teeth at six months, but bones are not recommended at any age.

6. Be sure to clip the kitten's nails when it is a few weeks old. Since kittens, and most cats, stay inside, their nails have no opportunity to wear down naturally. Long nails can tear things around the house and even damage the kitten's eyes.

These minor precautions can help you eliminate most of the problems that can give you and your kitten trouble.

THE FIRST NIGHT

On the first night at your house, a kitten may be a forlorn creature. It may indicate its loneliness and anxiety with a steady purring sound or with an attempt at a scream. There are, however, several things you can do to relieve its feelings of strangeness. Be loving, but firm. If the kitten fails to understand who is boss from the beginning, the grown cat will take over you and your house. Do not spoil it by running to it every time it whimpers.

Something warm—a hot-water bottle, for example—may make the kitten feel it is back at its mother's side. Or else wrap a towel or blanket in the form of a cat (approximately) and place it next to the kitten. The chances are it will be a source of comfort. If you use any electrical device for warmth, make sure the kitten cannot get at the wires. The older kitten will chew away until it is burned or shocked. Some veterinary surgeons recommend placing a clock nearby, so that the ticks will remind the kitten of its mother's heartbeat. Any device is good if it works and is safe. Once the kitten makes its break from Mother, it adapts readily.

THE KITTEN FROM BIRTH TO FOUR WEEKS

Let us now return to the newborn kitten or kittens. We are at the first hour on the first day.

If the litter is large—say, more than five, have the queen suckle in shifts of about three to four hours. This is better for her and for the kittens, especially the weaker ones, who might be left out. The rear nipples may be more plentiful than the others. This is good to know if you must rotate the kittens. Give everyone a chance at the fullest. Try to whisk away part of the litter when the queen is busy, or else the small kittens may miss a meal. Perhaps put a small identification tag on each so there is no chance of a mix-up. At this tender age (the weight of the kitten is about ¼ pound), each meal is important.

The newborn kitten must suckle as soon as possible. The queen's nipples contain colostrum—a substance that provides immunity against disease for the kitten until it can build up its own resistance. Colostrum, which is high in globulin, is nature's way of giving an animal a chance to survive when it is at its frailest. It is also somewhat laxative. Without the colostrum, the kitten is protected against feline distemper (panleukopenia, or feline enteritis) for only about a week, while with it the kitten is generally immune to this dread and wasting disease until its first inoculation, at about ten weeks.

If the litter is unusually large, the queen, no matter how diligent she is, may not be able to feed them all. Then supplementary feeding will be necessary. There are numerous ways of doing this, and I suggest several methods in the following pages. My suggestions for supplementary feeding can also be followed if the queen should die or if the kitten is separated from its mother and you have to bottle-feed. Since these methods can be somewhat time-consuming, you should know what you are getting yourself into.

You can, of course, always try to obtain a foster mother from the local RSPCA, but there are problems here. The foster mother may resist nursing kittens that she does not recognize as her own. You have to trick her by wiping some of her milk on the kittens and then staying with her while they suckle. Also, you must be especially careful that she is healthy, and even then there is no guarantee that she can handle the whole litter. Her own milk might be insufficient. Eventually, you may have to return to bottle-feeding.

Bottle-Feeding

Bottle-feeding a tiny kitten, is, on a smaller scale, not very different from bottle-feeding an infant. This is the course many of you will follow. A friend's cat queens, the friend wants to give the kittens away, and suddenly you find yourself with a newborn kitten. Usually, the kitten will be kept with its mother for a week or more, but you may possibly obtain it sooner. Whether you get it at two days or two weeks, you can feed it correctly by sticking to the following advice.

For the newborn kitten, you need certain equipment (most of which you will already have if there have been infants in the house). It is all very modest. You will need a baby-scale to check on the kitten's weekly gain. A regular scale may not register the gain in ounces that you can expect. Other necessary equipment includes:

> a measuring-cup with ounce gradations (standard kitchen equipment)
> spoons
> a mixing-bowl in which to prepare the formula
> a doll's baby-bottles and a doll's baby-nipples (regular baby-size nipples will be too large)

Keep a plastic eyedropper available for an emergency—even the doll's baby-nipples may be too large. Be sure the hole in each nipple is large enough to allow the formula to feed out steadily—neither too slowly nor in rushes. If the hole is too small, sterilize a needle over a flame and puncture the nipple until the hole is the size you want.

The formula itself can take many different forms. Several preparations approximate the queen's milk. Do not, however, use a straight cow's-milk formula—it may cause diarrhoea. The queen's milk is not the same as cow's milk, nor is it the same as human milk.

1. Use one of the prepared milks or milk powders on the market. You can buy them at chemists, pet-shops and department stores. Most of these commercial formulas simply need the addition of water to make them ready.

2. Another possibility is to take a powdered baby-milk and add regular cream, in the following proportions: 1 ounce of powdered milk, 1 ounce

of cream and 6 ounces of water. Or substitute the yolk of an egg for the cream.

3. Another formula involves diluting goat's milk (an especially rich milk) with equal amounts of water.

Whatever formula you decide on, your kitten should be given a vitamin-mineral supplement. Follow the directions on the label.

Make sure all equipment is sanitary, as the kitten, like a newborn infant, is helpless against common infections. Wash your hands before you prepare the formula, making sure the bottles as well as the nipples are thoroughly clean. Wash them with hot water and soap, using a bottle-brush to swab out the nipples and bottles. Avoid disinfectants—soap and water are sufficient. Be sure that no formula remains in the bottle from the previous day. Such a residue can grow bacteria and cause diarrhoea. Most of this is familiar if you have been around infants.

Whatever method of feeding you use, if the queen's milk is not available, be sure to keep the feed refrigerated until just before feeding-time. Do not make the feed for more than a day at a time. The amount depends on how many kittens you have. The newborn kitten should be offered ¼ to ½ ounce of feed the first day *at each feeding*. It may not drink this much—remember that the kitten's stomach is only the size of a walnut. You should feed the kitten four to six times a day—you must, of course, judge your own kitten's needs. Some newborn kittens take three feedings a day, because of a larger intake at each feeding; others up to six or eight. Thus, each kitten receives an ounce or more of feed each day. At least, offer that much.

Although the newborn kitten weights only ¼ pound, it gains rapidly to achieve a weight almost ten times that at two or two and a half months.

If the kitten is hungry, it will cry for food; if overfed, it will refuse the food. Always make more feed than you need; the demand will increase each day.

The bottle should be at about the same temperature as the blood temperature of the kitten itself. Figure on 100°F, and do not vary it more than a few degrees either way. The bottle should be warm to the touch but not hot. Sprinkle a drop of milk on your wrist to test it. Make sure the nipple is running smoothly and steadily. If the hole is too big, replace it; if too small, enlarge it.

This type of feeding, *used only when the queen's milk is unavailable*, must continue for about three weeks. Even if you do not have a scale, you can tell from looking at the kitten whether it is gaining weight.

Always be on the alert for the quality of the kitten's stool. At this young age, its bowel movements are a key to its digestion. If there is diarrhoea, regulate the formula so that its water-content increases, and then, as the diarrhoea disappears, go back to the original proportions. If diarrhoea should continue, be sure to consult your vet. He may prescribe a simple anti-diarrhoea medication, which is fine if there is nothing seriously wrong with the kitten. On the other hand, the kitten may have worms from birth, taken in while still an embryo. *Prolonged diarrhoea is very dangerous and should never be neglected.* The water-loss alone, leading to dehydration, can be fatal. If there are other kittens, keep them away from the droppings or they too might become infected.

Helping the Kittens
If the kittens have not been separated from the queen, she will take care of all their needs in their first hours. She stimulates them to make a bowel movement by lapping them and then cleans up afterward. Cats are meticulously clean when they are a little older, but the newborn kitten is not. It will, as mentioned, be blind for a week or more. While some 'foreign' pedigrees may open their eyes at five days, some cats will take twelve or more days.

But what if the queen is absent? Massage the kitten's abdomen with a piece of cotton, or else gently rub the genitalia until elimination takes place. The best time to do it is about five or ten minutes after a meal. The stimulation also serves to induce a burp, and this too is necessary, to prevent gas-accumulations. When helping the kitten, hold it over a container—you will save yourself a lot of cleaning-up. After a few days, bowel movements and urination will come almost automatically. Apply mineral- or baby-oil to the anal region after the kitten evacuates to prevent irritation of the skin.

Wipe off any faeces that cling to the anal region. If possible, keep orphaned kittens separate, so that they do not lick and chew each other. In the absence of the queen, they may irritate each other.

Weaning
Nearly all your work will occur in the first two weeks of the kitten's life. You have become the parental figure for that small ball of fluff. But unlike an infant, a kitten adapts very rapidly. By six weeks, it is able to take care of itself and has demonstrated a proportionally tremendous weight-gain.

After a couple of weeks of bottle-feeding, you can begin to prod the kitten on to dish-feeding. This is a gradual thing, of course. In fact, by the fourth week (some experts recommend a little later), it is a good idea to have finished weaning the kitten from the bottle or the teat. Start the weaning by very gradually introducing some solid foods into the diet—for example, a mixture of cereal and milk or cereal and the milk feed. If the queen is present to care for her litter, she will help wean them.

There are jarred baby-meats on the market, which you can offer in addition to, or instead of, cereal and milk feed. Or you can warm up some chopped meat and add crumbled cereal and cooked vegetables, mashed together. The kitten will love it and thrive on it.

Even if the queen is still willing to nurse, complete the weaning after six weeks. Also, willing or not, she may not have enough milk to supply the appetites of the rapidly growing kittens. See pages 37–39 of this chapter for some sample soft diets you can use when you wean your kittens.

Some Precautions
Certain minor disorders may arise, but you can protect against them with a little foresight. The kitten's navel, for instance, is very sensitive to injury and infection. You can try to keep it covered with a gauze pad, but the queen or

kitten will work it off. The best protection is to keep the sleeping-area very clean and to make sure the surface material is soft and not abrasive. That will prevent irritation, even infection. If you do suspect infection, call your vet. The infected area will need cleaning with an antiseptic, and perhaps the kitten will have to be treated further.

Worms are so common, particularly in kittens, that you should try to halt a possible infestation long before it becomes serious. One wormy kitten, unfortunately, can spread worms throughout the entire litter. Unless you remove the faeces right away, the other kittens in the area will play with them. If your kitten is alone, the chances of worms are lessened, but even so there are varieties that can be transmitted before birth. Many kittens have them as a congenital condition.

Do not yourself experiment with worm medicine. A medication that works with one type of worm is useless for another, so consult your vet, who will prescribe its correct medicine and dosage.

Some Problems
As mentioned above, one way worms are spread is that the kittens may eat the faeces of the others. This is a fairly common occurrence. Kittens become bored, and the faeces become playthings for them. Do not become alarmed, but discourage the practice by keeping the area clean. As soon as the kitten eliminates, remove the droppings. Or else stimulate the bowel movement over a container.

Provide diversion with some hard rubber objects. Toys of any kind without sharp edges and free of soft rubber are fine. Old knotted stockings, pieces of leather, a wrapped-up towel—any of these will keep the kitten occupied when it wants to play. Then, as the nails and teeth develop, provide a scratching-post—it will save your furniture and give hours of pleasurable activity.

Keep the children away from the queen at this time, especially when she is nursing. She is very possessive and jealous and may mistake the child's good intentions. She must be allowed to direct all her attention and energies toward the care of her litter.

Warn children about the delicacy of the kitten. Like an infant, a kitten has a soft spot on the top of its head, which remains until the skull bones grow together, perhaps at two or three months. The thin membrane covering the brain is elastic but easily punctured. In addition to this weakness, a young cat's bones, tendons and muscles are all generally delicate and subject to injury. A child's hard shoe, even from an unintentional kick or shove, can hurt the kitten, whereas the older cat will accept it as part of a game.

Before the kitten is weaned, the queen—if she is available—should have started and successfully completed the housetraining of the kittens. She will show them how to use the litter box. It should be in the area where she has nested and delivered her litter. Do not move it around, or you will confuse her and the kittens. In the event that the kitten is orphaned, you can do the job easily. After the kitten eats, after every couple of hours and after it awakens, put it in the litter box or pan you have provided. Pat and praise it after each elimination. If you see your kitten going in the wrong place, take a firm tone and indicate your displeasure. A few days of this, and a kitten is ordinarily housebroken.

Except under unusual conditions, do not bathe a kitten until it is six months old, preferably a year old. Some vets feel that a cat should never be bathed, even the mature cat. You can keep it clean with a washcloth or with cotton and baby-oil. A cat is fastidious about itself, and if the queen is taking care of the kittens, she will teach them cleanliness. Bathing of a cat of any age is a major undertaking, for it may suffer a chill or an upper-respiratory infection.

Incidentally, whether a cat's nose is hot or cold is not an indication of fever or illness. The nose may be dry because the cat is sleeping near a hot radiator or cradling it in its paws. The true test of health is not a cold nose but the general look: clear eyes, energy, healthy coat, 'thrifty' (generally alert) appearance.

If you have any doubts, take the temperature. The temperature, taken by rectum, should run around 101·5 or 102°F. This is normal, although excitement can elevate it. Also, normal may vary for each individual cat. Usually, an elevated temperature is accompanied by other signs: lacklustre look, vomiting and diarrhoea, either separately or together.

With weaning, your kitten is ready to make the major step toward maturity. In the next few months, it will gain much of its growth, move on to a steady diet, acquire its permanent teeth, learn a few forms of obedience— as many as you choose to teach, up to a point—and become your close companion and friend for the next fifteen or more years.

The following checklist of old and new points may prove useful if you have never owned a kitten before:

1. Be certain that a newborn kitten nurses right away and gets the invaluable colostrum. This protects it against infection.

2. Keep the kittens in a draught-free place.

3. Make sure all kittens, but especially those born small, are getting enough to eat. Supplement the feeding of those that are too weak to compete.

4. Maintain sanitation whether you have one kitten or an entire litter.

5. Feed the milk food (when the queen is absent) at body temperature (100°F) and do not feed too fast. Give a vitamin-mineral supplement as prescribed.

6. Check weight for growth. Also, be suspicious of trouble-signs: diarrhoea, eyes with pus, vomiting, blood in the faeces or in any other discharge, discharge from the nose, loss of energy and listlessness.

7. Clean up the litter box or pan after each elimination. There may be worm eggs that can infect the entire litter.

8. Start weaning by the third week—very gradually.

9. Watch out for minor infections near the navel and around the anus.

10. When the kitten is eight weeks old, see your vet if you suspect worms—a kitten without energy is not a good sign. If you catch it early, you can prevent an infestation.

11. Protect the kittens and nursing queen against small children.

12. Take care in handling young kittens—they are very fragile.

13. Avoid bathing a kitten until it is six months old or until after its permanent inoculations—if possible, avoid bathing altogether.

14. If the queen is available, let her teach the kittens about house-training.

15. Offer fresh room-temperature water to the kitten after each meal; if you leave it down, it may use the dish as a bathtub.

THE KITTEN FROM FOUR TO TWELVE WEEKS

By now, the kitten is amazingly along on its own course—able to handle regular food and housetrained. Your attention will focus on correct nutrition, inoculations and possibly worming. Also, you can accustom your kitten to its name, if you have not already started. As you follow this chapter, I discuss the correct feeding for the kitten until it matures.

At six weeks or thereabouts, your kitten has been weaned. There are several kinds of diets, each one with its good points. Some are easy to use, others more time-consuming. Choose one that fits your personal needs and time allotment. No matter which you select, you must be sure that your kitten is receiving sufficient nutrients for correct and adequate growth. *Any diet that enables a pet to grow into a healthy mature animal is a good one.* Spending a lot does not ensure a good diet, nor does spending only a little mean a poor diet.

Some Simple but Basic Nutrition Rules

Some of this information overlaps with the details in the chapter on nutrition. Turn there for further elaboration.

The growing kitten, as well as the mature cat, has certain dietary requirements. Hit-or-miss table scraps usually are insufficient. Friends' success stories with table scraps are not necessarily to be accepted; their pet may be undernourished and its life span shortened.

Contrary to common thinking, meat or dairy products are not the sole need of cats. They must have a balanced diet, of which protein foods such as meat compose thirty to thirty-five per cent for the growing kitten and as little as twenty to twenty-five per cent for the mature cat. Protein is essential, for it breaks down into several amino acids necessary for proper growth, to give heat and energy and to rebuild bodily systems. But a young kitten fed only lean meat, which is rich in protein, would deteriorate from malnutrition.

In addition to protein, a kitten needs fat, perhaps up to a quarter or a third of its nutritional requirements, with the mature cat scaling down to about twenty per cent. Not only does fat give an animal heat and energy, it also improves the skin, builds up resistance to disease and tones its nervous system. The chief asset of fat is an ingredient called linoleic acid, found in pork, lamb and beef. Even lard will supply it in ample quantity. This acid is required for adequate growth. Recent experiments in feline and canine nutrition have completely undermined the old belief that a cat needs only lean meat for energy and growth. A kitten kept on a low-fat diet tends to have dry skin: its skin may become scaly, its coat coarse. Further, resistance to disease is lowered.

Fat is also an excellent source of calories for the growing kitten. A kitten needs proportionately more calories than the grown cat. A growing young kitten may need four or five hundred calories a day (based on 150 or more calories per pound of weight), whereas the grown cat at 10 pounds will need fewer calories. Fat provides this in abundance. If you soak part of its dinner in bacon drippings—perhaps revolting for you, your pet may love it.

Of course, a cat's intake of fat does not remain constant throughout its life. With the older cat, you must be more careful of its caloric intake. As in a person, the older cat's metabolism slows down, and food is changed into harmful fat. But in the growing kitten, the metabolic rate is rapid. Fat keeps it going.

For bulk and energy—although not necessarily for food value, the kitten needs carbohydrates. At one time, carbohydrates were thought to be poor fare for pets, but this is not so at all. Carbohydrates, as in potatoes, rice and macaroni, are fine, *provided they are cooked*. The cat will have considerable trouble digesting them raw.

The Big Three are protein, fats and carbohydrates, supplemented by multiple vitamins and minerals. Incorrect feeding of your kitten can impede natural growth at a proportionately greater rate than would the incorrect feeding of a child. Cod-liver oil, incidentally, does not supply all the necessary vitamins and minerals—only A and D, and, unlike people, cats do not need vitamin C.

Vitamin A (found in grain, greens, liver, egg-yolk and other yellow-coloured foods) aids the body's growth, is necessary for correct vision and hearing, helps to prevent infection and gives tone to the skin. Vitamin B (found in meat, fish, vegetables, milk and egg-yolk) serves your cat in many important ways, all stressing general body health and endurance. It helps the liver, tones the muscles, gives appetite, even (some say) adds to fertility—although in cats this usually is not necessary. Vitamin D (found in bone-meal and assimilated from the sun's rays) helps to prevent bone diseases such as rickets. It provides good muscular co-ordination. Vitamin E (found in grain products) helps tone the muscles and is essential for normal reproduction. Both vitamins F and K, the first keeping the skin and coat healthy and the latter necessary for the clotting of the blood, are obtained in normal eating.

Like vitamins, minerals are essential. Calcium and phosphorus are bone- and tooth-builders, especially for the young kitten, whose bones are soft and pliable. They also help give your cat a healthy heart and, as well, solid muscles and nerves. Iron is a blood builder, while sodium, chlorine, iodine, copper, sulphur, magnesium and potassium are also important, especially for the kitten.

All growing kittens should be given a vitamin and mineral supplement to their regular diet. Check with your vet, and then follow the directions on the label. If you obtain a kitten from its owner or from a cattery, continue its current diet for a week or so, gradually leading the kitten into the diet you plan to continue. Or keep the old one if it meets your needs and is nutritionally sound. Most people like to experiment with their pets' diets, but too much change may find your cat balking. Also, as a rule of thumb, do not give more than twenty-five per cent of the daily diet in table scraps.

Three Types of Diet
I outline below the three kinds of diet. The variations are innumerable, of course. See also the chapter on nutrition for additional dietary information.

Canned Foods
Canned cat-foods are commercial preparations with a high moisture content—up to seventy or seventy-five per cent. They are low in fat content, for fat hastens spoilage. Since the kitten needs a hefty intake of fats each day, these canned foods will not fully supply its needs, although such foods will be sufficient for the mature cat. Supplement canned foods for the kitten with some fat and with a vitamin-mineral daily dose.

A single cat will eat about a can a day. If you have several cats, the cost can be considerable.

A factor for the growing kitten is that some (but not all) prepared foods do not provide sufficient calories. You can make up the difference with fats: fatty meat, margarine, butter. There is no precise way of judging how many calories your kitten needs, but in the fullness of its growth-spurt (at six or eight weeks), even a thousand calories is not excessive. This tails off considerably at maturity.

None of this should discourage you from using commercial foods. There has been considerable research on such products, and they are tasty and healthful for the most part. They are also easy to serve.

A way to handle the kitten at four to twelve weeks is to give a milk feed breakfast followed by a canned food. The milk feed may be cereal with evaporated milk (or whole milk if your kitten does not get diarrhoea). Since the kitten may eat three or four times a day, offer some variety. For its other meals, give it canned cat-food, perhaps supplemented by fat-products.

Dry Foods or Meal
These are almost entirely dehydrated products—you get exactly the bulk that you pay for, since there is less than ten per cent water-content. These are usually considered complete meals; theoretically, all you must do is add water and serve. But for young, growing kittens, the fat-content is too low. You should supplement the dry meal with bacon drippings, margarine, lard or fat from the butcher. Also, baked-in vitamins may lose some of their benefit; a supplement of that too may be necessary—check with your vet.

Dry meal provides sufficient bulk. With fat mixed in, it contains sufficient calories as well. When you serve it, soak the meal in the fat for the young kitten; less soaking is needed for the older cat. With the vitamin-mineral supplement and perhaps an occasional cooked egg, the diet is complete, but it is essential that a cat drinks plenty of water. A dry-food-only diet is not recommended by vets in the UK.

A Combination of Diets
If you want to spend some time on your pet, you may try a combination of

diets. Figure on about twenty-five per cent of (good) table scraps, some canned food, dry food and fat, all mixed together. On occasion, you might add an egg (cooked). This mixture, along with the vitamin-mineral supplement, will be nutritionally complete. If milk agrees with your cat, provide that as well. The danger here is not to exceed about twenty-five per cent in scraps.

From these three basic methods of feeding, most owners will choose either one or a combination of them all. Avoid highly seasoned foods at all ages. I have offered some feeding-procedures for the kitten from five to twelve weeks, from the time of weaning to middle growth. The amounts will vary with each cat—*I provide only average quantities.* At the early stages, offer as much as the kitten wants; if you see any signs of fat, decrease the amounts.

Some useful measurements:

cup = 8 fluid ounces
tablespoon = ½ fluid ounce
tablespoon = 3 teaspoonfuls
can of cat-food = between 6 and 7½ ounces

Diets for five or six to twelve weeks:
(Based on four feedings a day, at 8 a.m., 12 noon, 4 p.m., 8 p.m. Do not try to feed too much at any one time—the kitten's stomach is very small.)

Prepared (canned) food or baby-food (meats): one ounce (two tablespoons) per feeding, with some milk on the side.
Dry Feed or Meal: Do not give at this age.
Combination: One ounce of chopped meat, cooked lightly (mixed in with the drippings) per feeding; one ounce of canned food at another feeding; or one ounce of finely minced cooked chicken (mixed in with some fat) per feeding. Add a little grain—cornflakes or shredded wheat—to the mix, or else offer the cornflakes with a little milk added. An occasional cooked egg is fine. Give a vitamin-mineral supplement, according to directions on the label.

Although you may vary your kitten's diet, do so gradually. Sudden shifts may result in a choosy eater. If you have several kittens to feed, each one must have its own feeding-area and pan. (One warning: Siamese cats may have difficulty with cow's milk, resulting in diarrhoea. If so, then try other kinds of milk—goat's milk, for example.)

Let me also dispel a few ideas. No food in itself can bring on worms. A food that contains worm cysts may, but this is because it is infected. Avoid raw fish and raw pork in any event. Starch is fine as long as it is cooked. Do not worry if your kitten and cat eat rapidly—they have the juices to digest the food. Avoid bones with kitten or cat. Raw meat is fine (not pork) if your cat likes it. Some cats eat grass in order to vomit. If you give egg-white to your cat, make sure it is cooked; egg-yolk is good whether raw or cooked. Both the mongrel and the pedigreed cat have the same nutritional needs. A cat may skip a meal without being ill. If this recurs over a period of several days, then suspect illness. While a kitten needs a good deal of fat in its diet, do not overdo it—too much can make it ill.

Inoculations
(A fuller explanation of the diseases for which your kitten should receive inoculations can be found in the chapter on ailments. I repeat some of it here so that you have a sequence for the kitten.)

The main diseases for which protection is necessary are:

Panleukopenia (feline distemper), a viral infection of the digestive system

Rhinotracheitis, a cold-like ailment that attacks the eyes, nose and throat

Calici, an upper-respiratory infection, with mouth discharge and lung cough.

Other Considerations
In this period, up to twelve weeks, your kitten will adapt easily—to its litter box, its diet and its general surroundings. It will begin to have the physical development we associate with the mature animal.

By the fourth or fifth week, all its temporary (or deciduous) teeth will be in; in fact, by the second or third week, they have begun to emerge. These teeth remain with the kitten in part or full until it reaches about six months old. When the permanent teeth come in, the temporary ones drop out; if the kitten swallows any of them, do not worry. During teething, the gums may be bloody and sore. All this is normal. In all, your cat will gain thirty permanent teeth, although some cats have fewer. The permanent incisors should not be expected until three to four months, the permanent canines until five months, and the premolars until six months.

Ordinarily, dental development proceeds smoothly. Occasionally, the permanent teeth come in before the temporary teeth, or milk teeth, have fallen out, the result being overcrowding. If you notice this, bring it to the attention of your vet. The remedy is for him to pull the baby teeth. Have a mouth-check made when you go for the inoculations. Most vets will do a rapid check-up anyway. Teething-time is upsetting for your kitten, and it may cry or lose energy. This is natural. Your kitten's appetite may also fall off, and it may even suffer from diarrhoea. Usually, the period of discomfort is short, and most kittens sail through it easily.

Those painful teeth and gums will sometimes lead the kitten to gnawing. If you want to save your furniture, provide a tough piece of leather. Make sure it is something that cannot be shredded and swallowed. Although cats have less biting-surface than do dogs, they can work their way around things and then may swallow the pieces. A tough piece of leather will give pleasure and save not only furniture but slippers, shoes, scarves, magazines and books, newspapers and nearly anything else you leave around.

Another item of use is a scratching-post, an item available in any pet-shop, for your kitten's developing paws.

The young kitten is now a member of the household and may even respond to its name. If it is part of a litter, it is responding to its littermates. Be gentle in playing with it, since a kitten of three months is still fragile, with soft bones and an easily injured skin and coat. Kittens develop quickly, but their full motor skills mature fully only with adulthood. Of course, if the queen remains present, she is a great teacher, and kittens under her care will develop more rapidly.

Some Advice

When young, kittens are mischievous and destructive. You must take the same kind of precautions you would take with a small child. Do not leave small objects around; they can be swallowed. If you are careless about your possessions, they may end up in your kitten's digestive tract. Needles, pins, thread, very small building-pieces and so on can lodge in the kitten's throat, or else go down and cause an obstruction. If you suspect that your kitten, or cat, has swallowed an object, get in touch with your vet.

If you have a fireplace, keep it protected, or the kitten may use the ashes as a toilet area.

Furthermore, although kittens and cats have a great sense of balance, do not tempt them to be acrobats. They may try leaps they are not ready for.

Electric cords, if left exposed, might prove inviting to a bored pet; the shock can shock, burn and even kill your kitten if it tears through the insulation. If this does happen, disengage the cord from the outlet before touching the kitten, or else you too will suffer shock and possibly burns. If the kitten needs it, give it first aid for shock, and even artificial respiration (see Chapter 4, on first aid). Keep kittens away from electric cords by restricting them to a given area. The grown cat will tend to leave such matters alone.

Grooming

Since kittens and cats are naturally meticulous about themselves, grooming is an easy matter. They will usually lick away at any soiled spot on their coat. Even so, a cat cannot reach all areas, and a systematic combing is necessary, especially if you have a long-hair. The long-hairs shed a good deal, and the cat in grooming itself will ingest hair. That ingested hair will gradually accumulate inside into a ball and if large enough will create an obstruction.

Avoiding hair balls, however, is not the only reason for daily grooming. All cats, long- or short-haired, need grooming. Watch for accumulations of dirt in the corners of the eye, on the outer surfaces of the ears (*never* probe within), as well as the coat for parasites or their eggs. Go over the coat with a fine-toothed comb—this will flush out anything unusual.

If you do find fleas—not uncommon for both long- and short-hairs, a commercial flea-powder or spray should do the trick. One warning: cats constantly lick themselves, so if the flea-preparation is toxic, or contains phenol, it may make your cat ill. Make sure the label specifies that the preparation is for cats.

Grooming should be fun. If you find tangles or matted areas, do not jerk them apart; brush or comb gently. If an area resists that—such as a spot that has paint on it, cut off the matted hair. Turpentine or paint-thinner can be injurious to the skin and should not be applied.

Groom under the body and under the paws and tail; small knots can easily

TURN TO →
PAGE 65.

form there. Your pet may resist at first, but if you are gentle and persistent, grooming these areas will become part of a pleasant activity. You can avoid bathing by brushing and combing. It is rare that a kitten gets so messy that only a bath will solve the problem.

Incidentally, grooming also involves keeping the toenails trimmed. Since kittens do not wear their nails down on pavement or stone, their nails will grow and break off if not trimmed. The nails will also do considerable damage to your possessions and, possibly, to your skin. Keep them at manageable length. Use a nail-clipper but get your vet to show you how to cut them.

The Kitten in the Family

A kitten is the least troublesome of house pets, and by twelve weeks you are beyond most of the simple problems that do arise. Your attention to important details should take only a few minutes. Make sure you use the kitten's name so that the repetition will cause it to associate the sound or tone with itself. If you have small children, they will be enchanted with a young kitten or the entire litter. Any danger here is not from lack of attention but from too much. Until kittens fully develop their motor abilities, they must be handled gently. Too much activity, too much excitement and stimulation, will tire them and even make them vomit or put them off their food. Children should, of course, be allowed to play—that is part of having a small pet. They should simply be warned against handling the kitten too much.

THE KITTEN FROM THREE TO SEVEN MONTHS

If you bring home a kitten in this age group, then read the earlier sections on the younger kitten to gain your bearings. See especially pages 56–7, on inoculations. You should be sure your cat is up to date on these, and if not, do not let this go unattended. Follow the schedule for injections conscientiously. The previous section will also give you basic information about grooming, housetraining, correct nutrition and your cat's eating-habits.

With Children

Your kitten at this age is ready to become a close friend to your children. Its motor co-ordination has improved, and any pain from teething is just about over at seven months. You must still be careful about too much roughhousing, for the kitten is still small—perhaps 5 or 6 pounds—but it is ready to play. At times it may seem to want to be alone and should be left to itself. Part of the mystery of the cat is its desire to withdraw. Often this is interpreted as unfriendliness, but a cat is a far more private animal than a dog. While a dog thrives on human companionship, a cat has internal needs that make it withdraw. It enjoys the company of people, but it does not need them all the time, although individual cats differ widely.

Children should be warned not to pick up either the kitten or the older cat by the scruff of its neck. It should be picked up firmly with one hand under the chest and abdomen, the other steadying it.

END OF PAGE 40

By now the cat's name should have been repeated so many times that it responds. Be sure to use a short name, since the cat responds, probably, to repetition of sound rather than to anything else. Many people let their children name the cat, although others favour names that suit the origin. A Siamese, for example, will have an Asian-sounding name, a Russian Blue a Russian name, and so on. If you let your child name the cat, however, the two will probably have a long friendship; often, the name comes from a child's favourite nursery story, as 'Charlotte' might come from E. B. White's well-known *Charlotte's Web*.

Spaying and Castrating

See Chapter 6, on the reproductive cycle, for details about spaying the female and castrating or neutering the male. Spaying means that the female's reproductive organs are removed. Castrating means that the male's testicles are removed. For the male, this is almost always necessary, for an unneutered male will spray constantly and make it impossible for you to live with him. Spaying the female is a more difficult decision. Whatever you do, you should decide early. This is especially true for the male. Consult your vet as to the correct age, usually about 4½ months.

Spaying ends all sexual activity, as does castrating of the male. Spaying has been known to settle a temperamental cat down, although there is no guarantee of that. If you fear a sudden gain in weight after spaying, you can control it through diet.

If you plan on mating your female or male, then of course you leave your cat unneutered. This means that the female will 'call' whenever she goes into heat, which may be several times during the mating-season of eight or nine months. And the male, once sexually mature, will begin to spray.

Matters of Space

If you have more than one kitten or cat, then space could be a problem, especially if you want to keep them separate from the rest of the house. Whatever your arrangement, the particular area should be draught-free and light. Cellars and attics are too restrictive, and they prevent the cats' socializing. Their living-quarters should be on a par with those suitable for people.

Outside

Walking your cat on a leash in mild weather is highly recommended. But do not walk a kitten in poor weather, since its coat is not fully grown and the protective fat has not accumulated.

Car-Sickness

Some kittens get motion-sickness, and so the best thing is to acclimatize them slowly. Start with a short ride, then lengthen it, until the kitten becomes accustomed to the motion. If you cannot do it this way, then keep an old towel or piece of sheet handy; a damp washcloth is also recommended if sickness recurs.

If you must do a lot of driving with your cat, and sickness is chronic, then ask your vet for a prescription. Do not use a medication that works for you; it may contain ingredients harmful to the kitten.

When you notice your kitten or cat swallowing a great deal and starting to lick its lips anxiously, you know that it is becoming car-sick. Stopping the car to let the kitten breathe fresh air may help. Most cats recover, although some will drool and salivate. This should not, however, be a big problem for the owner.

Carrying-Box
Just as you accustom the kitten to riding in a car, so you should get it used to the confines of a carrying-box. If you ever wish to take it on a bus or train, you will need to do so in a carrying-box. You can find several different models in any pet-shop; be sure to get one roomy enough for an animal that will grow to 10 or more pounds.

Cats are adaptable, but they should not be shoved into a new situation without preparation. Place within the box something the kitten is familiar with—a toy, a piece of material, a teething-instrument. Let the cat or kitten come out whenever it wishes to, and keep the top open at first. Make it into a game and you will have no trouble.

Feeding the Kitten from Three to Seven Months
(Based on four feedings a day, at 8 a.m., 12 noon, 4 p.m., 8 p.m. Your kitten may thrive on more feedings than four or fewer as it reaches its sixth or seventh month.)

Prepared (canned) food or baby-food (meats): 2 to 4 ounces (4 to 8 tablespoons) per feeding, with some milk on the side.
Dry Feed or Meal: Do not give at this age.
Combination: 2 to 4 ounces of chopped meat, cooked lightly (mixed in with the drippings) per feeding; or 2 to 4 ounces of finely minced cooked chicken (mixed in with some fat) per feeding. Add some cornflakes to the mixture, or else offer some cornflakes with milk added. Give an occasional cooked egg; if raw, use only the yolk. Give a vitamin-mineral supplement, according to directions on the label. The 4 ounces mentioned in the serving will be far too much for the younger kitten, perhaps close to what the seven-month-old will eat. Kittens differ in their appetites and ability to hold food.

THE KITTEN FROM SEVEN MONTHS TO MATURITY
(Nine to Twelve Months)

Your kitten is now achieving its full size, although for many of the pedigree cats the coat has not attained its mature colour or its full texture. But for all types you can see what your kitten will look like as a cat.

Where does the kitten stand in relation to its needs? (1) It will soon be able to eat once a day. (2) Its permanent teeth are in, or almost. (3) Inoculations, except for the boosters, are completed. (4) Worming, if necessary, has usually been done. (5) If you have a female, spaying has taken place, or will at this time, the same for the male. (6) If you have a pedigree, you have decided whether you want to show it. You can, of course, decide later, but the earlier you make up your mind the better.

For most cats, showing is not a factor, and it has settled into the routine it will follow, as a house pet, companion, perhaps a hunter.

Watch your kitten's size to see if it has filled out enough. It should be lean and lithe, not plump. If it is gaining too much weight, eliminate all table scraps. Cut down somewhat on fats. Feed the same number of times a day, with once a day for the mature cat. Regularity is the best thing—familiar food, fed at the same time, a consistent diet. Most pets are creatures of habit, and the cat is no less so. If you feel your judgment needs bolstering, your vet can tell you if your kitten is growing the way it should.

Most people worry a good deal about being overweight or underweight. They should extend that same concern to their pets. As long as the kitten or cat obtains what its body needs, a certain slenderness prolongs its life and increases its chances of good health. Since most cats receive little exercise, their diet controls their weight. The best-looking pet is a lean, hard animal, and that pet feels at its best, also.

Sexual Maturity
If you have already had your female spayed, then skip this section; and if—as is likely—you have already had your male neutered, then also skip it. It does not affect you or your cat.

For owners still undecided about neutering their cat, I will provide some capsule information. By now, your female will have had at least one heat period in which she has 'called' out to the male. The male has himself long since become sexually mature—that is, ready to sire a litter, although the age varies for individual males and breeds. The female cat may have several heat periods during the mating-season, repeatedly at two- or three-week intervals. Her behaviour-patterns may change: she calls loudly and rubs against things and against you, and the size of her vulva may increase.

If she is not mated, this 'heat' may last for a week or ten days, or even longer. She will be receptive to the male at this time, and if not watched she will almost certainly become pregnant. Incidentally, there is a product on the market that can change the heat cycle without jeopardizing any future chances for reproduction. Ask your vet about it.

The male has by now made a nuisance of himself to express his sexual needs. He is always ready and if not neutered will spray a highly scented urine over things. This establishes his territory and rights. If allowed to roam free, he may disappear for days. The sexually mature male is aggressive and even belligerent if he suspects there is a female around. He will fight for possession. No matter how obnoxious he may seem on these occasions, he is simply fulfilling his way of propagating his species, which is to impregnate a female and produce a litter.

If you decide to mate your female, wait until she is at least ten months old. This gives her a chance to mature physically and emotionally. As for the male, if you want to mate him, wait until he is at least ten months to a year old—he, too, should first achieve physical and sexual maturity.

For further details, see the chapter on the reproductive cycle.

Controls

These are matters of choice, but some owners do not want their cat or cats to have the full run of the house and furniture. If you do not, then you must start early and be firm. Express a sharp *No* each time your cat leaps where it is forbidden. Clap your hands and lift the cat off. You must be persistent, because cats have their own way of handling things. Your firm tone should finally convince it.

Another decision is whether you want to allow your cat to roam—that is, if you live in the suburbs or country. A full male will disappear for days and even longer and possibly get into fights. The female, if left unspayed, will almost surely become pregnant. These are your choices.

My own recommendation is not to let your cat out to run free. There is always the danger of cars, which are the enemy of small pets. Your cat, while fast, may not be quite fast enough. I suggest that a cat be walked on a leash if you want it outside or tethered on a long line if you have a garden. If you live in a real country setting, however, then you can let your cat roam. I do not recommend putting a bell around its neck to warn birds—the bell can drive the cat crazy.

Feeding the Kitten from Seven to Ten Months (Maturity)

The feeding-procedures are basically the same as for the younger kitten. I would cut to two feedings a day, at 8 a.m. and 6 p.m. You should increase the amounts to 3 to 6 ounces a feeding, although by now you have a good sense of what your cat will eat. If you wish to use dry feed or meal, introduce it now, as a replacement for canned food or the combination diet. Make sure you add some fat—bacon, beef, butter—to the dry feed or meal. It has somewhat less fat than other foods. Always provide drinking-water.

On the advice of your vet, you may stop the vitamin-mineral supplement. He may suggest continuing it for another few months, however. I repeat that amounts of food are approximate. Three ounces may be too little for one cat, too much for another. Give a basically nutritious diet to keep your cat slender and healthy; do not cut away any one particular part of the diet, only the quantity.

Diets for Maturity

A cat is mature at twelve months—in terms of body size, bone development and weight. Only its coat may still be changing in length and colour. Its diet should continue as it is described above. Feed once a day and provide as much as is necessary to keep your cat lean, neither plump nor skinny. Try 6 to 7 ounces a day of whichever diet you have decided on, with a little extra fat, small amounts of milk (if digestible) and an occasional cooked egg (or raw yolk). Make certain that all basic needs are met, but do not overfeed. Make sure that your children are not feeding their pet on the sly.

This has been a long chapter full of dos and dont's. I will run through the major points, and you can use this summary as a checklist.

1. Prepare a draught-free area for the newborn kitten (or kittens).
2. Have on hand some basic equipment. For the new kitten without a queen to nurse it: doll's baby-bottles, a plastic eyedropper, doll's baby-nipples, a measuring-cup with ounce gradations, a mixing-bowl, perhaps a baby-scale.
3. Later on, for the growing kitten, get some toys made of hard rubber and a scratching-post for the kitten's developing claws.
4. Do not let children play too hard with the young kitten.
5. Have your cat's claws clipped by a vet if necessary.
6. Do not take the small kitten outside unless it is very mild weather.
7. Keep all items used by the kitten sanitary. Make sure the litter box is kept clean of bowel movements, and keep it dry by adding new layers of litter.
8. Periodically check the kitten's stools for signs of worms or other abnormalities—diarrhoea or blood. If you see such signs, call your vet.
9. Start weaning by the end of the third week if necessary and definitely in the fourth. Finish it by the sixth to eighth week. This is for owners who have the queen present and nursing.
10. Never attempt worming with home remedies.
11. Be careful of the unclosed spot on the top of the kitten's head.
12. Do not bathe a young kitten. By brushing and combing, you can keep it clean, and if the queen is present, she will do the job herself.
13. If you have doubts about your kitten's health, take its temperature with a rectal thermometer. Normal is 101 to 102°F.
14. Whatever diet you choose should be complete. The young kitten requires proportionately larger amounts of protein and fats. Give a vitamin-mineral supplement.
15. Your kitten receives colostrum from the dam. That gives it a temporary immunity to feline distemper. Inoculations are necessary for permanent immunity. See also the chapter on ailments.
16. During teething, from three to six months, check to see if everything is going correctly.
17. At about two months or sooner, work on naming. Walking the cat on a leash, if you plan to do it, should start at about three months.
18. If you plan to have your female spayed or your male neutered, follow the schedule on page 42.
19. The young kitten may become car-sick. It usually passes.
20. Accustom the kitten to a carrying-box in the event you need to use it.
21. Even if nothing seems wrong, your kitten needs a check-up every six months. The mature cat should be examined every year. Maintain the boosters.
22. Do not let your kitten or cat become overweight. It shortens their life. The ideal appearance is a slender, muscular and lithe animal.
23. If your kitten has not been neutered, expect the female to go into her

heat period at six to seven months; the male will show sexual interest after a few months.

24. Maintain daily grooming, brushing, combing and so on.

Owning a Cat: The Cat at Home

For those of you who have never had a cat before, what is it like to own one, or more than one? Does the experience differ from owning a dog or another pet? What is unique about a cat? Are there any emotional problems that might develop between you and your cat? Is there such a thing as voice and body language in dealing with a cat? Are there mysteries into which cats can enter, but not you as owner?

We can answer many of these questions. But for those that remain unanswered, we advise you not to fight against the 'will' or determination of your cat unless it is in matters of safety and training. Let your cat be itself. This point holds whether you have a pedigree or common cat, a long-hair or short-hair, a male or female.

If you do have a pedigree (a small percentage of cats in this country), there may be temperamental differences between one and another. Consider cats as part of a large family in whom certain traits overlap, as they do in people, but then consider the different breeds as you would different nations or races, where certain characteristics predominate. For example, the Rex is as slavishly devoted to its master or mistress as any dog; it is oriented toward people rather than to itself or other cats. The Abyssinian dislikes being enclosed, is very active and enjoys roaming free. The Siamese, if not neutered, will be especially demanding sexually, and both male and female will demand to be mated.

What about the well-known 'independence' of the cat? Are cats really so separated from the human world that they can ignore people? Many people judge cats from what they know of dogs; everyone knows that dogs are companionable and will, with few exceptions, devote themselves to their owner and family. Cats are not so openly companionable, but they are affectionate and they do indeed enjoy attention. A cat that is ignored as a kitten will develop much more slowly and may not develop fully. They do not, however, ordinarily enjoy the company of other cats and may, in fact, be quite jealous if attention is paid to another cat in the household.

In another respect, cats differ from one another considerably—they are not stamped uniformly out of a machine. Each cat has its own personality, so that some enjoy people more than others; some hold back, some must be enticed with voice or with gestures. They react often as people do, but there is in cats a core of independence that does create some reserve. Cats will not always be ready for play, as dogs are, and they are not always prepared to give of themselves. When they feel like it, they will respond to you and respond very affectionately, but they do have their own sense of when and where. Rather than calling them 'independent', I would label them 'individualists', and each has to be treated on its own terms. Go along with your cat, except in matters of health and safety, and do not attempt to make it into something foreign to its nature.

When mothering, cats are not selfish. They will take care of every aspect of their kittens' needs, and they will make sure that none of the kittens is lost. If one of the litter is defective, the queen will often lie on it and thus kill it, somehow sensing that the kitten is not normal and will not develop normally.

Unlike dogs, cats can make a great variety of sounds. Although it is not well known, they have a double set of vocal cords. One is called the 'superior', or 'false', and the other is the 'inferior', or 'true'. With these cords, the cat can make a sound that is an inaudible (to people) purr and a loud noise that sounds to us like a scream or shriek. In between, there is a large variety of sounds, from the calling that the female does when in heat to the purr that is characteristic of a cat we assume is satisfied. Often the purring of the nursing queen is a homing-device—a calling-in of the kittens. There may be as many as seventy-five to a hundred different sounds, a range that is second only to ours.

Part of the reason we think of cats as independent is connected to their ability to adapt very easily. Whereas the puppy has to be led along, on the model of the infant child, the kitten moves into its life with a minimum of difficulty. It can be litterbox-trained by the time it is weaned and seems to know exactly what it must do to survive. A kitten that has to fight for its place in the litter will make the most rapid progress; an orphaned kitten will be somewhat slower. What this means is that the closer the kitten and cat come to their natural state—fighting for their rights, the more rapidly they will come along.

Since the cat has such a unique personality, it has always posed a challenge for the owner. To live with it and relate to it is a distinct experience. Voice, gesture, body posture, manner—all these come into play when you try to relate to a cat. And you can take very little for granted.

THREE

Feline Ailments: A Complete Guide to Your Cat's Health

This chapter is intended as a reference. It is not the final word, and you should not try to take the place of a veterinary surgeon.

You see certain things wrong with your cat or you suspect an ailment, and you begin to check into it. Or else, your vet has examined your cat and you wish some additional information about what is right or wrong. You want to know what to expect. Or, in another sense, you may just want to acquaint yourself with what a cat is like medically, so that if anything does go wrong, you have some sense of things. For example, you might want to know what a cat's normal temperature is, or what a wheezing sound means if it continues, or why your cat is straining in its litter box, or how a cat's digestion works. Further, what vaccinations are necessary, and when?

I suggest that you read through the first section of this chapter, 'Symptoms of Illness and General Structure of the Domestic Cat'. In that way you can acquaint yourself with general medical considerations, such as symptoms of illness, the cat's physical structure and little warning-signs of ailments. Then, afterwards, read the rest of the chapter a little at a time, or consult it as necessary. It would be a mistake to try to read it all at once.

Throughout the chapter, you will notice I advise that in most cases you should see a vet when you recognize certain symptoms. However, a phone-call will often dispel your fears; a visit may not be necessary or even advisable. On many occasions the vet can advise you what to do at home. If, though, there is an emergency, do not try home treatment. Only a vet can help you.

SYMPTOMS OF ILLNESS AND GENERAL STRUCTURE OF THE DOMESTIC CAT

Although the domestic cat belongs to a species identified with the more primitive life in the jungle, it is an animal strikingly similar to us in its physical structure. Psychologically, if we can use such a term in reference to the cat, it is quite different, although many breeds of cats do become profoundly involved in human relationships, and some breeds even shun their own kind for relationships with people. Individual cats can differ as much as individual people, so it is not at all silly to think of your pet cat as someone in the family. When the cat is ill, the entire household is upset. When the cat is well, the household seems to function once again. Most of the time, you can expect your cat to be well. It is a hardy animal, not at all frail, as you may have been led to believe. Even the dainty-looking pedigree or a scrawny street-cat is quite tough.

It becomes sad, of course, when those we are attached to suffer from illness or disease. Our own lives are disrupted, and we go through our daily routines waiting for the time when everything will return to normal. However, with recent advances in veterinary medicine, you can be sure of one thing: whatever ailment or disease your cat suffers from will be treated with the finest medication and professional care. Medical advances in the last ten years have been as startling for cats as for people, and, in some cases, even more startling.

Whenever you recognize warning-signs, call your vet, describe the symptoms as best you can, and be ready to take your cat to him or her for examination. Then be prepared to follow carefully what the vet tells you to do.

You do a great disservice to your cat, or any other pet, if you attempt a home cure without professional advice, unless there is a clear emergency. You mean well in every instance, but you may mean too well. When you see your cat in pain or unhealthy in its look or manner, you wish to do something for it, immediately. The best way to proceed is to make your cat as comfortable as possible and wait until veterinary help is available.

Many home medicines that you would give to an infant or take yourself are potentially dangerous for a cat. Aspirin, which seems to be a miracle drug for both people and dogs, is harmful to cats. Other medicines may contain small amounts of certain drugs—strychnine comes to mind—that are harmful or even fatal to a cat. These are extreme examples, but the point is clear. Do not try haphazardly what you think or hope might work. Unless you have worked closely with cats for years, or grew up with them in the house, you more than likely do not know their reactions to medicines.

Another factor is your cat's weight. Owners often forget that a cat weighs, perhaps, 8 to 10 pounds, 12 to 15 at most, and therefore any 'adult'-size medication must be cut by a full nine-tenths. And if you have a dog in the house as well, you might try to give your cat the same dosage of medicine you give a much larger (or even a small) dog. Since the average dog is 25 to 30 pounds (except for the toy breeds), its medication will be two or three times that of the cat. On the other hand, you might figure that whatever dosage you give a small child cannot hurt a cat. Yet, once again, the difference in size is crucial; the child may be much heavier than a grown cat and considerably bigger than a kitten.

Your chances of killing your cat, or even severely hurting it, are small, but such a chance is there every time you become your own doctor. Why, then, should you take the chance of prolonging the trouble, making it worse, or even creating new problems? Saving money may be a factor, and it is a real one. But your cat's life may be at stake, and often simply a phone-call to the vet is sufficient. A visit may not be at all necessary.

As I suggested in Chapters 1 and 3, choose a vet who has a good reputation and inspires confidence. Do not be impressed by the newness of his equipment if you feel he will not give full attention to whatever goes wrong with your cat. His attitude and attention to detail count. He should really like cats and wish to help them, as we expect a pediatrician to take an interest in every child he or she treats. It is, after all, the person, not the equipment or the office, who will care for your cat when it needs help. The vet should also know his business. He does not need a bedside manner to inspire confidence. He needs to have the latest medical findings at his fingertips and to give you the feeling that he knows what he is doing. Veterinary medicine is moving very rapidly, and your vet should be on top of everything.

You should also insist on cleanliness when you choose a vet. His equipment, whether lavish or not, is a matter of his own method of practice. But cleanliness—of person, equipment and office—will inform you that he respects his profession, himself and his patients. You should want your cat, or any pet, treated only in sanitary surroundings.

Most people find a vet through a friend or relative or neighbour who owns or has owned a pet. Almost every community has at least one vet; most have one who limits his practice to small animals.

When your cat is ill, the best thing you can do is to be patient with it and give it attention and reassurance. Although a cat will often retreat into its own private world when something is wrong, it should still receive what support you can give. The chances of a serious illness are slight—although a few feline ailments can be acute—unless your pet has been ailing from birth or is very infirm. You do know that new medical techniques and new drugs will help it get well all the faster. So do not panic—illness in cats is usually less frequent than in people, and when it occurs, it is just as natural.

But how will you know if your cat is sick or getting sick? Will there be clear signs? And how severe must the signs be before you call in a vet?

If you have children or have been around children, you already know some of the signs of illness or discomfort. Although the cat cannot relate its ailments to you, you will notice a certain unhealthy look to your pet. A sick cat will mope around, even disappear into corners and shadows, lose its usual attentiveness and respond less frequently or not at all to the familiar routine of sounds and calls. Its eyes may lose their brilliance, and its coat may lose some of its gloss and appear dry and coarse.

Or your cat's appetite may decline, and if it does eat, it will be without its usual enthusiasm. It may become altogether indifferent to food. All this may be part of a general chance in behaviour. Your cat's bowel movements may become irregular, and it will have diarrhoea or constipation. You may notice a good deal of futile straining in the litter box. With diarrhoea, there may be only looseness, or there may be a watery, thin substance. There may be a change of colour to yellow or black or red (from bleeding). Bloody diarrhoea is, of course, very serious. The gums and tongue may appear pale or whitish, as though coated. This can be accompanied by dehydration—a loss of body fluids. The membranes around the mouth and eyes may appear dried out, or else the skin may not plop back into place when a fold is picked up. It returns immediately and firmly in a healthy cat, whereas in a dehydrated cat the skin remains separated from the body, in bulges. Also, the eyes may appear sunken, as though the cat has insomnia.

All these symptoms, or even some of them, can indicate a fever. The normal temperature for a cat is from 101 to 101·5°F, although if your cat is very excited or anxious, its temperature can fluctuate without any illness. It is a good idea to have a rectal thermometer available. Shake it down well below 100°, lubricate the tip in petroleum-jelly and insert half its length into the cat's rectum for two minutes. If there is resistance—which is quite possible, do not force the thermometer; work it in slowly, possibly rotating it as it goes in, until you feel the cat ease its sphincter muscle. *Make sure the cat is firmly held*, and do not let it sit on the thermometer. Either a higher or lower temperature usually indicates something wrong, serious or not—a low-grade infection, the presence of bacteria or a chronic condition. In kittens, incidentally, a lower temperature can be quite normal.

Some other signs of possible illness are accumulations of mucus around the eyes, a watery, thin substance, sometimes even turning to pus. Or you may notice some shivering, which may be from excitement or from illness. Shivering unaccompanied by other symptoms can be from a sudden change in temperature, from exposure to cold or from internal pain. In itself, shivering is not a reliable sign of an ailment; it will usually accompany other symptoms.

If your cat does have a fever, or if you see any of these signs, recheck every three or four hours, and if the condition persists or changes for the worse, you should call your vet. It is a good idea to keep track of the temperature if you take it more than once, so that you can give the vet an accurate account. Many illnesses begin in the same way, so it is all the more important that you give a full and accurate description if you want a correct diagnosis. Of course, no sure diagnosis can be made unless the vet sees your pet; blood tests and a stool examination may be necessary.

One of the surest signs of trouble comes with your cat's appetite. Watch for abrupt shifts. If its exercise and locale are constant—for sharp shifts there may create disturbances in the appetite without illness, its appetite after a year of age should remain more or less the same. A cat develops certain likings and then stays with its favourites. If it suddenly becomes ravenous and even an increase in its food does not satisfy it, there might be internal parasites. On the other hand, an unusually large appetite may have a natural reason: some females eat more (or less) when they come into their oestrus, or heat cycle; even a very happy cat that has enjoyed a good deal of attention and affection may eat more. On the other hand, a sudden indifference to food may mean infection or poisons in the system. Or you may simply have changed the cat's schedule and it is protesting by going on a temporary hunger-strike.

Most domestic animals are creatures of habit, and sudden shifts in their food or feeding-schedule will throw them off. Some variety is necessary, but abrupt changes may make your cat very finicky and you may suspect an ailment that is not present. All the cat may suffer from is a temporary attack of nerves or anxiety. A domestic cat 'survives' in the home by adjusting to its environment as much as a jungle cat survives by adjusting to its.

Coughing in a cat may result from a chill suffered in a draught, or it may be the first symptom of a whole range of possible ailments: worms, feline rhinotracheitis, upper-respiratory infection and pneumonitis. In itself, a cough may mean very little, perhaps a temporary condition that will clear itself. A cough combined with a fever, running nose, hoarseness, a lot of blinking or sensitivity to light, and abnormal breathing, however, indicates a severe illness that should be attended to by a vet without delay. The upper-respiratory infections, especially feline rhinotracheitis, can be quite serious.

Trembling and shivering in a cat may mean that it has been exposed to a draught and has become chilled, possibly with fever. Or it may mean poisoning. Has your cat been near fresh insect-powder, or have you used a spray that is harmful for pets? Has your cat perhaps got into the medicine cabinet or into the soaps? Like small children, cats are inquisitive and insistent, and they move with much greater agility. Then again, trembling in a pregnant queen or in a nursing dam (the mother queen) may indicate eclampsia, a disorder caused by a severe calcium-deficiency, which a vet can correct only by immediate injections of calcium.

Convulsions and collapse in a cat are, of course, frightening to any owner. They can result from poisoning, a very serious matter, or from certain worms—also serious, especially in a young kitten.

Some symptoms, however, will point to only a single ailment. If you notice, for example, that your cat is shaking its head or holding it at an unnatural angle, you can suspect ear trouble. It may have an infection, which your vet can correct, or fleas, mites or some other parasites. Or the ear flap might be torn or irritated.

Certain other annoyances, such as excessive scratching, may be cleared up by a medicinal bath (prescribed by a vet).

Then there are specific ailments that a cat is subject to usually only in old age—most kidney troubles, loss of sight, partial loss of hearing, the same afflictions that plague the human race. Yet, as we know from our own experience, many of these more serious ailments can be partially or completely controlled by medication or surgery.

If we allow for minor differences in skeleton and muscles, the cat is in fact strikingly like the human being in its basic make-up and in the illnesses that afflict it. Of course, some of its senses are far keener than ours—its sense of smell and hearing, for instance. And while we use our whiskers as a way of enhancing our appearance, the cat uses its as a supplement to its vision and hearing, somewhat like antennas in certain insects. While we use all our senses to orientate ourselves to our world, the cat focuses chiefly on two, smell and sound.

Although a cat's skin and hair are somewhat different from ours, they serve the same purpose: to protect it against heat and cold. And just as the races of man differ from each other in skin texture and hair quality, so does one breed of cat differ from another. The Siamese, for example, does not enjoy sharp changes in temperature and may suffer a chill in cold climates. Although cats normally do not live outside, those that spend more time outdoors than indoors do develop more resistant coats, longer, thicker and more protective. Of course, do not expect a short-hair to become a long-hair, but the quality of the coat does change if exposed to different climatic conditions.

When a cat sheds (heavily in the spring, but really all year round), it is renewing its coat for summer or winter. This is a natural process for the cat, and daily grooming will help you keep ahead of the hair fall and prevent the cat's licking off and swallowing the loose hairs. An excessive amount of such swallowing will result in hair balls, which can create internal problems that may need treatment. Long-hairs in particular, if not groomed regularly, will lick off the loose hair and develop hair balls. All cats shed as a way of ridding themselves of the old, dead hair. The hair is really a three-stage phenomenon: the old hair that is falling out, the new hair that is growing in and the hair that is doing neither. Different breeds obviously shed different amounts, with the long-hairs leaving a mat on furniture and rugs unless brushed regularly.

A cat's skin works rather the way ours does but not to the same degree. While our sweat glands regulate the body's temperature, only to a very limited extent does the cat's skin cool its body through evaporation. Its cooling-system works, rather, through radiation. Its tongue, nose and foot-pads also help to cool it off, but not enough to give it relief if it is closed up in a hot car, cupboard or attic. A cat may die of heat prostration or exhaustion in a situation that would only make a person very uncomfortable. In an enclosed hot space—such as a car under a hot sun, with the windows closed, there is nowhere for the body heat to go. A person would get rid of some of his heat by sweating, but a cat does not sweat through its skin.

But these are matters only of degree. The cat's body make-up is again similar to a human being's once we allow for certain elements that let the cat adapt to its own type of environment. The general muscular system is only one similarity between cats and people. The cat's digestive tract has the usual recognizable elements: from the mouth to the oesophagus, stomach, small and large intestines, on to the rectum. The digestive process is aided by bile from the liver (bile splits up fat into tiny globules) and a starch-digesting element from the pancreas. All this is quite familiar. But the cat's digestive system hurries things up—just as its teeth are more functional, serving to tear and shred rather than simply chew, all in the name of speed. If for some reason the cat wishes to reject its food, it has the ability to vomit voluntarily. Such rejection means a foaming-up at the mouth—something you will notice if you try to administer liquid medicine.

The principal difference between the nervous system of a cat and that of a man lies in the cat's reflex actions, which are faster and more co-ordinated and can be conditioned to a much greater extent than in man. Otherwise, the cat's nervous system is built on the same principles, with the brain serving as the source of learning and motivation and the spinal cord acting as conductor of impulses to and from the brain. As with people, there are several illnesses that severely strain and even damage the nervous system, among them rabies (relatively rare in cats) and feline distemper, or panleukopenia. Still other ailments are caused by the malfunction of a gland. We are all familiar with the symptoms of a thyroid disorder. When the gland secretes too much of its hormone, the cat becomes nervous, and when it secretes too little, it appears lazy. If other endocrine glands—the pituitary or the adrenals—or the pancreas fail to work properly, then the cat may go into convulsions, or fits. We often see trembling when poisons enter a cat's system, either through an insecticide or a snake-bite, for these directly affect its nerves.

The feline urinary system, also, is quite similar to man's. The chief organs involved are the kidneys, the bladder and the urethra. The kidneys filter waste material, the bladder holds the liquid matter, and the urethra carries the urine from the bladder. The urinary system of the cat, as in man, works with the digestive tract. That is, if something goes wrong with any one part, the disorder usually disturbs the entire system. You know that your cat may have a kidney ailment not only by the change in its urine but by the general decline in its appearance, behaviour and health.

A condition that seems fairly common in cats is urolithiasis, which will be described in detail later. This is a condition in which sand or a mucous plug form in the urinary system of the animal. Some cats appear predisposed to this condition, perhaps the result of an increased concentration of crystalline salts in the urine. It can lead to cystitis, an inflammation of the bladder; or urethral calculi, in which sand or a mucous plug lodges in the urethra. While serious enough in the female, the condition is most serious in the male, since the sand or mucous plug can lead to complete urethral blockage. The important thing is to recognize the symptoms (detailed below), so that you can take your cat to a vet as soon as you notice something seriously wrong.

The reproductive system for both male and female cats is very much like that of men and women, if we allow for certain small differences that originate in the cat's more primitive state. One of the differences is the presence of small papillae, or barbs, on the penis of the tomcat, the purpose of which is to stimulate the female and serve as a holding surface. This ensures that the mating takes, and may also force the female to ovulate soon afterward. The organs, however, are basically the same: in the male, the penis, testicles and prostate gland; in the female, the ovaries, uterus and vagina, and for nursing her kittens the mammary glands.

The rest of the female's internal organization is similar to a woman's, except for the uterus (which is Y-shaped), with the cervix and Fallopian tubes serving the same purpose. Of course, the female has an oestrus, or heat period, occurring during seasons and often lasting for some time unless she is mated. The female 'calls', or cries, during this time, and it can be an ongoing event unless she is mated or spayed. During her season, she is prepared to mate, and she will mate with several toms in succession; so if you are interested in selective mating, make sure your female does not roam, or else her litter will be made up of a composite of kittens. There are instances in which three or four different kinds of kittens have come from the same female.

This, then, is your cat in its general physical structure and development. It is not very different from us physically, although 'psychologically' the differences are great. Dogs, of course, work their way into human life much more closely than do cats. Although cats may share our happy and sad moments and may attach themselves remarkably to human company, they are nevertheless untouchable in some areas of their existence. The dog has somehow evolved to the near human state in its adaptability; the cat is still on the way. Thousands of years of domesticity have brought the cat closer to human beings, but it remains at least partially allied to its jungle cousins, the big cats, whose style of life is completely instinctive.

The cat is a remarkable phenomenon, as you know if you have lived with one, and you owe it to your pet to give it the best medical treatment you can. If you see it coming down with an ailment, or suspect sickness of some indeterminate kind, be prepared to act on your suspicion. And even if you have a perfectly healthy and functioning cat, it is always a good idea to have your vet give it a check-up every six months.

I indicated before that you should read this chapter through a little at a time, so that you have the general sense of what a cat's illnesses involve. You can then have a better idea of what a well cat is like and what to expect with a sick cat. Then, if you think it has a specific ailment, you can, through the use of the index, turn to the explanation of that ailment and find out what you should do. In this way you can alleviate the anxiety and nervousness that one usually feels when faced with the unknown.

VACCINES AND VACCINATION

The chief illnesses for which vaccination or inoculation is necessary are the following: panleukopenia (also known as feline distemper or feline infection enteritis), a viral infection that attacks the cat's digestive system; rhinotracheitis, a severe cold-like ailment that attacks the cat's eyes, nose and throat; and calici, which involves discharge from the mouth and a lung cough frequently accompanied by mouth ulceration. There are various types of vaccine in use in the UK against these infections; some are modified live vaccine, and others are killed vaccine. Your vet will recommend the most suitable for your cat or kitten and will advise you about booster injections. All cats and kittens shown under GCCF rules must have a current certificate of vaccination against feline infectious enteritis.

Panleukopenia (Also called Feline Distemper or Enteritis, even Cat Plague and Show Fever)
Feline distemper is a viral infection that attacks the cat's digestive system with extreme severity. It is almost always fatal to kittens and seventy-five to ninety per cent fatal to older cats. Usually, the virus incubates for a few days, and then some of the following symptoms may become evident. The cat loses all drive and energy and becomes lethargic. It may vomit, and there

will probably be discharges from the nose and eyes. Many cats break their litter-box training at this time, with diarrhoea or a bloody, watery stool, and will hang their heads, half asleep, over their water-bowl. If you take the temperature, you may find a fever as high as 104 to 106°F. There is, often, constant drooling and ulcerated mucous membranes of the mouth. Very often the afflicted cat will sit or lie quietly in a corner, and many cats simply vanish, as jungle animals disappear in order to die by themselves. One of the first warning-signals: if you see your cat vomiting persistently, see your vet immediately.

There is a severe weight loss as the result of dehydration, although by the time you notice such a loss, the disease has already ravaged the cat. Many of these symptoms, even the extreme ones, are indicative of several ailments in addition to panleukopenia. Often you cannot tell the difference between one and another, but your cat will appear so miserable that you should act at once. Your vet can tell by means of a white-cell count after a blood-test. The congestion spreads very rapidly once it catches hold, racing from intestines to liver, kidneys and spleen, so that the cat's insides are almost totally inflamed.

Where, you may wonder, does such a virulent disease come from? It is carried by the air, and any cat can catch it by breathing it in from an infected cat. It is also carried by excrement, urine and nasal discharges. One reason it takes hold so virulently in a cattery or kennel is that one cat can infect all the others even without contact. And the virus persists, remaining in the air for a month or more. Do not bring cats that have not been immunized into a house in which a cat has been ill with panleukopenia, even if plenty of time has elapsed.

The best way to handle this virulent disease is to make certain that your kitten or cat does not associate with other cats until it has received its immunizations.

Rhinotracheitis

Rhinotracheitis is an upper-respiratory infection, and it seems more common in kittens than in older cats, although it may attack either. Its symptoms are common to many upper-respiratory ailments: nasal and ocular (eye) discharge; sneezing, often violent and continued; a red throat; difficulty in breathing; perhaps drooling; a distinct loss of appetite; some coughing. An infected cat will fade away from its usual favourite places and very possibly hide.

Once again, prevention is everything here, since an infected kitten or cat may not survive a severe attack. And even a recovered cat can remain a carrier of the disease and inadvertently infect the rest of the litter or other cats in your house.

Vaccination serves as protection as soon as the natural immunity from the dam's colostrum becomes ineffective at six to eight weeks.

Calici

Calici is another upper-respiratory infection probably indistinguishable by the layman from rhinotracheitis or any other respiratory ailment. The symptoms are similar to those mentioned before: discharge from the mouth and tongue area, ulcerations in the mouth and on the tongue, a lung cough, high temperature—up to 104 to 106°F, loss of appetite (complete stoppage of eating) and severe depression. The cat may simply sit or lie in a corner and seem dead to the world. Since the symptoms are the same as for many ailments, you will not recognize calici in particular, but such symptoms indicate that your cat is very sick indeed and needs immediate professional care.

The best thing is prevention, by vaccination.

Rabies

Rabies is relatively rare in cats—far rarer even than in dogs. Because of our quarantine regulations, rabies is not present in the UK, and so the following paragraphs do not apply to this country but are included as a matter of interest only. Only animals about to be exported are permitted to be vaccinated here.

Since rabies is probably the best known of these virulent diseases, and the most feared, I will spend some time on it. Incidentally, although cats can have both the 'dumb' and 'furious' type of rabies, one sign of infection in cats is that they hide.

Rabies is a disease of the nervous system. It is a virus transmitted in the saliva of a rabid cat or another rabid animal. The usual way in which a person or a cat (or any pet) can get rabies is through the bite of a rabid animal, although contact of infected saliva with any skin lesion may transmit the disease.

A rabid cat has had the virus transmitted to its nerve tissues by the saliva from the bite of another rabid animal (cat, dog, fox, bat), and this virus travels eventually to the brain, where it causes an inflammation called encephalitis. Once the cat's brain is inflamed, its behaviour changes in one of two ways. The cat may become entirely lethargic (what is called the 'dumb', or 'paralytic', kind of rabies) or it may be overly excited (what is called the 'furious' kind).

In the dumb kind, the cat will sit around listlessly, utterly depressed and incapable of action. Often, its mouth is wide open, and its lower jaw hangs as if useless. The tongue drools saliva. In furious rabies, the cat may be irritated by everything that moves, and it may attack anything that moves. The cat is very alert and very anxious, hyperactive, with its pupils dilated. Paralysis will come later.

Some cats, however, will simply run away and hide.

What are the most common symptoms of rabies? The first signs may be no different from those you see in digestive disorders, injuries, poisoning or any infectious disease. Before the cat becomes either dumb or furious, there is usually a sharp change in its behaviour. A pleasant, companionable cat may become irritable, and a temperamental cat subdued. In most cases, your cat will show extreme restlessness. Its appetite will be disturbed, although it is difficult for me to predict exactly how. It may become ravenously hungry and yet appear indifferent to food. After a while, it may lose all interest in its food.

Some of the panic that a rabid cat suffers comes from its difficulty in swallowing. The rabies virus paralyses the nerves in the throat and jaw muscles—that is why we often see the jaw hanging open uselessly. Since the cat feels great thirst and cannot swallow, it becomes alarmed. Rabies was once known as hydrophobia ('fear of water'), but the cat does not fear water. It is simply unable to swallow it. Frothing may or may not occur; it by no means always accompanies rabies, although to the layman it seems characteristic of the virus.

As the disease develops, the cat's frenzy usually increases. In time, the brain is affected, but even before this happens the cat is filled with fear and frustration. Once the brain is inflamed, the cat usually dies shortly after. Rabies is considered a hundred per cent fatal in all animals and man if not treated immediately.

Because of Britain's quarantine laws, the country is free of rabies. Nevertheless, be wary of any cat or dog you suspect has rabies, and do not try to handle even your own cat if you should be in doubt. Keep your children away. Prevention of a bite is all-important. All suspected animals should be examined by a vet and quarantined if necessary.

EXTERNAL PARASITES

There are four external parasites that can attack your cat, and they are all annoying for it and possibly for you also. They are the familiar flea, louse, mite and tick (less common in cats). Of the four, the flea is the most common. Any of the four types may exist in small numbers or in infestations. They are called external because they attach themselves to the cat's skin, where they feed off blood, fluid in the tissues or the skin itself. Since in most cases they burrow in deeply, it is impossible for the cat to dislodge them by itself. In addition to the discomfort and annoyance these parasites cause, some carry disease with them. A cat heavily infested by parasites may even come down with serious illnesses because its resistance is lowered. These cases are rare but not negligible.

Fleas, for example, carry tapeworm eggs. Ticks, we know, may carry blood parasites. Lice in great numbers may suck the cat's blood and cause anaemia. Mites cause manges that can make a cat crazy with itchiness. Ear mites are particularly common.

External parasites multiply incredibly fast once they find a suitable host. Since the chief pleasure that a parasite gets is a meal, it resists ferociously any attempt to dislodge it, all the time biting and sucking. Many species have evolved a resistance to parasiticides.

Of course these parasites are by no means the only cause of skin trouble in a cat (or any pet). There are several other kinds of skin ailment that are persistent and troublesome. For these, see pages 84–93 for my discussion of skin problems. Like the parasitic variety, most of the others need veterinary treatment and advice. The general rule to follow is not to attempt treatment yourself. Many of these organisms are difficult to identify except under the microscope or by means of blood-tests. And if you cannot identify them, any home treatment, no matter how loving, is a hit-or-miss affair. You may think you are clearing up the condition when actually you are not. In the meantime, the organisms are multiplying. Ordinarily, a vet can determine the kind of skin trouble your cat has and recommend the correct treatment, although some skin ailments persist even under treatment.

Fleas

Fleas jump around, from one place to another, from one cat to another and even to a person. You can find fleas on nearly any part of your cat's body, although they do prefer the hairiest places: the neck, head, tail area and chest. They go after short-hairs as well as long-hairs, and even the cat confined in a flat is subject to them.

Flea eggs are dormant during the cold weather, and even if they are in an area where the cat usually sleeps or lies, it will not be troubled. With the coming of warm and humid weather, however, the eggs hatch. You may have noticed that your cat does a good deal of scratching during the summer and seems to have most of its skin troubles then.

Once awakened by heat and dampness, the flea egg hatches a worm. From this worm, or larva, eventually comes the flea, a very hardy fellow indeed. The flea simply waits until something warm comes along that it can jump on—your cat (or other pet) or you or someone else in your family. (It will not, however, remain on people.) The exception is the sticktight flea of poultry, rarely found on cats, which, instead of wandering around, lays its eggs deep down in the victim's skin, in little burrowlike ulcers it has made.

Fleas will make your cat scratch furiously. In time, it will not only wear away the hair in several places but also damage the skin, in some cases giving itself a case of chronic parasitic dermatitis.

Lice

Lice are somewhat less common than fleas on cats, but they do exist. They are host-specific, which means that a cat-louse will remain on the cat and not jump around. Lice do not roam the cat's body but dig into one place and remain there, sucking and biting until you flush them out. Once the louse settles, it makes the spot its permanent home, from egg state through adolescence and adulthood. Since the louse is so small, your chances of seeing it are slight. The louse is smaller than a pinhead, and it becomes lost in all that hair.

You can be pretty sure that your cat has lice or some other parasite when you see it using a lot of energy and determination burrowing into its coat with its paws, tongue and teeth. Its chances of finding such a small parasite are as slight as yours. Gradually its scratching may wear away the hair in the infested part, but by then the lice are deeply embedded. The parasites may also wear away the hair by attacking the follicles. As mentioned, the danger of a great number of lice is that, because they suck blood, they may cause anaemia in a kitten. Lice, too, can be passed on to members of your family when the cat sheds hair containing them or their eggs. They are harmless and will not stay on people but may irritate your nerves.

Mites

Mites are particularly troublesome because there are several varieties and they are difficult for the owner to detect. One type of mite—a cigar-shaped parasite—causes demodectic, or follicular, mange (red mange). A second type—a spider-shaped parasite with eight legs—causes sarcoptic mange, or scabies. A third type, the ear mite—the most common type with cats, infests its ear and may cause an ailment called otodectic mange. These manges are serious skin diseases that go further than discomfort for your cat. They can lead to serious complications. Demodectic mange spreads rapidly and may cause infections all over your cat's body. Sarcoptic mange results in a whole series of scabs, inflammations and bloody lesions. Otodectic mange may lead to permanent ear damage if not treated.

The mange mite, like many other parasites, with the exception of the flea, works its way into the cat's skin. It goes like this: it burrows into the small sac containing the root of the hair, and the hair falls out. This sac is called the follicle, thus the term 'follicular mange' for this particular kind. Many researchers believe that the mange mite can be passed at birth, although not by genes, but it cannot be passed from one cat to another. Everyone agrees, however, that demodectic mange cannot be transmitted from a cat to a person. Unfortunately, sarcoptic mange may be carried from the cat's skin to children and adults. Children, in particular, are exposed to it when they roll and play with their pet, or put their face up against the soft fur of the cat. The result can be an annoying rash.

In all types of mange, your cat will scratch violently at different parts of its body. Demodectic mange itself may be indicated only by general inflammation or by bloody pimples. Sarcoptic mange is evidenced by scabs, a thickening of the skin and extreme shedding of hair in the afflicted area. The cat may begin to smell sour. With otodectic (ear) mange, the cat will carry its head at a strange angle and shake its head. A black discharge is prevalent. The cat may even suffer loss of balance and show the symptoms of a general illness—listlessness and loss of appetite and weight—when not treated. You may notice only a general unhealthiness.

The definitive diagnosis for all mites can be made only by skin-scraping and microscopic examination.

Ticks

Although ticks are not particularly drawn to cats, they do frequent anything that moves, and a cat that lurks in woods or lives on a farm may pick up one tick or even more. The cat kept shut up in a flat need not worry. Ticks are extremely annoying because of their hardiness and endurance. The tick lives off three stages of hosts, and by the time it fastens on a person or an animal it is very practised indeed. Once embedded in the skin, it resists removal with the ferocity of a squatter fighting for his rights.

Ticks can be easily recognized because they look like flat, blackish-brown seeds, giving the appearance of small warts. Often the seeds have become greatly swollen with blood and are an ugly dark red. A serious infestation may lead to anaemia in your cat. The most common type is the sheep tick, which is found in long grass and which attaches itself to any animal or human. Ticks tend to seek out certain parts of the cat's body: the stomach area, the pads of the feet, the feet themselves and the folds between the legs and the body. Some varieties find the cat's ear a fine place in which to live. The tick seeks crevices in the cat, just as it looks for crevices in your house in which to lay its eggs and thrive.

The presence of more than one or two ticks is indicated by the persistent scratching and general misery of your cat. Unlike most other parasites, ticks can be identified without microscopic examination. They are rare on cats. I have never seen one.

General Treatment of External Parasites

Although the treatment for each type of parasite differs, there are two general procedures common to all. First, a vet must determine by examination exactly what parasite is involved. The treatment he recommends will depend, of course, on the diagnosis. Second, the owner must try to eliminate the source of the parasite by spraying and cleaning out the places his cat favours. The life-cycle of the parasite must be broken up, or else it will recur.

The vet will often recommend a flea- or tick-collar, powders, dips or sprays to eliminate the parasites already infesting your cat. If the case is advanced, the treatment, unfortunately, may be lengthy. As a general rule, the sooner an infestation is discovered, the faster it can be cleared up.

In addition, all owners should comb and brush their cat regularly. Not only will this prevent parasites, it will also prevent hair balls, the accumulation of hair in the cat's intestine that results from licking and swallowing. Regular combing and brushing or stripping of the old hair will add tone to the cat's skin and coat, prevent tangles in the long-hair and help remove parasites before they become solidly entrenched. Keeping the cat clean may not be the complete answer to parasites—especially if you let your pet roam in areas where such parasites abound, but it certainly helps to keep away these little armies of pests.

Cleanliness also means keeping the cat's quarters free of parasites. If your cat has the full run of the house, then this is more difficult, but spraying with a non-toxic insecticide may help. If your cat roams outside, there is not much you can do, since fieldmice and rats are secondary carriers of parasites that may in time find a home on your cat.

For a more detailed description of each external parasite, as well as the treatment for each, see the section on skin ailments, page 84.

INTERNAL PARASITES

One of the more common afflictions that a kitten or cat can suffer from is worms. Perhaps fifty per cent of cats have worms at one time or another, in varying degrees of infestation. Most kittens, even when turned over to an owner from a cattery or when purchased elsewhere, need to be examined for worms. If you notice some of the symptoms listed below, act immediately, because your cat probably needs worming, and the degree of infestation could be serious. In most cases, worming is completely successful, especially with periodic stool-examinations, and your cat will return to perfect health in a short time.

There are several common symptoms of worms. When you notice these symptoms, do not try to do the worming yourself unless you cannot take your cat to a vet. Certain worms are more dangerous than others, and a vet's diagnosis is essential. Different worms have to be treated in different ways. The patent medicines available at your local chemist's are generally aimed at specific types. Thus, the patent medicine you choose may be for a type your cat does not have and will do no good.

What are the signs of a worm infestation? A lot depends on how heavy the infestation is, of course. Your cat generally will seem lethargic, lacking energy and pep. It may appear ill without being really ill. Actually, it is quite ill in a quiet way, for the worms are parasites that live off the host's body and literally eat it up. The appetite of your cat will certainly be affected; there may be either a loss of appetite or a tremendous pick-up so that it stuffs itself. You may notice a bloated stomach, as if air had been pumped inside. Sometimes there will be diarrhoea, a watery and thin bowel movement; you may notice blood in the stool. When such signs appear, the worm infestation is serious.

Your cat's coat may also be affected, becoming dried-out and coarse in texture, especially if the infestation is heavy and neglected. A loss of weight can result, from a loss of fluids. If the infestation occurs in a kitten, the problem is serious, since even a small fluid-loss can result in partial dehydration. On occasion, the cat may vomit worms. It will look unhealthy. While it may not be suffering pain, it has lost energy and may drowse far more than usual; you may see it rubbing its body against the floor, as though trying to relieve a local ache. Do not expect too much of your cat at this time—it is temporarily ill, as much as if it had a more apparent illness.

Children, your own and their friends, should be kept away from a cat suffering from worms. A child who touches or rubs against the cat's hind-quarters and then inadvertently puts his finger in his mouth may become infected with worms, especially roundworms.

Most types of worms are relatively easy to treat, while some others are more difficult and require more care. If you see any of the above symptoms, suspect worms. You may be wrong, but to let the infestation worsen can turn an easy case into a difficult one. The best thing to do is to take a sample of the cat's stool to the vet for an examination, or to bring the cat in so that the vet can take a smear. The actual worming usually requires only one day and may have to be repeated in ten days, after which the stool is rechecked. Usually, a kitten under four to six weeks is not wormed unless its stool and vomit show signs of worms. The best time is at about eight weeks.

Later I will take up the internal parasites in greater detail. The description here is to acquaint you with the various types and, most of all, to alert you to some of the dangers. Different types of worms attack nearly every major organ—heartworms, intestinal worms, lungworms, stomach worms and so on.

Heartworms

Although heartworms in dogs have received more publicity than in cats, they can exist in cats as well, although rarely. (They have not been recorded in the UK.) I have never seen a case. The heartworms (also called filariae) are transmitted to cats by mosquitoes that have bitten an infected dog or cat. The heartworm was once localized, in wooded and rural areas, but it has spread to many regions of the United States, including the north-east. The mature worm settles in the heart and interferes with the circulation of the blood, causing breathing difficulties, loss of weight, a cough and even convulsions.

Intestinal Protozoans (Coccidia)
These are persistent intestinal parasites that bring on symptoms similar to those of many other feline ailments—especially diarrhoea. They can drain your cat's strength almost completely and, because of the diarrhoea, lead to dehydration.

NOTE: You have perhaps heard of this parasite because *Toxoplasma gondii*, one of its strains, gained a good deal of publicity recently. This strain can be contagious to pregnant women and affect the foetus. Although defects from *Toxoplasmosis* are very rare, such women should be careful to have their cat tested if they notice a general unhealthiness—certainly diarrhoea, loss of weight, coughing or any breathing difficulties, fever and lack of appetite. Also, do not feed your cat raw meat, and keep it in so that it does not catch rodents. (The stool and blood may be tested in healthy cats.)

Tapeworms
Although rare, these, also, can result from the eating of raw fish or meat, or from swallowing infected fleas and lice from mice and rats. They are difficult to eliminate, since the head, which attaches itself to the intestinal wall, must be removed, and the worm itself can grow to more than a foot in length. There may be several worms. You may recognize a worm or worms when you see what seem to be little progottids, like kernels of rice, around the cat's anus. These are pieces of the tapeworm, but their presence does not mean that the infestation has cleared up or been eliminated. The head itself must still be removed, or the worms will remain.

Whipworms
While very rare, whipworms settle in the cat's colon and intestinal tract (the cecum). They cause the same symptoms associated with other types of worms: diarrhoea, both chronic and acute, loss of blood and extreme intestinal irritation, so that your cat is uncomfortable and uneasy.

Ascarids, or Roundworms
These worms are the most common type in cats. They are a white, slim worm, about 1 to 4 inches in length, which develops in the intestine and is found in the cat's stool. They live by absorbing food-value from the digestive juices of the cat. They are often found in kittens, since the queen can pass them on to her litter through the blood.

TURN TO PAGE 65 →

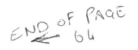
Fluke Disease

This is a disease that derives almost solely from the eating of raw fish. Flukes are parasitical worms that harbour a virus-like organism that attacks the cat's lungs, liver and small intestine. Some of the symptoms are similar to those of a respiratory illness, if the worms settle in the lungs, and to an intestinal illness if in the intestines.

Hookworms

Hookworms live off blood and are particularly dangerous if they infest a kitten. They attach themselves to the intestinal wall, where they suck the cat's blood and, with it, its energy. The results are diarrhoea, weakness, loss of weight and severe anaemia, if neglected. The kitten is especially susceptible to anaemia.

Lungworms

This type of worm attacks the lungs and gives symptoms similar to those in respiratory diseases. Since you cannot see these worms in the stool, your chief signs will be your cat's cough and general malaise; there may also be nasal discharge, fever and loss of appetite. A cat can be infected from eating crayfish.

Kidneyworms

These attack the organ they are named after. Very rare, they can cause symptoms similar to those of other types described above.

What to do about Internal Parasites

1. One of the biggest mistakes an owner can make is to try to worm a cat without professional help. All worming must be done by a vet or under his close supervision. You can give your cat a patent medicine only if you know what kind of worm is involved.

2. If no vet is available and will not be for some time, then you may have to give a patent medicine. Follow directions carefully, but keep trying to find a vet.

3. If you notice worms or suspect them and cannot see a vet right away, then give your cat a bland diet of starch (rice, barley or noodles) and cooked hamburger meat. Avoid bulky foods that encourage a loose stool (such as raw meat, raw vegetables or uncooked grains). Once the worming procedure begins, feeding will depend on the type of worm being treated and the kind of medicine being administered, as well as the degree of worm infestation. These will differ for each cat and for each attack of worms. Ask your vet for information about feeding and fasting. Many vets have a printed schedule for you, one that fits your cat's condition. After worming, continue the bland diet suggested above for a week or for as long as is recommended.

4. For the protection of the cat as well as for the protection of everyone else in the house, keep your cat's living-areas clean. Scrub the floor with a strong (non-toxic) disinfectant—this is especially for those who keep

their cat or cats in a limited space. Change the cat's drinking-water several times a day. Disinfect all pails and feeding-dishes. Remember, worms will not disappear the moment a vet treats your cat internally; all aspects of its life must be treated.

5. Do not try to worm a sick or weak cat. The worming procedure itself involves toxic medication, and the cat or kitten needs strength to maintain itself. Ask your vet about building up a pet that has been severely weakened by worms.

It will be difficult for you to ignore the fact that your pet has worms, for the cat will almost always call it to your attention. Incidentally, worm infestations seldom leave any lasting effects if the worms are identified early and completed eliminated. You must be careful to continue treatment when necessary, for worms, like any other parasite, are persistent. With modern equipment and medication, however, the vet can quickly determine what kind of worm is involved and prescribe the proper treatment.

CIRCULATORY DISORDERS
(Affecting the Heart and Blood Vessels)

As you know from human beings, the circulatory system involves the heart and blood vessels. Heart disorders and blood ailments in cats are very similar to those in people, and often the causes are also similar. Incidentally, heart disorders in cats are not very common. A few cats have congenital heart disease (the result of incomplete closure of valves in the heart), creating a condition similar to that of the 'blue baby'. Some kittens may now be operated on for such ailments and recover.

One of the most common signs of a heart ailment or condition in your cat is a cardiac cough, a sound that sounds like an upper-respiratory cough. If your cat becomes excited, it may hack, and when calm it may not. Or it may cough all the time. Everything depends on the actual condition and the degree of severity. Such a heart ailment is rare.

Some symptoms you may notice are that your cat seems winded or gasps for breath; breathing appears rapid. There will be loss of vitality; quickness to tire; weakness of pulse; a murmur, or shushing noise, in the chest cavity; even a blueness of tongue and gums.

An enlarged heart also causes a weakness. Enlargement means that your cat will restrict its activities—do not encourage anything strenuous, such as undue excitement or running and jumping.

Also, an old cat, like an older person, should not suddenly be forced into violent activity. Any cat past seven or eight should not be treated as if it were an energetic kitten. The heart is regulating it into old age, and the cat should be permitted to set its own pace—it probably will anyway. Most of this is not 'medical knowledge' but common sense, applicable to house pets as well as to people.

Accidents that affect the heart are almost impossible to cure, although advances in cardiology are so breath-taking that even here we might expect a breakthrough. Occasionally, heart surgery for an accident will save a cat; rapidity of treatment is, of course, essential.

With modern methods of diagnosis by means of electrocardiographs and audio-visual recorders and with new medication available, heart disorders may be successfully handled today. Consult your vet.

Anaemia
When the haemoglobin (red blood cells) in the blood is reduced by illness, bleeding from an accident, hookworm or some other cause, the cat has anaemia. Cats have a sensitive bone-marrow structure and thus can suffer anaemia from any disease that seriously depresses the marrow. One reason, in fact, that aspirin is bad for cats is that it affects the bone marrow, as well as irritating the stomach.

Since the red blood cells carry oxygen from the lungs, their breakdown or reduction will lead to certain obvious signs: the cat's tongue and gums will become whitish, unhealthy-looking, as will the mucous membranes of its eyes. Its appetite may decline, and the general condition will be one of weakness, listlessness and depression. Your pet may sleep more than usual. Its body will become drawn and thin, the coat lacking in lustre; its eyes will seem sunken, as though pulling out of the head cavity.

Anaemia may also result from internal or external parasites. The symptoms here are similar to those from anaemia that derives from other causes. You may notice a rise in temperature, loss of appetite, a reddish discolouration of the urine, extreme listlessness and depression, pale lips and gums or increase in pulse rate and respiration. Any of these symptoms (which may also seem to derive from other diseases) should send you to a vet immediately.

The veterinary treatment of anaemia involves supplements of iron in the diet: plenty of meat (especially liver), iron pills, liquid iron or injections of liver. Even a blood-transfusion may be called for in particularly bad cases. Once the red cells are built up again, you will notice a steady increase in your cat's vigour. The bright look in its eyes will return, the coat will regain its lustre, the appetite will pick up and its body will begin to fill out.

Ascites
Ascites is an ailment usually associated with the older cat, but it can occur in the younger animal as well, although less often. It is an accumulation of fluid on the abdominal cavity, the result of a defect or malfunction in the liver, heart or lungs. Since a defect or malfunction is more common in the older cat, ascites normally develops then, if it develops at all. In some cases you may notice an unnaturally swollen abdomen and shallow breathing. The condition is serious and calls for immediate professional treatment. Ascites is not itself the disease or ailment but a symptom of a larger malfunction or defect.

Haemorrhaging, Clotting, Rupture of Blood Vessels
One of the more common and recognizable blood-vessel ailments is haemorrhaging, or bleeding. When this happens as the result of an accident or other complications, follow the directions in Chapter 4, on first aid.

In certain other cases, blood clots can form, especially after a severe accident or after surgery. If you neglect a clot in a vital vein, it can block the passage so that blood does not flow. Eventually the area without blood can turn gangrenous. (For haematoma, an ear haemorrhage that clots, see the section on ear disorders, page 82.)

A stroke is the result of a rupture of a blood vessel in the brain. It is not common in cats, but it is possible. The chief sign of a stroke is the cat's inability to stand steadily on its hind legs, and a tendency to circle in one direction. If it ever does occur, it would be more likely in the older cat. The after-effects vary according to the severity of the attack. A limb may be either temporarily or permanently paralysed, depending on the degree of circulatory disturbance. Many cats recover completely from a stroke, but the cat's age, its general health and the size of the brain area affected all have something to do with recovery-time.

Oedema

Oedema is relatively rare and usually seen only in older cats. If there is a circulatory disturbance, large accumulations of fluid may form in the tissues—sometimes in the lungs but more often in the legs, causing a swelling of the tissue. When you push your finger into the skin, it will not bounce right back. You will notice an indentation, possibly for several seconds. To avoid disintegration of the tissue, a vet must give the condition immediate treatment.

DIGESTIVE DISORDERS

The digestive system of a cat, like a person's, starts with its mouth and ends with its anus. The mouth and teeth, throat, oesophagus, stomach, intestines, liver and rectum are considered part of its digestive system.

Several ailments affecting this system are localized—such as trouble with the teeth or an abscess in the mouth—and can be cleared up with a minimum of difficulty. Others that are more serious or persistent could require more extensive treatment and a longer convalescence.

These ailments will be accompanied by many symptoms that you are now familiar with: vomiting, possibly blood-flecked; drooling, as a sign of nausea; diarrhoea, also possibly with blood; severe constipation or diarrhoea; a bloated stomach, the result of gas accumulations, with the skin over the stomach stretched taut; the presence of undigested food in the stool; a strong or unusual odour in the faeces and urine; a rise in temperature; possibly the presence of worms in the faeces; a general depression and unhealthiness in the cat's appearance, including a poor-looking coat; listlessness and exhaustion.

As far as your cat's digestion is concerned, there are only a very few things your cat should not eat. I do not recommend bones of any kind or raw meats and fish. Although a cat's digestive juices work on bones rapidly, nevertheless bones can injure the throat or create an obstruction if swallowed whole and even when chewed can cause constipation. Raw meats and fish, especially if fed as the sole diet, can also cause worms. Also, avoid spicy food. While spice in itself will not create a digestive disturbance, it does increase the intake of water and serves no real function. There may be discomfort and even vomiting. The best foods for your cat, perhaps on a fifty-fifty basis, are commercial (canned) preparations supplemented by some fat and a little cooked fish or meat. A cat may seem a choosy eater, but it usually is not if presented with a simple basic diet.

Abscesses (of Mouth)

The usual place for a dental abscess is at the very end of the tooth root, deep within the gum. Its presence may result in a fever, or the cat may show symptoms of pain. The abscess itself is a collection of pus. Receding gums, a blow on the mouth, or broken teeth may leave openings for bacteria to enter, and occasionally tooth abscesses form. The condition is very painful and should not be neglected, for it can lead to a general body infection. If it occurs, it will usually happen to the older cat.

When there is an abscess, your cat will almost always make you aware of it. It will try to avoid using that side of the mouth with the affected tooth when it eats and will hold its head at an angle while eating. It will shake its head and paw at its mouth. Loss of appetite and fever are often present. There may also be a discharge on the gum line of the tooth.

Also, cats will occasionally develop a swelling under the eye, which may rupture and discharge pus. This condition—called dental fistula—is usually symptomatic of a tooth abscess, usually in the upper third premolar. Extraction of the tooth is the only cure.

Constipation

Although constipation is more frequent in the older cat, it can be seen in cats of any age. Constipation occurs when solid waste-products build up in the cat's intestine and for some reason cannot be eliminated easily. If you have a long-hair, one direct cause of constipation can be the formation of a 'hair ball' in the cat's intestine. (I treat this under 'hair balls', page 73, as it is an important cause of constipation, blockage or obstructions.) Hair balls are not really balls but strung-out clumps of coat hair of various dimensions, sometimes extending from the mouth down into the intestine. It results from a cat's grooming itself and swallowing the loose hairs. One way to prevent such a condition is frequent grooming and adding a tablespoon of lubricant—such as mineral-oil or petroleum jelly—to your cat's diet as needed.

But constipation can, of course, result from several other factors. In the older cat, in particular, constipation can be present, since the slowing-down of intestinal movements (loss of muscle tone) occurs and more fluid is absorbed from the faeces. For cats of all ages and both sexes, a poor diet can cause constipation—just as it does in people. Little exercise, too much dry food or hard foods, and the conditions for constipation are established. Another serious cause of constipation might be an obstruction in the intestine, something more serious than a hair ball, such as a tumour or some foreign object the cat has swallowed. As you know, cats are curious experimenters, and many strange objects can end up in their throats (stuck there) or in their stomachs and intestines. String can even get caught around the tongue.

When constipation occurs infrequently, your cat may need only a mild laxative—a teaspoonful of milk of magnesia for the average-sized cat (about 10 pounds), or even oil from a sardine tin (when it is *not* olive-oil), which your pet will probably prefer to mineral-oil. *Do not give other human laxatives or tonics*, as some contain substances (aspirin derivatives, for example, or strychnine) that even in small doses can be harmful. If your cat is still constipated after a couple of days, the waste-product is probably so impacted and solid that a mild laxative will not penetrate. You should then consult your vet. Do not experiment with laxatives.

If the constipation results from lack of bulk in the diet—the most likely condition—you can rectify it easily by including roughage (leafy vegetables, bran). If it is caused by old age or lack of exercise, add a lubricant such as mineral-oil or white petroleum-jelly to your cat's diet.

If your cat swallows a small ball or other toy, the object can partially block the passage from the stomach to the small intestine. This is very rare. Call your vet immediately. *Never* give a laxative or attempt home treatments (such as an enema) if you suspect a foreign body.

Sometimes constipation is the direct result of illness. Depending on the particular ailment from which your cat is recovering, its treatment must be regulated by a vat. After an operation, for example, a cat may become constipated from just lying around and because of a break in its regular feeding-habits. In such a case or in a similar one involving recovery from an illness or operation, do not attempt to treat the constipation yourself.

On occasion, the cause of constipation is deceptively simple. The cat's anus might be caked with faeces attached to the hair, creating a wall that nothing can penetrate. Normally a cat will groom itself, but sometimes this condition can develop anyway, especially when the cat's owner does not make grooming a frequent event. A washing with soap and warm water will remedy the condition. On still other occasions, the very sluggish or listless cat may develop constipation, and some walking-time on a leash may help. At other times, while the cat's diet may be adequate nutritionally, constipation can still result, and what is needed is a change of diet. Sometimes something as simple as a shift from one canned product to another, or from one meat to another, can bring results.

Diarrhoea

When your cat has a watery or bloody loose bowel movement, the condition is called diarrhoea. If your cat simply has a softly formed stool, it is not diarrhoea, although it may be an early stage of the condition.

Like any ailment that persists or recurs, such as vomiting, continuing diarrhoea is usually a symptom of a serious ailment, although it may be a temporary condition or result from a simple cause. Nearly every feline ailment may cause diarrhoea: panleukopenia or distemper, intestinal parasites (worms), poisons (from eating plants), foreign objects in the digestive tract, partially decomposed food, even nervous disorders.

If the diarrhoea occurs as an isolated event and your cat otherwise seems healthy, it is probably a minor stomach or intestinal upset. Or it may be that, for some reason unknown to you, your cat is emotionally upset—yes, this can occur in cats. Also, diarrhoea is not unusual in very young kittens—say, up to two or three months. Of course, if a kitten of that age or older has persistent attacks of diarrhoea, you should be on the alert. If the elimination contains mucus as well as fluid, there is surely something wrong and you should consult a vet. And if the stool contains blood, your cat needs immediate professional care. The normal colour of the bowel movement is light to dark brown, but of course it can vary with the kind of food that is eaten.

When diarrhoea is infrequent, it may simply indicate a mild stomach-upset, of the kind people occasionally suffer from after a heavy meal or some excessive drinking. A good remedy for control, recommended for both pets and children, is Kaopectate or milk of bismuth, if you can get your cat to take it. It helps to settle the stomach and normally stops any mild diarrhoea. Give a scant teaspoon of Kaopectate for the average-sized cat three times a day and after each bowel movement. If it does not work or if your cat resists it, consult your vet.

Regulate your cat's diet during attacks of diarrhoea. You can withhold food altogether, for as long as twenty-four hours. Avoid too many fluid foods, such as broth or milk, which may cause diarrhoea even under the best conditions. Feed cooked starches such as rice or macaroni with meat, or even baby-foods.

Sometimes the diarrhoea is only one symptom among many, and you will note many other signs of illness. The diarrhoea itself will be persistent, turning yellowish or tarry, while the cat also vomits, loses its appetite, has a fever, experiences mucous discharges from its eyes and nose and seems generally depressed and miserable. When some or all of these signs occur, you should call in your vet immediately.

Enteritis (Intestinal Inflammation)
This is a simple disorder and not to be confused with panleukopenia, or feline distemper. It is sometimes difficult to control.

Inflammation or infection of the intestine may come from several sources: poisons or bacteria from putrefying food, from worms or from sharp objects (pins, needles) that have been swallowed. Such an infection, whatever has caused it, is called enteritis and is usually accompanied by diarrhoea or foul-smelling bowel movements.

The intestine is a particularly sensitive area and is therefore easily irritated. All food must be processed through the intestine, and it is the place where most types of worms are found when and if they exist. When anything goes wrong in the intestine, there is some indication in the bowel movements. They may show worms or mucus from the intestine itself, and they are good indicators of the condition of the colon. If pieces of food come through in solid form in the stool, that will inform you that your cat is not digesting that food.

Most intestinal ailments require professional care, especially if they continue into a second or third day. While the cat is recovering from such an ailment, a bland diet is usually recommended: rice, meat, baby-foods.

Disorders of the Oesophagus

The oesophagus is the tube from the mouth to the stomach. If there is something wrong with the cat's oesophagus, it will have a good deal of trouble swallowing, which is the chief symptom. Many of the troubles with the oesophagus in cats *derive from accidents*, not illness, and many of them require first-aid treatment.

Some typical ailments or conditions involving the oesophagus are inflammation or injuries caused by caustics (lye or rat- and roach-poisons), acids and poisons, ruptures, fistulas, foreign objects, a blow or an enlargement that causes pouches or pockets to form. Even string, if swallowed, may lodge under the tongue, causing severe damage to the tongue. All these injuries or ailments require medical treatment. Cats with such injuries should be given no food or liquid until the condition can be cleared up by medication or surgery, as necessary. If you continue to feed your cat, the chances are it will eat nothing or may vomit what it does eat.

Foreign objects caught in the oesophagus and not removed may injure the lining and increase the damage. When such objects are caught in the throat, your cat will not eat; it cannot. Any oesophageal injuries caused by the objects in the throat, or by acids or caustics, and other similar afflictions are handled in Chapter 4, on first aid. After you administer the emergency treatment indicated there, call a vet at once.

Anal Fissures

Anal fissures are cracks in the skin around the anus, sometimes the result of too much straining during a bowel movement, or an injury in the area that fails to heal. Since constant bowel movements to not give the fissure or crack much opportunity to heal, a soft diet—cooked oatmeal, rice, meat—will ease the bowel movements. Ask your vet about treatment if the condition fails to heal. Mineral-oil added to the food will also help to lubricate the stool and reduce strain. After a couple of weeks (or sooner), the tear should be sufficiently healed to allow a return to the cat's normal diet. If not, consult your vet; in persistent cases, cryo-surgery may be necessary.

Flatulence (Gas)

'Flatulence' is simply a big word to indicate that your cat has an accumulation of gas in its stomach or intestines, which might make it pass wind more than it normally would. Very often large amounts of proteins—such as hard-boiled eggs, meat and cheese—will cause gas. Also, strong-flavoured vegetables, such as cabbage, turnips, cauliflower and onions will produce flatulence. If you watch these proteins and vegetables in your cat's diet, you can control the accumulation of gas. Sometimes small amounts of milk of magnesia work as an antacid and provide relief. If your cat is old, however, the condition can be a normal part of the aging process.

If flatulence persists and becomes really offensive, you should consult a vet. An antiflatulent medicine may help. A chronic gas condition might indicate stomach or intestinal trouble that requires treatment. Sometimes it accompanies diarrhoea, which itself needs to be treated.

Foreign Objects (in Rectum)

Sharp objects can work their way through a cat's body and become lodged in the rectum and do considerable tearing damage. A pin or needle, for example, may come through the stomach and intestine, become lodged in the cat's anus and then cause an obstruction in the rectum. As the cat strains, the pin or foreign body works into the rectal lining, causing severe pain. The cat may call out when it evacuates, and you may see blood around the anus or blood in its stool.

Unless you know what is wrong, a professional check is necessary. Home remedies may only aggravate the condition. *Do not* give an enema if you suspect an object in the rectum. It is wedged in, and will only do additional damage if the cat strains. Also, do not attempt to remove such an object; you may cause a laceration with severe bleeding.

Gastritis

Gastritis is an inflammation of the stomach lining caused by over-eating, eating of spoiled food or garbage (for the cat that roams) or the presence of indigestible food or objects in the stomach. It also accompanies several serious ailments, such as feline distemper and upper-respiratory infection, and is often seen in advanced uraemia. The symptoms are vomiting and an irregular appetite. In acute cases, the cat may feel pain when you touch its stomach. A vet must determine what treatment should be given.

Treatment usually involves diet-control: the feeding of bland foods such as broth, boiled chicken, soft-boiled eggs and cereal and milk (if the cat can digest it) in small amounts three or four times a day. If the condition is acute, all food and water should be withdrawn for twenty-four hours. Give your cat ice-cubes to lick if you withhold water.

Hair Balls (in Stomach)

As I mentioned before, the cat that licks off a good deal of its coat and swallows the loose hairs may develop a hair ball in its stomach. Such an accumulation is not really a ball but a loosely formed mass of hair that can string itself out throughout the cat's intestines. When the mass becomes large and firm, it blocks the digestive track, leading to vomiting and constipation due to intestinal obstruction. If the cat vomits the hair, that is a partial or complete solution to the problem, or it may indicate that the problem has not developed to any dangerous stage.

The best 'solution', however, is prevention. With a long-hair, frequent grooming is necessary, and if the cat tends to have the problem, the introduction into the diet of some mineral-oil, or white petroleum-jelly, or even oil from a sardine tin (as long as it is not olive-oil) will help it 'pass' the loose hairs that make up the ball. Also, ask your vet about commercial hair-ball preparations, which often work to prevent the formation of the hair ball.

You cannot always recognize that the cat has a hair ball, although if your cat vomits up hair, you know the potential condition is present. When the ball is extensive, it interferes with digestion in the intestine, and your cat will become ill. You will notice fever, loss of weight, loss of appetite, a dryness to the coat, a generally unhealthy look. There may also be constipation, lots of straining without results. By this time, the lump may be extensive and no longer respond to medication or diet-control. Drugs can control the infection, but only surgery can remove a sizable lump. Surgery is, of course, a last resort, and your vet can try using other methods before resorting to it. He can treat with oil, medication and sometimes instruments. Once the hair ball has caused an impaction, home remedies are no longer effective, and a vet must decide on a course of treatment.

The best way of handling this, as I have suggested, is *prevention*: frequent grooming (especially of the long-hair) and the introduction of mineral-oil or white petroleum-jelly into the cat's diet if it is prone to this condition.

Infection of Salivary Glands

The salivary glands, which secrete saliva, might not function correctly for a variety of reasons. As the result of an injury, the ducts leading from the glands into the mouth can become stopped up. Cysts may form under the tongue because of interference with the gland secretion. If your cat's neck appears swollen or if there is swelling under its tongue, a salivary-gland cyst may well be the reason. Only a vet can diagnose the condition, which could also be a number of other things. Surgery is necessary in many of these cases. These cysts are rare.

Intestinal Impactions

Intestinal impactions are blockages or accumulations of indigestible material in the intestine. If left around, nearly anything can find its way into your cat's intestines—pieces of toys, pieces of rubber, cellophane, leaves, needles and string. To this, add hair balls, which are described above. Cats will often consume these unlikely items even when they are otherwise receiving a well-balanced diet. Kittens, in particular, will try to get into everything and consume what they can. Part of it is curiosity.

These objects can and do create a digestive problem. They may, in fact, block the intestinal tract so that your cat is in real difficulty. Treatment for impactions of this kind must be left to a vet. A laxative here is useless and may falsely lull you into thinking you are helping the condition when, in fact, you are not and cannot. In very severe cases of intestinal impaction, surgery is usually necessary, especially if the foreign object cannot be passed.

An impaction is not easy to diagnose. Usually, the abdomen is taut and stretched tight, and the cat seems listless and depressed. It may assume strange positions to relieve the pain. Your chief clue, however, is constipation. The condition may call for hospital care and surgery.

Intussusceptions

The condition known as intussusception is a telescoping of the intestine into itself. While it is relatively rare in cats, it can occur. When this happens—and the reasons for it are not always clear, the food passing through the intestine is blocked. The blood-supply to the telescoped part is also cut off.

You will probably not know when a cat has this condition, but you will notice many symptoms of illness. The symptoms are, incidentally, similar to those of appendicitis in a person. The abdomen itself will become very sensitive; your cat may vomit frequently, perhaps after every meal if it eats. As a result of the inflammation, the temperature will rise. Dehydration occurs. The faeces may be bloody and are almost always watery, or bowel movements may stop altogether. Correction of the condition calls for immediate surgery.

Jaundice
Jaundice usually occurs when some growth blocks the bile duct or disease interferes with the normal secretion of bile. The symptoms are orange urine—which can signal many ailments besides jaundice—and yellowish colouring of the skin and the whites of the eyes. Like all other liver ailments, jaundice requires professional care.

Liver Ailments
Cats can have liver trouble. Whenever your cat has something wrong with its liver, you can usually tell by the colour of its eyes. The whites will turn yellowish, as will its gums and skin. Furthermore, the urine will be orange, and the stools may be grey or black and sticky-looking. However, since certain foods will change the colour of the stool, this in itself is not always a dependable symptom.

Do not neglect any condition involving these symptoms.

Some worming-medicines when given in large doses, as well as certain toxins, can cause liver damage. Certain insecticides may, if consumed over a period of time, cause liver trouble. The symptoms are grey or black stools, a yellowish colour to the skin, and general depression and listlessness. See Chapter 4 for the first aid in the event of an emergency. If there is no emergency and you see these symptoms, consult your vet.

Rectal and Anal-Gland Trouble: Anal-Gland Impactions
Cats may have anal-gland problems. On each side of the anus, situated inside and below the anus itself, are the anal glands, which secrete a yellowish fluid. It is an accumulation that carries over from the cat's wild state—which the skunk still retains to frighten away possible attackers. Because cats are domesticated and exercise little, their glands sometimes tend to retain the secretion, causing irritation and sometimes leading to abscesses. They are very painful, and the cat tries to help itself by rubbing and licking the affected parts, or by causing friction on its hindquarters. Sometimes the abscesses will break open, discharging pus and blood. Take your cat to a vet for the treatment of any swelling near the anus.

Do not try to break the abscess-filled sacs yourself. The secretion is particularly foul, and you will not correct it. Only a vet should do this job. He will exert pressure in the right way to express the sacs. This should clear up the condition, and your cat will stop irritating the areas. If the glands fill up again, the symptoms may return and your cat will need further treatment.

Haemorrhoids as we understand them in a person are also present in cats. Sometimes, of course, the swelling of the veins in the rectal area will return to normal. Constipation may make the anus swell, but as soon as regularity returns, the swelling goes away. This is very rare.

Stomatitis

Stomatitis has nothing to do with the stomach. It is a common inflammation of the oral cavity, usually occurring in the fold of the tongue or the cheek. There may also be lip ulcers, generally of the upper lip, although they may occur in other places on the lip or body. Blood disorders, foreign bodies, infected gums, tartar or a chronic disease can cause stomatitis. Symptoms may be loss of appetite, excessive salivation, halitosis (bad breath), continued pawing at the mouth, some crying and possibly fever. Since these symptoms are similar to those for many other ailments, professional attention is necessary. See your vet.

Throat Ailments

A cat may suffer from several different kinds of throat ailment, and one way to detect the problem is to pick up a change in its cry. When a cat's throat is ailing, its characteristic cry or meow sounds different.

Inflammation of the pharynx (the link between the oesophagus and the mouth cavity) is called pharyngitis. Inflammation of the larynx (the so-called voice box) is called laryngitis. Neither kind of inflammation will in itself indicate what is wrong with your cat. Soreness or pain there usually accompanies other symptoms of a more serious ailment.

There will certainly be other signs of trouble: vomiting, running nose and eyes, loss of appetite, fever, perhaps difficulty in swallowing, or general depression and lack of vitality. If you notice any of these signs, take your cat to a vet, who can determine whether it is a purely local thoat ailment or part of some other problem. Do not attempt any home remedy, such as you would try with a child. Aspirin, for example, which relieves discomfort in a person, is not suitable for a cat. Many other home remedies that seem suitable for a throat ailment contain aspirin derivatives also.

Tooth Problems

A cat has thirty teeth (twenty-six as a kitten), although it is normal for any given cat to have fewer than the full complement. This is not a problem, unless the cat has lost many teeth because of illness or because of lack of care. The teeth of a cat are intended not for chewing but for ripping, grasping and shredding—just like the teeth in the larger jungle cats.

Your vet should check your cat's teeth in his regular examination. The most common problems are pits, discolouration, worn enamel, breaks, an accumulation of tartar, or calculus, where the tooth joins the gum, and gum abscesses. Cavities of the kind people suffer from do not usually trouble cats. Tooth problems in general—except for tartar—are infrequent, unless the cat gets into mischief or a fight and cracks a tooth.

A very bad mouth-odour may mean a tooth problem, or it may mean a digestive upset, in which case the sour smell comes from the stomach. If the odour persists, and your cat seems otherwise healthy, the problem may well be a dental one. This is particularly true for the older cat. Its teeth may need no more than a cleaning.

A cat has all its permanent teeth by the time it is six months old. Some cats take longer, some less time. Usually, however, the permanent teeth are set in the three-to-six-month period, and the deciduous (kitten) teeth are pushed out. The kitten teeth must be extracted if they interfere with the thrust of the permanent teeth. If your cat eats a reasonably balanced diet, including minerals, it should have no trouble with its teeth until it is much older, and very likely not even then.

A large accumulation of tartar on the teeth will often cause bad breath. Although a little tartar may be offensive to look at, it is otherwise harmless. A lot of tartar, however, can lead in time to further dental trouble—recession and gum infection. An unattended infection can lead to complications. To remove the tartar, a vet usually anaesthetizes the cat and then cleans its teeth. They should be done once a year if needed.

You can yourself try to keep your cat's teeth clean by washing them a few times a month with a piece of cotton dipped in milk of magnesia. If all this strikes you, and your cat, as too much trouble, you should let a vet do the job his way.

If your cat roams freely and loves hard objects, it may over a period of time wear down its teeth. The best of teeth are no match for metal and other such items. By the way, when the enamel is worn away, cavities are possible in the small rutted areas where the surface of the tooth is gone. For the cat confined in a flat such difficulties will be very rare.

There really is not much you can do about worn teeth. Broken teeth, however, are another matter. If your cat cracks a tooth in a fight or in play, or in trying to get into one thing or another, then it should have professional treatment. A cracked tooth can often lead to trouble; it must be extracted before it causes infection and great pain.

Tonsilitis

When a cat's tonsils bother it, it may run a fever, refuse to eat or gag and vomit a great deal. The ailment (rare in cats) may, of course, go beyond the tonsils themselves. An infection in the mouth may cause tonsilitis (inflammation of the tonsils), a condition that can be treated with antibiotics. The condition needs professional care.

Tumours of the Mouth

Although tumours are described in a separate category in this chapter, I mention mouth tumours because you can possibly see them yourself. Other tumours develop internally and are beyond your powers of diagnosis.

A cat's mouth, like a person's, is subject to tumours. If you see any growth or if your cat has any difficulty in eating, have your vet check its mouth. Since gum tumours become easily irritated, they should not be neglected.

There are several types of gum tumour that are troublesome and may be malignant. They should be removed if they are found. They interfere with eating and generally bleed.

Worms

Before I describe the important types of worms, I will repeat some of the signs that indicate worms in your cat. Also, see pages 62–6. Usually, you will see these signs only when there is a fairly heavy infestation.

1. Weakness, listlessness, general depression
2. Diarrhoea, with or without blood, or thin bowel movements
3. Dry and coarse coat, loss of lustre
4. Bloated stomach (not in all cases)
5. Vomiting, with or without the presence of worms
6. Sleepiness, loss of vitality (a lazy cat will become even lazier)
7. Frequent rubbing of body against the floor

Ascarid, or Roundworm (Common Worms in Cats)

The ascarid, or roundworm, is one of the most common worms in kittens and grown cats. It is white and slim, about 1 to 4 inches in length, and it develops in the intestine. There are cases in which roundworms infect the kitten before birth. When attended to early, roundworms are relatively easy to eliminate if the infestation is slight. They are, however, particularly dangerous for young kittens, since they lower resistance by absorbing the food-value from its digestive juices.

Fluke Disease

Flukes are parasitic worms that harbour a type of virus-like organism that makes the cat severely ill. If your cat is fed a good deal of raw fish—salmon, snails, tuna, trout, it may get fish-poisoning, or what is called 'fluke disease'. In several parts of the country where fishing is still good and the tendency is to feed house pets on the catch, there may be some fluke disease.

The most common signs are similar to those of an upper-respiratory ailment: discharge from the eyes and nose, diarrhoea (often bloody), dehydration with great thirst, loss of appetite and evident loss of weight. The disease is very serious, and the best prevention is not to feed your cat raw fish. Boil it and remove the bones, and then it becomes a fine, nutritious food.

Hookworm (Rare in Cats)

The hookworm is so called because of its mouth (buccal) hooks, which clamp onto the cat's intestinal wall. The worm is one of the most dangerous, especially for kittens, because when it attaches itself it sucks blood. If it is not removed, it may seriously weaken your cat, causing anaemia.

The rare cat with hookworms will become depressed and exhausted and will suffer from anaemia, and may have blood-streaked stools. In some instances, especially when the condition has gone unnoticed for a long time, the cat may need a blood-transfusion. Since hookworms multiply rapidly and can deplete the cat's blood, the anaemia that results can be debilitating. A kitten can have hookworms before it is born.

Intestinal Protozoans (Coccidia)

You should be aware of coccidiosis, one of the most common of intestinal parasitic infestations. They are found in the alimentary tract. It is particularly dangerous if neglected because it weakens the cat by lowering its resistance to other diseases.

The symptoms are familiar: chronic diarrhoea (often with blood), rough, coarse-looking coat, depression and general exhaustion. When the attack is particularly severe, the cat will seem to have a cold. It will cough, its eyes will water and its nose will run. It may also have a slight fever, about 103°F. After treatment, you should wash everything the cat has soiled, as re-infection is possible.

The cause of intestinal protozoans is mainly the eating of raw or under-cooked meat or of rodents that harbour the infection. This is particularly true of the strain known as *Toxoplasma*. Occasionally, this infection has shown up in people and been attributed to transmission from the stool of an infected cat. The stool should be disposed of immediately, before it becomes infectious, but the more common cause in people is the same as it is for cats: the eating of infected raw meat.

Tapeworm

One of the most difficult parasites to eliminate is the tapeworm, which infects both the younger and older cat. The head of the tapeworm, which is attached to the intestinal wall, must be removed. The worm itself may be 6 inches in length.

The cat shows its discomfort with diarrhoea. If not treated, it may vomit, become listless and rub its hindquarters persistently against a hard surface as though suffering from an itch. The proglottids (small flat white or pink pieces of the tapeworm ¼ inch in length) might be found in the stool. When they dry around the anus, they look like kernels of rice. Since the head remains attached to the intestinal lining of the cat, the appearance of pieces in the stool does not mean that the parasite has been eliminated. Such infestations often require periodic treatment (under advice from a vet), for the worms are hardy and resist complete removal.

Fleas and lice are carriers of one variety of tapeworm, so if your cat is in an area with fleas and lice, eliminate them through spraying. Also, cats that eat rodents may have tapeworms.

(Incidentally, the so-called stomach worm causes symptoms similar to those of tapeworm, but without a faecal examination you do not know which infestation your cat suffers from. Stomach worms are very rare in cats.)

Thelazia

This worm is found in the conjunctival sac beneath the third eyelid. Cats living in wooded areas are more prone to it. (Thelazia has not yet been recorded in the UK.)

Whipworms

The infection of cats with whipworm is rare and may be non-existent in the United States and the UK.

EYE DISORDERS

Ordinarily, your cat's eyes are as hardy as your own. You should, except under very special conditions, expect little trouble. A few eye ailments, however, are hereditary: in particular, glaucoma and cataracts.

One of the first signs that something is wrong with your cat's eye is a chronic discharge that goes beyond the usual 'washing out'. Along with this discharge, the cat will paw and scratch at its eyes and shake its head. A clear discharge may mean a deficiency and can sometimes be corrected with a vitamin-mineral supplement. Scratching and pawing may, however, indicate that there is a foreign body in the eye, or a scratch on the cornea, or trouble with the third eyelid, which all cats have, or a simple inflammation of the eyelids.

If any of these symptoms appear, get in touch with your vet right away. Do not try any home remedies beyond wiping away the discharge with a sterile piece of cotton soaked in an eyewash. Until you know what the trouble is, you will not know what to do. Also, you might accidentally aggravate or irritate the condition.

Cats that roam free in the country or suburbs might pick up several nuisance eye ailments. The country cat running free may have its eyes scratched by branches and twigs or whipped by tall grass. While the city cat is exposed to fouler air and dust in larger quantities than its country cousin, the city cat has fewer opportunities for direct eye injuries, especially if it is confined in a flat.

Cataracts (Not Common in Cats)

Cataracts are a partial or complete opacity of the crystalline lens, that part of the eye just behind the pupil; they give the eye a china-blue colour. Cataracts may occur in the older cat but are rare. They can also be inherited or caused by an injury, which is rarer.

In some cases, the cataracts may be slow in developing, but the condition often means a gradual worsening of sight until the cat goes blind. Since blindness develops very slowly, the cat may live out most, if not all, of its life with some sight.

Conjunctivitis

On the inner surface of the eyelids is a mucous membrane that keeps the eye clear. When the membrane becomes inflamed, the cat is suffering from conjunctivitis. Usually the condition is caused by a foreign body (fumes, wind, dust, smoke, pollen) or by bacterial infection in the eyelid.

Conjunctivitis is characterized by tearing, inflammation and sensitivity to light—any of these or all three.

If the cause is simply a foreign object and you can remove it with a piece of sterile cotton, wash the eye out with warm water or an eyewash after you have done so. Sometimes an eye-ointment is soothing, but it is best to consult a vet before you put anything in your cat's eyes.

Removal of the foreign object should clear up the inflammation in a day or two. If the redness persists longer, the eye needs a vet's attention. If you do not see any foreign object in the eye, do not probe around *and do not try any home remedies*.

A particular kind of conjunctivitis is follicular conjunctivitis, a chronic

type that is difficult to clear up. It is characterized by follicles in the conjunc-
tiva (the mucous membrane lining the inner surface) of the third eyelid that
do not respond readily to treatment and may take months to clear.

Glaucoma (Rare in Cats)

Glaucoma involves an increase in pressure in the eyeball. When such fluid
cannot escape normally, the eyeball becomes enlarged. There is an
accompanying impairment of vision and eventually a loss of sight. The
disease may be congenital, and it often appears only after a cat enters middle
age, although it can occur at any time. If glaucoma develops in only one eye,
its removal may save the other. But even here there is no guarantee. Sometimes the condition responds to treatment, and removal is not necessary.

Sad as blindness is, your cat will not be helpless. Through its nose and
whiskers, it remains accustomed to familiar surroundings.

Progressive Retinal Atrophy

Progressive retinal atrophy is a hereditary eye disorder and leads to
blindness, often beginning as night-blindness. Your vet can check your cat
for this condition. There is no treatment.

Enlargement of the Third Eyelid

Next to the nose, in the inside corner of the eye, is a tissue called the
membrana nictitans. The third eyelid (the nictitating membrane) becomes
inflamed when conjunctivitis is in the eyelids. The eye may discharge
profusely. This is a condition for your vet to diagnose, since the symptoms
are so similar to other eye ailments, especially follicular conjunctivitis.

Eyelid Abnormalities

Inverted eyelids, or entropion, is a condition that is usually congenital. The
eyelid is actually inverting, creating pressure and irritation on the eyeball. If
diagnosed early, it can be surgically corrected before any permanent
damage is done. Everted eyelids, or ectropion, is the opposite condition
from entropion—here the eyelid turns out. Ectropion is rare.

Eyelid Ailments

There are few specific lid ailments; most of them are associated with injury
to the eye. If there are pimples, warts, infected glands or other irritants on
the lid, the problem may involve the eye, which will reflect the condition. Do
not attempt home treatments.

Keratitis

This is an inflammation of the cornea (the transparent tissue that covers the
iris and the pupil) in which the cornea turns a bluish white. The white of the
eye may turn reddish or red at the same time. If the cornea is ulcerated, it is
possible to see a small hole in it. This is a condition that usually accompanies
a serious illness or results from an injury. Keratitis needs immediate
treatment.

EAR DISORDERS

If you suspect ear trouble, the best thing to do is to leave the ear alone and call a vet. While many cats do suffer from ear ailments, far more have their ears injured by over-anxious owners who probe too far and accidentally damage the sensitive ear canal. If you must do something, be sure not to put any object in the ear, certainly nothing sharp or pointed.

If the surface of your cat's ear appears dry, you might wipe it with baby-oil or some mild ointment. Or if the surface seems too moist (from a mild discharge), you might dust it with antiseptic powder, after cleaning with an ear-wash. But these provide only temporary relief. If the condition persists, the treatment must come from a vet. Incidentally, if you suspect that the ear is infected (you can judge from the symptoms listed below), do not use any medication or insecticides you may have around the house. They may irritate the ear and can possibly create a worse condition. They certainly cannot cure it.

Some of the more obvious symptoms of ear ailments are pus-like discharge, black caking around the canal just inside the ear, frequent shaking of the head and pawing away at the ear, holding the head at a strange angle so that you think your cat has gone mad, a strong, cheesy odour coming from the ear, or heavy waxy material and matted hair on the ear surface. The ear is often red and inflamed.

The most common ear trouble in cats stems from mites—maybe fifty per cent of cats suffer from ear mites at one time or another. Such an infestation leads to otodectic mange, which, if unattended, can result in permanent ear damage.

Probably no single condition will present all the symptoms I have listed, but if you see one or more, suspect trouble. The cat's head angle and a strong, cheesy odour should warn you. Sometimes, the cause may be no more than an insect-bite, or it may be a minor ulceration, a small pimple, that will clear up by itself. Whatever the trouble, a cat will worry the spot until you and it are frantic.

With all ear conditions, it is better to be over-careful rather than neglectful. Neglect of a relatively simple matter may lead to something more serious.

Haematoma

A haematoma is a swelling that contains blood. Haematomas sometimes occur in the middle of the skin of the ear flap. They result from a sharp blow that ruptures blood vessels in the ear. The shaking and scratching that accompany otitis, or an ear infection, can lead to haematomas. The swellings, which will possibly distend the ear, must be operated on by a vet. It is a relatively simple operation. Your cat will show its extreme discomfort by shaking its head, crying, pawing and scratching at its ear(s).

Do not expect your cat to co-operate if you try to examine the flap. The spot is very often extremely sensitive to the touch. If you do get close, you will see that the ear is swollen and inflamed. If you neglect a haematoma or any growth on the ear, you are taking a chance with your cat's hearing. Often such ears resemble the cauliflower ears of a prize-fighter—sometimes even after an operation.

If you cannot see a vet immediately, put a stocking or covering over your cat's head so that you protect the ear from further irritation from the cat's feet. (Do not cover the cat's nose with the stocking.) Swabbing with baby- or mineral-oil might relieve the pain, if your cat lets you near it. Do not give aspirin, as you might with a child who has an earache.

Infection (Otorrhoea or Otitis)

Infection or parasites can cause a condition known as otorrhoea or otitis, a painful inflammation of the skin of the external ear canal. The infection may come from excessive probing or result from irritation by foreign material such as water, bacteria or fungi. A cat so afflicted will scratch and paw at the ear, shake its head, lose its appetite and become irritable. The inflamed skin bleeds easily, and quite possibly the cat will not let you near the painful area.

For temporary relief, soothe the area with sterile cotton soaked in mineral-oil or baby-oil. Do not probe inside the ear, and see a vet.

Occasionally, a cat will suffer from an inflammation of the middle ear, called otitis media. It may come in either of two ways: from an infection of the external ear passage or from infection in the nasal passages by way of the eustachian canal. The most common symptoms are pain, fever, ear discharge, circling, head-tilting and possible loss of balance (vertigo). Immediate veterinary treatment is called for.

Mites

Ear mites are parasites that settle in the ear and lead to chronic irritation. As I mentioned before, they are very common in cats, afflicting up to fifty per cent of them at one time or another. The symptoms are similar to those for otitis. The cat will shake its head and scratch violently, as though it wants to rip off its ear. Sometimes, excessive scratching will make the entire area bleed. There is a waxy, dark secretion, as well as a sour, cheesy odour.

Mites are difficult to get rid of, and they may return after treatment. Also, there is the possibility that your cat, through excessive shaking and scratching, will cause haematomas in the ear flap (described above). You can temporarily relieve your pet's misery by swabbing the ear with baby-oil, but a permanent cure needs treatment and then scrupulous cleanliness.

Wax

Although the symptoms are no more than an occasional shaking of the ear and some pawing, you can see that something is obviously bothering your cat's ear. The condition may be any of the above, or something as simple as too much wax in the ear because of infection or inflammation.

There are home remedies, but they can end up doing more harm than good. You may have read that you can remove wax by pouring in some mineral-oil and then massaging the outside of the ear until the wax softens and falls out. You may well succeed in dislodging the wax. But you might also injure the ear canal by rubbing the hardened wax against the sensitive interior. You may also be trying to remove wax in the ear when that is not what is bothering your cat.

It is far better to have a vet take a look. If there is an accumulation of wax or an infection, you will learn precisely what to do. This includes medication, how to massage the ear and what to watch for in the event of a recurrence.

INTEGUMENTARY (SKIN) DISORDERS

Skin ailments in cats—as you can see from the Contents—are as extensive and varied as those in people. Cats are allergic; they draw parasites such as fleas and lice (although ticks only infrequently); they can get serious afflictions such as tumours and extremely minor conditions such as dandruff. They can, on occasion, even become bald. Sometimes their skin ailments can be traced to a hormonal imbalance, or they develop an eczema or dermatitis that defies diagnosis and treatment.

A cat's skin and coat is a sensitive, accurate indicator of its health. Usually, when its skin is clear and well toned, you can assume that your cat is at the peak of condition. A well-groomed cat—one that is combed and brushed daily—stands the least chance of suffering from a skin ailment, although grooming does not make it immune.

Each skin ailment brings with it its own symptoms, but there are certain signs common to all. When you see these signs, do not attempt home treatment. Such conditions are difficult to diagnose and often require laboratory tests to determine their exact cause.

Nearly all skin ailments are accompanied by some of the following symptoms. There will be severe itching—you will possibly notice that first. The cat will be scratching almost constantly, until often parts of its coat are worn away. You will see pus-filled pimples, inflammation in one or several areas. The skin itself will thicken and coarsen, in time flake or scale. Sometimes there will be little more than an angry-looking rash, with little scabs forming, or else an extreme dry spot that the cat scratches and irritates. One or all of these are danger-signals, which you should heed.

If you own a long-hair, matting may result in skin problems. Daily grooming will help there. Also, the older cat is more prone to skin ailments because it grooms itself less—although this depends on the individual animal.

Allergies
A cat may be allergic to an endless number of things. If an allergy does appear in the form of a skin condition, it may usually be traced to something in its home or neighbourhood: possibly a new food, perhaps an insect, dust, pollen, a particular plant or flower, certain chemicals in the soil or paint, even its own bedding. Some cats are allergic to vaccines, serums and milk-products (which produce diarrhoea). Others are literally allergic to themselves—to certain conditions that their own bodies produce.

An allergy may be apparent in the same way as any of the other skin ailments, with inflammation, swelling or puffiness around the face, itching, hives, pus-filled pimples, irritation, thickening of the skin, flaking or scaling, perhaps loss of hair.

Treatment can take time, since diagnosis is not always easy; the specific cause must be found or else all remedies are symptomatic. Very often an allergy will look so much like other skin ailments that identification is almost impossible.

Often, too, allergies will disappear with time. To soothe the irritated area while the cause is being determined, wash it with mild soap and warm water and apply oils or lotions recommended by your vet.

Bee-Stings (Rare in Cats)
This applies only to the cat who roams freely, not to the cat confined in a flat. Occasionally a cat will be allergic to a bee-sting, which can lead to difficulty in breathing. Along with the breathing difficulty, you may see the classic symptoms of allergy: swelling of lips and face, puffiness around the eyes, general discomfort and irritation. If your cat reacts in this way, you should call a vet immediately.

Flea Dermatitis
A cat infested with fleas will wear away the hair in many places and eventually damage the skin with its furious and persistent scratching. The case can then develop into chronic flea dermatitis.

Although you will notice the severe itchiness as well as the damaged coat, you will probably not be able to diagnose this condition. It calls for professional treatment, which may involve dusting with powder or internal medication. See the section on fleas (pages 88) for the details of treatment.

Solar Dermatitis
Solar dermatitis affects only white cats with white ears that are in the sun for long periods of time. It is a form of skin inflammation of the nose and ears (caused by the sun), which the cat aggravates by pawing at its nose or ears. The condition is localized in its nose, ears and eyes, and the skin surface around them.

You can recognize this type of eczema from the lesions or pustules (pus-filled pimples) that form in the area, as well as from the inflammation of the eyes and from scabs or scales on the nose bridge. There will probably also be a loss of hair in the region and even some bleeding. The first step in treatments is to keep the cat out of the sun.

As with all types of dermatitis, there is not much you can do yourself except relieve the cat's discomfort with applications of skin-lotion or mineral-oil on the nose and skin surface, and a mild eyewash for the inflamed eyes. But actual treatment must be left to your vet.

Urticaria (Hives)
This occurs very infrequently in cats. Hives are large, inflamed areas on the skin, like gigantic puffed-up pimples. They indicate that the cat is allergic to something. You can relieve some of the itchiness caused by the hives by applying cold packs. But if they persist, as they well may, you can correct

them only by treating the allergy itself with antihistamines (as recommended by a vet) and by removing the cause.

Infectious Ailments

Infectious skin ailments in a cat are somewhat common, although some—such as ringworm and chin infection—are seen more frequently than acne. Like most skin disorders, the infectious type has several common symptoms: pustules, inflammation, itchiness and dead-looking coat. All these conditions—acne, pimples, chin infection and impetigo—are basically the same.

Acne

Acne results from an inflammation of the skin glands. It occurs on the chin and the edges of the lips. Dirt gets into the pores, and when the bacteria multiply, red, pus-filled eruptions can be observed. It is usually a mild condition in cats, and cleanliness plus a recommended lotion should clear it up. A really bad condition may need further treatment from a vet. If your cat has a collar, the friction against the neck may combine with dirt to cause eruptions.

Chin Infection

A cat may irritate the skin on its chin, and when the surface of skin opens, bacteria can enter and cause an infection. Cats that dribble or eat messily may have food particles stuck to them; then, if the skin cracks, it is open to infection. This, if minor, can usually be treated by daily washing with a mild medicated soap and warm water. Any infection that persists must receive a vet's treatment.

Impetigo

This is not common in cats, but it does occur. When it appears, it does so on the less hairy parts of the body: lips, chin, even belly. You can recognize it by the isolated pustules, or pus-filled pimples, that characterize the condition. Usually, the pustules will break open easily and lend themselves to rapid cure. Your vet can recommend an antiseptic powder or lotion to clear up this trouble. The cat should be kept clean and dry.

Ringworm

You may at first confuse ringworm with one of the mange parasites (described below), but there are significant differences. Ringworm is more or less localized and is so called because the infected area is in the shape of a small ring or circle, growing larger and larger as the infection spreads. The ringworm lesion, however, may not be precisely a circle; it may be oval, although the general shape is roundish. Incidentally, there is no worm involved in ringworm. It is a fungus.

Your vet has a lamp called a Wood's light, which gives some lesions a greenish colouration under its glow and can help in identifying a fungus. The fungus can also be identified by growing a culture in the laboratory.

Ringworm usually attacks the outer layer of the cat's skin. There it settles into the follicles, or hair sacs. Loss of hair distinguishes ringworm from mange parasites, but at first the hair may not fall out. Instead, the hair in the infected area becomes dry and coarse; the skin underneath is also dry and scaly, much like a person's scalp when he suffers from severe dandruff. Eventually the hair will fall out when the infection is neglected, but even then the affected area is left with a short stubble.

Before the hair falls out, the infected area usually looks like a slightly raised platform of scaly matter. It may also take the form of small bloody pimples on the less hairy parts of the cat's body, such as the belly. However, look for ringworm on every part of its body. When the hair falls out, by the way, that particular spot will probably not give further trouble. But then the infection spreads to a nearby area, with the same results.

If you suspect ringworm or fungus, be particularly careful, because you and your children may get it. One really unfortunate characteristic of ringworm, incidentally, is that a cat may be a carrier—it may not be infected and yet it still can spread the infection. If your cat has been around any pets that have ringworm, this is a possibility.

When you treat the cat, be sure to use rubber gloves, which should then be sterilized in alcohol or in hot water and soap. The best method of care, once your vet has determined the condition, is first to clip the hair in the afflicted area for spot treatment. (The entire body may have to be so treated.) Then wash the lesion of the 'ring' with mild soap and water in order to soften and loosen the scabs. The next step is to apply a fungicidal ointment or another recommended solution to the lesions and let them dry. If the cat tries to lick the treated areas, you might have to put an Elizabethan collar on it (see page 139). You may accompany this treatment with oral medication prescribed by your vet. Both may be necessary to gain a quick and complete recovery.

REMEMBER: Ringworm is catching. Do not touch your face with your rubber gloves, and keep your children away from the cat and from any of the material you used to treat the cat.

Rodent Ulcer

Although the precise causes of rodent ulcer remain unclear, it can be a persistent skin ailment and cause considerable discomfort to your cat. Like many skin ailments, it has a raw, reddish, irritated look to it, and the skin may feel thickened. It is located mainly around the lips, in the form of ulcers. The condition may result from irritation, when the cat's teeth rub against its lips or from prolonged licking of a given area. Your cat may lose all appetite and stop eating if it has a severe rodent ulcer.

Rodent ulcer needs professional treatment. This could be a cancerous condition.

Parasites

External parasites are one of the most common causes of skin disorders in your cat. Fleas, lice, mites and ticks (rare) can create ailments that are difficult to treat and cure once the infection becomes generalized. The chief sign of all infestations is scratching, persistent and furious. That will be your clue. There may also be inflammation, lesions and bald spots. All such parasitic conditions need professional treatment. Attempts at home treatment may aggravate a case and cause the condition to spread.

Fleas

The chief characteristic of the flea is that it runs around in the hair and may jump. In this respect it differs from the other external parasites, which burrow into a particular place and remain there until they are dislodged. If you have ever picked up even a single flea while travelling, or even in your own home, you know how annoying those little bites prove to be. Imagine several fleas moving around on your cat's skin and nipping it insistently. And a few fleas may soon become dozens. Fleas also may carry the eggs that give your cat tapeworm, adding complications to mere discomfort.

There are three basic kinds of fleas: the human-flea, the cat-flea and the dog-flea. They will all hang on to any warm animal or person, with all finding the ears and their rims and the abdomen a most congenial part. Expect to find fleas in nearly any part of the cat's body, although they do prefer the hairiest places: the neck, head, tail area and chest.

Flea eggs are incubated in heat and dampness, and they hatch during the summer. The life-cycle of the flea is about thirty days, and the best way to treat your cat is twofold: break up the cycle and eliminate those fleas that have already hatched.

Once a vet has seen your cat and diagnosed fleas, there are several ways of dealing with them: medicated baths, a powder or a flea-collar (probably the best treatment). If your vet recommends dusting, make sure that you work the powder into the skin. If it simply lies on the surface of the coat, it cannot do much good. Avoid getting any in the cat's eyes and nose. Do not use a powder without consulting a vet, for cats are very susceptible to chemicals, and you can assume they will lick at whatever substance is on their coats.

You may also dip or spray the cat. Once again, if you use a spray, make sure you use one that is non-toxic, and be sure to protect your cat's eyes from the spray. If you use a dip, follow the same precautions. Let the solution dry. If you rub the cat dry right away, you eliminate the flea-killing powder of the dip. Keep the cat in a warm, draught-free area until its coat is dry; this is especially necessary for the kitten.

If you use a flea-collar, be sure you read the label. Your cat may be allergic to it. Whichever method you use, you will have to comb out the dead fleas. Have the cat stand on some newspaper (you may need some help for this) and then comb carefully. The dead fleas will fall out. When you think you have them all, wrap up the newspaper and burn it. If the cat is seriously infested, you may have to repeat this treatment several times.

You must also disinfect all the spots where your cat spends most of its time. If it has a definite sleeping-place, spray this area or wash it down with the same chemical compound you used on the cat. You should use the chemical in a stronger solution on the bedding. Try to spray everything—even furniture that the cat sleeps on, or its blanket. Everything that might harbour the fleas—rugs, couches, hairs, all crevices and corners—must be sprayed, and sprayed often, or else the fleas will continue hatching. Like roaches and other vermin, with a heavy infestation, they are difficult to dislodge.

If your cat has a definite resting- or sleeping-place, it may be a good idea to spray there even if you do not suspect fleas. A few minutes of prevention will serve you well.

Lice
Unlike the flea, the louse burrows into one place and remains there sucking and biting until you flush it out. Since the louse is so small—smaller than a pinhead, your chances of seeing it are small. But your cat feels the louse in its skin and sometimes scratches violently trying to dislodge it. Gradually the scratching may irritate the skin, but the louse simply burrows more deeply, right into the hair follicles. When this occurs, the hair will be worn away in the infested area.

A large infestation of lice is dangerous for a kitten, for lice suck blood and can possibly cause anaemia. The louse, if permitted, will live out its entire life-cycle on your cat, with the female producing large numbers of eggs. Those eggs will then hatch in about a week and become adult lice in three weeks—a fantastic rate of multiplication.

A nursing queen should be watched carefully for lice and other parasites. If she has lice, her kittens too will become infested, and then you will have a handful of trouble. While she may be able to cope with a large infestation, the kittens are in no condition to do so.

Frequently you will not be able to discover the cause of the persistent scratching and biting. But your vet can recognize the parasite and clear up the condition. One method is an insecticide dip.

Mites and Manges
Mites cause two different kinds of mange: demodectic, from a cigar-shaped parasite, also called follicular; and sarcoptic, from a spider-shaped parasite with eight legs. They are very seldom found in cats, and I mention them here only because you may have heard of them in connection with other pets.

Another kind of mite may cause otitis, an ear inflammation that is described under 'Ear Disorders' in this chapter, page 83.

Cats do suffer from mange, and a progressive case means a more extensive treatment. It may be necessary to clip the cat's hair very short and bathe the cat in a medicated solution. Frequently, this treatment must be repeated, for the mange may recur. If you do use a bath or spray, make sure your pet's eyes are protected. This can be done with a few drops of mineral-oil or an application of a mild eye-ointment in each eye.

You might find that your cat's condition is getting worse in the first stages of treatment. Hair may fall out, and the chances of baldness are ever present. If you begin treatment soon enough, the infected areas may soon grow the same fine coat that your cat always had, unless the mange becomes generalized. Postponement of treatment could lead to permanent baldness in the spots where the lesions formed. However, even when you catch it early—as soon as you see a rash, itching or the lesions themselves, a cure is often long and difficult.

Notoedric Mange

The notoedric mites produce a dermatitis of the ears, head, neck and lower parts of the legs. The diagnosis is made from mites or their eggs, and the treatment is generally successful.

Ticks

I will give you a full description of the tick, but it is not very common in cats; I see it only infrequently.

The tick is an annoying parasite because of its hardiness and endurance. Once embedded in the cat's skin, it hangs on tenaciously. The most common tick is called the sheeptick. A severe infestation can cause anaemia. It looks something like a small wart or a flat, blackish-brown seed and in some stages becomes a dark red. Ticks look for crevices and corners to settle into, and these crevices may be in your cat (or other pets) or in parts of your house. Their favourite spots on the cat are the stomach area, the pads of the feet, the feet and the folds between the legs and the body. Some varieties make their home in the cat's ear, usually in the external ear canal.

The general treatment is to dip the cat in a medicated compound, one of those recommended for fleas and lice. Or else you might try a tick-collar. Do not, under any conditions, take any action without consulting a vet.

When the infestation is small, some owners may try to remove the ticks themselves. There is a definite way of doing it to protect both your cat and yourself. If you reach into the cat's coat to pry off the ticks, you may break off the head from the body, or *vice versa*, causing a skin infection.

Here is how to do it correctly. First, wash the infected area with alcohol. The tick does not like to move, and it takes a strong liquid to loosen it. When you have dislodged it somewhat, place the tweezers squarely over it and lift it off. Be careful not to pull off any part of the tick's body. It is best to place one leg of the tweezers under the tick's body, so that it is separated from the cat's skin by the width of the tweezer. Place the tick directly in the toilet and flush. Do not assume that it is dead simply because it appears dazed. Ticks have considerable recuperative powers, like other parasites.

Tick-control is the best way of dealing with the entire problem. Control of the tick will also probably result in control of other major parasites. If your cat has a favourite sleeping-area, spray that. Of course, if it roams freely in the country or suburbs, there is nothing you can do by way of prevention except try a tick-collar.

Traumas

Traumas are wounds, injuries or breaks in the skin. They can result from accidents or simply be part of the daily life of the cat. The house cat or the cat kept in a flat is not likely to suffer such an injury, although some cats do attempt leaps they cannot make.

Abrasions

For abrasions, see 'Closed Wounds', page 131.

Capped Elbow (or Hard Elbow)

This is very rare in cats, since they are not heavy. Capped elbow is a callus that develops on the cat's elbows from resting on a hard surface. This thickening of the skin is normal and is nature's way of protecting the area from constant irritation. Occasionally, however, the hardening may make your cat uncomfortable. If this should happen, rub some mineral-oil into the elbows to soften them. You might also give your cat something soft to lie on. If the thickening is severe—this is extremely rare—and fluid accumulates, surgery may be necessary to relieve the condition.

Cuts

For cuts, see Chapter 4.

Tumours

Tumours in general are covered later in this chapter (page 115). A tumour—whether on the skin or elsewhere—is by definition an uncontrolled growth of tissue. Very often you will feel these growths right under the surface of the cat's skin. They seem like small, pliant, doughy balls that under pressure shift in the fingers. Any lump or growth is potentially serious, and if it grows, however slowly, then it should certainly be removed. If you feel such a lump, call it to the attention of your vet.

Benign

If the tumour or growth does not spread or recur after removal, it is called non-malignant or benign.

Malignant

When a growth or tumour spreads or if it recurs, it is said to be malignant or cancerous.

Baldness (Alopecia)

Usually, it is the older cat that suffers from baldness, although some internal or external parasite or disease can affect the skin and coat at any age to cause baldness. A cat's coat on occasion will nevertheless become thin in several places without any apparent reason. The bald spots may themselves be small, localized areas, or they may appear on whole sections of the body: the ears, hind legs, head. Baldness may be congenital.

Unless there is a specific cause—digestive trouble, diabetes, friction, internal or external parasites, contact with acids and other chemicals, dietary or hormonal imbalances, the condition may have been inherited. And just as suddenly as the coat has become bare, it may in some cases grow back to its normal condition.

Chemical Burns

For chemical burns, see Chapter 4.

Dandruff

When the skin flakes, dandruff or dry skin results. It may be a perfectly normal condition, for when the skin replenishes itself the old skin flakes away. When you see dandruff on your cat's coat, give it a good brushing. In time the dandruff should stop accumulating. Often, it is simply a seasonal event.

If the dandruff persists, however, there may be some reason beyond the natural shedding of skin. The cause may be dietary—is your cat receiving sufficient fat? Cats need a fairly high proportion of their diet in fat, and without it their coat will dry and peel. Or perhaps you have been washing it with a strong soap, or a soap it is allergic to; irritation has made the skin flake. Even sleeping in an excessively warm house over a radiator may dry out the skin.

If your cat scratches persistently at its skin and makes it flake, there may be parasites, not simple dryness. If the dandruff persists, a vet should examine your cat, as he would for any skin disease. Only he can tell through observation or laboratory tests if the cause is dietary, hormonal, parasitical or seasonal.

Lick Dermatitis
Some cats lick their skin so much that they create a serious inflammation that is difficult to cure.

Non-Specific Dermatitis (Eczema)
'Eczema', or 'non-specific dermatitis', is a comprehensive term for skin conditions or irritations that cannot be clearly defined. By general agreement, the word 'eczema' is best used to mean an ailment in which the skin shows either wet or dry patches: what we call moist and dry eczema. The causes of eczema have not been fully determined, and therefore the term is itself arbitrary. Eczemas can be difficult to treat; they often prove persistent.

Moist eczema is a skin condition in which moisture is discharged. The afflicted area then becomes scaly and pimply. The cat scratches the spot and irritates it still further. Although it looks angry and painful, it is sometimes easier to clear up than the dry kind.

Dry eczema is a skin condition in which moisture disappears from a given area, causing an itchy spot that the cat scratches and irritates. It may spread rapidly, with the result that the hair falls out. In long-hairs, it may spread invisibly for a long time. Moist and dry eczema may occur in any type of cat, and both types appear to be more prevalent in damp, warm weather.

Eczema attacks suddenly. One day your cat's skin is normal, and the next day it is scratching away at an ugly red moist patch. Home remedies such as medicated powders or calamine lotion provide only temporary relief; the condition must be treated by a vet. Treatment may take some time, for eczema frequently disappears only to re-appear shortly afterward. It is easy to confuse eczema with other skin ailments, and even after the condition has been determined, it is still very hard to diagnose the precise cause.

Researchers have suggested several possible causes of eczema. Dietary deficiencies are one of the more obvious possibilities, especially deficiencies of vitamin A and fats. Other theorists suggest damp and heat as possible causes, while still others believe a hormonal imbalance or even an infestation of parasites to be the cause. When parasites are a definite cause, the condition is called parasitic dermatitis. Other theories claim that an organic breakdown—say, in the kidneys or the digestive system—may be at fault. A further possibility is an allergy, but little is really known on this subject. The allergy may be to a food, a particular soap or the cat's bedding. Such is the range of possibilities.

Eczema proves to be a baffling condition. When a vet says that your cat has an eczema, he really means that there is no other skin ailment present and the cause is unknown. He will try to cure your cat through internal and external treatment, but the condition may hang on for a long time. External lotions and medication might soothe the condition, but until the internal factors are diagnosed and dealt with, there can be no permanent cure.

While eczema is not transferable from a cat to a person, once the treatment begins, your cat may possibly need treatment for a long time by your vet. If your cat persists in scratching its sores or licking away the medication, you may have to put an Elizabethan collar on it (see page 139 for a description).

Dry eczema, incidentally, is never helped by frequent baths. Frequent bathing will, in fact, make a cat's coat more dry, and this may actually aggravate the eczema. Regular combing and brushing will help keep the coat soft and healthy, but even such care cannot prevent eczema if there is an organic reason for it.

ONE FURTHER WARNING: Avoid bathing a cat with *any* skin disease, but if you must bathe it, do so only in a medicated bath as recommended by a vet.

Hormonal Imbalances
Sometimes a skin disorder can be traced to a lack of hormonal balance in your cat, especially when the ailment resists all other treatment. In such a case, your vet may recommend injections or hormones in an attempt to clear up the condition. He may recommend spaying (of the female) or neutering (of the male) if it has not already been done.

Neurotrophic Dermatitis
Neurotrophic dermatitis is an inflammation of the nerve endings that causes extreme sensitivity and pain. Diagnosis and treatment must be done by a vet. It is relatively rare.

MUSCULOSKELETAL DISORDERS
(Muscles, Bones and Joints)

Unless your cat suffers a serious injury in a fall or car-accident or is born with a congenital defect, you should not expect any serious trouble with its muscles, bones or joints until it passes middle age, at seven or eight. There are, of course, many minor ailments, such as infections, abscesses, irritations and sprains, that you might expect, especially if your cat is very active and adventurous. Accidents or infections may cause inflammation and loss of movement. But the cat's musculoskeletal system is hardy until it becomes subject to the degenerative processes of old age—provided it has received good nutrition throughout its life.

Degenerative Changes (Aging)
On rare occasions, a cat will suffer the loss of movement in a joint because of infection, accident, inflammation or excessive connective tissue. Ankylosis, or stiff joint, the name given to the ailment, calls for professional care.

Arthritis
Inflammation of the bone at a joint is called arthritis. Older cats suffer from arthritis much more than do younger ones, although it may afflict cats of any age. With arthritis, a cat feels pain on walking and jumping. There may be swelling around the joint, and the cat's discomfort will be more severe in damp weather.

The condition must be treated by a vet. Although treatment for a person with arthritis consists of periodic use of aspirin, this can be used only with caution in a cat and only under the supervision of a vet. Warm packs on the joint may help relieve pain, if it is severe. Restrict the cat's activity if possible and keep it in a warm, dry area away from draughts.

Bursitis
Inflammation of the capsule (the bursa) that the joint moves in is called bursitis. The treatment and home care are the same as for arthritis.

Infections
Bone
A bone infection (called osteomyelitis) is usually caused by a secretion of pus. A cat may develop osteomyelitis from an infected bone fracture, from bone surgery or from bites from other animals. The cat that roams freely is particularly susceptible to cat- and other animal-bites. Severe dental infection can also lead to osteomyelitis of the jaw.

Cats with the condition usually have fever, pain and swelling in the afflicted area, and they avoid moving the infected limb. One of your first signs will be that the cat favours the limb. Treatment should begin immediately if the limb is to be saved.

Joint
Bacteria lodging in a joint as a result of an injury may cause an infection. The enclosed area will generally swell, and the joint naturally becomes extremely painful and sensitive. The symptoms will be the usual ones for an infection: pain (the cat may favour the area, particularly if it involves a leg), swelling or inflammation, redness (wherever you can see through the coat) and heat. If the infection is neglected and goes untreated, your cat may run a high temperature, lose its appetite and become depressed. Until you see a vet, restrict your cat's activity (it probably will not be too active at this time anyway) and relieve its pain with wet compresses or pads on the sore area. Do not give aspirin without professional advice.

Muscle Abscesses

A muscle abscess is a formation of pus in the muscle tissue as a result of an injury. It is caused by bacteria and often leads to the destruction of the tissue. The muscle itself is usually inflamed, swollen and very painful; the cat will favour it. There may also be a fever.

You will have trouble recognizing this ailment, because its symptoms are similar to those of many other musculoskeletal conditions. If you notice any of the above signs, see your vet at once. Muscle trouble, even a bruise, needs immediate and careful attention. If neglected, the unused muscle may cause a chronic lameness. Cat-bites are the usual cause.

Tail Irritations

Cats sometimes suffer from infection or sores under the tail. The tail might interfere with bowel movements in some cats and the skin become irritated. To relieve the irritation and prevent any possible infection, you should apply a mild antiseptic, oils or medicated powder daily.

Rickets (Nutritional)

Rickets is a disorder in which the bone formation is poor. It affects pets and people, although it is somewhat rare in cats. It is caused by a sub-standard diet, especially by a lack of vitamin D and calcium and phosphorus in the kitten's diet. It may also result despite the correct diet because the cat is unable to assimilate those foods that prevent rickets, although this is rare.

Rickets is characterized by irregular development of the bones, particularly the long bones in the legs. A cat with rickets often has enlarged joints in its legs and walks on its wrists and ankles: hind legs high, front legs low. When the nutritional deficiency is severe, other parts of the body are also affected; the head and jaw may bulge strangely. In addition, the cat will look unhealthy. Its coat will lack sheen, and its eyes will be dull and bulging.

If caught early enough, rickets may be treated successfully with a balanced diet of mineral supplements, vitamins A and D, meat, eggs and milk. If the treatment comes too late, however, the damage is done, and the cat's bones may remain soft and break easily.

Many owners may acquire a kitten with rickets and not know it until the cat is grown. In such cases, the cat must lead a gentle life, because the weakened limbs can break even under normal stress.

Traumas

Dislocations

A dislocation is a displacement of one or more of the bones making up a joint, and it may occur at the hip, the knee, the toes, the jaw or any other joint. For details of symptoms and treatment, see Chapter 4.

Fractures

A bone fracture is a broken bone. For the different kinds of fractures, their symptoms and their treatment, see Chapter 4.

Hernias

Hernias may be of several kinds, and a cat can suffer from any one of them. All types are characterized by soft swellings that appear in the general abdominal area. The hernia is itself a protrusion or bubble of tissue or organs working through an abnormal opening in the abdominal wall, the navel or the diaphragm (the partition between the chest and abdomen). In an accident, a traumatic hernia may develop. All hernias need immediate professional treatment, or they will lead to more trouble.

I will describe the different kinds of hernias, so that you can be on the alert for any swellings that appear. You probably will not be able to recognize some types. The umbilical hernia is the most common in kittens and is generally hereditary. It is characterized by a lump or swelling that comes through the abdominal wall at the navel, where the umbilical cord was once attached. The lump may be a single small bubble or it may be extensive (several inches). The larger type usually requires immediate surgical correction.

Car-accidents may cause diaphragmatic hernia, a break in the wall (or diaphragm) between the chest and abdominal cavity. For the cat that does not roam outside, this is unlikely. When this happens, the abdominal organs work their way through the tear in the diaphragm, exerting pressure on the heart and lungs and seriously interfering with breathing. There is no treatment except surgery, which should be performed as soon as the diagnosis is confirmed by X-ray. This is usually an emergency first-aid situation.

The female and sometimes the male may suffer from inguinal hernia, the result of a tear from a structural defect that allows the intestines to pass into the inguinal region, sometimes called the groin.

While inguinal hernia occurs more frequently in the female, the perineal hernia is more prevalent in the older male. A tumour or an enlarged prostate gland but most often chronic constipation may cause your cat to strain when at stool. Whatever the cause, the strain may create a tear in the rectal muscles in the pelvic region, through which intestines can then pass. There is usually a large swelling around or on either side of the anus. By the time this occurs, your cat has the hernia. If you notice excessive straining, or if you see your cat repeatedly trying to move its bowels, you should have it examined; a perineal hernia is a slim possibility.

Sprains

A sprain occurs around a joint when, as the result of a sudden twist or wrench, the ligaments are stretched or torn. A cat that tries acrobatics that it does not succeed in carrying out might suffer a sprain. For details of the symptoms and treatment, see Chapter 4.

Cancer

Bone cancer is rare and almost always inoperable. Generally, if possible, the diseased bone is amputated. Many of these malignancies spread throughout the body if unchecked, carried by the blood, a process called metastasis. An abnormal swelling or an unexplained lameness may indicate this condition. The diagnosis is made by X-ray or biopsy.

British Short-Hair

DOMESTIC BREEDS

Balinese, Chocolate-Point

Rex, Cornish, female

Rex, Cornish, male

Long-Hair, Bicoloured

American Short-Hair, Silver Mackerel
Tabby

Burmese

Dr. Myra Hinman

Balinese, Blue-Point

Lieselotte A. Grimes

Siamese, Seal-Point

Carol Keller

Havana Brown

Tortie-and-White (Calico), Long-Hair

Maine Coon, Odd-Eyed White

Chinchilla

Birman

Russian Blue

Abyssiniań,
Sorrel (Red)

Patricia A. Webber

Chartreux

Helen Gamon

Manx

Marjorie Lomoriello

Angora

Japanese Bobtail

Korat

Egyptian Mau, female
(Oriental Spotted Tab[

Long-Hair, Smoke

The incidence of cancers of different types in cats can be high. Cats develop many different types of tumours, and some occur more frequently than others. Skin and skin-related tumours are among the most common, but tumours of the mammary gland (breast tumour) are also very common. Leukaemia (which is being diagnosed more frequently) has been noted, whereas lung and colon tumours occur less frequently.

Feline Leukaemia Virus Diseases

The feline leukaemia virus (FeLV) is a major cause of death among cats. FeLV infects the rapidly growing cells of the blood and lymph system and causes several fatal feline diseases in addition to being indirectly responsible for several other feline diseases. Fortunately, much is known about the virus and how it is transmitted from cat to cat, and this knowledge can be used by cat-owners to protect their cats from infection.

Probably the most well-known FeLV disease is leukaemia or lympho-sarcoma (LSA)—a cancerous disease of the white blood cells. The signs of LSA are, unfortunately, not specific for LSA or consistent from cat to cat. The signs that are most frequently seen are pale gums, enlarged lymph nodes, difficulty in breathing, lack of appetite, listlessness and a poor coat. In addition to LSA, FeLV causes non-regenerative anaemia, a progressive disease characterized by pale gums, weakness and weight loss; an enteritis-like disease, characterized by bloody diarrhoea and weight-loss; and 'fading kitten syndrome', a disease in which newly-born kittens do poorly and die from various bacterial infections one or two weeks after birth.

The virus is also suspected of causing some foetal abortions and resorptions as well as several proliferative and degenerative bone-marrow disorders. FeLV is an immunosuppressive virus; that is to say, it reduces the ability of the cat's natural defence (immune) system to provide resistance to other viruses and bacteria. As a result of this immunosuppression, FeLV-infected cats are more liable to infection from other agents and are more likely to die from these infections than are uninfected cats. In fact, more FeLV-infected cats die from these 'immunosuppressive diseases' than die from LSA.

In the last six years much has been learned about how the virus is transmitted from cat to cat. It appears that the primary route is via the saliva, which may contain as many as one million infectious virus particles per millilitre. Biting, communal grooming and the communal use of feeding-bowls are thus the most likely ways in which one cat can infect another. However, the virus is present in the blood and urine of infected cats as well as in the saliva, and cat fleas and litter pans are therefore other possible routes of FeLV transmission. FeLV is also shed into the milk from infected queens and can pass across the placenta from the mother to the foetus. It should be pointed out that most cats in the general cat-population are not infected with FeLV. It is thought that the virus is spread in the cat-population primarily by close, prolonged, direct cat-to-cat contact in multiple-cat households or catteries rather than by brief contact between uninfected and infected cats.

The prognosis for FeLV-infected cats is very poor since most infected cats will develop one or other of the FeLV-related diseases. No cure is available for any of these diseases, and they are invariably fatal. A few infected cats are resistant to disease development, but these cats are 'carrier' cats and are a constant source of infection for other, uninfected, cats.

Although the FeLVdiseases cannot be cured, they can be prevented by preventing the spread of FeLV. This is done by testing all the cats in a household or cattery, as well as all the cats being exchanged between households and catteries, for FeLV, using a simple and inexpensive blood-test. Once all the infected cats in a household have been identified, they are euthanized or isolated from the uninfected cats. The household (and especially the feeding-bowls and litter pans) is then thoroughly cleaned with detergents and the uninfected cats are 'quarantined' for three months before being re-tested. If all the uninfected cats are still uninfected after the quarantine period, the household is considered to be FeLV-free. Another, and probably more acceptable, method of preventing the spread of FeLV would be vaccination. It has been found that a few cats are naturally resistant to FeLV infection, and this finding has given rise to hopes that it will be possible to develop an FeLV vaccine. Several research groups are currently investigating this possibility, but a safe, effective vaccine will probably not be available for several years.

The public-health risks of FeLV are unknown. The virus can grow in human cells in the laboratory, but there is no evidence that FeLV can cause disease in humans. However, some people who have lived or worked with infected cats have been found to have antibodies to the virus and might, therefore, have been infected with FeLV. In view of the uncertainties regarding the public-health risks of FeLV, euthanasia or isolation of all FeLV-infected cats should be considered.

If you suspect that your cat has been exposed to an FeLV-infected cat or has an FeLV disease, your vet will be able to take a blood sample for an FeLV test and may be able to determine if your cat has an FeLV disease.

Feline tumours are similar in many ways to human tumours, which are thought to be caused by a combination of factors such as viruses, radiation, chemical carcinogens, genetic predisposition, hormones, nutrition and the immunological status. Cats with tumours can be treated with drugs, radiation and surgery, and by stimulating the natural defence (immunity) system of the body to attack the tumour cells. As with human cancer, the response of feline tumours to therapy varies, depending primarily on the tumour type and on the extent of the disease. Some tumours can be cured with therapy, while in others treatment does not result in cure, and the best that can usually be achieved is an improvement in the quality of life.

NERVOUS DISORDERS

The nervous system of the cat, like that of man, centres in the brain and spinal cord. From these central areas, like branches on a tree-trunk, runs the complex network of the nervous system. The brain is, of course, the central repository of all motivation. What the brain commands, the rest of the body does. If the brain is troubled in any way, the entire body responds accordingly. Brain damage or inflammation (encephalitis) can throw the cat's entire nervous system off balance.

Certain diseases directly attack the cat's nervous system. Since the system is so delicate, prevention of such diseases is the only way to ensure a healthy cat. Rabies leaves no survivors. There are also diseases of lesser intensity that attack the nervous system only temporarily, such as eclampsia, the result of an imbalance of calcium and other minerals in the queen's nervous system during pregnancy or nursing. Poison may also attack the nervous system.

How can you tell when the nervous system has been affected? The clearest indications are excessive shaking, rapid breathing, convulsions and paralysis. While many of these conditions are frightening, some may clear up, provided they are treated in time.

Convulsions, or Fits

A number of things can bring on convulsions and fits: disease, excessive heat, accidents, poisons, nervous ailments, inadequate diet, over-excitement, parasites, worms and high fevers. A fit is characterized by foaming or frothing at the mouth; champing of the jaws, as if the cat were chewing gum and salivating; thrashing of the feet for no purpose; stiffening of the muscles so that the body quivers and shakes; and even unconsciousness.

Do not panic if you see your cat having a fit. Any cat that has a fit should be examined by a vet.

The fit itself is not generally the ailment. All you can do si to see that the cat does not hurt itself. Remove any objects that may prove injurious, but otherwise leave the cat alone. It may accidentally bite or scratch you. When the fit subsides, try to keep the cat wrapped warm if it will hold still, and be sure it does not bite you. Do not feed directly after a fit.

A fit may be simply from nervourness, and its reasons may defy analysis, but it generally points to something more serious that can be diagnosed and treated. A heavy infestation of worms, for instance, may lead to fits if not treated. Often you will not recognize the real ailment until the fit tips you off, and even then a vet may have difficulty diagnosing the condition.

Encephalitis

Encephalitis is an inflammation of the brain that accompanies some of the more severe feline diseases, especially viruses. When the virus reaches the brain, the result is inflammation. The cat may lie down and pedal with its feet, as if bicycling. The other signs are also obvious: convulsions, possibly with frothing; twitching of muscles; partial or complete loss of vision; rapidly fluctuating temperature, from very high to near normal; confusion in the cat as to where it is; partial (sometimes complete) paralysis; possibly excessive urinating and defecating.

By the time encephalitis has developed, your cat will probably be under professional care for the primary disease.

Meningitis

Feline meningitis is similar to the disease in people. It is a viral or bacterial inflammation of the material covering the spinal cord.

The afflicted cat may go into a stupor or become rigid. It loses all sense of direction, whines as if in pain and seems to retreat into itself. All movement seems to be very painful. Its eyes, too, may be affected, and it will not be able to control them. Meningitis is an ailment that needs immediate professional treatment, and even then the cat may not recover.

Neuritis

Inflammation of the nerves results in a condition known as neuritis. It has a wide range of causes and symptoms. It may cause considerable pain in the cat, and you will notice difficulty in its movement, particularly in cold, damp weather. This may be your only sign. The condition needs professional treatment, since correct diagnosis is very important. Do not give aspirin unless a vet advises you to.

Paralysis

An accident to the brain or spinal cord or a disease may cause paralysis, or immobilization.

Certain accidents can damage a section of the brain, and the result is partial paralysis, depending on the extent of the damage. A sharp blow on the spine or a crunching smash that fractures a vertebra causes sufficient damage in some cases to bring on paralysis. A herniated disk that separates the vertebrae may also cause paralysis.

Paralysis may come on slowly as well, from disease or from a cerebral haemorrhage. Recent advances in medicine, however, have made many cases treatable, whereas in the past such ailments were considered hopeless. The chief advance has been in surgery, which is still often the only remedy, and post-operative care.

Convalescence from paralysis is usually slow, once again depending on the cause and the extent of the damage. For those cases in which surgery may help, the decision whether you wish to go through with an operation depends, of course, on you. Even successful surgery may mean a very slow recovery period, always with the chance that recovery will be less than complete. Many cases are not treatable.

Poisoning

All poisoning, whether food or chemical, may affect the nervous system. For emergency treatment, see page 132.

Tetanus, or Lockjaw (Very Rare in Cats)

Tetanus is a severe infection that may occur when a puncture wound is not treated properly, as in a bite or a nail puncture. This can happen to the cat that roams and gets into fights. At a certain stage in its development, tetanus will cause a generalized muscle spasm. Very often in this state the cat will stretch in a grotesque way: lips, mouth, head. Everything stiffens unnaturally, as though it were turning to stone. Get it to a vet immediately, but even then recovery is rare.

REPRODUCTIVE DISORDERS—FEMALE

In the female, the reproductive system consists of all those organs that are concerned with giving birth: the ovaries, uterus, mammary glands, cervix, vagina, vulva, clitoris and Fallopian tubes. When everything is going well, all these organs work together in harmony. The female's season of heat may come several times yearly; she conceives then, if you mate her, and sixty-one or sixty-two days later (more or less) she has a healthy litter, which she proceeds to take care of. For most females, this is the natural cycle of life. It is only the exceptional case that causes difficulty, but it is the exceptional case that you may be interested in.

One problem with the domestic house cat is that she is enclosed and her normal cycle has been disturbed. She has little exercise, and she has little opportunity to make use of her heat periods to reproduce—unless she roams freely. As a pet, most of her natural responses are limited. To some extent, female difficulties can result from this, although most ailments may be cleared up through new medical procedures and drugs.

Eclampsia

Eclampsia is an ailment that afflicts pregnant or nursing queens when their supply of calcium and other minerals is disturbed. When she is pregnant, the foetuses will absorb her calcium and other minerals for their own needs. Similarly, when the queen nurses her litter, they will suck her breasts, and unless there is a calcium and mineral supplement she may lose what she herself needs. The chief preventive is to give a vitamin and mineral supplement, plus calcium, to the pregnant and nursing queen. Also make sure that milk is available—if she can digest it. The condition, generally, is more common in the nursing queen than in the pregnant female.

The signs of eclampsia are unmistakable. The queen will start excessive panting and shaking, and she may go into convulsions. She will possibly have a wild look in her eyes. Her temperature will rise; her mouth becomes rigid. When you see these signs, be sure to call a vet and describe the symptoms. He will sometimes have to inject calcium, steroids and sedatives to return her to normal. Relief is very rapid in most cases.

If the queen has eclampsia, remove the kittens and do not let them suckle for two or three days. Feed them prepared milk or formula with an eye-dropper. When the condition occurs in the pregnant queen, the kittens may be born with a mineral-deficiency. Prevention is the best treatment. It is rare in most cats with today's diets.

False Pregnancy (Pseudocyesis)

In false pregnancy, the female shows many of the symptoms of real pregnancy: expanded belly, sensitive and even swollen breasts, a need to make a nest for her litter, even pseudo labour—but there is no pregnancy. This is a condition that can occur after a sterile mating. It usually terminates after five to seven days.

Ask your vet about hormonal injections to relieve the condition, especially if it recurs. The only permanent cure is a hysterectomy.

Infections

Although most female difficulties seem to focus on the uterus, the vagina occasionally will give some trouble, especially if there is an injury to the vulva. Since the vulva is exposed, it may be irritated by foreign objects. The country cat may scratch her vulva on rocks or brush or even barbed wire. The open wound might become infected, leading to infection of the cervix and the uterus. You will then see a discharge of pus and blood, and the cat may have difficulty in urinating because of the pain.

There are also the usual injuries that a pregnant queen might suffer when her breasts are filled with milk. Even before she is ungainly and slow, her nipples might be injured by sharp rocks, sticks and other foreign objects. (Obviously most of these possibilities do not exist for the cat kept in a flat.) When she is pregnant, you should take particular care to see that she avoids injury. Any severe wound should receive immediate professional care—there is always the danger of infection if the wound is of the puncture type. See 'Open Wounds,' page 131, for what to do if your pet, pregnant or not, suffers a cut or laceration.

Mastitis

When the nursing queen's teats become inflamed and swell up as a result of infection or inflammation, she probably has mastitis. At first the milk may be removed easily, but then it suddenly stops; the infection follows.

The glands will be hot to the touch, and the queen may feel severe pain. This is a condition that needs immediate professional treatment. During the infection, the secretion coming from the teat may make the kitten sucking it sick. While most kittens will refuse the teat when the milk is infected, there is no guarantee that they will. Also, the queen will be in danger, as the infection may spread throughout her body.

Metritis

Metritis is a condition in which the uterus becomes inflamed and swollen. It generally occurs six to eight weeks after heat. It may also occur during queening, right after queening or at almost any time. It affects only unspayed females. One of the reasons for spaying a female is, in fact, to avoid an ailment such as metritis.

Pyometra

Pyometra is an accumulation of pus in the uterus, perhaps as a result of a hormonal imbalance or infection. It occurs more often in mongrel females over five years of age, most frequently in the middle-aged cat between eight and nine. It is accompanied by thirst and increased urination, vomiting (of solids and even of water), a rise in temperature, pain and swelling in the abdomen, and loss of appetite. The cat will sometimes have a discharge from the uterus, as though in continual heat. These are symptoms common to many ailments, but with pyometra the female's hindquarters may give off a sickly-sweetish odour if she is discharging.

Structural Defects

A female may have certain structural defects that you are ignorant of until she has a litter. A queen with a pelvic obstruction or with a uterus that cannot accommodate kittens should not have been mated. X-ray examination will reveal any pelvic defects before mating. In most cases, however, the mating will take place, as the majority of owners will not have their cat X-rayed for this purpose. Therefore it is always a good idea to have a vet on call when your queen is ready to deliver. Then, if she does have trouble queening, she can get professional help should she need it. Even a Caesarean section may be called for.

See Chapter 6 for the details of what to do when queening-time approaches.

Tumours

The unspayed, mongrel female may develop tumours in the mammary glands, particularly as she grows older—say, after seven or eight. Such tumours are noticeable because of visible lumps or swellings in the breast area. As soon as you notice anything unusual, you should have a vet check them.

Tumours of the ovaries are also a possibility. (The spayed cat, of course, does not have this problem.) With this condition, the heat period is thrown off balance. There may be excessive bleeding or discharge, or no discharge at all. The heat may last an excessively long time, or there may be periods with no heat at all. Generally, the cat is constantly in heat. Such an abnormality calls for a professional check.

REPRODUCTIVE DISORDERS—MALE

Cryptorchidism

Cryptorchidism means that neither testicle of the cat has descended. A cat with this condition is generally sterile because the undescended testicles have never developed or else body heat has destroyed the reproductive cells of the testicles. Otherwise, your cat is unimpaired—and since most owners of males have them neutered, this should not be a problem. However, you should consult a vet, because undescended testicles are always removed to prevent tumours developing in them and also to prevent male cat odour. See also 'Monorchidism', page 104.

Ailments of the Genital Organs

Injuries to the testicles are very rare indeed, since the majority of owners have their male cat neutered very young.

Injuries to the penis are also rare, although penile haematoma can sometimes be caused by rough manipulation. Most of the time an injury will respond to first-aid treatment (see Chapter 4). There are few ailments to which the penis is subject, except perhaps for tumours, and these too are very rare.

Monorchidism

Monorchidism means that only one of your cat's testicles has descended into the scrotum. The condition is hereditary, and there is nothing you can do about it without professional help. Such a cat is not necessarily sterile, and he may pass on the defect to the male kittens in any litter.

Usually an operation is performed to remove the testicle before it gives trouble or causes male cat odour. Since most males are not used for stud purposes, you need not worry about its inability to reproduce.

Prostatitis

The prostate gland may become enlarged, especially in the older cat, through either infection or hormonal imbalance. The resulting condition is prostatitis. In the neutered male, the gland atrophies.

The gland normally rests in the cat's pelvic cavity below the colon (large bowel). As long as it remains normal, it serves its function in the reproductive system. When it swells or becomes inflamed, however, it compresses the rectum. The result is pain during defecation, and constipation. The cat may be reluctant to sit and may find walking difficult. Since most males are neutered when young, cases of prostatitis are very rare.

If your cat has not been neutered, such an infection is possible. The symptoms are a rise in temperature, restlessness, general irritability and a favouring of the entire area. If you do nothing to relieve the condition, your cat may have a bowel movement with pain.

RESPIRATORY DISORDERS

The respiratory system consists of the nose, sinus, windpipe (trachea), pharynx, larynx, bronchial tubes and lungs. Cats are subject to most of the common respiratory ailments: coughs, sinusitis, bronchitis, laryngitis, rhinotracheitis and calici. While cats do not suffer from the common cold as we know it, they do get something very similar—an upper-respiratory infection. All these ailments, when severe, require professional treatment, especially now that antibiotics are used with such good and quick results.

Many respiratory ailments have common symptoms: discharge from the nose and eyes, rise in temperature, shallow and rapid breathing, generally a dry or hacking cough, loss of vitality and lack of interest in food. There may also be sneezing, although sneezing by itself can also mean an allergy or a sensitivity to dust rather than an infection.

WARNING: Your cat's nose is not an indicator of illness. A dry hot nose does not mean sickness and a cold nose good health. Other indicators are much more important.

Vaccination prevents many respiratory infections.

Asthma

Asthma is a chronic breathing difficulty that occurs more often in the older cat, although by no means exclusively. It is characterized by wheezing and a deeply based cough. Breathing may also be shallow, interrupted by bouts of coughing. A damp climate can aggravate an asthmatic condition.

Sometimes a sedative—recommended by a vet—will help relax your cat. Injections and oral medication may relieve the condition temporarily.

All types of cats are equally susceptible to asthma, although the over-weight pet is more disposed to it.

Coryza

Coryza is similar to the common cold that all of us experience. It is a relatively mild upper-respiratory ailment characterized by sneezing, nasal discharge, loss of appetite, a low-grade temperature (usually not higher than 103°F) and soft stools (usually not diarrhoea). Usually it runs its course in a week or less. But if the discharge is heavy, then it may lead into something more serious that needs professional attention.

Inflammation

If your cat has received the combined vaccination, it is protected from the fiercest of the upper-respiratory inflammations: rhinotracheitis and calici. But it can still suffer from inflammation of the trachea, pharynx, larynx or bronchi. Usually, these result in a scooping, wheezing cough. The cat seems to have something in its throat that it wants to bring up. It may even foam or froth at the mouth in its frenzy of coughing or gagging.

All these respiratory ailments are generally infectious. They may last for weeks or months and if neglected can lead to complications. If ignored, the cough irritates the already inflamed areas, which in turn causes more coughing.

Do not give home remedies, but let a vet prescribe what is best. Since a cough can indicate a variety of ailments, it should be attended to as soon as you recognize its persistence. Give it forty-eight hours at most to clear up. Do not let a cat that is coughing roam outside.

Lung Ailments

There are several lung ailments that a cat can suffer from. Since you will not be able to diagnose any of these conditions yourself, I will give a short rundown of the possible diseases. All are characterized by difficulty with breathing—usually short and rapid breath accompanied by a rasping sound—and by coughing.

Two very rare lung ailments are feline tuberculosis and emphysema. You should not expect your cat to have either one, but I mention them in passing. Feline tuberculosis can usually be confirmed only by X-ray and other laboratory tests. Its chief symptoms are coughing, loss of weight and depression. Emphysema involves the breakdown of the lung cells, or dilatation, as they accumulate air pockets.

If your cat by chance has either of these lung ailments or any of those described below, it will be hard for you not to notice them. In addition to the laboured breathing and hacking cough, your cat will appear unhealthy and depressed. A good deal of its energy will be going into the sheer effort of breathing, and its heart will be under extra strain. The condition needs immediate professional care.

Pleurisy

An inflammation of the membrane covering the lung and adhering to the chest cavity is called pleurisy. It is characterized by sharp, harsh respiration. Sometimes pleurisy follows or is present at the same time as an attack of pneumonia. Such inflammation of the lung area generally produces a cough and often fever. In another form of pleurisy, the chest cavity may fill with fluid. This is known as hydrothorax or chest-fluid pleurisy. It is accompanied by shallow breathing, as though the cat cannot get enough air no matter how hard it tries. Fluid presses the lung so that it cannot expand to its full capacity.

Pneumonia

Pneumonia is a lung ailment in which the tissues become inflamed, thickened and watery. At one time pneumonia was a persistent killer of cats, but antibiotics and prescription drugs, as for people, have prevented many fatalities. It is important to treat pneumonia early.

There are several kinds of pneumonia, including parasitic, but all are characterized by a rough, hacking cough, discharge from the nose, shallow breathing—like a kind of chest vibration—loss of appetite and a high fever. Frequently the nasal discharge will be ropy and greenish, perhaps even flecked with blood when the infection is severe. These are your danger-signals, for pneumonia and for most upper-respiratory infections. The cat needs prompt professional care.

As with any respiratory ailment, keep your cat out of draughts and do not let it outside. Feed an easily digested diet and try to make it eat. Baby-foods are recommended at this time, including protein cereal mixed with warmed milk (if digestible by your cat) and also egg-yolk and milk.

These are only temporary matters. Only a vet can tell if the pneumonia is accompanying another illness or exists alone.

Tumours

Tumours in the lungs or general chest cavity may have the same symptoms as tuberculosis: shortness of breath, coughing, loss of weight, depression. They are diagnosed by X-ray and by laboratory blood-tests.

Upper-Respiratory Infections

Cats can suffer from what we call a cold—coryza (described on page 105) is such an ailment. Generally, the cat's nose and eyes run with a thin mucous discharge; there may be a slight fever and chills. Your cat may also cough and sneeze. If there is no more than a slight upper-respiratory infection, the condition may pass in a few days. Keep your cat out of draughts and do not let it out.

The symptoms of an upper-respiratory infection can indicate something more severe—rhinotracheitis or calici if your cat has not been vaccinated. Then the symptoms will be more intense, and the cat's misery will be obvious. It may not eat or want to move, and it might sleep constantly. A cat this sick may also stay out of sight.

URINARY DISORDERS

The cat's urinary system consists of the kidneys, ureters, bladder and urethra. The kidneys filter waste-material, which would otherwise poison the cat's system; the ureters carry the urine from the kidneys to the bladder; the bladder in turn holds the liquid matter, which is carried away in the urethra and eliminated as urine.

While all urinary problems can be serious, I have outlined in great detail one ailment that is potentially the most serious of all: it is called feline urolithiasis and appears below, page 110. I describe feline urolithiasis at length, and you will see that some of its symptoms overlap those of other ailments, such as stones and bladder disorders. But feline urolithiasis is of such potential danger for a cat that you should have available a complete description of its symptoms and emergency treatment, even if this involves some duplication of other information.

Kidney Troubles
In the normal course of events, your cat should not suffer from a kidney ailment until it is old. In cats over eight or nine, the incidence of kidney ailments rises, although it can, of course appear before then. In cases where age is not a factor, kidney trouble may result from a severe illness that places an excessive burden on the kidneys.

Other factors that might cause kidney ailments are food poisons in the system or poisons or insect-spray the cat has swallowed. Although it appears to recover and seems well, its kidneys may be affected because the poison has damaged the cells. Since this organ is very delicate, it can be permanently damaged well before any distinct symptoms of illness begin to appear. A very sharp blow like a kick may injure the sensitive tubules of the kidneys. When some are destroyed, a greater burden is placed on the rest, and the kidneys are unable to function properly.

Inflammation of Kidneys (Nephritis)
There are many symptoms of inflamed kidneys (also called nephritis): chiefly vomiting, as well as increased thirst and increase in urination, sensitivity in the general back area, actual pain when pressure on an area around the kidneys is applied, loss of appetite and general unhealthiness in the form of blurred eyes and depression. The cat's urine may change colour, to orange or red. In some instances, when stones are present, the cat may have great difficulty in urinating. It might strain and strain in order to pass a few drops. When the condition worsens, the cat may have trouble walking, or faint, or go into a coma. With neglect, nephritis becomes chronic or long-term, and your cat's chances of complete recovery are lessened.

If you notice any of these symptoms, call a vet. Your cat may not have a kidney ailment at all. Your only signs may be thirst and difficulty in urination, and these can indicate many other conditions, or even nervousness. Some females when they go into their heat periods urinate very frequently, often apparently without control. This may last for a short period or for a week or two.

When an acute kidney ailment passes into a chronic condition, the attacks are frequent over a long period of time. There may also be difficulty in walking, as though the cat's entire back area were in pain.

A kidney ailment may throw your cat off its litter-box training. Although most cats are fastidious, when their kidneys fail to function correctly, irritation may make retention of urine impossible.

There are certain dietary precautions you should take with kidney trouble. Highly seasoned food is generally not recommended for even a healthy cat; it should never be given to a cat with a kidney ailment. Since table scraps are usually spicy, or at least contain salt and pepper, avoid giving them if the cat is ill. A heavy meat diet is not recommended either, since large amounts of protein will excessively burden the kidneys.

Consult a vet about your cat's diet. A prescription diet is available for the cat with kidney ailments, although you may have trouble getting your cat to eat it. If your cat balks, you may have to resort to tricks to persuade it to eat. One method is gradually to remove the regular food and replace it with the special prescription diet.

Stones

Some cats have kidney stones for years before showing any signs. Then suddenly they begin to pass blood in their urine, or they find urinating extremely difficult. At this time your cat may cry when it urinates, or walk with a humped or arched back. It may even hold itself in a urinating position for much of the time without being able to urinate. The condition is very rare, but it is very painful when it does occur.

Do not confuse kidney stones with bladder sand, which is much more frequent and which collect in the bladder, where they may occlude or close off the urethra and prevent urination. Kidney stones ordinarily have to be removed by surgery if X-rays show them to be present. If not, there will be recurrent attacks. On occasion, they can be aggravated by sudden and violent exercise, which results in the shifting of the stones. Of course, the stones can move at any time, even while the cat is resting or sleeping. The condition is very rare.

Like all kidney ailments, kidney stones have symptoms similar to those of many other conditions. If your cat cries when it urinates or if it humps over when walking, it may well have some other illness. If you see this, you should call your vet, for your cat is obviously suffering and in need of medical aid. The vet can give treatment to relieve pain temporarily. You should not give aspirin to tide your cat over an attack. The only permanent cure is an operation to remove the stones, and sometimes a kidney, followed by a special diet and medication after the stones have been analysed.

Bladder Ailments

My description of urolithiasis below will overlap with some of the material in this section.

There are several bladder ailments, most often found in the older cat. Unless your pet is hurt in a fall or a car-accident, or possibly is kicked hard, the chances of a bladder ailment are slight. However, any cat may suffer a bladder disorder if it gets chilled or wet. Owners who let their cats run free outside could have this problem.

The most common bladder ailments involve dribbling, sand and infection (called cystitis). Dribbling usually occurs in the older cat, but it may also afflict the younger one, and both sexes indiscriminately. It may also occur in spayed females, usually as they grow older. Dribbling results when the cat is unable to hold its urine. The reason is ordinarily a loss of tone in the sphincter muscle of the urethra, which controls the flow of urine. It may be caused by sand in the bladder, or possibly by an infection.

Dribbling is, of course, a nuisance for the owner. It may also be annoying for such a fastidious animal as the cat. Before you can do anything about dribbling, a vet must determine the cause. If the condition results from loss of tone in the sphincter, the chances are the cat is old and there is not much that can be done except diet and water control. Sometimes medication works. If the reason is that the female has lost control because of spaying, then hormones may be injected or given orally. This injection provides a substitute for the secretion of the now missing ovaries, and it may help. You may choose to stay with the dribbling rather than give hormonal treatment. If your cat dribbles because of an irritation or an infection, your vet may give antibiotics or some other medication to try to correct the condition.

Along with dribbling, the presence of stones in the bladder is occasionally seen in cats of all ages. The most obvious symptom is that the cat will have trouble urinating, or there may be blood in the urine. The male and the female will squat and strain, to release only a few drops, or may pass blood with the urine. The fact is that a stone or sand is plugging the small opening between the bladder and the urethra, like a barrier at the mouth of a hole. Or in the male, sand may enter the urethra and serve as a dam shutting off the passage of urine, especially at those places where the urethra is small in diameter.

Although this is very painful for your cat, do not administer aspirin without a vet's advice. Usually, the female will find it easier to pass this sand from the urethra than the male will.

Not all bladder-stone conditions are the same, however, and each case needs separate treatment. The stones themselves (or calculi—accumulations of mineral matter) are very small and cause irritation. The calculi also differ in smoothness and roughness, and they do not always settle in the same place in the cat's urinary tract. That is why some cats have no difficulty with bladder stones, while others must have the stones removed. You will probably not be aware of the condition until your cat has trouble urinating or urinates with blood, and by that time the stones will most probably have blocked the urethra. When that occurs, treatment followed by surgery is the only way to relieve the blockage.

Cystitis is a severe inflammation of the urinary bladder—caused by infection, sand, diet or even body chill. It seems more prevalent in females than in males. With cystitis, your cat may cry when it urinates, and it ordinarily urinates frequently, possibly with blood. Many times increased urination is the only symptom.

As the inflammation worsens, your cat will develop the general symptoms of an infection: perhaps a rise in temperature, loss of appetite and depression. Quite often, however, cystitis is a local infection without any fever. Antibiotics may clear up the inflammation in short order, provided there are no other complications. Cystitis may recur; it is difficult to obtain a permanent cure. Bladder rupture can be caused by a kick, a passing blow from a car or a fall from a window. Falls are more common than you might think. This is very serious and if not treated immediately is usually fatal. The cat will react by losing its sense of equilibrium and collapsing. Surgical care is needed quickly. In most cases, the cat dies from shock.

Renal Dropsy (Hydronephrosis)

Hydronephrosis is a collection of urine in the pelvis of the kidney. This condition leads to an impairment of the organ, which in time leads to atrophy of the kidney structure. The basic cause is an obstruction to the flow of urine, whether congenital or acquired. One kidney or both may be affected.

The chief symptoms are difficult to distinguish from other ailments: vomiting, pain upon touch, enlargement of the general area. Treatment must come from a vet as soon as you notice any irregularity. Surgical removal of the kidney may be indicated, provided the other kidney remains unaffected. This condition is very rare.

Uremia

Uremia is a condition caused by the accumulation in the blood of waste-products normally removed by the kidneys. The cat continues to urinate—in fact, generally more than normal. Many people falsely believe that with uremia the cat stops urinating.

Uremia usually causes a severe reaction: nausea, vomiting, dizziness and, in its final stages, convulsions and coma. The cat's breath may take on an acrid odour, somewhat like ammonia. The older animal in particular is subject to uremia. When the condition develops, your vet is the best judge of whether treatment is possible.

Urolithiasis (Also called Feline Urolithiasis)
Every cat-owner should read this section through:

A condition that is seen very commonly in cats is called urolithiasis. Although not well known to the layman, the ailment has been known to vets for a long time. Since it is serious—and if neglected can prove fatal, the owner should be alerted to spot its symptoms and to act quickly.

None of this is intended to make you panic if your cat is suddenly ill. Not at all. Simply be alert if you note symptoms of straining at urination, which looks like constipation with much effort, blood in the urine, pain in the kidney-bladder area (general sensitivity), loss of appetite or else eating and vomiting, and a lack of interest in personal care or grooming itself. Usually, many of these symptoms are combined. Isolated vomiting or straining is not a reason for concern. But if you notice a combination of these signs, then your cat may be suffering from urolithiasis.

First, What Is It?

Uro-lith-iasis: the condition of small stones, sand or calculi forming in the urinary system of the animal. The sandy material is caused by an increased concentration of crystalline salts in the urine. The reason why this occurs in some cats and not in others is still unknown. Certain cats, however, seem predisposed to the condition, and it often recurs. That is, there is apparently no permanent cure, as, say, there is a cure for other organic conditions.

Three serious conditions or ailments may result:

1. **Cystitis**, an inflammation in the cat's bladder, which may be caused by bacterial or viral infection, or by sand (or calculi).
2. **Urethral calculi**, in which sand, a mucous plug or stones lodge in the cat's urethra (the tube that extends from the bladder to the tip of the penis, or in the female to the urethral opening).
3. **Renal calculi**, in which sand or stones form in the cat's kidney, causing nephritis (or inflammation of the kidneys). This is very rare.

Cystitis—a bladder condition—seems the most common. There is no rule of thumb you can follow to determine whether your cat will be susceptible. For example, neutered cats do not seem to suffer from the condition any more than unneutered cats, although young adults do seem more prone to the condition than do kittens or much older cats. It is relatively rare in cats under one and over four years of age, even though it may occur in a cat of any age. Young males seem more disposed, at one to three years old, but these are statistical averages only and certainly not definitive. We see more cases in the winter and early spring.

Symptoms

For *any condition* deriving from urolithiasis, you should be on the alert for:

1. Difficulty or pain in urination; straining as though constipated.
2. Frequent expulsion of small amounts, in many cases just driblets, of urine, often bloody, in sinks and bathtubs, on kitchen floors and in other strange places, as if the cat has forgotten normal housetraining.
3. Loss of vitality and loss of interest in grooming, playing or eating. The cat may suddenly seem lazy.

These symptoms become apparent for both females and males, but in addition to these the male has something more serious to contend with. Because his urethral opening (that tube extending from bladder to penis) is much narrower than the female's, he may suffer from partial or total blockage of the urinary tract. Mineral crystals (sand or calculi) simply block the passageway, and the male cat cannot urinate (this condition is somewhat rare in the female).

He will constantly lick his penis in an attempt to clear the obstruction, and he will use the litter box fifteen or more times a day. You may see him walking up and down the house after each try. Finally, he may just sit in the litter box and not move, or hang his head over the water-bowl. You may think he is constipated, which is misleading—always suspect urolithiasis.

Causes
Most vets now believe that certain factors aggravate feline urolithiasis, while other factors help to control it. Bacteria, viruses, stress, the kind of food your cat eats, vitamins and heredity all play an important role in causing and aggravating the condition. Airborne viruses, for example, have been known to carry the ailment to healthy cats, and high bacterial counts have appeared in infected cats. High-ash diets and dry cat-foods seem, also, to contribute to the condition. On the other hand, antibiotics have done a good job in controlling urolithiasis when bacterial infection was one of the factors causing it; and lots of water, low-ash diets (2·5 or 3·0 in commercial cat-food) and vitamin C or other acidifiers have helped to diminish the ailment.

The exact causes of urolithiasis are complex and as yet unknown. Until we have more information, many of the causes we think are responsible (vitamin-C deficiency, high alkaline content in the urine, high-ash and dry-food diets, bacterial and viral infections, stress and heredity) should be viewed as predisposing factors. That is, they make the cat much more susceptible and open to the condition. And several of them may even be responsible, because they show up whenever the cat is sick (bacterial or viral infection, urine with high alkaline content).

Dangers of the Condition
In the male, if total urethral obstruction is not treated immediately (within twenty-four to forty-eight hours at the latest), it will lead, first, to loss of appetite, if not a downright aversion to food; then to dehydration, weakness, depression, vomiting, coma and finally death. Since the poisonous products in the blood cannot be eliminated in the urine, uremia results; and at a certain point, bladder or kidney damage cannot be reversed. The condition is so serious that cats suffering from urethral obstruction get first priority in treatment, and when well enough they should have surgery if the condition has occurred before and the vet recommends it.

What to Do
The first order of business is to get in touch with your vet. This is not a problem for the layman to try to solve. If, however, your cat is obstructed and you cannot get to a vet or to a hospital within forty-eight hours, take the following emergency action:

1. Manipulate the penis to try to get the obstructing material from the urethra. Begin from the body and work your way down to the tip, rolling the penis gently but firmly between your fingers.

2. An alternative method is to apply a cotton pad that has been soaked in warm water; apply directly to the penile area and repeat three or four times.

3. You can tell if you are successful, with either method, if you see a white- or blood-tinged substance coming out from the tip. If you have got everything out, urine will begin to flow, and this will give temporary relief.

4. If you have got everything out, or think you have, and your cat still cannot urinate, gently compress the abdomen on either side, in the flank area. The swollen bladder feels like a small orange.

REMEMBER: *Compress gently so as not to rupture the bladder.*

Once you have relieved the obstruction, do not consider the condition as having disappeared. See your vet as soon as possible. The methods listed above are only for emergency purposes.

Recovery Time
Once your vet has diagnosed and treated the ailment, I suggest that you do the following:

1. Give your cat plenty of fresh water.

2. Feed it a low-ash diet. Check the label on commercial cat-food, if you use it, and do not buy any that contains more than 3·0 in ash, 3·5 at the most if you cannot find the other.

3. Do not feed ground-up bones, sardines or milk, and dilute all food with a little water and then add a small amount of Vitamin C powder.

4. Keep dry cat-food to a minimum, especially if you have a male cat and he tends to have blockage. There is no solid evidence that dry cat-food leads to urolithiasis, but it may aggravate the condition.

All these precautions will help your cat in everyday life. But the condition often recurs, and no cat that has had urolithiasis is safe from bladder inflammation or a blocked urinary tract. If you have a female, urolithiasis or the presence of sand is troublesome for you and potentially dangerous for your cat, but it will not immediately threaten her life unless she is blocked. The male, however, is more likely to suffer total obstruction, and therefore his situation can lead to serious complications and even to death. If your cat suffers from recurrent attacks and is unable to urinate, consult your vet about surgery, which may help in many cases.

SPECIAL CATEGORIES

Abscesses
Abscesses are swellings caused by a collection of pus and are quite common. They may appear nearly anywhere. They may result from several things: insect-bites, dog- and cat-bites, vaccinations or improperly draining wounds. A cat with an abscess usually runs a fever, and you can be sure that

the general area will be sensitive. It will pull away whenever you attempt to see or examine it. The cat may also be irritable. If anyone happens to touch it on or near an abscess, it may scratch or bite.

Abscesses must be drained, and only a vet can do it correctly. You may squeeze the sore spot yourself, but if you extract only part of the accumulated pus, the abscess will recur.

Cysts

Cysts are not to be confused with tumours, even though the cyst takes the shape of a growth. The cyst is a capsule, or saclike body, that is filled with fluid. It occurs in the tissues and forms lumps that appear right under the cat's skin. Cysts may form in several organs as well, particularly in the ovaries and sometimes the kidneys. There they settle into the tissue of these organs; when in the ovaries, they sometimes cause partial or complete sterility.

Cysts do not necessarily upset your cat's health, although if they form in the ovaries they will upset the female's powers of reproduction. Some outward signs may be frequent heat periods or heat of long duration, or no heat at all for a year or more, and sometimes frequent urination. When large enough, cysts may interfere with your cat's normal functions, especially if they are sublingual (under the cat's tongue). Your vet will decide whether they must be surgically removed.

Diabetes

A cat may suffer from diabetes, properly called diabetes mellitus. (A second type, called diabetes insipidus, is unknown in cats.)

Diabetes mellitus is a chronic disease of the metabolic system associated with insufficient insulin. This results in too much sugar in the blood and urine, progressive loss of weight, extreme hunger and thirst, and exhaustion. Eventually the cat will begin to lose weight, becoming gaunt and unhealthy-looking. There are several causes of diabetes mellitus, most of which involve damage to the pancreatic islet cells, usually from another disease. Diabetes is ordinarily much more common in middle-aged and fat cats and nearly always more common in males than in females.

Your vet can keep your cat alive by checking its urine and blood regularly, giving injections of insulin and instructing you how to do this. In most cases, a cat can resume a normal life with proper medication. Diabetes mellitus has been diagnosed frequently in cats.

Frothing

Frothing in itself is not an ailment. Motion-sickness may bring it on, even on a short car-ride. Occasionally frothing accompanies an ailment, or it may simply be a particular cat's way of reacting to fright. Sometimes frothing will occur during a fit. If this is the case, let the cat alone until the fit is over, and then call your vet. The fit is probably signalling a serious disorder that needs immediate treatment.

Tumours

Tumours or growths may appear on nearly any part of your cat, but particularly on the breasts of females. A tumour is, by definition, an uncontrolled growth of tissue.

If the tumour or growth does not interfere with the workings of any vital organ and is not spreading, it may be non-malignant, or benign. Very often you can feel these growths or tumours right under the surface of the cat's skin. They have the consistency of small, pliant doughy balls that under pressure shift in your fingers. Whenever you feel one, call it to the attention of your vet even though it may prove to be unimportant. Any lump is potentially serious, and if it grows, however slowly, then it should surely not be neglected.

The older cat in particular will suffer from growths, whether non-malignant (benign) or otherwise. If your cat is over seven or eight, you may find some growths under the surface of the skin without any further symptoms. They should nevertheless be checked. All old cats are subject to warts, for example, another kind of growth that is usually not dangerous. They should be removed where possible. Warts are ordinarily non-malignant growths, usually rough to the touch. Sometimes your cat will scratch the wart until it becomes raw and bleeds, and surgery becomes necessary.

When a growth or tumour spreads, it is said to be malignant or cancerous. Not all such tumours are of equal seriousness, and some cats who had them removed have gone on to live long lives. Malignant tumours can take several forms, depending on what kind of tissue is involved. Sarcomas, for example, are made up of embryonic connective tissue from the mesoderm, while carcinomas are malignant growths of epithelial-cell origin. Cancer is a term applied to all malignant growths.

All females are subject to breast tumours, and therefore as soon as you see any signs of a swelling, call your vet. I certainly recommend regular examinations of your cat after it passes (say) seven, and not only as a way of checking for tumours. You never know what illness might be detected that could be corrected in its early stages. If your cat appears to be losing weight and its coat seems dry-looking, these may be other symptoms of a tumour. X-rays of the lungs will ordinarily show if a tumour is invading other organs. Bone tumours are rare in cats.

Vomiting

Most owners worry when their pets vomit. It is, surely, one of the most disturbing of sights and leads the average owner to fear the worst.

Many things may cause vomiting, among them stomach or intestinal ailments of various kinds. Some occasional vomiting, however, is usually nothing to worry about. The cat has the power to vomit whenever it wishes, and many times it simply wants to regurgitate something that is unpleasant. If your cat is unusually nervous or highly-strung, it may demonstrate its nervousness by vomiting whenever something bothers it.

This type of vomiting is not serious. If your cat seems fine and settled after it has vomited, you know that the cause is isolated and temporary. You might skip its next meal, if it is to come soon, and cut down on water for a few hours. If, however, the vomiting persists or falls into certain clear patterns (regularly after eating or drinking), your cat is probably ill.

Persistent vomiting, with or without blood, is a symptom of nearly every cat disease, from kidney trouble to inflammation of the intestine. Vomiting may accompany worms, obstructions in the digestive tract, poisons or toxins in the system, and nearly every kind of liver, stomach and digestive ailment. If the vomiting is caused by poisons, follow the first-aid procedures outlined in Chapter 4. Usually, when vomiting indicates a condition that requires immediate attention, it is associated with a fever or with some inconsistency in the cat's bowel movements (possibly diarrhoea). Also, your cat may appear depressed or unusually subdued. All these signs add up to the fact that it needs treatment by a vet.

Acupuncture

Acupuncture, the system of treating the energy flow and balance in an ill person, has now become part of the practice of veterinary medicine. Considerable research has gone into the attempt to discover the chemical, biophysical and neurophysiological mechanisms that will explain acupuncture therapy. The aim of all such research is to see how effective acupuncture treatment can be in veterinary medicine as well as to collect data on treatment procedures. So far, it has become clear that many ailments of all kinds—from arthritis to skin diseases to diarrhoea—have been aided by acupuncture, even after other more traditional forms of therapy have failed. Some vets practise acupuncture.

THE SICKROOM

Like a sick person, a sick cat needs quiet and rest. Like a person, a cat usually knows the limits of its energy, and it will separate itself from all the activities it sees around it. Most cats will remain inactive until recovered, although some may attempt to overtax themselves. You should make every effort to confine a sick cat to the room it is most used to, difficult as this may be.

Very often your cat will be sent home from the hospital with a definite routine to follow. You will be under instructions from the vet that should be carried out with a minimum of interference. If you can confine your cat, so much the better for you and it. Children should be discouraged from any rough handling.

If an isolated room is not possible, then a quiet, draught-free corner is fine. Make sure that plenty of air is circulating and the area is clean. Also, remove all rugs and valuable furniture. Keep in mind that the convalescing cat may not have full control over its elimination. Newspapers are the best covering for the floor, and old sheets or blankets for the furniture you leave. A large box is very helpful.

If the area is excessively light, make sure that curtains cover the windows. Some illnesses—upper-respiratory infections and conjunctivitis, for example—make your cat's eyes sensitive to light. On the other hand, the room or corner should not be completely dark and depressing.

The room temperature should be about 70°F. Do not overheat the room or the cat may catch cold when it leaves the area. The room should not be cool either, or your cat might contract an upper-respiratory infection in its weakened condition. Draughts should be avoided at all costs. If the room must be aired to eliminate a musty or bad odour, take the cat into another room of the same temperature. Then bring the original room back to 70°F before returning the cat.

These and other precautions may seem bothersome, but they are certainly worth the trouble. The more careful you are and the more closely you follow your vet's advice, the sooner your cat will return to health.

If the illness has been severe or if the operation has required a long convalescence, then the cat's room or area should be organized something like a hospital room. If, however, the period of home treatment is to be only a few days, you might not wish to shift your house around.

The primary consideration is the cat. Does it need absolute quiet? Can you give it the attention it requires? If you are already burdened with children, can you take on a patient? Do you have space? If the burden is too great, then you should leave the cat in the pet-hospital until it fully recovers. Home nursing can be time-consuming, especially when cats reject medication and special diets. Some cats will miss their owners if you leave them in the hospital; others will not mind at all. This is still another judgment you will have to make when you decide whether or not to try home treatment.

In my chapter on first aid, I indicate what a cat's typical medicine-cabinet should contain. I refer you to Chapter 4 for this information.

A WARNING: Do not haphazardly administer any medicine that you happen to have around and think might be useful. Every medicine that you keep in your cat's medicine-cabinet or first-aid kit must be specifically for cats if it is to be taken internally. Do not keep a general 'pet' medicine cabinet, since each pet has different needs. Aspirin may be helpful for one, dangerous for another. Certain medications, such as Kaopectate, which is safe for infants, and milk of magnesia, a mild laxative, are ordinarily safe for all. But medicines and tonics that you might take yourself are not to be given thoughtlessly to your cat. Some tonics, for example, contain small amounts of strychnine, which a person might absorb with no ill effects but which could be very harmful to a cat.

Furthermore, do not use old medicines and pills that you have felt reluctant to throw out. You may well make your cat worse by administering them as a possible cure. If, in fact, you do give anything to your cat, make sure you scale it down sharply. You weigh perhaps ten to fifteen times more than a cat, and a normal dose for you would be lethal to your pet.

Above all, follow precisely the directions that the vet gives you. If you are told that your cat should receive medication at certain hours, you cannot skip one time and give a double dose at another. The dosage is set so that a uniform amount of medication is maintained in the cat's bloodstream at all times. If you forget its medicine at the proper time, the required amount decreases, and the cat receives less benefit from the medication for several hours. For the sake of your cat's health, you must be precise and prompt, and you must want to do everything possible to help it.

If you have any doubts about your ability to handle your cat during convalescence or during the necessary period of treatment, you should leave it in the hospital.

Procedures

There are several checks you can make on your cat to see if it is recovering. If you telephone your vet, he will want to know certain things. It is a good idea to keep a rough chart—something, perhaps, that approximates the chart of the doctor and nurse in a hospital. You can make it a simple affair, or you may wish to make it more detailed.

Some of the items you should note daily are the cat's temperature (taken rectally—leave thermometer in for two minutes) in the morning and evening, its breathing (rapid or slow?), its bowel movements (how many, loose, hard, bloody?), appetite (good, poor, fussy?), urination (frequent, infrequent, colour, smell?), eyes (sensitive to light, discharge, inflamed?), muscular control (weak, able to move?), general condition (alert, interested, depressed?), nose (any discharge, bloody?), any vomiting? These are the most common signs in a cat that is now or that has recently been ill. There may be still other things that you notice. Write them down and mention them to your vet. He may not think of everything to ask, and if you can tell him of other symptoms you have observed, by all means do so.

Taking the Temperature

You take a cat's temperature the same way you would take a child's. Use a regular rectal thermometer. Shake it so that the mercury is below the cat's normal temperature. Figure on normal in the range from 101°F to 102°F. There is no fixed figure for normality, since excitement, a good deal of activity and a high outside temperature can raise a cat's temperature, just as it does a person's. Certainly anything over 102°F should be considered a fever, or make you suspect that a fever is developing. Listlessness and a hot body should warn you. Dip the thermometer in petroleum-jelly so that the tip is covered. Insert it gently in the cat's rectum and make sure the cat does not sit on the thermometer or move violently. You may need a second person to help. Leave it in for two minutes. Wash it in cool—never hot—water after you have registered the figure.

Giving an Enema

It is not easy to give an enema to a cat. You may have trouble, and if you expect it, your job may be a little easier to handle.

Before you give your cat an enema, you should have a go-ahead from the vet. Many sick cats may need only a mild laxative, and that might be the first step. If that fails, you may have to follow with a suppository or an enema. Also, not all sick cats need an enema. You should check on your cat's bowel movement to make sure that it has not had an elimination. Then after consultation (a phone call) with your vet, go ahead with the enema if necessary.

Although cats are small, they are elusive, and you will probably need a second person to help restrain your pet. The cat may be too weak to resist, but this is something you have to determine. The cat that is unable to stand will probably give in quietly.

It is best to use a Fleet enema, which is prepared and disposable. It is complete with everything you need and obtainable at nearly all chemists'. The nozzle, incidentally, is already lubricated. You may add more petroleumjelly or mineral-oil if you wish. Place your cat in the bathtub. Since the enema usually works fast, the best place is the tub, which you can wash out. If you have a large,portable rubber tub, such as those used for infants, you may prefer that. The bathtub is best, however, because there is space for the cat and it will not foul its coat.

Insert the nozzle carefully and gently in the cat's rectum—this may not be easy to do. Administer half the contents of the bag. Try to reassure the cat with soft words and gestures; this is a trying experience. When the bag is half empty, remove the nozzle rapidly from its rectum, which should be elevated at a 90° angle. If its legs will hold it after the enema, make it stand up so that the bowel movement does not soil its coat.

If the cat's coat has been soiled, do not give it a bath. Soak a washcloth in warm water, wring it partially dry and wipe off the coat until it is clean. Dry with a towel. If the skin becomes wet, make sure it is thoroughly dried. Before taking the cat from the bathroom, check to see that there are no draughts or windows open near its sleeping-area.

Feeding a Sick Cat

A sick or injured cat presents a problem in feeding. Cats can be very choosy eaters, and unusual circumstances can make them turn away from food completely. The shock that accompanies many sicknesses and diseases, the lack of exercise, the general psychological depression that goes with inactivity and loss of muscular control, the weakness that follows upon an operation or a serious ailment—all these will destroy the healthiest of appetites.

Somehow you must deal with this. Since the recovery of your cat depends on its eating nutritious food, it must, if necessary, be force-fed. Usually such a drastic step is not necessary. You can encourage it to eat by simply varying its diet and giving it more tempting foods than usual. Try chicken, chicken liver, steak, boiled fish or canned sardines.

On many occasions, your vet will recommend a diet. For the cat with a kidney ailment, there is a special prescription diet, but cats do not like it, and you may have trouble there. For special reasons, the diet may be a liquid one, or it may be high in protein or in carbohydrates. Whatever it is, you should not add to or subtract from it.

If the diet is a liquid one, you may want to feed your cat teaspoonful by teaspoonful, for it may not want to eat if it is very ill. In that case, the liquid, whether beef broth, milk (if digestible) or soup, must be forced in gently but firmly. *If restraint is necessary*, one person should hold the cat with a large towel around its neck and under its chin, the legs firmly grasped. The other person opens the cat's mouth and compresses the lips. Then the food is administered bit by bit.

The very weak cat might even have to be bottle-fed. On other occasions it is better to use the lip-pouch method (see below for detailed instructions), the same way in which you usually give it liquid medicine.

With a soft or solid diet, small amounts of food placed on the back of the tongue will often force it to swallow. Stroke your cat's throat if it has difficulty in getting the food down or tries to spit it out. You might even put food on your finger and let your cat lick it off. This sometimes does the trick, although the food so lovingly given might be regurgitated the next moment.

If you feel that this is a trying time for you, remember that it is also a difficult period for your cat. If you have to feed it by force, you can be certain that it is unhappy at the situation. Try to treat it calmly and gently. If you appear unsettled and irritable, that will only make the cat fight back even more. Tension and anxiety are ordinarily contagious. Do not jam the food into its mouth, do not scream, do not push and rush it.

If you are under no special orders from the vet about feeding, there are several ways you can make your cat's food more attractive. At least you can try. Mix whatever you happen to be feeding in beef bouillon or in chicken broth. If you want to feed chopped meat, shape it into small balls and try feeding from your hand. Soak any solids in beef broth or milk (if digestible). Keep all foods at room temperature. Under the best of conditions, cats dislike cold food.

For the cat who has trouble keeping its food down, a beef bouillon diet is nourishing and usually easy to digest. Do not try to give large quantities at any one time if your cat has trouble in holding its food. Feed it often—four or five or more times during the waking day. If vomiting continues, of course consult your vet; some food must be consumed and digested. Usually, however, the vomiting lasts for a short time, and then the cat can gradually be out back on solids: mushy cereals, baby-food, chopped meat, boiled chicken, canned sardines, even regular cat-food if it can be blended with table food.

During the convalescence, give your cat a vitamin-mineral supplement. If it does not mind having it mixed with its food, give it that way. If it objects—by refusing to eat or by bringing it up, give the supplement as you would medicine, by the lip-pouch method (see below for details of the procedure).

Some ailing cats suffer from diarrhoea, and their diet should be planned to curb the diarrhoea while providing nourishment and strength. Such foods as boiled rice, cheese (especially cottage cheese, which is easy to digest) and boiled milk—if your cat can digest it—ordinarily serve this purpose. Your vet will probably recommend special treatment if the diarrhoea continues.

If your cat regurgitates its food and then shows interest in it, this is perfectly natural. You should not interfere. If the cat has vomited because its digestive system is upset, it will not go near the regurgitated food. But if it is interested in the food, then it should be allowed to eat it.

The most important thing for you to keep in mind is that a sick cat must eat, and it must do so with a minimum of anxiety and nervousness. Your job is to see that this comes about.

Administering Liquid Medicine
The best way to give a liquid medicine is to have your cat run up to you, open its mouth wide and let you pour it down toward the back part of its tongue. Unfortunately, no cat will do that, and most cats will, in fact, foam it right back if you attempt force. Liquid medicine is not easy to administer.

The second-best way is to mix the medicine with the cat's food or mix it with other liquids that it generally likes. If the medicine is not particularly foul, this method might work. The chances are good, however, that it will not. Cats are highly suspicious, particularly when their noses tell them that something foreign is in their food. If you have extra of both food and medicine, you might try the method on the chance that it will work. Do not be too optimistic.

The third method is the 'force' method. Incidentally, whatever you do with liquids, *make sure you do not force them down your cat's throat*. They may get into its windpipe and cause considerable trouble. Liquid in the lungs can cause pneumonia, or at best a serious congestion. The best method is the lip-pouch way, which is safe and virtually infallible unless your cat manages to foam the liquid back at you.

Lip-Pouch Method
First, place the medicine in a spoon, or better still in a large eyedropper. Grab its lower lip (without hurting it) in front of the corner of its mouth and pull it out, without forcing. This forms a pouch or pocket. Pour the medicine slowly into the pouch, a very little at a time, close the pouch, and let the cat swallow. Lift its muzzle up if it hesitates about swallowing, and then it has little choice. The liquid will go through its clenched teeth down its throat. Repeat until all the medicine has been swallowed.

Sometimes a cat will see it is useless to resist after it receives the first dose—but do not count on that. On the other hand, some cats will see the medicine coming and fight to avoid it, or foam it back. Often you will need a second person on hand to hold the cat's head and paws while you form the pouch and pour in the medicine. Do not wrench the cat around or wrestle with it, and yet do not be timid. Gentle forcefulness is best.

Some measurement equivalents are as follows: a teaspoon of liquid is about $^1/_6$ ounce; a tablespoon is about ½ ounce or 5 cc; a dram is about the same as a teaspoon; an ounce is 30 cc, and a cup is 8 ounces.

Giving Pills and Tablets
When the time comes to give a pill to your cat, you might try to sneak it in. Put the pill in the cat's food and hope that it gets gulped down. Some cats will take it, but most will not. Those who will not, usually smell the medicine—it may be odourless to you but not to your cat.

The next step is to 'force' the cat, once again taking care not to hurt or upset it. If you seem frantic, the cat will react frantically. Try not to let on that it is giving you trouble.

Once you have its confidence, grasp the muzzle and squeeze the lips against the teeth, your thumb on one side and your fingers on the other. As you apply pressure just forward of the corners of its mouth, the cat will open its mouth. It has little choice, since resistance begins to hurt. Push its lips between its teeth so that if your cat decides to play rough and bite, it will bite its own cheeks. You now have the mouth open, and you will have one hand free.

Tilt the head backward and upward. That will open the lower jaw and provide you with an excellent target. Make sure the teeth are covered by the lips, and with your free hand place the pill, capsule or tablet well back in the mouth, toward the base of the tongue. Do not toss the pill in, or you may flick it into the windpipe and choke the cat. After the pill is settled on the back part of the tongue, close the mouth firmly. When the mouth is closed, hold it tight to prevent the cat's spitting out the pill. Then rub, stroke or massage its throat. Lift up the muzzle at about the same time. The cat has little choice but to swallow. When it does, the pill goes down.

If you feel you cannot handle this alone, then have a second person nearby to administer the pill while you do the holding, or *vice versa*.

Keeping the Sick Cat Clean

Cats are so fastidious about grooming themselves that even the sick cat will keep itself clean. However, it may be so sick and weak that it cannot do so adequately. Your job here depends on what your cat can and cannot do.

If your cat can get up and walk, it probably will use the litter box. If it finds moving difficult, then you may have a clean-up.

First, make sure that it rests on a washable material—rubber sheeting or washable sheets and blankets. These may have to be changed often, particularly if your cat has diarrhoea or urinates frequently, or even vomits in its sleeping-area. You can, of course, put a nappy or two (for double thickness) on the cat; this sounds ridiculous, but it does save a lot of cleaning-up for the cat that is almost helpless. Make sure the nappy is fastened securely, and that no open pins are around. Change the nappy as soon as it is soiled or the cat, like an infant, will get a nappy-rash to add to its problems.

The cat itself now has to be cleaned. If it soils itself or if it wears a nappy, there is still the problem of cleaning it. You cannot bathe a cat while it is undergoing treatment. Bathing is a dubious business even under the best of conditions, and you should not be doing it now. Wherever it is soiled, wash off with a mild soap and warm water. After you have dried all wet spots, comb out the hair.

If your cat has diarrhoea, its hindquarters will probably be matted and dirty. This area requires frequent washings to prevent discomfort or a rash. You might, under these circumstances, trim the hair. It will grow back in time.

The cat's nose and mouth should be kept clean of discharge, particularly if it has a respiratory ailment that keeps a mucous discharge on its face. With warm water, clear away any hard or caked matter around its eyes, ears or nose. If the eyes are inflamed, apply a mild eye ointment. If your cat has a condition that causes vomiting, keep its mouth area fresh and clean, and wash out its mouth and teeth with a cloth. It will feel better after this attention.

Keep the coat combed and brushed. The cat will enjoy it, and the coat itself will benefit.

A cat that is too weak to move around can, like a sick person, develop bed-sores. The only way to avoid them is to be sure that the cat turns over several times a day. This condition seems remote, but it is possible.

If your cat is very uncomfortable from the heat, sponge it off with a wet washcloth and dry it off with a towel. Never soak a sick animal, and watch out for draughts. You can cool off a healthy cat in the same way.

Bandages

For the application of dressings and bandages under emergency conditions, see Chapter 4.

If your cat has been bandaged, and the bandage works loose, you should get in touch with your vet. Dressings and bandages are a tricky business, and you may not replace them correctly. Unless there is no possibility of professional help, you should not attempt to re-bandage a cat.

Usually the vet has arranged the bandage so that it cannot be torn or pulled off. Occasionally the cat through sheer persistence will be able to break through the bandage and get at the wound. The danger then is not always from the cat's mouth but from bacterial infection in the general area. Sometimes the vet will provide an Elizabethan collar (see page 139), which prevents the cat's getting at the wound with its mouth.

You should have some bandage and tape around, but any re-wrapping that you do is temporary. If bleeding starts, this is an emergency situation, and you must act. See 'Treatment of Arterial Bleeding', beginning on page 126, for how to apply pressure directly on the wound. The chances of your having to do this except in accidents are slim.

By now you recognize that a sick cat is a large responsibility, especially if the cat is very weak. You must do everything for it, but if your feeling for your pet is strong, such help is in the nature of things. Your reward will be a cat that is once again strong and active.

FOUR

First Aid for the Kitten and Cat

First aid is emergency treatment for your cat until you can obtain professional help. It is only a stopgap measure; it is not the final step. The function of first aid is to save your cat's life, not to cure the condition. In almost all cases, your cat will need further treatment, sometimes lengthy and extensive.

What are some first-aid situations? They can be numerous: falls, burns, broken bones, heavy bleeding from an accident, multiple injuries from a car-accident, severe shock from electric cords, insect-bites and stings, drowning, animal-bites, eye injuries, poisoning.

The function of this chapter is to give you some information about your role until professional aid is available. Most of the information is simple, since you are not a medical expert and you probably do not have sufficient equipment at hand. I recommend that you keep some first-aid materials stocked, but most owners will have only a few of them available when an accident occurs. You must act quickly and confidently, and I hope that the information here will help you do just that. You must judge what requires immediate attention—severe bleeding, for example, comes before a broken bone. And you must learn not to give up—many cats have been saved after lengthy exertion.

1. All severe bleeding needs immediate care. Whenever you see heavy bleeding, try to stop it in any way you can. See 'Treatment of Arterial Bleeding', page 126, for directions.
2. Any bar to free breathing must be removed. Make sure the cat's nose and mouth are clear.
3. Let the cat lie where the accident occurred. Attempts at removal—unless absolutely necessary—may aggravate a serious condition.
4. An accident brings severe shock. Make sure your cat is warm—cover it with a blanket or whatever is handy (towels, newspapers, your jacket).

5. Any visible wound should be covered with a clean dressing. This is discussed later.

6. Do not give any water. Liquids can aggravate an internal condition or make the cat choke.

7. While you give emergency treatment, make sure that someone calls a vet or makes arrangements to take you and the cat to a vet.

RESTRAINT

An injured cat may have to be restrained. Its claws and teeth can do damage to anyone who tries to help. A cat in shock or in great pain simply does not know what it is doing. One of the best forms of restraint is for a person to hold the cat with a large towel around its neck, the legs grasped firmly; or else wrap the cat in the towel, immobilizing the legs. That takes care of the claws. You can then expose the area that needs treatment. If the cat is inclined to bite, then hold a towel lightly over the mouth.

CAR-ACCIDENTS

This will not be a problem for flat- or house-dwellers who keep their pets inside. Few cats roam freely, but for those who do, being struck by a car is always a potential danger. The chances of a cat's surviving such an accident are small. Sometimes a car strikes at an angle and throws the cat, causing only shock. But usually the situation leaves little hope for recovery.

If your cat is struck, you can expect the following kinds of injuries: internal bleeding, shock, bad cuts and lacerations, broken bones, concussion, brain haemorrhage, unconsciousness. In addition, there will be injuries that you should ignore for the moment: bruises, abrasions, dislocations and things of a relatively minor nature.

You must work quickly to help alleviate the major injuries. I will discuss some of them, and by following through you can see what to do, whether a car-accident is involved or whether the injury is caused in some other way.

BLEEDING

If your cat is bleeding seriously from a car- or other accident, do not move it unless you have no other choice. Apply restraint—use a towel or blanket. The cat is probably in shock, and the covering will also serve to keep it warm. Sometimes the bleeding is internal, and you can spot this by checking the cat's gums. They become white if there is internal bleeding, usually from a ruptured organ. Also, the eyes will become white.

Internal bleeding has other signs as well, but you might not notice them in the moments after an accident. The pulse may change sharply, becoming either feeble or very rapid. The skin of the legs becomes cold and clammy. The cat is feeble, almost dead, its temperature falling below normal; the extremities will be cold, its respiration rapid and shallow. There may also be gasping, shivering and shaking.

If you suspect internal bleeding—that is, if external signs are few but the cat seems listless and depressed, then you must act quickly. Try to find some kind of support for its body (a board or a blanket made into a hammock, for example), and get it to a vet. Although moving the cat may aggravate an internal condition, there must be fast treatment.

If there is no vet available, then keep the cat quiet—it will probably be in shock. Give it nothing to drink, and wait for professional care. There is really nothing you can do about internal injuries.

If the bleeding is external, you must move to stop it. Look for seeping or surging blood; leave all minor cuts and lacerations alone. There are three kinds of bleeding:

1. **Arterial:** Bleeding from an artery. This is bright-looking blood, very red and spurting in jets. If the cut artery is deep inside the wound, the wound will fill rapidly with blood, like a cup filling with water. This is very serious and must be controlled.
2. **Venous:** This is a seeping kind of bleeding, from a vein. The blood is dark red, and the flow is steady, not in spurts.
3. **Capillary:** Bleeding from a capillary. You will notice a steady oozing kind of bleeding from several spots on the surface of a wound. This type usually stops by itself and is the least serious.

Treatment of Arterial Bleeding

The most dangerous form of bleeding is arterial—bright-red blood spurting out. Since a cat's supply of blood is limited, this is your top priority item. One method is for you to place your finger directly on the cut artery, inside the wound, and apply pressure. If you have a clean handkerchief, put it over your finger, although infection from dirt is not the major concern now. The bleeding must be stopped; infection can be treated later.

A second method is to apply a pad with pressure and bandage over the wound.

Still another method is the application of a finger at a pressure-point. The trouble is that the pressure-points *are not easily located*—there are, in all, three of them. The first occurs just above the elbow joint. Pressure here will stop haemorrhaging from wounds below the elbow by controlling the brachial artery. A second point is found on the femoral artery as it passes over the thighbone, on the inside of the thigh. Pressure here prevents bleeding below the thighbone. The third point is on the carotid artery and jugular vein, which pass on each side of the neck above the shoulder. Pressure here can stop haemorrhaging in the extremities.

For serious limb or tail bleeding, a tourniquet is another method, but the tourniquet must be released every ten or fifteen minutes. While it will usually work well, a layman often mades it too tight or not tight enough.

I recommend use of pressure with a finger or a piece of gauze and bandage as the best methods to stop arterial bleeding. This bleeding is almost impossible to stop.

Treatment of Venous Bleeding
Apply a gauze pad and a tight bandage directly over the wound.

Treatment of Capillary Bleeding
Usually, capillary bleeding stops by itself. It is the least serious of the three types. If it continues, apply gauze and bandage over the wound, or a styptic pencil (if you have one), which contracts the blood vessels, or compress the wound with a pad and cold water. Ice applied directly also works. Once the bleeding is under control, keep your cat quiet and cover it—there may be shock accompanying the bleeding. Call a vet, since you cannot diagnose the extent of the injuries.

SHOCK

When there is some failure in the blood's circulation, the result is shock. Shock can be caused by many things: loss of blood (as in a severe accident), emotional upset (also from an accident), great pain, severe vomiting, exposure to extreme cold (for instance, if the cat falls into icy water), fear, starvation, damage to tissues or a blow to a vital organ (also from an accident or a fall). Car-accidents are the main cause of shock, although many cats attempt to defy gravity and suffer grievous falls.

A cat suffering from shock may look as if it is asleep or may appear semi-conscious. A good deal depends on the severity of the condition, but its breathing can be rapid and shallow, the gums and inside of the lips usually whitish. The body will be cold, the pulse feeble and rapid, the temperature low. Since shock makes the muscles relax, your cat may have no control over its bladder and bowels. Shock can be a cause of death, and it must be treated as an extremely serious condition. If help is not immediately available, first lower your cat's head below its body and try to raise its temperature with warmth: blankets, any kind of covering, a hot-water bottle if one is available. Keeping the cat quiet should not be difficult, since shock leads to a deadly-still condition.

If the cat's breathing is very weak and shallow or in some other way irregular, try to give a stimulant. If the cat cannot swallow, let it sniff spirits of ammonia if you have it in your first-aid cabinet. When there is a long time between breaths, you know that your cat is having difficulty breathing. Warm liquids are good treatment for shock. If the cat is too weak to lap the liquid, try the lip-pouch method (page 121). If the cat gags or retches, stop.

REMEMBER: If you suspect internal bleeding because of a severe accident (car, fall, massive blow), do not offer liquids of any kind. They are harmful if there are internal injuries.

FRACTURES

Any cat hit by a car will probably suffer from broken bones, what doctors call a fracture. A bone can be broken in many different types of accident: by a car, a severe blow like a kick, from a fall (rather common) or even from a bullet or blunt instrument.

Types of Fractures, or Broken Bones

Fractures can be of three types: simple, compound and comminuted. A simple fracture means that a bone is broken; compound, that a bone is broken and the skin and muscles punctured or torn by the bone. Bacteria can enter and cause infection. Comminuted means that there is a break in several places, what is called a multiple fracture. There can always be additional factors, such as an injury to an organ (brain, lung, kidney, liver) or to an important nerve, blood vessel or joint.

Signs

If your cat has had a severe accident—car, blow or fall, you can suspect a fracture and begin to look for one (or more). The cat will lose the use of the broken limb, and if it is not a limb but another part, the cat may still not be able to walk, or it will walk with an unnatural gait. You will also see swelling and inflammation in the area of the fracture, and if it is compound there will be bleeding where the bone has come through the skin. Although you may think that the cat is in great pain, often shock has set in and deadened the pain. Other signs may be a deformity at the point of fracture—the limb may hang strangely. A cat with a broken limb that does not receive adequate professional care may end up with a deformed limb. This happens when the muscles contract and cause the bone ends to override each other, leading to a shortened and deformed limb.

A fracture, which in itself might not be serious, can become a real problem if you are careless. Particularly in a car-accident or fall, a broken rib can pierce a lung. Or even a simple leg fracture, which is easily tended, can become compound or comminuted (break into several pieces). Most of your responsibility, as outlined below, is to immobilize the afflicted parts until you can obtain professional help. You should, of course, try to obtain such help as quickly as possible. In the meantime, cover the cat with blankets, newspapers, whatever is handy, to warm it up from the inevitable consequences of shock.

General First Aid for Fractures

These are always moments of panic, but you should keep a clear head. If you see a bone coming through the skin, or a strange set to the rib cage, you will wonder what to do first. First, seek help. Whatever else you do is temporary.

1. Seek professional help.
2. Do not move the cat unless it is clear that the spine is not affected.
3. Approach the cat warily—it may need to be restrained with a blanket or towel. It may be in great pain and try to attack anyone who comes close, including you.
4. If you do find that a fracture is present (the bone coming through the skin, inflammation, bleeding, limb immobilized), then handle the broken part as little as possible.

Only if a vet is *not* available should you try to do something yourself. First, keep the limb from moving with a splint, which is difficult to apply. You can improvise a splint from many different types of material: tree branches, pieces of wood, stiff leather, pipes, heavy cardboard, even pencils. As long as the object is firm and of sufficient length to keep the joints above and below the fractured bone from moving, it will work as a temporary measure. Once the splint is in place, treat the cat for shock—warmth, quiet, rest.

Here is how you work with a splint. You first wrap the limb in cotton or a bandage. If only newspaper is available, use that. Pad the splint with soft material so that pressure can be applied evenly; without padding, the bare splint will not fit snugly against the broken limb. Place the padded splint against the limb, making sure the splint ends extend above and below the fractured part. Bandage the splint and the limb together firmly but not tightly. Do not restrict blood circulation. Remember—this is not the cure for a broken limb but a way of keeping it still until help is available. A vet will apply traction and set the bones, or he may have to operate if the fracture cannot be reduced.

If bandages are not available, improvise as before—use tape, strips of cloth, handkerchiefs, socks, a tie, a belt. If the accident occurs on the road or away from home, you will have to be ingenious about finding suitable materials.

SPRAINS

If a joint is suddenly twisted or wrenched so that the ligament is stretched or torn, the result is a sprain. The most common signs are swelling and tenderness, plus sharp pain if anything touches the joint. You probably cannot tell a sprain from a fracture, but you should handle as you would a fracture anyway.

The treatment is the same as for a fracture. That is: *restraint* if the cat seems violent, treatment for shock and calling a vet. In a serious accident, a sprain may be the least of the problems and should be left alone while you attend to more important injuries. However, a fall may result in a sprain or sprains and little else.

DISLOCATIONS

A dislocation is caused by sudden violence, such as being struck by a car. It means that one or more of the bones that form a joint is knocked out of place. The most frequently dislocated bones are at the hip, knee, toe or jaw. A cat that attempts a leap and misses may suffer severe dislocations.

The chief signs are similar to those for a fracture and a sprain: loss of movement or use of the limb; deformity (the limb may stick out or bulge); very possibly inflammation around the joint; considerable pain if the afflicted limb or joint is touched. With a knee dislocation, a cat will hold its leg up in a flexed position and will not put its weight on the limb. With a hip dislocation, one leg will appear shorter than the other, so that it swings when the cat walks.

A dislocation can be helped only by a vet. If you diagnose the condition—and it may seem no different from a fracture or sprain, simply try to make your cat comfortable. Place it in a restful position so that the injured part is not further strained; then cover it and keep it quiet. Apply cold compresses—ice-cold water, a cold-water bag or ice cubes wrapped in a dishtowel or washcloth—to relieve pain. The cold helps relieve pain temporarily. If you attempt to remedy a dislocation, you can do real damage to the ligaments and muscles. X-ray is necessary here.

STRAINS AND RUPTURED MUSCLES

These are further forms of damage that you cannot diagnose because the symptoms are similar to those for several conditions. A stretched muscle or tendon is a strain. When the muscle is torn, it is ruptured. This condition will seem little different from a sprain, dislocation or even fracture. There will be lameness as well as tenderness, and the cat will hold its leg up so that no weight is placed on it. If the back muscles or tendons are injured, from a bad fall, the cat may become partially paralysed. With paralysis, there is no pain. The hind legs are generally involved.

DRESSINGS AND BANDAGES

Probably you will not have dressings or bandages around your house, unless you keep a first-aid cabinet for small children. Nevertheless, you should know something about them in the event that the need arises. Your use of dressings and bandages is for temporary relief.

A dressing, which can be either wet or dry, is a covering applied to a wound or an injury. A dry dressing usually consists of folded pads of gauze and is used to protect a wound, to apply pressure to stop bleeding (a first-aid device) and to prevent infection when medicated. The ideal dressing is sterilized, but in the absence of a sterile dressing you can improvise with a clean handkerchief or any other sanitary piece of cloth. The dressing should be held in place by a bandage.

The wet dressing (also called a compress) may be applied either hot or cold (room-temperature). If it is applied to an open wound, the wet (cold) dressing is usually first soaked in an antiseptic solution (such as witch hazel or half peroxide and half water). A cold dressing is applied to relieve pain and to control any internal bleeding. If you do not have a regular compress, a handkerchief or dishtowel folded several times to give thickness serves the same purpose. Make sure it does not drip after it is soaked in cold water. Hold it in place with a bandage. A hot compress is used to relieve or reduce swelling and inflammation. Follow the same procedure as above, only use very hot water instead. Wring the cloth dry.

One bandage used frequently is a roller bandage, usually 4 to 6 yards long and 1 to 3 inches wide. Bandages are used to keep dressings or splints in position—they should not themselves be the cover for the wound. They also exert pressure and help reduce or prevent swelling or bleeding. They help to support a bone that is strained or dislocated.

Roller bandages should be rolled tight and evenly, and when using them, allow only a few inches to unroll at a time. Bandage from below upward and from within outward, over the front of the injured limb. This way you can make sure the bandage will be an even spiral. As you roll the bandage over the limb or splint, apply each successive layer so that two-thirds of the preceding layer is covered. Roll firmly but not so tightly that circulation is impaired.

WOUNDS

Closed Wounds

Ordinarily, emergency first aid involves open wounds—deep cuts that bleed heavily, for example. But treatment of closed wounds is also called for, although not usually on an emergency basis. Closed wounds do not penetrate the entire thickness of the skin. A blunt object, for instance, can cause a contusion or bruise—this is a closed wound. Small blood-vessels are ruptured and the soft tissue beneath the skin is damaged. The most common signs are pain, swelling, heat and discolouration. If the skin in the area is somewhat loose, the swelling may be great; where the skin is taut, the swelling may be slighter but the pain much greater.

Treatment calls for a cold compress with a firm bandage on the afflicted part to limit the area of swelling. If the swelling is already there, the application of the cold compress will relieve pain. Do not bandage in this case.

Another kind of closed wound is the abrasion, or sore. Such wounds can be very painful, but they are ordinarily not emergency matters unless they cover a good part of the cat's body. Usually, they involve only the loss of some surface layers of skin. With a severe abrasion, the nerve endings in the skin may be exposed; this can be very painful. Such wounds often become filled with dirt, grime and matted hair and become open to infection.

If you choose to treat this condition, clip away the hair around the abrasion. Use a clean pair of scissors. Wash with mild soap and warm water until the wound is cleaned out. Then apply a mild antiseptic solution such as witch hazel or half peroxide and half water.

Open Wounds

In an open wound, the break in the skin or mucous membranes leads to a break in the soft tissues immediately beneath it. Open wounds can be divided into several kinds.

1. **Incised wounds:** From a sharp cutting-instrument such as a knife or a piece of glass, causing a clean-cut wound that bleeds freely.
2. **Lacerated wounds:** From kicks by people or farm animals, barbed

wire, bites, collisions with a car, causing a tearing wound. It is irregular in shape, with the edges of the skin ragged and uneven. The amount of bleeding depends on the vessels that are cut.

3. **Puncture wounds:** From sharp-pointed instruments such as nails, pins, thorns, hayforks, bullets, fishhooks and similar objects. Bleeding is ordinarily slight, and the wound might be overlooked. The danger is infection if the wound is neglected.

Treatment of an Open Wound

An open wound not only frightens you, it may panic your cat because of pain and shock. Before you examine the wound and attempt first aid, use restraint as described on page 125.

Sometimes the object that has caused the wound is still there and can be removed. If it can be done easily, do remove it, particularly if it is something that might cause further damage. As soon as you have removed the object, follow directions described under 'Bleeding', pages 125–6. Any severe bleeding must be stopped while you are waiting for professional care.

Once the bleeding has been stopped, or staunched, you must try to prevent infection. This is true of open or closed wounds, for either type has been caused by objects that are themselves full of bacteria. If you can, cover the wound with a sterile gauze pad soaked in antiseptic, and bandage it to keep it on. If no gauze pad is available, use a handkerchief or a piece of dishcloth.

For open wounds, as for all first-aid treatment, remain calm and think first of what you can do to help your cat. The initial help right after an accident may be the crucial time between life and death. Remember that first aid, important as it is, must be only the first step toward treatment. Any accident that causes a minor injury may have also caused a major one; while you believe that your cat is recovering, you may have overlooked something important. You must call in a vet to make a full diagnosis and to prescribe treatment unless the condition is very slight.

HOME ACCIDENTS

Poisoning

You must be careful, or else your cat may poison itself with one of the many germicides, insecticides, detergents, corrosives or medicines on the market. If left around they become available to one of the most curious animals alive, the kitten or cat; if swallowed, they can lead to serious poisoning or death. Since cats are small and have a delicately balanced system, it does not take much of a dose to poison them. Also, remember that cats can get into nearly anything that is left exposed, since heights do not deter them as they would a dog or an infant.

A cat is poisoned almost always by accident. There are several ways it can happen. Your cat may eat garbage that has become poisonous refuse, or chew plants that contain poisonous elements or have been sprayed, or eat poisoned food intended for insects and rodents. What are the symptoms of poisoning? Many of them are similar to the symptoms of other ailments: trembling, even convulsions, a drooling mouth, abdominal pain, cringing, rapid, shallow breathing, vomiting, depression, eventually coma. The poisoned cat may vanish, to suffer out its misery alone.

The severity of the reaction depends on the amount of poison consumed. With some poisons, the symptoms become acute almost immediately; with others, weeks may pass before you realize that your cat is poisoned. It may be ingesting small amounts of poison and gradually poisoning its system, so that the symptoms you can recognize take a long time to develop. Small amounts of lead from paint can do this. *And do not forget house and garden plants.* Cats like to eat plants, and many can prove poisonous to the cat's system—for example, philodendron, lily of the valley, oleander, foxglove, daffodil, monkshood and ivy.

Whenever you recognize the problem, you must act quickly:

1. Give an emetic (to make the cat vomit): hydrogen peroxide. Mix equal parts of hydrogen peroxide and water. Administer 1½ tablespoons. Vomiting should occur in a few minutes. This is the best emetic.
2. Take your cat to a vet right away.

There is little else you can do. A cat will fight any other attempts at treatment. It is very difficult to make a cat vomit.

Identifying the Poison

Identification is, of course, difficult, unless you know for certain that your cat has been chewing house or garden plants. I will describe the most common poisons—to help you, mainly, with prevention.

1. **Plants.** Many plants are in part or whole poisonous to cats. The leaves of philodendron, for example, are poisonous, while only the bulbs of daffodils are poisonous. The symptoms are those listed above.
Treatment: Emetic, immediate care by a vet.
2. **Lead** is an ingredient of paint, and the cat is poisoned from licking wet paint or drinking out of old paint-tins. Also, your cat can become poisoned if it absorbs the lead arsenate in sprays used to kill insects and vermin. Kittens are especially prone to this. There are two kinds of lead poisoning:
Acute: The symptoms are trembling, laboured breathing, cramps, bloody diarrhoea, muscular weakness, convulsions and coma. The acute form occurs when the cat consumes large amounts of lead compound at one time.
Treatment: An emetic followed by immediate care by a vet.
Chronic: A chronic condition results when small amounts of lead are consumed over a long period of time. The chief symptom is a bluish discolouration at the margin of the gums. This is rare with cats—the acute form is much more common.
Treatment: Immediate care by a vet.
3. **Arsenic** is found in rat- and insect-poisons. The symptoms of arsenic

poisoning include loss of appetite, intense thirst, pain in the abdomen, vomiting, bloody diarrhoea, depression, rapid breathing and complete collapse.

Treatment: Immediate care by a vet.

4. **Insulin** poisoning occurs in cats receiving home treatment for diabetes. An overdose of insulin can send the cat into unconsciousness. Diabetes mellitus is more common in the middle-aged or older cat, but it can strike a cat of any age.

Treatment: Immediate care by a vet.

5. **Warfarin** and **Antu** are rat-poisons, and they can work on your cat in much the same way they affect rats. Symptoms of Warfarin are bleeding from the nose, bloody diarrhoea and vomit and hair-loss after a few days.

Warfarin Treatment: Immediate care by a vet.

Symptoms of Antu poisoning are vomiting, difficulty in breathing, diarrhoea, progressive listlessness and collapse.

Antu Treatment: Immediate care by a vet.

6. **Phosphorus** is found in rat- and roach-poisons. Poisoning usually develops slowly, sometimes taking several days. The symptoms are extreme irritability and restlessness, violent stomach pains, vomiting of greenish-brown material, a garlic-like odour in the breath, bloody diarrhoea, swelling of the tongue, yellow skin (jaundice) and extreme lethargy and depression. The vomit will glow in the dark, the result of the phosphorus.

Treatment: Immediate care by a vet.

7. **Alkalis** (corrosives) are found in cleaning preparations and drain-cleaners. The symptoms resemble those found in other cases of poisoning, *plus* the fact that the cat's mouth and throat are burned.

Treatment: Immediate care by a vet. You will not be able to get the cat to swallow an emetic.

8. **Medicines** and **Tonics** (intended for people) bring on symptoms described above for other poisons. Sleeping-pills and sedatives will put the cat to sleep; you may at first see it staggering around.

Treatment: Immediate care by a vet.

9. **DDT** is contained in flea-powders and insecticides. Some of these are now off the market, but many homes still contain such preparations. The symptoms are similar to those listed above for other poisons. There may also be muscular twitching.

Treatment: An emetic followed by immediate care by a vet.

10. **Strychnine** is contained in some rodent-poisons, in poisoned bait, in poisoned rabbits and rats and in some medicines that people thoughtlessly give to cats. Small amounts of strychnine that are harmless to people can be deadly for a cat. The symptoms of even a tiny dose are: increased respiration, frequent yawning, nausea and vomiting, spasmodic twitching of muscles, convulsions; the corners of the mouth will be drawn back, or the jaw locked; the eyes—with dilated pupils—will protrude, head and tail will be drawn upward in pain, and your cat may wear a vicious look. If convulsions occur, death is near. Any sharp sound

will make the cat go into convulsions—this is one way a vet can diagnose strychnine poisoning.

Treatment: Immediate care by a vet.

With all cases of poisoning, rapid treatment is your byword. Give the emetic if your cat will swallow, but most important of all is to get it to a vet. All first-aid situations involve a rush of events, but poisoning, like severe bleeding, needs a cool head on your part and fast treatment. It is not common, however.

Burns and Scalds

A long-haired cat has a natural protection against many of the burns that a person may suffer. Nevertheless, a cat, whether long-haired or short-haired, can be burned or scalded from boiling water, soup or coffee. Or the cat, curious as ever, may nose itself into something that leads to a severe burn. Burns and scalds come from three basic sources:

1. Excessive heat from direct flame, hot solids, steam, boiling liquids, such as water, coffee, soup, oil or tar or from a direct fire in the flat or house, or a car-accident.
2. An electric current. The kitten in particular may chew through a wire that is connected.
3. Chemicals in sprays, acids and alkalis or corrosives. Cleaning-agents are a chief source of such burns.

Types of Burns and the Cat's Reaction to Them

Burns vary greatly, of course, in their surface extent and depth. You judge by the surface damage, for if the surface is not badly burned or scalded, the skin and muscle underneath cannot be severely burned. *A burn is considered major when a large skin area is affected.* If the burn goes deeper than the skin, it is also major. Deep burns extend through the skin and may affect muscles, fatty tissue and even bones. Such burns are considered very serious, and the cat's reaction will be severe.

1. A cat with severe burns will go into shock. See the section on shock on page 127.
2. Toxic poisoning and infection are always potential dangers from burns and scalds. The body absorbs the poisonous products of the cells damaged by the burns, or poisons from the organisms that multiply on the surface of the burn may spread throughout the entire body. A burn that is neglected can lead to a general poisoning of the entire body.
3. Death may follow from severe and extensive burns as a result of shock, toxic poisoning or infection—or from a combination of all three.

Treatment

Your treatment will vary depending on the degree of the burn. A superficial burn may mean simply that you cut away the hair in the afflicted area, and then gently apply mineral-oil or petroleum-jelly, burn-ointment or a similar preparation that you already have or can buy at the chemist's. Tannic-acid jelly is very useful here.

First-degree burns usually consist of a few blisters on a small surface of the skin. Treat as you would any superficial burns. If you are unsure of the severity or if the burn looks angry, consult your vet.

If a quarter or more of the cat's skin surface is damaged, the burns are considered extensive and require a vet's care immediately. First aid in the meantime includes protection against infection and treatment for shock— these are the real dangers at this stage. The treatment for the burns them-selves is beyond your help and must be left to professionals. You may do serious harm by applying grease, flour, baking-soda, iodine, hypol or any ointment you may have on hand. You should cover the burned or scalded area with a clean, dry dressing—sterile gauze, sheet, towel or handker-chief—and bandage it to keep it in position. Keep your cat warm, dry and quiet—the best home treatment for shock.

Burns Caused by Chemicals

Chemical burns should be treated differently from burns caused by direct flame, boiling liquids or hot solids. If the burn is caused by a corrosive acid—such as an alkali, bathe the affected part with an alkaline (*not alkali*) solution. Here is how you make an alkaline solution: add a tablespoon of baking-soda (bicarbonate of soda) to a pint of warm water. Washing-soda (sodium carbonate) can be used in the same strength. If you have neither, wash the afflicted area gently with milk of magnesia.

Sometimes the burn is caused by a corrosive alkali—such as a garden lime product, and in those cases, brush out the cat's coat. Use long rubber gloves so that you do not get it on yourself. Bathe the burned area with a solution made by mixing equal parts of vinegar and water.

Once the acids and alkalis have been neutralized, apply to the burned area tannic-acid jelly or hypochlorite solution, which you can buy at any chemist's. This is only the first step. All burns may become infected without professional care. Most burns are fatal to a cat.

Loss of Consciousness

A cat may suffer from loss of consciousness for many reasons. I have already discussed some of them. Shock, for example, is a chief cause. Under 'Ailments', I mentioned eclampsia, which is caused by a lack of calcium or a mineral imbalance in the nursing queen. Poisons can also cause loss of consciousness, as can severe bleeding. Most of the time (except for eclampsia) loss of consciousness or fits of fainting will result from an accident. Some common ones in and around the home are:

Brain Injury

Any hard blow on the head can obviously cause unconsciousness. A cat may suffer a concussion as the result of a fall, a blow or being stepped on. It will fall on its side, and its breathing will become slow and shallow—accom-panied by a weak pulse and enlarged pupils. Its body may feel cold, the inside of its lips become pale and whitish. **Treatment:** Keep the cat quiet and warm until the vet can examine it.

A blow or fall can also cause compression, which is a very serious condition. The usual signs of compression—depending on the part of the brain affected—will be a radical interference with the cat's sense of balance. It may not be able to walk straight. Also, it may bleed from the ears and nose; vomiting is common. The pupils may be unequal in size, and they may show great sensitivity to light. **Treatment:** The same as for shock. Provide warmth (with a blanket or a hot-water bottle wrapped in a towel) and quiet. Call a vet immediately.

Haemorrhaging or bleeding in the brain causes what is called a stroke, or apoplexy. A stroke comes on suddenly, resulting in partial or full loss of consciousness. It is relatively rare in cats. If still partially conscious, the cat may vomit, show great excitement and try, unsuccessfully, to stand. It may hold its head to one side, while the eyeballs move uncontrollably. You cannot see any external sign of trouble with this condition, and so you must react to the cat's unusual behaviour. **Treatment:** Rest and quiet, no stimulants. Allow small amounts of water if the cat can swallow; do not give water to an unconscious cat. Call a vet immediately.

Sunstroke and Heatstroke

Heatstroke or stress can occur if you leave your cat in a parked car on a hot day—it may be in a shopping-centre or in your own driveway. Even if the outside temperature is moderate, the heat inside the car may be great if the sun shines on it. Such a stress is particularly hard on kittens, overweight cats and the older animal. But it can occur with a cat of any age, and it may happen outside on a hot day as well as in a car.

The most common signs are rapid breathing, severe and loud panting—as the animal attempts to catch its breath, vomiting, weakness in the legs, staggering, collapse, an extraordinarily high temperature (over 105°F) and a staring expression without any focus.

At any of these signs, you have a cat in real trouble. The first thing is to bring down the temperature by taking the cat into the shade, cooling it and sponging it with cold water. If at all possible, give a cold-water enema—that cools immediately. If you have a tub available, fill it partially (not too deep, as the cat may be fully conscious) with cold water and immerse the cat. Afterwards, dry it thoroughly.

Electric Shock

As I mentioned before, kittens bite through attached electric wires and suffer shock, if they are not killed outright. Since a kitten is so small, the shock is enough to kill it; if not, then it will become paralysed. *Do not touch it* until you have unplugged the wire or unless you are wearing rubber gloves. Keep children away. You may be able to push the cat away with a stick. **Treatment:** For a shock, warmth. If the cat has stopped breathing, administer artificial respiration, which is described just below. If there are burns, treat them as the directions above indicate.

Suffocation

Suffocation is caused by exposure to smoke or gas. Remove the cat immediately to fresh air. If it has stopped breathing, or if the breathing is very feeble, give artificial respiration according to the following directions.

The most effective method of artificial respiration is to apply mouth-to-mouth breathing. Cup your hands to form a cone and breathe directly into the cat's mouth and nostrils. Continue until the cat starts to breathe.

The other method is to place the cat on its right side, with its head and neck extended and its tongue drawn forward. Place your hand over the cat's ribs, right behind the shoulder blade. With a sudden but gentle movement, press downward, and this will compress the chest and expel air. After this sudden movement, relax immediately to allow the air to rush back into the lungs.

Wait about five seconds (count one-two-three-four-five) and start again. Keep up this pressing and releasing twenty to thirty times per minute until the cat begins to breathe. If you have experience in giving artificial respiration to people, follow the same procedure with a cat. Make sure you maintain a smooth and steady rhythm.

Once you see the cat is breathing, treat for shock, with warmth. Do not try to force liquids down the cat's throat. Even if you overcome the cat's efforts, it may go into the lungs.

Heart Attack or Circulatory Failure

The older cat may lose consciousness because of a heart attack or a circulatory failure. This is rare, of course, but possible. In many cases, a heart attack will be accompanied by a slight coughing. Often the cat may stand perfectly still or sway a moment, its eyes glazed.

In serious cases, the cat may scream out and fall. The pulse is very rapid, and the breathing at first shallow. The cat's tongue will be very dark—the result of blood leaving that part of the body; as circulation returns to normal, the tongue will turn lighter.

Treatment: When the cat returns to consciousness, keep it warm. Check with your vet for further treatment.

Fits, or Convulsions

I have already described fits and convulsions in the chapter on ailments (page 99). But since it is often a first-aid situation, I will repeat some of the information here.

Fits derive from several conditions: poisoning, worms, epilepsy, sharp allergic reaction, anaemia, brain diseases. A fit may come on suddenly, with the cat screaming out or going into a convulsive spasm. Its jaws may chatter, it may foam at the mouth, and it may lie on its side while its feet paddle away. Muscles often twitch, and the breathing becomes very excited and rapid. There may or may not be loss of consciousness. The bladder and bowels will become uncontrollable, and your cat will probably soil itself. A fit ordinarily lasts a few moments or five to ten minutes, and sometimes fits follow each other rapidly.

Treatment: Do not panic, although the situation is very unpleasant. The important thing is to get your cat to a vet once the fit subsides. If you are at home, move the cat to a dark corner and keep everyone else away. To pick up a cat that has had a fit or fits, cover it with a blanket—it may try to bite or scratch. A vet may be able to help in some cases.

OUTDOOR ACCIDENTS

If your cat does not leave the flat or house, there will be little opportunity for an outdoor accident. But many cats have some limited freedom in the summer, when their owners go away with them and let them roam for part of the day. I discussed car-accidents before, and here I will present a few of the other things that can possibly happen. Most of them do not, but for first-aid reasons you should be prepared.

Drowning

To help a cat that is drowning, you must open up the air passages so that it can breathe. The best way to do that is to dangle the cat by its hind legs to let the water run out of its nose and mouth. Pull the tongue outside, as that helps breathing. Even swing the cat around if necessary—remember the air passages must be cleared or the cat will die. Once the water is out, apply artificial respiration as described above, under 'Suffocation', page 138. After the cat is breathing normally, dry it by rubbing briskly. Cover with blankets for treatment of shock.

Bites and Cuts

The cat that runs free in either the city or the country is bound to tangle with other animals, and from that you can expect bites and cuts. Simple cuts or abrasions are no cause for alarm, since the cat will lick them clean. But deep wounds must be treated, for infection is always a danger. Let the cat lick the wound, and wash it out with soap and water; then apply an antiseptic such as peroxide.

Sometimes the cat irritates the wound by constant attention, and it will not heal. You may have to put an Elizabethan collar on your cat to keep its mouth away from the wound. The collar fits snugly around the cat's neck and provides a protective shield. It looks crazy, but it does work. Here is how you make one. Start with a piece of stiff cardboard and cut out a large circle. In the centre of that, cut out a smaller circle that will fit neatly over the cat's head. Do not allow any play around the neck. The collar should be wide enough so that the edges extend out and make it impossible for the cat's muzzle to reach its body. Then make some holes in the collar so you can fasten string from it to the cat's own regular collar. This will keep it from slipping off. If all this seems too much trouble, then ask your vet about rubber collars that can be inflated. Do not use the collar unless your vet recommends it.

Some bites from other cats are puncture-wounds, and since they close up easily, they look as though they are healing. But infection can set in if they fail to drain correctly. The result can be abscesses and infection. Try to keep such wounds open. Restrain the cat with a towel, since it will not like this, and then insert cotton tips dipped in peroxide into the bites. Remove scabs to prevent surface-healing under which the wound may fester. If you find all this too much—and it is no longer simply first aid, ask your vet to attend to it.

Bee- and Wasp-Stings
A bee- or wasp-sting, or several such stings, can send a cat into shock. The pain is also considerable, and before you attempt treatment, restrain the cat. Use a cold compress on the bite or bites, if you can find them under the cat's coat. If there is swelling, use a warm compress and follow it with an application of petroleum-jelly.

Several stings can make your cat lose its breath—probably an allergic reaction. Get it to a vet immediately for an injection to counter the toxic effect. This condition is rare.

Snake-Bite
This is a *rare* occurrence, but if your cat runs free in the country, it is possible. The only dangerous snake in the UK is the adder.

It is unlikely, however, that you will be prepared to treat snake-bite. Your only recourse, then, is to get your cat to a vet immediately for an anti-venom injection and further therapy. *Quick action is essential.*

Frost-bite
A cat that roams may disappear for some time and return frost-bitten. The tips of the ears or the end of the tail—sometimes the paws—will feel dry and leathery. Do not rub the frozen area with snow or any rough material. Gradually thaw out the affected area, or the entire cat, with your hands, a blanket or any soft object available. Be gentle because you can easily tear or bruise frozen tissues. Sometimes, the tips of the ears slouch.

Lameness
The cat left outside for a good deal of time may suffer lameness from a foreign object lodging in its paw. You will see it favour the injured paw, which may also bleed and swell.

If you are sure that the injury is not a fracture but a foreign object, first restrain the cat and then try to remove the object. The more common objects are thorns, glass, nails, tacks and splinters, most of which can be removed with pliers or tweezers. After removal, wash the part thoroughly with warm water and a mild soap. Let the cat lick the area. If there is swelling, soak the foot in warm water.

This will do unless the cut is really deep. If it is, there will be continued swelling, the formation of pus or a failure to heal. In that case, take the cat to your vet.

Injured Tail
You may be surprised to learn that accidents often result in injuries to the cat's tail. Sometimes it is only a bruise, which can be treated with compresses soaked in warm water or witch hazel. If it is a break, however, as would

happen if the tail were caught in a car door, then it must be seen by a vet and probably amputated. An even more common accident is that someone inadvertently steps on the cat's tail while it is sleeping; this can crush it and require the help of a vet.

Objects in Mouth and Throat

This is a condition that applies especially to a kitten. It takes a foreign object—small chicken bone, needle, pin—and tries it out in its mouth. If it attempts to swallow the object, you can have a first-aid situation. The kitten or cat may choke or gag. Often, you can force the mouth open by pressing the thumb and forefinger of one hand into the cheeks. Reach in and try to remove the object with the fingers of your other hand.

Occasionally, the sharp object will have descended into the throat. The cat will gulp repeatedly and refuse food or water. If a pin or needle with thread is involved, it may do considerable damage. Call a vet for help.

Eye Injuries

The cat which never leaves the flat will probably never suffer an eye injury. But the country cat may—from brush and tree branches, from fights with other cats or animals, from accidents in which the socket itself may be injured. If the injury is only a scratch or minor laceration, bathe the eye in an eyewash. If you have any doubts, call your vet, especially if the cat seems to be in pain.

For a foreign object in the eye, such as dust or grime, simply wash it out with sterile cotton soaked in an eyewash. If that does not remedy the situation, call for professional help.

If an injury occurs that you cannot determine, keep the eye moist until you can take the cat to a vet. Pads of cotton soaked in warm (not hot) water are helpful. An eye-ointment, if you have it, is also recommended. Pull down the lower lid of the eye and apply a little ointment on the lid or in the eye itself.

In a severe accident—a car-accident or a blow to the head, the eye may be forced from the socket. Here the only thing you can do is to keep the eyeball moist until a vet examines the cat. Keep the socket itself free of dirt. For any treatment, you will need restraint for the cat.

Ear Injuries

Like eye injuries, ear injuries are rare in the cat kept inside a flat, but the country cat may suffer from them. Lacerations and bruises are the most common forms. A minor laceration needs only a washing-out with a mild soap and warm water followed by an antiseptic. Any continued bleeding or discomfort calls for a vet's help. If the cut or bruise seems extensive or deep and becomes inflamed, do not attempt home treatment.

OTHER INJURIES—INDOOR AND OUTDOOR

These are miscellaneous injuries, from accidents. In many cases, you will not have time to diagnose what is precisely wrong, but you can recognize general signs of trouble and act accordingly. As you can see from most of the accidents listed above, your chief treatment is to stop bleeding and then apply warmth to handle shock.

Abdomen

Any open abdominal wound is very serious and needs immediate care. In the event such care is unavailable, wash the wound or the protruding section with water or a mild antiseptic and push it inside. Use your hand or a towel as a sling to keep it in place. Before you do this, unless your cat is unconscious, you must use restraint.

Treat for shock: warmth, quiet, but no liquids. If the cat is conscious, you may let it lick ice.

Nose

A blow, a kick or an accident can injure the cat's nose, causing it to swell. If there is bleeding, apply a cold compress. If the bleeding continues or the cat seems in considerable discomfort, call a vet.

Larynx

The larynx is the passage through which air reaches the lungs, and any severe injury to it can cause suffocation. A blow, a kick, a sharp object swallowed or an accident can cause such an injury.

An injury to the larynx causes pain and swelling, also noisy and laboured breathing. If punctured, the larynx will give off a hissing sound, with bubbles of blood oozing from the wound.

Treatment: If there is bleeding, first apply restraint and then a cold compress on the wound. Do not give liquids if there is an open wound. You need a vet's care at once.

Lungs

Like other organs, a lung can be injured by a sharp blow, a kick or an accident, or even by the penetration of a broken rib. In a severe accident, a collapsed or injured lung is not unusual. Even though you see no external blood, haemorrhaging may be occurring internally as a result of the injury. What you see are breathing difficulties, irregular breathing, possibly coughing of frothy, bright-red blood. There may well be shock and considerable pain for the cat.

Treatment: This calls for immediate veterinary care. In the meantime, treat any external wound after applying restraint. Wash out the wound with mild soap and warm water and then apply an antiseptic. If bleeding is heavy, follow the directions above (under 'Bleeding', pages 125–6) for treating it. Keep the cat warm, with blankets and a hot-water bottle. Do not give any liquids.

DIGESTIVE UPSETS

The various digestive upsets a cat can suffer are general indigestion, bloat, constipation and diarrhoea. I have described all of these in the chapter on ailments. Most of these conditions are temporary and require control by means of diet. If you notice any continued swelling of the abdomen, bloody vomiting or diarrhoea, or a lot of rubbing of the stomach on the floor or crouching, then professional treatment is called for.

MISCELLANEOUS ACCIDENTS

There are always unforeseeable accidents that do not fit into a particular category; one of them is your kitten or cat's swallowing pills—sleeping-pills, slimming-pills, or whatever. Since more and more people are taking pills, there is a better chance than ever before that they will be left lying around. This can be very serious if a large number are consumed. If you see any pills missing, try to make your cat vomit at once with an emetic. If it is too late and the cat is unconscious from sleeping-pills or energized by slimming-pills, take it immediately to a vet.

ONE WARNING: If you try to make a semi-conscious or unconscious cat vomit, make sure that you do not force the emetic into its throat. This is difficult to avoid.

Car-sickness, while not really a first-aid situation, needs care. I discuss it above, but the best treatment is not to feed your cat before a trip and to hold down its water intake also. If this does not work, then consult your vet about prevention with a tranquiliser for motion-sickness.

A FIRST-AID KIT FOR CATS

I will list only the most basic items.

1. **A rectal thermometer** (wash it in cool water only) and petroleum-jelly for lubricating it.
2. **A germicide** (peroxide or witch hazel) to wash off whatever a sick cat uses, as a protection for you and your children. Also, a mild soap, for washing off the hair.
3. **A Fleet enema**, pediatric, which is far easier to use than one you must prepare yourself.
4. **Sterile cotton**—which you probably have anyway—for washing out ears and eyes.
5. **Mineral-oil** as a laxative.
6. **Kaopectate**, as a control for diarrhoea.
7. **Activated charcoal**, as an antidote for poisons. Or you can use hydrogen peroxide, mustard powder or salt. Charcoal is best, however.
8. **An ointment**, of tannic acid or some other, for burns.
9. **Cotton-swab sticks**, for cleaning out eyes and nose.
10. **Peroxide**, or any other mild antiseptic for dressing wounds.
11. **Adhesive tape.**
12. **Aromatic spirits of ammonia**, for shock treatment.

All these can be put into a handy bag and carried along if you go on a trip. If you live in the country or plan a holiday in a remote area, you might consider taking along a **snake-bite kit** (for your cat, yourself, your family or any other pets).

Some handy measurements:

1 tablespoon = ½ ounce
3 teaspoons = 1 tablespoon
1 cup = 8 ounces

FIVE

Nutrition

Even if you know a good deal about human nutrition, you may know little about what your cat needs nutritionally. You should start out fresh and learn about your cat. Put a halt to all your assumptions. Even as basic a food as milk or dairy-products may be harmful to your cat under certain circumstances. Although milk generally is an excellent source of nutrition, some cats are allergic to it and develop diarrhoea on a dairy diet. And fish, if fed raw, can lead to serious ailments. Similarly, a steady diet of liver may prove too rich and lead to diarrhoea.

Begin with calories. The caloric need of your cat is proportionately greater than for a person. A sedentary person may get along well on 1,500 to 1,800 calories a day, if he or she is of average size with a job that requires relatively little exertion. Yet the average cat uses about 300 to 350 calories a day, and weighs in at 10 pounds, 12 to 15 if exceptionally large. If scaled up for a person, that would amount to over 3,000 calories a day, so you can see that a cat needs proportionately far more calories than a person, considering its body weight.

Basic requirements: a cat usually needs more fat and protein than either a person or a dog, proportionate to its total number of calories. Although many of the cat's basic requirements remain something of a mystery, we do know that fat and protein are very necessary items in its diet.

We tend to forget that a domestic cat is an unnatural object in nature's pattern for animal life. The wild cat roaming free and living off the land was assured of a complete diet from its kill, or else it died. By catching its most common prey—rats, mice and other small animals, the wild cat ate an entire cycle of food: skin, bones and insides, as well as meat. It gained protein and fat, calcium and various minerals and vitamins. By eating the stomach and intestines of its catch, it ingested everything it needed for its health and well-being.

When the cat was domesticated, its needs did not change, but they were met with home feeding. Many of these home meals satisfied the owner but did not fulfil the cat's nutritional needs. A cat fed on a steady diet of fish or meat could suffer from a severe calcium deficiency and have a weak bone structure. A cat fed a straight diet of liver or other offal could develop an excess of vitamin A. Finally, a cat given a straight dairy diet—milk, cream, butter, yogurt—can develop a severe chronic diarrhoea, because of an excess of milk sugar (lactose). The things we often think of as typical 'cat food' may prove detrimental if they become the entire diet.

We must also cope with the fact that certain aspects of the cat's needs remain as yet undiscovered. We are not at all certain of the minimum or maximum vitamin and mineral needs of the cat, although we have determined these factors with people and dogs. What all this means is that you must take some care in providing your cat with a *balanced diet*, which means the correct multiples of protein, fat, calcium, carbohydrates (for calories) and vitamins and minerals. It is not very difficult.

Your aim in feeding your cat is to give it everything it needs for good health without making it fat. A lean and healthy-looking pet is one who lives long and enjoys an ailment-free existence. Cats do not, on the whole, exercise very much, unless they are allowed to roam free, as farm cats are. But the city cat spends most of its time resting, sleeping, lying around. Therefore overfeeding is as bad as poor feeding. All cats are the same in their needs, since, unlike dogs, they do not appreciably differ in size. One cat may be 8 or 10 pounds, while another is 12, but basically they are of comparable size and have comparable food needs.

To give you a working formula, your cat—which I assume falls within the range of 8 to 10 pounds—needs around 350 calories a day. But this is only an estimate. Different cats have different metabolic rates, just as people do, and you should find the exact caloric intake that suits your pet best. Once your cat is grown, you should aim at a hard, muscular, lean look—the cat should be a miniature panther in silhouette and movement.

What, then, goes into a cat's dietary needs? Remember that this is for the adult. The care and feeding of the kitten appear in Chapter 2.

FATS

The proper intake of fats for people depends partly, of course, on their intensity of activity; the more active they are, the more fats their body can absorb without itself becoming fat. So with cats. The active cat—say, a farm cat or a street-roamer—needs relatively more fats per body-pound than the sedentary pet, since fats provide energy and heat.The average cat needs fifteen to twenty per cent of its diet in fat, with the active farm cat perhaps using even more, although these are estimates only and must be regulated according to the needs of the individual. Fats are not the only source of energy, since protein and carbohydrates also provide it, but fats permit the proteins to work on other parts of the body, building stronger muscle and tissue. It is better to have fats converted directly into energy than to use proteins as an energy source.

Fats also serve a variety of functions besides providing heat and energy. They keep your cat's coat and skin in good condition; they slow digestion down and make it more complete. Fats help a cat to grow to its full potential, and an inadequate intake of fats can lead to a stunting of growth. Many owners are reluctant to feed fat-products to their pet and think that it may be a poor diet item. On the contrary, a cat thrives on a balanced fat-intake.

Fat-intake can even be equated to a cat's temperament. On a dry-food diet without sufficient fat in it, a cat may become nervous and irritable, for its energy source is partially cut off. Such an animal starved for fats gains its energy from protein and carbohydrates, which are, physically, far less economical. But temperament is only one factor. Skin tone and coat tone will suffer from a diet too low in fats, and such a cat will also probably be more subject to ailments. It could well lose that energetic and healthy look that a pet should have.

There are three fatty acids in fats that a cat should have: linoleic, linolenic and arachidonic. The chief of these is the first, linoleic, and fortunately this is one of the easiest to come by because it is found in most meat products, in suet, in corn-oil and in butter. The importance of the other two is less obvious, but they are still necessary. They are found in various oils and in animal fats.

While most commercial pet-foods contain sufficient fat for a dog, they are often insufficient for a cat. The commercial dry foods, which are excellent in other ways, should be supplemented. Check the amount of fat on the label, and remember that an active cat needs twenty per cent or more in its diet.

If you feed your cat a commercial dry food, supplement it with one of the following: bacon-fat, cooking-oils, butter. The amount should be about 2 ounces (or 4 tablespoons) of fat per pound of dry food, a little less if you are mixing the fats with semi-moist food, which already has some fat content. None of this is exact; as I mentioned, it all depends on your particular pet. The kitten may need proportionately more fats, the adult cat less. You achieve a balance when your cat seems healthy and vibrant, its coat and skin tone good, its body sleek and hard.

If you feed your cat a predominantly meat diet (which I do not recommend), do not cut away all the fat. Very often, the cheap cuts are preferable, since they have a higher fat-content. If you feed your cat from table scraps, include the fat that you have cut off from your own meat. Do not feed huge amounts of fat or fatty products; be reasonable, and make sure your cat gets what it needs in moderate amounts.

Special circumstances may call for a change in diet—in fats and in all other ingredients. The very thin kitten or cat should be built up with a fat-rich diet, *as long as it can absorb the extra fats without vomiting or suffering from diarrhoea*, and only until its weight and health come up to expectations. Similarly, the pregnant queen and nursing mother will require larger amounts of fats than she will under normal conditions. On the other hand, the very fat or overweight cat will need smaller amounts, for it has stored great quantities and can draw upon the reserve. The very active cat—one who works on a farm or is allowed to roam free—may need still larger doses of fats to give it energy, although the free-roaming cat is probably living off other small animals and acquiring what it needs that way.

Every owner will find that he can make suitable adjustments simply by looking at his cat and taking the necessary steps towards raising or lowering the fat-intake. Unless you feed your cat an immensely large amount of carbohydrates, you can control its calories by controlling its intake of fats.

PROTEINS

Most owners are knowledgeable about the protein needs of their cats. It is, in fact, the one ingredient nearly everyone knows about, since we assume a pet needs meat or fish, foods that are rich in protein. But one thing many people do not realize is that cats require a diet particularly high in protein. The average mature cat requires about twenty per cent of its diet in protein, while the growing kitten may need about a third of its diet in protein. Since most commercial cat-foods provide about fifteen per cent or more protein, you may well need a protein supplement for the growing kitten, but probably not for the mature cat.

Proteins operate in cats the same way they operate in people. Specifically, protein helps body-growth and repair. Without it, the cat's body gradually deteriorates, and its physical processes slow up. Its resistance to infection is lowered, so that it may seem ill or ailing much of the time.

Proteins are themselves compounds made up of various amino acids, some twenty of which have been identified. When your cat eats foods containing proteins, its body breaks them down into component amino acids and then rebuilds them into the right combination of proteins it needs for growth and repair. Those amino acids not used for such protein-building are further broken down and transformed into heat and energy.

The only way a cat can obtain protein is through the eating of fod that already contains protein. When it roamed free, the cat enjoyed a protein-rich diet from its kill.

Some foods are better sources of protein than others. Milk, meat, eggs and cheese (foods that nearly all cats eat and like) are rich in the kind of protein the body needs. But some of these foods cause side-effects in individual cats. A large amount of milk or milk-products (cheese, yogurt, cream, butter) can give a cat diarrhoea; some cats need only a little in the way of milk-products to suffer from diarrhoea. Sometimes, yogurt works well while plain milk or cream creates the disorder. Eggs are also an excellent source of protein, but they should always be fed *cooked*; the white, especially, might create a digestive upset.

A food such as corn, while good for the cat, does not contain all the essential amino acids, and the rare cat fed mainly on corn may suffer from a dietary deficiency. The same is true of rice, potatoes, wheat flour, peas and several other foods—all of them are rich in some proteins but not in all the essential ones. A cat whose diet is made up chiefly of these items should be given a daily protein supplement—fatty meat, for example.

CARBOHYDRATES

Nutritionists have not been able to demonstrate that a cat needs carbo-hydrates as an essential part of its diet. But in day-to-day feeding, carbo-hydrates form a good part of the bulk of a cat's diet and do provide calories. They furnish a good supply of energy and allow the proteins to be used in body-building. Up to a third of a cat's diet may be carbohydrates. If there is significantly more, other essentials such as proteins and fats may be crowded out of the diet.

Carbohydrates are found in sugar and starch foods, such as potatoes, chocolate, whole grains, corn, milk, sugar and rice. Potatoes, rice or corn is fine if your cat likes it and does not get fat. However, never give it a raw potato. Uncooked starch is difficult for it to digest, and such a diet of raw starch can cause severe diarrhoea. If a cat is fed raw grain, it will probably pass it whole in its bowel movement, as its digestive system usually cannot handle it. Prepared cat-foods contain cereals already baked or cooked in some manner, so that they can be absorbed.

WATER

We take water for granted, but it is essential for your cat to have access to it at all times. Cats need about a pint of water a day, although they can obtain most of this in their food. However, if you give your cat a predominantly dry-food diet—that is, a commercial dry food, then be sure to have plenty of water available. If you feed a moist or semi-moist food diet, commercial or otherwise, then your cat is probably obtaining most of its water intake there. If your cat is sick, or suffering from diarrhoea or from attacks of vomiting, a plentiful supply of water is even more important. Either keep it available (changed daily) near its litter box or else put water down three or four times a day to see if your cat is thirsty.

VITAMINS

Although the precise level of vitamins essential for a cat's health is not known, it has been well established that vitamins are necessary. When cats ran wild, they ate their prey and in that way gained their vitamin needs.

A vitamin is an organic substance found in very small quantities in natural foods. For many years vitamins have been recognized as essential to a pet's health, just as they are essential to a person's well-being. Vitamin deficien-cies in your cat may result in a great many health hazards. All aspects of its health are affected: from its general metabolism to hearing, vision, fertility, muscle control, kidney function, blood clotting and skin and coat health. All depend upon a sufficient quantity of various vitamins.

If your cat eats a well-known brand of cat-food, it is receiving all the vitamins that it needs. You may have to supplement it with fats or protein, or both, but manufacturers of the major brands have been careful to include essential vitamins. The kitten, however, will need a supplement of vitamins and minerals (any one of the several brands on the market) because of its rapid growth rate. So too will the old cat if it no longer gains benefit from its food. Also, the pregnant queen and nursing mother will need vitamin and mineral supplements, as the drain on her body is greater than nature can replace.

But suppose you feed your cat chiefly from the table. Then there is always the chance that its diet is haphazard and its vitamin intake will not include all the essentials. Of course, some cats thrive on strange foods and even stranger diets, but you cannot assume your cat will be one of them. The cat fed on prepared canned food, or on a dry-meal diet with a fat-supplement, will gain necessary vitamins and minerals. Make sure that the commercial food you use mentions a large amount of vitamin A (1500 to 2100 IU).

A cat on a straight meat diet may need a vitamin-and-mineral supplement, for meat lacks minerals such as calcium and phosphorus, and certain kinds are deficient in vitamin A. Lean meat, in addition, lacks essential fat. As you read through the analysis below, you can check your cat's diet against the essentials.

Vitamin A
Cats need a good deal of vitamin A in their diet, since they cannot synthesize it from other elements. Vitamin A is necessary for growth, good vision, adequate appetite, skin tone and health, nerve health, coat lustre, good hearing, digestion, prevention of infection and a number of other important functions. It is found in most yellow foods such as egg-yolks, carrots, butter and corn, as well as in liver and many green vegetables and grains.

Just as you want to avoid too little vitamin A, so you want to avoid an excess. An excess—say, as a result of feeding your cat a steady diet of liver—can sometimes lead to crippling bone-deformities. The chances are excellent that if you feed your cat a complete commercial food, there is sufficient vitamin A. Supplement it by eggs (cooked) or liver twice a week. Liver should be fed in small amounts, an ounce or two being sufficient.

Cod-liver oil, an excellent source of vitamin A, used to be recommended. but this has given way to a more general vitamin-mineral supplement. Nothing, however, should be administered without a vet's advice. You must not give excess dosages.

At one time a cat given large amounts of mineral-oil to relieve constipation or to prevent formation of hair balls suffered a loss of vitamin A through absorption. At present, mineral-oil is supplemented with vitamin A so that such a loss is no longer possible.

Vitamin-B Complex
Cats seem to require a high proportion of vitamin B, what we also found in their requirements of vitamin A. This group includes B_1, thiamine; B_2, riboflavin; B_6, pyridoxine; and B_{12}. Vitamin B in its various forms is needed for the adequate growth and health of most vital organs. It also stimulates appetite, prevents anaemia, adds to muscle tone and aids in regular bowel movements.

Thiamine is found in meat, while milk and yeast are rich in riboflavin. Pyridoxine is in liver, egg-yolks, fish, vegetables and milk; and all foods containing protein have vitamin B_{12}. The vitamin-B requirement for cats has not been fully established in all its phases, although the need is definitely present. Since several of the vitamin-B elements are destroyed in the high heat used to prepare commercial cat-fods, be sure the food you buy has been supplemented with B vitamins, or else supplement it yourself with some of the foods listed above.

When a cat lacks some of the vitamins in this group, it may suffer from a niacin (nicotinic) deficiency. Do not confuse this element with the nicotine of tobacco. The tobacco element is poisonous, while nicotinic acid, niacin, is necessary for your pet's health. A cat suffering from a thiamine deficiency will have 'black tongue', or pellegra. The mucous membranes of its mouth will become very sensitive, and its tongue will take on a purplish-blackish colour. The cat will become much leaner, almost skin and bones, nervous and extremely irritable and out of sorts. It may die if untreated. Treatment consists of improving the diet, with a stress on foods that are a good source of vitamin B.

Vitamin-B elements are necessary for the functioning of the heart, liver and nerves. They tone up the muscles and provide for satisfactory digestion and lactation. They promote growth in the younger cat and keep up the blood of the adult cat. Kidney and bladder functions may also suffer from a deficiency of the vitamin. And if you plan to breed your female, a vitamin-B deficiency can affect fertility; the same is true for the male.

Your mature cat will get its vitamin B from commercial cat-foods, although the kitten and pregnant (as well as nursing) queen will need a vitamin-mineral supplement. If you have any doubt, check cat-foods with your vet and find out what he or she thinks about the need for such a supplement. A straight meat diet will, of course, give sufficient amounts of vitamin B, although it may be inadequate in other respects; so will table scraps. If you feed (cooked) eggs, liver or grains to your cat, it will gain sufficient vitamin B that way. A diet of dry meal mixed with meat fat will provide adequate vitamin B as well as other requirements.

Vitamin C

We know from novels and stories, or from personal experience, that people with a vitamin-C deficiency will develop scurvy, but recent research indicates that mature cats synthesize their own C. In the rare case of an imbalance that might result in scurvy, the cat will respond rapidly to vitamin C, which is found in abundance in fruits and vegetables. But this should not be a concern.

Vitamin D

Kittens need vitamin D *and* calcium and phosphorus to develop strong, sturdy bones. A deficiency can result in the ailment called rickets. This is a condition in which the bones do not calcify correctly and as a result become bent or bowed. Teeth, too, may be affected by the deficiency, forming irregularly and breaking through the gums later than they normally would.

These bone-deficiencies may be caused not only by a lack of vitamin D but also by an insufficiency of minerals. Normally, a vitamin-D deficiency alone will not cause these conditions.

For the mature cat, commercial foods provide adequate amounts of vitamin D, as do good grades of dry meal, which contain irradiated yeast and bonemeal. Either of these foods, together with some exposure to the sun, will be sufficient to provide the vitamin. The pregnant queen, the nursing mother and the kitten itself, however, all need extra amounts of the vitamin, and a vitamin-mineral supplement will supply that.

Do not dose your cat with excessive amounts of vitamin D or the results may be undesirable: hardening of the tissues, deformation of the teeth, poor growth, bloody diarrhoea, great thirst and depression or prostration. To be certain, ask your vet if a supplement is necessary, and do not indiscriminately give this or any other vitamin to your pet.

Vitamin E

Vitamin E is lesser known to the public, but it appears to be necessary for normal reproduction and lactation (secretion of the queen's milk before and during nursing). There also seems to be evidence for its need in toning the muscles. Wheatgerm supplies the cat with the necessary small amounts of this vitamin, and all vitamin-mineral supplements also include it.

Deficiencies of vitamin E, in the course of normal feeding, are very rare. It sometimes results when tinned tuna is the sole diet, or when the diet is high in polyunsaturated fats. If such a deficiency does occur, it results in a (rare) inflamed condition called steatitis; the symptoms include those of many other ailments: loss of appetite, fever, immobility and pain. Since you will recognize only the general sick condition, your vet will have to diagnose the case as a vitamin-E deficiency.

Vitamin K and Others

Research indicates that a cat, like a person, needs vitamin K to make its blood clot. When the blood fails to clot properly, severe anaemia may follow. In Warfarin poisoning, which leads to such bleeding, vitamin K is injected to coagulate the blood. Vitamin-K deficiency does not seem to occur in cats under normal conditions.

There are several other elements that may serve some purpose in the cat's diet. Two of these are pantothenic acid and folic acid. They are not major considerations for the owner, although pantothenic acid is necessary for good growth and a healthy appetite. It is found in liver, yeast and crude molasses, and a cat seems to have sufficient amounts if the rest of its diet is balanced. The same is true of choline (not to be confused with chlorine). Folic acid, which some owners may be familiar with, is a necessary ingredient of haemoglobin.

Two other elements that the cat appears to obtain without any special feeding are biotin and inositol; the requirements for these are very low.

None of these should give you any concern.

MINERALS

For a cat to enjoy a well-balanced diet, it needs adequate minerals as well as vitamins. If you fed your pet a commercial moist or dry food, the chances are that it is getting all the minerals it needs. If, in addition, you give your cat a vitamin-mineral supplement, you can be sure you are filling its basic requirements.

Cats need the following minerals in varying amounts, some of them quite small: calcium, phosphorus, iron, copper, potassium, magnesium, sodium, chlorine, iodine, possibly sulphur, manganese, cobalt and zinc. This is an impressive list of needs, but actually most of the requirements are met simply with a balanced diet. The chief items are calcium and phosphorus (usually considered together as a unit) and iron.

Calcium and Phosphorus

For rapidly growing kittens, supplementary calcium and phosphorus, along with vitamin D, are necessary for good bone, blood and tooth health. The same is true for pregnant queens and nursing mothers; their need for these two minerals is far greater than the requirement of the mature cat who is not bearing kittens. In fact, one danger is too much calcium and phosphorus in the diet, which can lead to abnormalities in the bone-development of the kitten and grown cat as well. There should be a balance between the two minerals and vitamin D.

Milk is rich in calcium, as are bones and bonemeal and alfalfa meal. Phosphorus is found in bones, cereal and milk. Since I do not recommend ever giving a cat bones of any kind, the minerals should come from bonemeal, grains and milk—what the cat can expect to derive from a complete commercial food.

If table scraps form the chief part of your pet's diet, there is some chance it will not get enough minerals, particularly calcium and phosphorus. Scraps should not, in most cases, compose more than twenty-five per cent of the daily diet, and even less is desirable. The exception would be when the scraps are themselves carefully selected for vitamin and mineral content, but it is the rare owner who has the time to do this. Also, costs can soar—feeding the cat will become like feeding a child.

Prepared cat-foods, both the moist canned variety and the dry kind, contain adequate amounts of calcium and phosphorus, sufficient for the mature cat. (Vitamin-mineral supplements are in order for the growing kitten, the pregnant queen and the nursing mother.)

Iron

Iron is needed only in very small amounts, but it is essential for building red blood-cells and for keeping the kitten or adult cat healthy and active. It is found in meats, especially in liver and other inner organs, as well as in egg-yolks and cereals, especially the bran. Inadequate iron in the cat's diet can lead to anaemia. The pregnant queen—as a precaution against anaemia—must be given a vitamin-mineral supplement. For the adult cat under normal conditions, the iron included in most commercial foods should be sufficient for good blood health.

Other Minerals

Several of the other minerals—copper, cobalt, magnesium and potassium—are also necessary for good blood and bone health, but they are needed in such small quantities that most cats receive their requirements in their normal diets. Unless your cat is fed a highly unusual diet without any variety, such as a steady fare of tinned tuna, it will pick up these necessary minerals. For example, iodine, sodium and chlorine are in ordinary table salt, an ingredient of nearly every food preparation. Sulphur is found in meat and egg-yolks, and potassium in the blood of meat.

The mineral requirement of cats has not been fully established, but minerals compose less than five per cent of your cat's body, with calcium and phosphorus forming more than half of this small percentage. The remaining third or so of the five per cent is composed of other minerals mentioned above, with a relatively important one such as iron being only a few hundredths of a per cent of the body's weight.

If you have any doubts about the diet you give your cat, and especially your kittens, consult your vet.

If you wish to feed your cat fresh food because you do not believe in the commercial varieties, a diet of meat supplemented by cereal, an occasional egg, occasional milk (*if it does not cause diarrhoea*) and perhaps some liver twice a week should keep your pet healthy and energetic. If you feed a vitamin-mineral supplement, first check with your vet, and follow the directions on the label. Do not overdose.

REMEMBER: If you buy a preparation designed for human consumption, you must scale down any dose you give your cat. Even a preparation designed for infants and children must be sharply scaled down. The average cat weighs 10 pounds, and therefore should receive a tenth of an adult dose, and perhaps a fifth of a child's. It is much better to use a supplement designed specifically for pets.

OTHER CONSIDERATIONS

There are no indications that eating-habits differ among the various breeds or that pedigree cats require a different diet from the regular house cat. All cats, regardless of background and breeding, have the same food requirements in terms of vitamins, minerals, calories, fats, proteins and carbohydrates. The internal structure of one cat is the same as the internal structure of another. Feeding-habits only seem to differ because some people prepare their cats for a variety of foods while others stick to one diet.

A cat will thrive on the same diet repeated every day for the rest of its life, *provided that the diet is balanced and complete.* In fact, many cats become established in their eating-preferences, and if you shift their diet around too much, they may stop eating for some time. Some cats may go for a week or so without food.

If your cat has become accustomed to a particular diet and then stops eating, there is probably something medically or emotionally wrong with it. It will not lose its appetite because it is bored with its food, unless there is a sudden shift of ingredients. Many owners, of course, get pleasure from varying their cat's diet and providing little delicacies and surprises. Such attention is part of the gratification in owning and enjoying a pet, and it is understandable. But you should recognize that your cat will thrive on a single diet that meets its essential needs. Excessive variation may, in fact, throw off the cat's health, leading to temporary diarrhoea or vomiting, for its digestive system has been accustomed to one kind of food and then must readjust to another. Your cat's health is best preserved by a balanced diet that remains basically similar day after day.

HOW MUCH TO FEED

In a land of plenty, not only people over-eat. Owners gain great enjoyment from feeding their pets well. But the healthiest cat is the one that remains lean and lithe, with a muscular, panther-like look and a sleek coat. As I have indicated throughout, there is no precise formula for all cats, any more than there is for people. Metabolism differs, activity differs, basic needs vary considerably. I can only give you some average figures. You must watch your cat's weight and adjust amounts as necessary. These figures and amounts are for the adult cat weighing 10 pounds, perhaps a little over that. This is not for the pregnant queen or the nursing mother. For the kitten in its various stages of development, see Chapter 2; for the pregnant and nursing queen, see Chapter 6.

For the moderately active grown cat, you can figure on about 300 to 350 calories a day, certainly no more unless the cat is extremely active. The average cat kept indoors in a flat is hardly active at all and would need no more than 6 or 7 ounces of food a day. If you give your cat a good deal of milk, one pint (16 ounces) supplies the entire caloric intake the cat needs— but I would not try to supply all the calories with milk alone. If you feed milk, even a cup furnishes half the caloric intake of your cat—and it leaves only enough room for a few ounces of solid food.

You should aim at a more balanced diet. A steady intake of milk may well cause diarrhoea, and the cat does not need that much calcium; it can use some bulk and other vitamins and minerals that are not present in milk. A bored cat may eat as much as you put in front of it—the meal becomes the major event of the day. Not all cats are self-regulating. But the healthiest animal is the one that eats the minimum it needs to stay active and happy. If you overfeed your cat, you shorten its life and create the chance for ailments it might not otherwise suffer from.

PRESCRIPTION DIETS FOR OLD CATS

All the information above applies to the normally healthy cat. For the old cat suffering from urinary problems that may come with old age, you must take other measures. A prescription diet (called c/d) for such a cat is obtainable only from your vet. The price is more than most prepared cat-foods cost, but often no more than a home-prepared diet. The one difficulty is that your cat may not enjoy it, and many cats, after a lifetime of certain food habits, will not readily take to a prescriptive diet.

If your cat has any kind of chronic ailment, whether it results from old age or otherwise, discuss its diet with your vet. For the ageing cat, excess weight may become a problem, but that is easy to control if you cut its daily food intake by about sixty per cent until the desired weight is achieved.

COST FACTORS

Since I do not know how much you, as owner, wish to spend on feeding your cat, I can only make some general statements that I hope will be useful to you. I will mention some diets that cost a moderate amount, or very little, or a good deal. My estimates are for an average-size cat, of about 10 pounds. Sometimes cats are abnormally large (up to 25 pounds) or small (no more than 6 or 7 pounds), and their needs will vary proportionately, but they are the rare case.

If you have an average-size pet, then a moderately priced diet would consist of a major brand of prepared cat-food supplemented by fats, vitamins and minerals (if recommended by your vet), with perhaps an ounce of liver a couple of times a week. This is by no means the cheapest way to feed a cat, for the tinned food is fairly expensive to begin with and is more than two-thirds moisture. One tin daily may possibly not provide enough caloric intake for your cat and may have to be supplemented with fats. But this is an easy way to solve the food problem—open a tin each day and add some (cooked) fats, and that may be all you need.

A far less expensive method of feeding is dry meal, 4 ounces of which will be sufficient for your cat's caloric intake. Some brands are complete in themselves, although I recommend adding fat to them, maybe from the table. Dry meat can be obtained in bulk, and the animal fat that you add is easy to come by from any butcher. Such a diet is perfectly sound, as long as you are sure the meal you use is a complete diet. These brands have been laboratory-tested and tried for many years. Since the high heat under which such dry foods are prepared burns out some of the vitamins and minerals, be certain that the one you buy has them added or baked into it. If you feed your cat a dry food, be certain you have water available, for there is little moisture in the meal itself. Veterinary opinion in Britain does not favour an entirely dry-food diet.

A variation on the above diet could be two-thirds dry meal mixed with one-third tinned food, with some fat added. This would be a middle ground, and it might prove more palatable for your pet. A cat fed on it from an early age will eat it without hesitation.

If you are an owner for whom cost is not a factor, then I recommend a home-prepared meal. Fresh-ground sirloin is great for your cat if it contains some fat and if it is supplemented by an occasional cooked egg (two or three weekly), some cereal or grain (cooked) for bulk, some milk or bonemeal for calcium and perhaps an ounce or two of liver each week for minerals and vitamins. Fresh food is not necessarily better for your cat than the prepared tinned or dry diets. But many owners, especially now with the interest in organic and fresh foods, feel safer when feeding their pet this way. This is a matter of choice, not necessarily medically better. Simply be sure the diet is balanced and complete.

If you plan to feed your cat on fresh food, you may wish to check the precise requirements with your vet, or you can check my list of the cat's needs and estimate yourself what it should receive. One of the vitamin-mineral supplements on the market can satisfy any of your fears about the cat's additional needs here.

A WARNING: Very lean or muscle meat should not be the sole basis of a fresh diet. Nor should fish or milk. You do the cat a disservice if you feed it only the fine cuts of meat you like. A cat needs a more balanced diet than lean meat or fish (especially tinned tuna) provides.

You can make your cat's diet as simple or as complicated as you wish. If you have time and patience, then by all means cook fresh food every day. Do not, however, vary your cat's diet too much. It manages best on a steady, balanced diet. If there is change, it should be because of some real need—either illness or a nutritional deficiency. Once you have found a satisfactory diet for your cat, its appetite remains constant and there is no need for you to tempt it further.

LIST OF POINTS TO CHECK

1. Do not ever feed a cat bones. Even ground-up bones, while nutritional, can lead to constipation.
2. Make sure you choose a complete diet when you feed your cat, and supplement it with some extra fat—as long as your cat remains sleek and lean.
3. Serve all food at room-temperature, not ice-cold. Cats do not take to cold food.
4. With dry foods, you can serve them as they are, but make sure ample drinking-water is available.
5. You might mix in some leafy vegetables with your cat's food—the cat likes them. Also, some catnip is recommended, not for nutritional purposes but because it seems to reduce flatulence (gas in the intestine).
6. Do not buy the cheapest products on the market. Be sure to check the ingredients and the level of protein, vitamins and minerals. Some cheaper brands are inexpensive because they are deficient, or else they contain large chunks of ingredients, which indicates incomplete mixing or grinding.
7. Do not assume that milk should be your cat's whole diet. Do not be surprised if milk or dairy-products create diarrhoea.

8. The fat you add for energy may be butter, corn-oil, meat fat, margarine and so on.

9. Never feed raw fish. Raw meat seems all right, but then your cat should be accustomed to it from the start. Keep away from tinned tuna—it is not a balanced diet, and a cat once started on it will never want to stop.

10. Occasional vomiting is no cause for alarm. Chronic vomiting means either an ailment or that the cat's food does not agree with it. Under these conditions, see your vet.

11. Check with your vet before giving a vitamin-mineral supplement. And if you do give one designed for human consumption, be sure to cut it proportionately to the cat's weight.

12. Do not over-indulge your cat—either with food or with vitamin-mineral supplements. A healthy cat should be lithe and lean, with good coat and skin tone. An over-indulged cat may become soft and sluggish, factors that shorten its life and expose it to illness.

13. The best diet is a *complete* diet, no matter what its components may be. If your cat thrives on what you give it, then you are doing the right thing. If it does not, then rethink what you are doing.

SIX

The Reproductive Cycle: Breeding, Pregnancy, Queening

The mating instincts of both male and female cats are exceptionally powerful, and so if you choose not to have your female spayed or your male neutered, you will be involved in the reproductive cycle. That means breeding, planned or otherwise. If you have a pedigree cat and wish to breed it selectively to another pedigree, this chapter is for you. And if you have a house cat that has haphazardly mated, this chapter is also for you. Often the original reason for owning a cat is to breed from it. But whatever your reason, this chapter will provide a step-by-step explanation of the cat's breeding and reproductive cycle.

Since the female cat will have the pregnancy, the queening and the care of the kittens, the owner will have a lot to contend with. But the owner of a male or stud also has his problems, since the male is only temporarily satisfied by mating and will continue to make a fuss until he can mate once again. In the meantime he will spray the house or flat with his 'odour', which can make living with him rather difficult.

If you want a cat simply for companionship, as many people do, then mating it is not really for you. You may have cramped living-quarters, or a limited income, or be too busy professionally for the trouble of watching over a litter of kittens. Of course, such an experience has its own rewards. What is marvellous to watch is the queen taking care of kitten as it emerges from her uterus and then her diligent care of each growing kitten until it is weaned. These are remarkable aspects of the natural process, of the female going through a ritual that is observed by every size of cat, whether domestic or jungle-oriented.

In fact, unless you are a professional breeder, the deliberate decision to mate your female should be made for the sake of the pleasure you will have in raising the kittens—that is, if the mating is not by chance or error. When the litter does come, it will make work for you, but the work will be rewarding. Of course, if you fear the arrival of kittens, perhaps foresee possible disaster or feel anxiety about the entire enterprise, then this is not for you. You should have your female spayed or your male castrated, and enjoy them as companions. But if you are enthusiastic about the prospect, even while you recognize the annoyance that will develop, then by all means go ahead. In a sense, if you do not have your cat neutered, you owe her or him at least one litter.

One of the first things you must do—and this may sound strange—is to determine the sex of the cat. Obviously, if you bought it at a pet-shop or from a breeder, you know its sex from the time of purchase. But if you picked up your cat as an orphan or from the RSPCA or some other organization, it is very possible you took over a 'cat', without knowing its sex. Here is how you do it, and you can use this information to determine the sex of any kittens you acquire, or when you buy a cat, to make sure you are getting the sex you want. Lift up the tail (gently) and take a look at its rear end. The female will have two darkened spots or holes, the round one being the anus and below it a vertical slit. That is the vulva. Think of it as the small letter 'i', in which the top dot is the anus and bottom part is the vulva. In the male, the anus and bottom dot representing the tip of the sheathed penis are both round. If the kitten is older or matured, the testicles can be seen or felt below the anus. But in the very young male kitten, you have nothing to go on but the two round dots: anus and tip of penis. In male cats, the testicles are not so evident as they are in male dogs and most other animal species.

Once you know the difference, you should know something about when they mature, when they should be mated and what, if any, problems are involved in breeding them.

But first of all, do cats need to be mated to have a normal life? Can you keep your female or male without neutering and still not mate them? Some authorities believe that an unmated female (one not neutered) will suffer emotionally and physically, and some of these authorities feel that the female should be mated more than once a year. Under this theory, you could find yourself with two or three litters a year (each pregnancy takes about nine weeks) in order to keep your female functioning normally. What this amounts to is a warning that you should have her spayed if you cannot face the prospect of a constant flow of kittens. Since most people want no more than a kitten or two, spaying would seem the only solution.

As for the male, an unaltered male will prove a nuisance unless used often as a stud. Since the male, once mature, is almost always ready for a sexual encounter, you really have no way of holding him down except through neutering. And even fairly frequent mating—in the back alley or on the side roads in the suburbs—will provide only temporary relief. As long as he remains without a female, the male will howl, shriek, rub himself, masturbate, pace up and down and spray with his urine on rugs, furniture and anything else available. The smell from spraying is extremely strong, tomcat urine being known for its 'musk', which means the smell that comes from activity in the testicles.

So here once again you have a decision: mate your male often or else have him neutered. One alternative, if you have the space, is to confine him in an outside kennel where he has his own run. Keep in mind that he will still cry out frequently and prove a disturbance to the neighbours. If you live in the country or on a farm, then there is no such problem. The male cat living separated from the house, with all his furnishings made of washable material, can remain unaltered and stable. Over ninety per cent of males are neutered, incidentally.

THE FEMALE

The female cat, like all females of the animal species, undergoes an oestrous cycle, which is another way of saying a heat season or period. It is *only* during this season that she will be sexually active. The male, as we have mentioned, has no such cycle, and thus is active at all times once he has reached maturity. The female comes into her first oestrous cycle sometime after six to seven months, although there are stories of earlier ages, even four months having been cited. The average number of seasons for the years is two to three, but this varies with the individual female. You may, then, have a female who 'calls' (is 'in heat') as little as once or twice or as much as ten to fifteen times. And the calling itself may last for three to five days, or it may stretch out for as long as two or three weeks. Certain females, especially Siamese, appear to be more sexually active than others and may give out the sexual song or call on almost a steady basis for more than half the year; another female may call for only a few days only once or twice during this period.

In this period the female will become more affectionate than usual; she will rub against you, attempt to masturbate and lick under her tail (where there may be some discharge from her vulva, which may also be swollen).

What is happening chemically inside the female is this: just before her oestrous cycle begins, the ovaries are preparing for pregnancy by secreting hormones. The interior walls of the uterus become suffused with blood, and eggs begin to develop in each ovary. The female will not ovulate without copulation. Ovulation usually follows about a day after copulation, and at this point the female is no longer receptive to the male. But if you leave her free, she will in the period before ovulation begins copulate with any male cat, and her resulting litter may combine many different kinds of kittens, depending on the males who serviced her.

Once ovulation begins, the ova, or eggs, pass out of her ovaries and move down the Fallopian tubes (oviducts), where the male's spermatazoa move up to meet them. When they meet, fertilization occurs, although it does not always take. When professional breeding is done, with a professional stud, usually the male and female are encouraged to copulate more than once to make certain that fertilization takes. Once fertilized, the eggs pass into the two forks or horns of the uterus, where they attach themselves and begin, as embryos, to develop into foetuses that will become kittens. With some physical modifications, the process is similar to what occurs in human conception.

THE MALE

While most of the action occurs in the female, the male should not be forgotten. While many male cats seem sexually interested in mating long before they reach maturity, they should not mate before they are close to a year old. I am talking now about mating in which you desire a particular kind of litter, and not mating just to relieve the male physically.

The male, or tom, is usually very aggressive in seeking out a female, but in actual copulation he may be uncertain. When professional mating takes place, the female is usually kept around the male for a day or two before any attempt is made to bring them together. And she is almost always brought to his territory, or else he may be too nervous or uncertain to perform. Confronted by a female in season, most males will, of course, respond, but it is not the instantaneous matter that most people think it will be. The tom must feel he is on safe ground.

Part of his temporary uncertainty is surely connected to the 'domestic' role cats now play, as distinct from their past roles when they roamed free. The free-roaming tom played by the rules of nature, and he marked out his territory by spraying urine scented with his 'musk' allure. Once his territory was so marked out, he would defend it, as other males would defend their space. A female in season who strayed into any of these areas would go to the victor, after the rest of the courting and mating ritual. Most male cats no longer run free, or if they do, it is mainly on farms. As a consequence, they do most of their spraying indoors if left unaltered.

MATING

The actual mating is a ritualized affair. While the male circles her, the female will do a dance of sorts—stamp her paws, rub against the floor or ground, crouch, brush against him. When they are ready, the male bounds over to her and pinches or even bites the back of her neck with his teeth. She raises her back end, exposes her swollen vulva and balances herself of her front end.

Actual copulation is quite rapid, without the 'locking' of penis and vagina common to dogs. However, the tom does have a barbed end to his penis— little barbs that cover the very tip of the penis. When the penis is pulled away after sexual climax, the barbs are activated and irritate the internal wall of the female. A possible explanation of the cry or scream that comes from the female at climax may be attributed to the action of the barbs, which are apparently very painful. In any event, the barbs seem to be an essential part of feline copulation and may well have something to do with conception. This aspect of feline anatomy is still not clear.

After copulation, the female may become very active and try to attack the male. She may swipe at him or go after him and on occasion become vicious. Breeders often provide a shelf or perch to which the male can jump to get away from the female's anger. This condition is temporary, however. The cats will groom themselves, lick themselves off and, if permitted, go at it again and again. If the female is free to roam, she may well mate and conceive with another male.

Some Advice

If you own the stud, you should give the female a couple of days at least on the male's territory. Do not try to rush things, as the stud will not always react right away.

If you own the female, plan on allowing her two or three days away—copulating on the second or third day of calling is usually best. If you are mating her for show purposes, or because you want the best possible kittens of their type, then you may have to take her some distance. Figure on several days, therefore.

The way to locate the stud service, if you want to mate a pedigree female, is to buy *Fur and Feather* or to visit a cat show and meet the breeders. Another method is to consult the cat fanciers that are listed near the end of this book.

It is advisable to visit the owner's house or the stud's living-quarters, for your cat will stay there until the pregnancy is reasonably assured. You want to be certain, of course, that the stud is free of any unwanted ailments, just as the owner of the stud will want proof that your female does not have feline enteritis, is free of parasites and has received her inoculations.

Once you are satisfied, if you have gone this far with the process, then arrange a fee with the owner of the stud. This may be a monetary fee, as it normally is, or pick of the litter, or some other arrangement agreeable to both owners. Put the agreement in writing. And also make some provision for the possibility that the pregnancy will not take. This can happen, and it may become the source of some contention if payment is made in advance without that contingency in mind.

If you are shipping the female by train or even plane, then arrangements must be made for pick-up at the stud's end and for the return trip. If you own a house cat and think that these arrangements are ridiculous, keep in mind that breeding for owners of pedigree cats is very serious business indeed. And it should be. The only way certain types of cats can be held to their standard, or the standard improved, is through careful selective breeding; and such care takes time, money and effort. Serious breeding is not for everyone, nor should it be; but for those who enjoy it, it can be highly rewarding.

If you feel you can turn your pedigree female into a steady money-maker, the chances are you are wrong. A single female, even if she produces two or three litters a year, requires a considerable outlay—for stud service, for veterinary fees for the kittens, for worming and so on. The only real profits that do come—and even they are only rarely sizable—result from running a full establishment and keeping the stud. A stud service is, in terms of profit, a better business proposition than breeding the female. But even the stud requires a considerable outlay, such as a good piece of ground away from neighbours, a kennel and run area, quarters for the females and other considerations. For most people, breeding is not a business proposition but one of love for cats and for a particular breed.

After Copulation

Copulation has occurred. You are reasonably certain the female is pregnant. By the way, if she gets pregnant as the result of a stray male, this litter will not in any way affect future litters. Also, if she is impregnated by a pedigree stud and also by a stray male in the same calling period, she may have a litter of mixed kittens, some from the stud and some from the stray.

Once impregnated, the female should lead a normal existence. Do not treat her as delicate or unusual. *This is a natural process for the queen.* Allow her normal exercise and her regular diet, and when you see that her appetite increases, adjust her food upward. Make sure she is getting plenty of protein and calcium, and if your vet advises it, put her on a vitamin-mineral supplement. Let her eat as much as she wants. Normally her food-intake will remain proportional to her body-weight. If she gains too much during pregnancy, you can cut her down once the kittens are weaned. The best way to increase food is to provide an extra meal—say, breakfast. Do not try to pile it on at one sitting.

What will be the positive signs of pregnancy? First, as I mentioned, the female's appetite will increase, and with that you may note a marked increase in food-intake. Second, at the third week or so, her nipples will turn a pinkish colour. Third, she may show a marked friendliness and affection. Not until the sixth week will an X-ray turn up evidence of the kittens, and by then, or shortly afterward, her belly will begin to swell noticeably. Kittens are such tiny foetuses that it takes nearly two-thirds of gestation time for them to become evident. Normal gestation time is nine weeks, sometimes a little more or a little less. Breeds differ, as does the same female during first or later pregnancies. But sixty-three to sixty-five days is what you can count on, and if you wish to alert your vet to the event, in case your cat needs help, then use that figure.

Before the kittens are born, prepare the box where the queening (you hope) will take place. See the chapter on kittens, pages 25-7, for that information. You should at this time acquaint the queen with this box area and try to keep her mind on it. She has her own instincts, which may mean using your bed or laundry pile for kittening—these choices are, of course, mysterious. In any event, you should try to locate her for the event where you think best. It may or may not work.

One other thing you can do is this: as the time of birth approaches, you may have to clip the hair away from the nipples and vulva. This may be necessary if you have a long-hair, for the hair will interfere with the kittens coming out of the vulva and then trying to get at the nipples. This is also cleaner, as well as easier.

As the female comes to term, her reaction may be anything from high spirits to extreme quiet. She is unpredictable, and different breeds, as well as different house cats, react differently. If you notice her sticking to a particular spot, you may suspect that she will make this the place for delivery. The best thing, unless she is frantically hyper-active, is to let her be. If she is hyper-active, consult your vet about a sedative.

BIRTH

Cats handle queening with little fuss and are among the most fastidious and efficient of mothers in the animal kingdom. For the most part, you can expect to do little or nothing. The rest should take place as a natural event. If you are anxious, make certain a local vet is available, and this is a good idea even if you are not nervous.

How will you recognize labour when it does come? The contraction of the female's uterus will show in movements of her sides. There may also be a sudden display of anxiety, highly-strung behaviour, restlessness, pacing. She may squat over her litter box and try to evacuate; she may salivate or have a dry mouth, indicating nervousness. She may scratch away at her post or whatever is at hand, or chew up favourite toys. You may notice some or all of these patterns at the onset of labour. The movement of the queen's sides, however, is the most reliable indicator. *At this time, make sure she cannot get outside.* She must be confined to some area from which she cannot escape.

You can expect three or four, perhaps five, kittens, although this can vary. Sometimes a litter is only one or two, but extremely large litters are rare. Kittens at birth weigh ¼ pound or less, and so your cat is carrying about one pound of foetuses. Since she weighs about 10 pounds, at most, she is carrying one-tenth of her weight in kittens. This would be the equivalent of a normal-sized woman carrying a 10- to 12-pound baby—almost twice the size of most babies. So she is, relative to her size, heavily burdened.

As time for birth begins, the queen will strain, as though at stool. She may strain like this for some time—first-time mothers may have some initial difficulty in expelling the first kitten, or else it may work out smoothly, without too much effort. Leave her alone to do the job, unless you see her straining hour after hour without any results. Kittens generally are born head first but, like babies, can occasionally come out as breech births—end around. When this occurs, the kitten may get stuck, as the opening is more suitable for head-first birth than for a body-first. If a kitten is stuck, and this is rare, it can often be freed by a gentle pull with a clean cloth. Be very gentle and try to grasp well up on the kitten's body. If this does not work, then a vet will be needed to help with forceps. You should not expect to have this problem, although it is possible.

Normally, the procedure goes like this. As the time comes for the first kitten to appear, the cat begins to heave and strain. The kitten may appear almost at once, or, more likely, when it is part of the initial litter, after several minutes or an hour. When the kitten comes out, it is enclosed in the birth sac, and it is not breathing. To allow it to breathe, the cat must clean off the amniotic sac, the thin skin or bag in which the kitten is born. The cat will bite through this and clear away the passages around the kitten's nose and mouth. At the same time, she will break the umbilical cord connecting her to the kitten. This is a crucial stage of the delivery. If the cat does not break the amniotic sac or membrane, you must do it, or else the kitten cannot breathe. It may prove too tough, or after a hard delivery, the queen may be too tired at this stage; or else another kitten may come so fast she does not have sufficient time.

Break through the sac and then with a piece of disinfected towelling or cloth rub away all the obstructive matter around the kitten's mouth and nose. This is the most important step, for without it the kitten may suffocate. One other important thing: be sure to keep track of the placenta (afterbirth) for each kitten. Attached to each kitten as it comes out will be the placenta— it will be connected to the umbilical cord, and it can be recognized as a reddish hunk of matter. During pregnancy, it served as the food-supply for the foetus. This must be expelled from the cat during delivery, for any part of the placenta may cause an infection if not expelled.

The queen may decide to eat the placenta, or she may simply let it alone. Eating of the placenta stimulates lactation (milk production). She may first clean off the sac from around the kitten and then turn to the placenta, or she may reverse the procedure. What you have to concern yourself with is: (1) that the queen breaks through the amniotic sac of the kitten so it can breathe; (2) that there is a placenta located for each kitten. Under normal circumstances, the procedure should go smoothly. I run through the entire procedure below, and you can follow step by step.

Through instinct, the queen recognizes that several steps are necessary for the survival of the kitten. It must breathe, it must be cleaned off and then it must be fed. These are procedures that are followed with human infants and nearly all other species in the animal kingdom.

Usually the second kitten does not come along until the queen has had sufficient time to take care of the previous birth. These intervals between births also give her time to rest; it is an exhausting procedure, since she must do all the work and the litter may run to four or five. Eating of the placenta may give her strength, although some queens prefer not to eat or drink during the entire process. Give only small amounts of water during this time, although she may be panting and seemingly thirsty. She is gaining nourishment from what she is cleaning off and eating, and it is sufficient for the time being.

The intervals between kittens may be a matter of minutes or of several hours. Breeds and individual cats differ. Another factor is whether the litter is the first (usually slow) or a later one (usually faster). The length of time involved should not concern you unless the queen strains and works very hard without producing any results. Also, the litter may be large, and that in itself takes time. There are natural protections built into the mechanism of animal birth, and in most instances they work as intended.

Difficulties in Delivery

I have already mentioned several of the difficulties that may occur during delivery, and I have given some of the ways in which you can help. *As you follow these steps through, you will see that they all have a solution if the problem is not too difficult.* If it is, however, then do not hesitate to call your vet.

1. Make sure you have a vet in the general area alerted to the birth of the kittens. You may not need help—and frequently just a phone call will be enough, but one should be available just in case you do.

2. The first problem may be that the queen strains and strains and nothing happens after several hours. This is an abnormal circumstance. Try to calm her, because the exertion may make her anxious and even frantic. Speak soothingly. Do not become frantic yourself. If nothing is really happening, call your vet for advice.

3. The birth instead of being head first may be a breech birth—in which the foetus's rear end comes out first. This is usually a more difficult kind of birth because of the larger bulk coming through the vaginal opening. Here you may assist by gently pulling with your hand covered by a clean washcloth or dishtowel. Since the foetus will be slippery, a rough-surfaced cloth is best. If you can obtain no result, or if you fear injuring the foetus, then consult your vet.

4. Once the foetus is delivered, you must be sure the amniotic sac is removed so that the kitten can start to breathe. If the queen is too exhausted, or for some reason remiss in this, then break through it yourself, with a gentle tear so as not to injure the kitten. With a piece of clean cloth, wipe away the mucus around the mouth and nostrils. Dry off the kitten and put it next to the queen so that it can begin to suckle.

5. Make sure that every placenta is accounted for. The placenta is the reddish mass attached to the umbilical cord, and it should be expelled. The placenta, or part of it, if left in the queen may cause a uterine discharge.

6. The umbilical cord, connected to the kitten's navel, must be cut. Normally the queen performs this operation, but if she fails to, then with a pair of scissors that you have sterilized in alcohol snip it off about an inch or so from the kitten's navel. Do not be afraid of causing pain; there is no feeling in the cord area at this time. Usually you do not have to tie the end—it will bleed a drop or two and then dry up, eventually dropping off.

7. If the cord continues to bleed, which is unlikely, you will have to tie it. The best thing is to loop a piece of string or thread around the hanging cord near the bleeding end. Pull it tight as you would a tourniquet. The tourniquet should stop the bleeding very quickly. Eventually, when she notices it, your cat will pull the string off, but during queening, she will be too busy.

8. If a kitten does not begin to breathe once the mucus is removed from around its mouth and nostrils (either by you or by the queen), then you must follow a firm course of action. If you do not, the kitten will die. Hold it firmly, with its head down, and swing it gently in an arc, stopping suddenly so that centrifugal force can push out any mucus that is blocking the air passages. Since the kitten will be slippery, wrap it in a clean cloth. This should work.

If it does not, rub its rib area vigorously to stimulate breathing. Do not push in as the rib cage is delicate. You can even try artificial respiration.

If none of this works, pull gently on the umbilical cord and rub the body with a towel, concentrating on the rib area, pressing lightly on the chest. Keep at it for several minutes. You may be successful, and the kitten will start to breathe. If you fail, it could not have been saved anyway.

9. Occasionally the umbilical cord has already broken away from the sac

when the kitten is born. It is then attached at its other end to the placenta. This is all right if the placenta is expelled with the birth of the next kitten. If you see this has not happened, often you can locate it with your hand wrapped in a clean cloth—that is, if the queen allows you to interfere.

10. On rare occasions the foetus becomes stuck even when it is a head-first birth, and you may have to give some help. Try to reach toward the foetus's shoulders, or below the head, and pull ever so gently. Try to set up a rhythm with the queen's labour contractions; if you move against her rhythms, you will do little good and perhaps even some harm. Be very careful of the kitten's head and neck. Do not twist the neck.

11. If the queen is too occupied elsewhere to clean a kitten off, you should do so. It is essential that it be dried off. Use a clean towel and rub vigorously (without pushing in). This is also good for its circulation.

12. If the queen does not start to suckle her kittens, put them right at the nipples. It is absolutely necessary for the kittens to get the first fluid, or colostrum, for that gives them temporary immunity against disease. Make sure all the kittens have a turn at the nipples—smaller ones may fall by the wayside.

As I have pointed out, your assistance will probably not be required. Cats make excellent mothers, and their deliveries are usually free of incidents.

After the Event
After the queen has delivered two or three kittens, or even one, she may be finished with delivering. You really cannot be sure, especially if the births have been strung out over several hours. If she seems to be resting and you think the end has come, feel very gently around her abdominal area, checking with your fingertips for lumps or bulges that may be more kittens. If you had an X-ray of her taken in the seventh week or later, then you may know how many kittens to expect. But if you did not and suspect there are more inside, you should call your vet. The chances are that if the queen is settling down with her kittens, the event is over. It is not a good idea for you to stick your finger into her vagina to see if there is another kitten there. You could do some damage, to her and to the kitten.

This should have been a pleasant time for you. Thousands of years of domestication have not blunted the queen's instincts for perpetuating the feline species. Her attention to detail is remarkable, but if she missed a point or two, you were present to help out.

Post-natal Care of the Kittens
For this information, turn to Chapter 2, where I deal with the care of the kittens from birth. If they have their mother, you will find what your role should be. If they should be orphaned kittens (where the mother is not to be found), I also have information for your role. Probably you will need the sections on what to do, if anything, when the queen is present and nursing.

Post-natal Care of the Queen
Although the kittens are born with eyes closed—and will remain that way for

nine to ten days, they will find their way to the nipples, and the queen will nurse them. Shortly after delivery, she will probably want to relieve herself, if she has not already done it during queening. Her litter box should be nearby, so she can do it and return rapidly to her litter. It is, of course, possible that in expelling her kittens she also evacuated, but cats are so fastidious that unless she is out of control this will not occur.

All her attention will be on her litter. *Do not remove any of the kittens.* In the rare instance that the queen ignores her kittens, you will have to take over, as I describe it in Chapter 2, but you can normally expect her to do the whole job—feeding the litter and cleaning up after them. This is not a good time to bother her. If the household is a noisy one, try to keep down the din, or else she may become upset. If you have a dog, keep it away.

Make sure that every kitten has a turn at her nipples. The number of nipples is usually sufficient for all but the largest litters.

Your role in this really falls into three parts:

1. Make certain that the queen and her litter are allowed peace and quiet. Small children should be allowed a look but no fondling or picking-up at this stage. The kittens are too delicate, and the queen is too anxious about them. The kittens should be touched only if they are not getting enough time at the nipple. The queen, indeed, might well scratch or bite anyone who tries to play with the kittens. Like all animals, a nursing cat can be unpredictable here.

Another thing: if the male who impregnated the queen is available, do not bring him in to see the kittens. He will not know them, and the visit has no meaning; bringing him in could, in fact, create an ugly situation. The queen may sense an enemy and attack him or abandon the kittens in her frantic search for somewhere to go.

The best thing is a tranquil period that lasts several days until a definite routine has been established.

2. The second thing you must be certain of is something I have already mentioned. Very often the smaller kittens, or 'runts', get closed out from a nipple or for one reason or another are simply not getting enough time feeding. At this stage, a lack of food—the kitten weighs no more than 3 or 4 ounces—is very serious; plus the kitten needs the antibodies in the queen's colostrum. If you see any kittens that are being shoved aside or overlooked, place them at a nipple. If they still will not feed, then you must do it with an eyedropper or drops of milk on your fingers or palm. See Chapter 2 for how to feed the orphaned kitten. The neglected kitten is, in a sense, orphaned.

3. The final thing you must watch out for is the food-intake of the nursing queen. She will probably eat an enormous amount, up to three times what she is accustomed to. You should arrange to give her food whenever she wants it. The main part of her diet should be proteins (meat and cooked fish), fats and calcium—cow's milk *if she can digest it* or some kind of dairy-product if she is unable to take milk itself. Siamese are often unable to digest cow's milk. Often goat's milk works well. You should also give her a vitamin-mineral supplement, for the drain on her body is enormous.

Weighing perhaps 10 pounds, she is feeding three to five kittens who will double and triple their weight before weaning.

The best thing is to follow the diet you were giving her up to the time of kittening, but give her unlimited amounts. You can tell how much she is eating and simply give her a little more. If she finishes that, increase the supply.

If you follow these three precautions, everything should proceed normally.

Some Tips

Immediately after the queening, it may be a good idea to keep the food light. Labour has taxed her, and there was probably a good deal of nervousness. Some chopped meat in its gravy, or milk (if she is able to take it) with a raw egg, is a tempting dish. Start the vitamin-mineral supplement right away, or simply continue it from her pregnancy days.

In a short time, the queen will indicate that she has returned to normal. Except for nursing her litter, she will exercise normally and re-enter into the activities of the house. The recovery, unless there are complications, is extremely rapid. Nevertheless, keep down the excitement and do not let anyone threaten the kittens even in play. If she seems generally lazy, let her be. Different females react in different ways, and laziness is simply her way of recovering. If she seems listless, however, for several weeks after recovery, then be sure to consult your vet. And if she is not eating well, also seek professional help. Tests may be necessary.

A vaginal discharge may continue for several days—this is perfectly routine. The discharge contains the lining of the uterus to which the placenta was once attached, and it is being naturally eliminated. If it seems to continue for more than four or five days, or if it becomes unusually heavy or thick, then check with your vet. And if you see no discharge at all, your cat is probably licking it as it appears. This, too, is normal.

Another thing you might watch for is any abnormality about the breasts. The breast area should be swollen—that is normal, but if there is infection, there will be extreme sensitivity. If you touch around the area, the queen will jump with pain. This is a serious condition, and if you suspect some trouble, consult your vet. An infected breast is serious for the queen and can lead to the death of the kittens. They may catch the infection and fail to receive their proper nourishment.

The breast milk will last two or three weeks, unless the litter is exceptionally large, and then it will possibly be exhausted much sooner. Under normal conditions, you should begin weaning the kittens from the queen by the end of the third or the beginning of the fourth week. The queen will, by then, become indifferent or begin to push the kittens away. Of course, some queens continue to nurse on and on, and their milk-supply seems inexhaustible. But even when this occurs, you should wean the kittens and get them on a regular diet. My advice, as I mention throughout this book, is to put the kittens on a diet that you intend to keep. (See Chapter 2, for diets of kittens at various ages.) Once you have settled on one when the kitten is very young, stick to it.

I now mention a few things that really fall outside this chapter, which is on mating, pregnancy and queening in their normal course. One of the strange and rare phenomena that happen now and then is false pregnancy. You may have a female who after a sterile mating shows all the signs of pregnancy, physical as well as psychological symptoms. But there is, of course, no pregnancy, since she was not impregnated. It would seem the female is compensating for her lack of a litter by 'creating' one by herself, a circumstance that is seen not only in the human world but in the animal kingdom as well. Her teats will swell, her appetite will increase, she will begin to swell up with a paunch, and she will even make a nest for the kittens. In addition, she may become snappish and antagonistic, scratching at things. If so, keep your children away, or she may in her anxiety scratch or bite.

The false pregnancy lasts about five weeks, perhaps as long as two months. The pregnancy was purely psychological, probably based on a hormonal imbalance. It is rare, but if you are disturbed by it, discuss it with your vet. If it recurs several times, the only way to deal with it is through spaying.

Another condition, this one related to real pregnancy and queening, occurs when the female begins to call again for a male even while she is still nursing a litter. This is rare, but possible, and it may occur when the kittens are only a few days or a week old. Occasionally when this does happen, the mother's milk will begin to dry up—she physically changes so as to make herself ready for her new pregnancy. If this occurs, and you are not alert, the kittens may be sucking steadily but not gaining sufficient nourishment. In that circumstance, you will have to provide supplementary feedings. (See Chapter 2, for how to feed an orphaned kitten.)

Make sure that your cat while nursing does not run outside, or else she may possibly become pregnant again. This would be far too soon, for her condition is somewhat run down from the exertion of labour and queening, followed by nursing. You should figure on a litter a year, if you want all those kittens. Two a year is a considerable physical burden on the female.

For determining the sex of the kittens, see page 160.

Once the kittens are weaned, cut down on the queen's food-consumption. She may have grown accustomed to the extra rations, and if you let her indulge, you may end up with an overweight pet. This does her no good. Bring her food portions back to what they were before she became pregnant. Eliminate the vitamin-mineral supplement on the advice of your vet. He may wish to see her to determine if she is in sound condition. If all of this sounds too cautious for you, remember that when animals lived in the wild they died if anything went wrong. You keep your pet alive by diagnosing any abnormal condition and rectifying it.

At this point, pick up the care of the kittens, in Chapter 2.

SEVEN

The Older Cat

When your cat ages—say, passes its eighth year, you should not feel that your enjoyment of its presence and company will diminish. These years can be among the best for you and your cat. By this time it has become an active participant in every aspect of your family or single life and knows your routine, as well as you know its routine. Although a cat will not demonstrate the slavish devotion of a dog over the years, it has definitely attached itself to you and, in its way, shows its loyalty and devotion. Cats are not the impersonal creatures that common talk makes them into.

Generally, most cats that were healthy to begin with and received a good diet and attentive medical care throughout their lives can be expected to live from twelve to fifteen years, and in many cases much longer. The eighteen-to twenty-year-old cat is not so unusual now that we know about correct diets and enjoy new developments in medical science. One certain thing: you should not begin to treat your cat as aging or old until it begins to send out signals that it is slowing down. Some cats are as perky in their twelfth year as they were in their third, whereas others seem to slow down at a relatively early age—much like people, who have different metabolic rates and rates of development and decline.

Just what are the characteristics of old age in a cat? Are they similar to those in human beings? What are the equivalent ages of cats and people? What evidence will you have that the aging process has even begun? What precautions, if any, should you take with your aging pet? How long can you expect the house cat or the different breeds to live? Can special treatment—diets or exercise—appreciably prolong the life of your cat? These are some of the many questions that cat-owners ask me all the time. Not all of them have precise answers, since cats do differ, but I will try to answer them and many others during the course of this chapter.

As I mentioned above, the cat of twelve to fifteen years is not at all unusual.

There is no difference between male and female in this respect. Nor is there any difference between a cat that has been neutered and one that has not, or between one that has been mated and one that has not. The cat by one year has matured, and so it is equivalent to about the first fifteen of a person's life. After that, each year of a cat's life is roughly (very roughly) equivalent to five or six of a person's, so that a cat of ten is about the same as a person of fifty-five to sixty. You can see that the cat of fifteen is quite old in human terms.

A cat that has led a happy, secure, balanced and stable life will usually enjoy a longer existence. This is not always true, of course, since some old alley fighters who struggle their way through life can turn out to have a very strong hold on a long life. But we are speaking of averages. The cat that has no outstanding illnesses, or if it had, illnesses that were promptly cared for, will live out its entire allotment of years. The cat that has suffered through serious diseases, such as feline enteritis, may have its life cut short no matter how good your treatment is in subsequent years. Its constitution has been weakened, and there is little you can do about it. Preventive medicine is perhaps more important than any other factor if you wish your cat to live out its years. Inoculations, boosters, special attention to symptoms of illness—all these are factors in prolonging life and in postponing the decline that comes with old age.

Correct nutrition—proteins, fats, calcium—for the kitten will extend into the later years, giving it sound bones, good teeth and excellent muscle tone. The cat's diet should not lead to overweight, for this will in turn lead to a heavy, sluggish cat and shorten its life. Besides correct nutrition, a draught-free place for the cat to sleep in will keep it free of arthritis and rheumatism, conditions to which any older animal becomes prone.

Certain indefinable factors also help to keep the cat longer-lived. Although a cat does not appear to be responding directly to the personality of its owner, a nervous and anxious household will take its toll on its pets. Studies are still inconclusive, but the general feeling is that the cat will react with faulty appetite, digestive problems, even heart ailments when the household creates a sense of insecurity. The cat may try to compensate for what it cannot understand by over-eating or losing its appetite altogether.

Even though independent, a cat likes to know what to expect, and a household in which everything is topsy-turvy will upset its pets. Keep in mind that a cat may never leave the flat or house in which you live, and therefore it is responding at every minute to what goes on inside. Mixed-breed cats, incidentally, are as susceptible as purebreds to tenseness and anxiety in the home. Some breeds may be more highly strung than others, but they are all affected by an unsure atmosphere. These things, in turn, shorten life or speed up the aging process.

The more we learn about pets, the more we see how they integrate themselves into the life of the household. You may think your cat is unresponsive, but it is aware of gesture and tone and attitude. In the kitten, in particular, poor treatment and an unrelaxed atmosphere may lead to a very nervous and sick animal. Although at the time the kitten may appear to be concentrating on sheer survival, it is nevertheless being affected, and there is some reaction. Like children, cats are sharp observers of the home situation, and to some extent the cat's psychological as well as physical condition will determine how long it lives.

For all the higher animals, there is a process called homeostasis, a tendency to regulate the internal equilibrium of the body. Such elements as body-temperature, composition of the blood, metabolism, pulse-rate (heart-beat) and blood-pressure are all kept in balance. As the individual person or animal ages, the delicate balance that we take for granted in youth is upset or, at least, impaired. We take it for granted in youth because it seems to be working automatically. But during the aging process, the living organism no longer responds in the same way to heat, cold, exercise and other stimuli. Certain compensatory elements are necessary to restore the equilibrium that the body once possessed. It is to provide such compensation that we give the older cat special attention, *when it needs such attention.*

Most of the time the aging process in an animal occurs over a period of several years, so gradually that it is almost imperceptible. The exception would be when a severe illness or accident ages your pet rapidly. Usually, however, the effects of aging do not all appear at the same time or in the same degree of intensity. While one change is noticeable—perhaps a duller coat or loss of back-leg muscle tone, another may not occur at all.

SOME SIGNS OF OLD AGE

What, then, are some of the ways you know your cat is aging? The older cat tends toward heaviness or leanness, depending on the amount of exercise it gets, and, of course, on the individual cat, whether pedigree or mixed breed. As the cat's metabolism begins to slow, an unchanged calorie intake can well lead to excess weight. A cat of 8 or 10 pounds can begin to edge toward 12 or 14, a proportionately tremendous increase, equivalent in a person to 30 or 40 pounds. On the other hand, the aging process can lead to digestive upsets—vomiting, diarrhoea, constipation—that result in loss of weight. A cat of 10 pounds can go to 9 or 8, or less. None of this means that all cats go through either phase; some appear as youthful as ever at eleven or twelve, whereas others begin to lose their sparkle and tone at seven or eight. Sometimes congenital factors are involved, and there is simply nothing you can do about it except give your pet good care.

The skin glands of the older cat become less active, resulting in drier hair, sparse hair growth on the abdomen or other parts of the body, even a certain scaliness of the skin. The sheen and smoothness of the young cat's coat begin to disappear, and the hair around the muzzle turns white. The aging cat can even become bald. The skin may tend to thicken in places. Calluses may form on the hocks (the bone on the hind leg forming the joint that is the cat's true heel), on the elbows (the joint above the forearm on the front legs) and on other bony areas. Even the pads on the feet may thicken, forming a horny spur that must be cut away. Since cats are not heavy, they do not develop corns, but their nails may become brittle.

Constipation is another condition the older cat may suffer from, due partially to a slowing-down of bodily processes and, usually, less exercise. Whatever the cause, be on the look-out for chronic constipation, whether in the older or younger cat. Also, make sure you do not confuse simple constipation with a serious condition a cat of any age can suffer from: feline urolithiasis (see page 191 for a description).

Digestive upsets, if they exist, are part of the systematic slowing-down that takes place over a period of time. Corresponding disabilities occur in the cardiovascular (heart), respiratory and genito-urinary (kidneys, bladder, uterus, ovaries, testicles) systems. These are evident in the cat's shortness of breath after exertion, in its lessened resistance to disease and stress, in dribbling in females, in the cat's decreased ability to stand extremes of cold and heat,in loss of muscle tone, sometimes in increased thirst (as apart from the thirst that accompanies a specific illness) and in slowness of recovery and repair after illness.

The female's teats may begin to sag with the nipples becoming enlarged and wrinkled. The unspayed female, particularly one who has never been mated, may develop tumours, cysts and cancer of the mammary glands. Skin tumours become more prevalent in both males and females. With the decrease in skin tone and the resultant dryness, the skin becomes less supple, more subject to disease and parasites. All these, when they do occur, are gradual processes. Do not expect your pet, male or female, to develop suddenly all these conditions; and many individual cats glide through old age with a minimum of difference in their appearance.

There is, also, the possibility that your cat will become increasingly deaf, and blindness, the result of cataracts or other afflictions, is also seen in the older cat. Eye-discolouration is not uncommon.

Even teeth may give the aging cat trouble. Although a cat's teeth are exceptionally strong, they may develop tartar. More common than tartar is a general erosion, a loss of enamel, perhaps sensitivity or gum recession, leading to possible infection and loss of teeth. If your cat has gnawed excessively on hard objects, bones or stones, its teeth may be worn down more than those of a cat who was accustomed to relatively soft foods and few bones. The teeth should be scaled (the calculi and tartar removed) to avoid gum recession—much as human teeth must be cleaned periodically.

Hernias may also appear. In the male, what is called perineal hernia occurs when the muscle weakens and ruptures, allowing the intestines to cause a pouch at the side of the anus. It is not very common, however. Many times the hernia is caused by chronic constipation, from the daily straining at stool, which puts stress on the muscles of the rectal area. The condition can be surgically repaired if it is serious.

In addition to these possible afflictions, there may be growths, prostatitis (not commonly seen because most males are castrated before their prostate gland can become inflamed), pyometra (pus in the uterus), ascites (fluid in the abdominal cavity), anaemia, otitis (ear-infection), increase in body and mouth odour, lameness, nephritis (kidney inflammation), Kidney ailments are especially prevalent and may have been present at times in the younger cat but went undetected because they were not acute.

In more general terms, your older cat will probably sleep more, begin to develop a sunken-in forehead and find its hind legs beginning to weaken.

I will discuss in detail most of these and other ailments, but before that I want to assure you that veterinary medicine can now treat with some degree of success virtually every affliction your aging cat may suffer from. Once surgery was not even attempted on the older pet, but now new techniques, modernized anaesthetics and more advanced knowledge in the field of post-operative care make surgery a procedure that you need not fear. If your cat does suffer from any serious ailment in its old age, you can be sure that modern hospitals are ready to take care of it, that vets are fully aware of the recent advances in their profession and that the life of your cat is held precious by all who care for it.

As your cat grows older and certain physical activities bcome harder for it, or it suffers from aches and pains that are entirely new to it, it may begin to behave in a different way or seem 'strange'. An older pet becomes less adaptable to change, and it will expect the house routine to continue as it has always known it. Even the shifting of dinnertime for an hour or so may prove upsetting. Your cat may not eat, or it may cover up its food or throw it around out of sight. As it slows down, it may need more reassurance— despite the fact that cats usually preserve a degree of independence. Since they were originally not clannish, they do not become this way even later in life, but they do require reassurance. If you bring another cat or pet into the house, there could be considerable resentment. A good deal of scratching of rugs and furniture may occur, or even some mischievous avoidance of the litter box. Such resentment may not be strong, but with individual cats that have enjoyed the run of the household, there can be nasty flare-ups. If you bring in a kitten or a puppy, be sure it is not bullied by the older cat.

If you do bring a young pet into the house against the day when your old cat will no longer be around, then do so carefully and discreetly. Do not concentrate all your attention on the new pet. While its beguiling ways will charm the entire family, do not slight your old cat, whose feelings will be injured by the new centre of attention. Assure it constantly that it stands first in your affection. Do this by plenty of play and patting. Spend more time, perhaps, than you normally did when you had only a single pet. Sometimes, if the situation is handled well, the arrival of a new kitten or puppy gives the older cat a second lease on life. It will teach the newcomer tricks and get it used to the new environment.

If your old cat becomes aggressive or irritable, do not think any the worse for it. It may be suffering twinges of arthritis, or one of several other ailments, all of which can make it feel anti-social. A cat does not usually complain—it may, in fact, withdraw altogether, and its periods of fretfulness may be your only clue. If you see that such behaviour continues and you cannot locate a particular reason—no signs of fever or diarrhoea, for example, then consult your vet. It could be the aches and pains of aging, and medication may prove beneficial.

Even if it causes you some inconvenience, try to keep your cat's surroundings as much the same as possible. Familiar smells and sights offer it assurance, even when its senses become less sharp. Like people, most pets as they age dislike any sudden shifts in locale or routine. The cat's sense of smell becomes its way of *knowing* and compensates if the eyes and hearing are beginning to fade. Even in matters as simple as the frequency of its meals, if you have accustomed your mature cat to one meal a day, then stick with it unless there are medical reasons for some change. If your cat is used to one meal with a late (or early) snack, then continue that. Even in the wild, where it was once believed that the large cats led a haphazard existence, it is now known that they follow definite patterns of behaviour, in their eating- and sleeping-habits as well as in mating.

The older cat needs some exercise. If you walked it on a leash, as some people do, then continue to do that, If exercise took other forms, such as play-periods that the cat is accustomed to, do not stop. Perhaps a little less exuberance is called for but certainly not complete cessation. You should try to keep your older cat trim and firm. Of course, if you exercised your pet very little—which is normally the case for flat-dwellers, then do not suddenly begin. Control your cat's muscle tone and weight through diet, chiefly, and do not attempt hard exercise with a cat unused to it.

You can really give your cat a psychological blow if you suddenly kennel it or board it out. The pet used to being boarded out while you go on holiday will accept it. But the old cat who has never been boarded out, or only infrequently, will sense something wrong, and it may go on a hunger-strike or become a very fussy eater. Some cats, of course, react more unfavourably than others, and some breeds resist it more firmly.

Many catteries do not like to take older pets, as they create several problems. If you must leave your cat temporarily or permanently, make sure that you give the cattery-owner a list of instructions, which he will attempt to follow as far as possible. This special attention may cost you a little more than his minimum daily charge, but it is worth it. Leave with your cat, as you would with a child, its favourite toy or blanket, whose smell will remind it of home. Try to have the same diet maintained, with the same number of feedings; this, too, will provide continuity and blunt the effects of the sudden shift. If your cat does change in behaviour after it has been boarded out, do not blame the cattery-owner. He has probably done all he could, but the aging cat will almost always react adversely to sudden changes in its routine. This does not apply, of course, to all cats in all circumstances.

GENERAL CARE

This section is devoted to the general care of the older cat that does not suffer from any specific ailments resulting from old age; I discuss the ailments later on.

1. When your cat passes six or seven years, keep in touch with your vet a little more than you usually would. Do this even if there is no history of illness. Little things have a way of developing. A six-monthly check-up is a way of making sure that nothing serious is developing. Also, your vet

may be able to give you some additional advice about the care of the older cat.

2. Do not make any unexpected or sudden physical demands on the older cat. That is, do not begin to exercise it madly; if it is accustomed to exercise, continue it. But do not let your cat get too worked up or exhausted. Keep stress to a minimum. If the weather is hot, keep it indoors. Make sure plenty of water is available. In the cold, you might consider a coat if you take your cat outdoors. The long-hairs have plenty of protection, but the short-hairs may be chilly, and the older cat's heating-mechanism is less efficient than it used to be.

3. Cut down on the calorie-intake of your pet as it grows older. Since most cats receive little exercise, unless they are on a farm, you can assume that as they age they will need less fat-content. Remember their nutritional needs remain constant, but their calorie-intake can be decreased by anywhere from five to fifteen per cent. Do it gradually and watch your cat carefully to see what is happening to its weight. If you cut drastically, you will have a ravenous pet. If your cat does seem terribly hungry, then break the food into two meals. But there should be no weight-increase—your cat should maintain the same weight throughout its life span. If it is overweight to begin with, do not fear it will starve. It can live off the extra flesh until it comes off.

4. The chances of a cat confined in a flat getting worms is very slight, but if your cat is at all active outside—on a farm or allowed to run free in the suburbs or the country, then worms are a real possibility. Take a stool specimen to your vet about every six months to be checked for worms, even when you see no evidence of worms.

5. As your cat gets older, groom it more. This applies to the long-hair and short-hair varieties, to the pedigree and mixed breed. Frequent grooming stimulates the skin, keeps it fresh and gives the coat a more vital, vibrant look. Since age definitely affects the skin texture and quality, the older cat picks up parasites, fleas and ticks more readily, and careful grooming will help eliminate them. Grooming is a matter not only of appearance but of health as well. Parasites can deplete the older cat's strength and lower its resistance, whereas the younger cat might have shrugged them off as a nuisance. To improve skin tone for the older cat, your vet may recommend supplementary vitamins and minerals as well as food-additives. But no matter what the particular case, all cats of every age need daily grooming, and the older cat most of all.

6. Keep your cat's nails trimmed. You can either have them trimmed by the vet or do it yourself according to his directions. If your cat is active outside, the nails may be worn down and need less attention, but if with age your cat roams less or seems less inclined to exercise, then the nails will become long much faster. For the cat kept in a flat, the nails grow rapidly, since there is little friction on rugs or wooden floors. Very long nails that go unattended may affect its gait. Also, you want to prevent broken or ingrown nails; the latter is particularly painful. Of course, if your cat has been declawed, there is no problem; some owners prefer to do this to save furniture and rugs. In Britain declawing does not, on the

whole, meet with veterinary approval, and cats which have been de-clawed may not be shown under GCCF rules.

7. Although cats usually regulate themselves very adeptly, you should watch out for the older cat—in fact, a pet of any age—in very hot weather. Make sure there is circulating air and plenty of fresh water available.

If your cat seems to be suffering in some abnormal fashion—vomiting, heavy breathing, inability to stand or wobbling when it does stand, then you can suspect heat prostration and call your vet. In the meantime, spray your cat with cool water or even place it in a basin of cold water, keeping the water shallow. The older cat will be more susceptible to heat prostration than the younger one. The condition is very rare.

8. A cat's teeth usually cause little or no trouble. Cats do not ordinarily suffer from cavities if they have had a balanced, nutritional diet, and their teeth do not break off. But there can be bacterial infections or simply the wearing down that comes with age. Cavities, calculi and tartar can develop in the older cat. If you suspect tooth problems—if you see your cat favouring one side or the other, or shying away because of pain or discomfort, keep it on a soft diet and get in touch with your vet. An extraction or other treatment may be necessary. But this is not a usual problem, except in older cats.

9. If your cat's eyes run and if the vet has assured you that there is no ailment, simply wash out its eyes periodically with a good eyewash. Follow directions on the package. Sometimes soaps or dyes used in the home may cause the cat's eyes to tear.

10. Be alert for any general listlessness or exhaustion in your cat, some-thing that goes beyond the natural decrease in energy that age brings. The causes may be of several types, of course, but one of them is anaemia. Anaemia is a condition in which the red corpuscles in the blood are either reduced in number or become deficient in haemoglobin, and the result is loss of energy. A vet can easily tell by means of a blood-test and give your cat medicine or injections that will bring his blood back to normal.

11. You should avoid bathing the older cat, unless the conditions are perfect—warm indoors or outdoors and no draughts. Bathing is not really necessary, and the older cat may become chilled and sick. Daily grooming and the cat's own fastidious cleanliness should be sufficient. If there is matting from food or other causes, use a wet washcloth or sponge and then dry off the spot. If your cat has been outside in the rain or snow, dry it off when it comes inside. If you use a soap to wash it, buy a non-irritant variety. It may cost a little more, but you will not use much of it.

12. A real possibility for the older cat, as for nearly all older pets, is some kind of kidney malfunction. I describe the full range of kidney malfunc-tions and symptoms in the chapter on ailments. Here let me say that, if you notice marked increase in water-consumption along with an increase in urination, you should suspect a kidney ailment, although it may not be present. Any extreme thirst is the sign of some possible trouble, and you should consult your vet. Make sure your cat has a plentiful supply of water. The condition may be very minor, or it may require treatment. Sometimes a cat will 'lose' its fastidiousness about urinating in its litter

box, because it does not have immediate access to it. The cat has not lost its housetraining, but it is under terrible pressure and cannot hold its urine. Make sure that a cat with a kidney ailment has easy access to the litter box inside, or access to the outdoors if it normally roams.

13. If your cat shakes its head as though it wants to rid itself of something, suspect ear trouble. It may be simply a parasitical infestation, or it could be a more serious condition. It may be a gradual loss of hearing—older cats do suffer from deafness, although it is uncommon.

14. Be on the alert for any rise in temperature—check the eyes for discolouration (reddish) and the tongue for whiteness. There may also be a general lack of health. If you suspect a fever, take your cat's temperature. Grease the thermometer lightly with petroleum-jelly and insert it gently into the cat's rectum; hold the animal tightly and wait two or three minutes. Normal is in the range of 101 to 102°F. By the time your cat is older, you know what temperature is normal for it and can act accordingly. A couple of degrees of fever can be serious, or it may indicate that your cat is in the early or intermediate stages of some illness. A high temperature in an older cat, as in an older person, is more dangerous than in a younger animal.

If you find a fever present or developing, keep track of the temperature and call your vet. A fever that is allowed to run its course for several days may lead to serious consequences. The fever may be nothing serious, or it may mean that your pet is incubating an illness or infection.

15. Like people, cats suffer digestive problems as they get older, and one of the manifestations of such a problem is chronic constipation. It is not serious, but it should be attended to, since it is unnatural and leaves a good deal of poisonous waste in your cat's body. Constipation can result from many causes: sluggish digestion, insufficient exercise, decreased peristalsis (movement of intestine), lack of coarse food in the diet (bulk or roughage) or hardened faeces in the intestinal tract. You may think your cat is constipated when it suffers from an anal irritation and simply chooses not to evacuate, in order to avoid pain. Or else, it may be suffering urolithiasis, which may cause the cat to strain for hours in its litter box.

Unless there is an organic breakdown, some bulk added to the diet usually clears up constipation. In fact, there should always be bulk in your cat's diet—I recommend it in the section on the kitten, and it should be continued throughout the cat's life. A few tablespoons of cereal may relieve the condition. Or try milk of magnesia. Many owners of long-hairs, and some owners of short-hairs, periodically give mineral-oil or vegetable-oil, so as to avoid the formation of hair balls. The oil also lubricates the system and prevents chronic constipation.

Often an increase in the number of meals (the same daily ration divided into several portions) with roughage will relieve constipation. The cat's digestive organs have less to work on at one time and may, therefore, be more efficient. If none of these methods is effective and your cat's constipation continues for several days, call in your vet. Temporary constipation is not at all serious, but chronic constipation may be cause for alarm, and it may also be the symptom of something more serious.

16. Sometimes the older cat dribbles, the result of the weakening of the muscle structure. If this occurs, your vet may perhaps recommend treatment.

17. The older cat may urinate more frequently. Since cats are meticulous about keeping themselves and their surroundings clean, they rarely miss using the litter box. But be on the alert for such an increase, and keep the litter box clean. The increase in urination may be the result of a weakening in bladder control—the muscles generally relax and make retention that much more difficult. Also, the older cat may tend to drink more water than usual, and that leads to increased urination. If your cat has a real problem here, it may be a good idea to keep more than one litter box around to prevent accidents.

18. Ask your vet about a vitamin-mineral supplement for the older cat. It may not eat as well as usual or absorb nutrients as efficiently. Sometimes supplements are necessary, but do not give them on your own, and do not use those taken by people.

19. Watch out for warts. They are easily removed, but do not confuse them with other tumours, which create different problems. A wart is usually a small hard protuberance on the skin, frequently rough and raw from the cat's scratching at it. It is probably caused by a virus and can be removed surgically or even eliminated by a vaccine. Also, do not confuse a wart with a tick embedded in the cat's coat. The tick can be removed, since it is embedded and not part of the skin. Ticks are rare.

20. You may notice small growths developing on your cat's skin as it grows older. Most growths, if caught early, can be removed without any harmful effects. Also, many of them are simply fatty tissue—unpleasant to see but harmless. However, some growths, if left unchecked, might develop into large tumours, which are far more difficult to remove. Sometimes one growth is removed for purposes of a biopsy, and if it is non-malignant, the other growths can be left alone unless they keep increasing in size.

21. If your cat seems to be blinking a good deal, look at the eyelids. Occasionally tiny growths will form on the edge of the lids, and these are, of course, troublesome. A vet can remove them or recognize any other eye-disorder that may be developing.

22. General digestive upsets may occur in the older cat when its intestinal action (peristalsis) is slowed down. The symptoms are discomfort, diarrhoea, vomiting and inability to absorb food, resulting in loss of weight, perpetual hunger and general ill health.

To combat this general condition, which is not connected to any particular ailment or disease, dietary changes may be necessary. If so, keep your cat off all gas-producing foods, such as vegetables, liver and kidneys. Instead, provide foods that are easily digestible—for example, chopped cooked meat, chicken and lamb. Your vet may recommend a dietary programme.

These twenty-two points describe general conditions: various aspects of your cat's health that are unconnected to any particular ailment. They tell you of some things you can expect in the aging cat, and most of them are no more than the natural processes we associate with any animal or person growing older. What works well in the younger animal begins to work less well in the older animal. In the discussion of ailments below, I will describe in somewhat greater detail those internal disorders that cause the dangers you notice in your cat. Many of these ailments require immediate attention. Others are simply symptomatic of the aging process and are not responsive to treatment.

AILMENTS OF THE OLDER CAT

Never try to handle any serious ailment in the aging (or even younger) cat. Home remedies are not only ineffective—they can be outright dangerous. As soon as you notice a symptom, consult your vet. If you act quickly, especially if the ailment is serious, you may add years to your cat's life. Surgery, if necessary, is now performed on older animals with a high degree of success. New medication and new developments in post-operative care also contribute to longer life. Certainly, kidney malfunctions, tumours, growths, inflammations, heart disorders and abscesses need immediate treatment if you want your cat to survive.

Kidney Disorders

Kidney ailments (for additional detail, see 'Ailments', Chapter 3) are rather common, running from one kind in which the cat urinates frequently to another kind (more serious) in which it retains the urine. The most common kidney ailment is nephritis, which is an inflammation of the kidneys. Nephritis may become more prevalent in the older cat. There are two types: acute and chronic.

If your cat is very thirsty and empties its water-dish more often than usual, you should suspect that a kidney ailment may be developing—or it can be something else. Take your cat to a vet for diagnosis.

Once diagnosed, acute nephritis calls for several precautions and immediate treatment. Provide water in small amounts, but frequently, and do not encourage your cat to exert itself too much. Avoid all foods that will increase thirst—ham, bacon and other salty foods (not highly recommended even for the healthy cat) or any spiced foods that you may give as table scraps. Restrict your cat to its regular rations or put it on a prescriptive diet. What the young cat ate and thrived on, the older cat may find too difficult to digest.

If the condition is chronic (not acute) nephritis, some of the symptoms may be a sharp increase in urinating, a generally unhealthy look, indifference, loss of weight, perhaps vomiting, bad breath, difficulty in walking and a dull coat. A cat may well survive with this ailment, but it needs immediate treatment by a vet. If you neglect the condition, uremia may develop.

In the meantime, provide plenty of liquids at frequent intervals in small amounts: water, broth, skimmed-milk if it agrees with your cat. Always take the chill off liquids; room-temperature is the best.

For both chronic and acute nephritis, a prescription diet may be necessary, although cats do not like it. If your cat refuses it, then a non-meat, high-carbohydrate diet is recommended: rice, pasta, honey, sugar.

Such kidney ailments may well throw your cat off its housetraining, so perhaps keep more than one litter box available if you have a lot of space.

Dribbling

If dribbling is the problem, your vet may recommend treatment; it may be a symptom of some specific disease. However, unless it is connected with some other disorder, dribbling is part of the aging process in which the cat's sphincter muscle loses its tone, and nothing can be done about it.

Tumours and Growths

Tumours and growths are fairly common in older cats, as in all older animals. They are seen in unspayed females who have never been mated and occur in the mammary glands. They also occur in spayed females. If you notice a lump forming or even a persistent swelling or inflammation of the breasts, alert your vet to the condition. The two breasts in the inguinal region (near the groin) seem to be more subject to tumours and growths, for they are usually the most active and therefore the ones most easily irritated. A vet might be able to control a tumour, if it is inoperable, through hormone injections or other treatment.

If the growth turns out to be malignant, then, of course, it will recur. After surgery, your cat may live to a ripe old age, provided that the growth has been completely removed. With modern methods of surgery and recently developed techniques, you should feel no qualms about surgery.

For the male, tumours in the genital area are rarely seen because most male cats are castrated at an early age.

Tumours are possible in nearly any part of a cat's body, both male and female. When you brush or comb your cat, you may notice small growths on the skin. If these persist—a pimple will go away in time, take your cat to the vet for an examination. Removed early, tumours, malignant or not, can be controlled, and your cat can live happily for many years. As I mentioned before, many of these growths are simply fatty tissue and harmless, although unsightly.

Deafness

Cats do suffer from deafness as they grow older, although it is fairly uncommon. If your cat begins to cock its head in a strange manner or paws at its ears persistently, you should suspect an infection or the beginning of one. Very possibly by the time you notice that something is wrong, the canal leading to the inner ear needs cleaning. Or the ear may be irritated, in which case the wax or collected dirt must be wiped out. As long as you do not try to dig into the ear yourself, you cannot do any damage. For a surface irritation or accumulation, use a piece of cotton dipped in baby-oil. If the difficulty seems acute, consult your vet immediately.

It is part of an animal's nature to worry a wound, and often your cat will try to relieve its discomfort by clawing at what is bothering it. A spot already infected will worsen, for the claws can carry bacteria into the wound.

If your cat has an infection in which the lining of the ear is involved, it must be treated by a vet.

Warts, also, may grow within the ear, and minor surgery under anaesthesia may remove the trouble.

Despite all your care, however, the aging cat may gradually be growing deaf. It does not realize it is growing deaf, and its other senses have already started to compensate. Your sudden approach from behind may startle it; or if it is awakened from a sound sleep, it may instinctively claw. If there are small children in the house, be sure to warn them not to startle their pet. If you have an infant crawling or just walking, keep it away unless the cat clearly sees the child coming.

ONE WARNING: With a deaf cat, it is better not to let it roam. Although its other senses can usually take over, nevertheless it may not hear a car coming in time to get out of the way.

Arthritis

Arthritis is another ailment the older cat may suffer from. Unfortunately, aspirin or aspirin compounds should not be given to a cat, unless your vet advises it. Aspirin can make cats very ill because it is irritating. One way to help is to restrain your cat to a warm dry spot, away from draughts. Also your vet may recommend medication or injections to alleviate the pain of those stiff joints that cause the discomfort. If your cat seems out of sorts and irritable as a result of arthritis, bear with it and let the vet help it whenever possible.

REMEMBER: No aspirin, unless specifically recommended by a vet.

Prostatitis

In the older male cat, there is the recurring problem of an enlarged prostate, known as prostatitis, although this is rare, because most males are castrated. The enlargement of the prostate gland may lead to difficulty in urinating. If he cannot pass his urine, the bloodstream will retain toxic products. If you notice that your cat is having difficulty in passing urine and that he is constantly trying, you should suspect a prostate disorder. Of course, another kind of ailment may be the cause.

An enlarged prostate may also affect the cat's bowel movement because the gland presses on the large colon and makes elimination painful. This can lead to a toxic condition and also to troubles such as irritation around the anus. Any kind of straining at stool is a trouble sign. He may be suffering from stones in the kidney, which can block the passage of urine to the bladder. In the male, the stone may also pass from the bladder into the urethra, making it impossible for him to pass urine. Surgery may be required before your cat regains his ability to urinate properly.

Female Ailments

The female may suffer from some specific ailments, such as metritis (an acute inflammation of the uterus, often with bloody discharge) and pyometra (an accumulation of pus in the uterus). Pyometra is a condition more prevalent in unmated females as they pass their fifth or sixth year. Its symptoms are similar to those of many other ailments: greatly increased thirst and urination, vomiting, loss of appetite, abdominal swelling and perhaps pain in the abdominal area, as well as fever. The vagina will often give off a sickly-sweet odour. Metritis, if untreated, can lead to pyometra. Its symptoms may be vomiting, thirst, little appetite and rise in temperature. There may be a bloody discharge from the vagina. Both pyometra and metritis need diagnosis and treatment by a vet and sometimes require surgery for correction.

Abdominal Swelling

Any abdominal swelling that is more than a collection of fat or the temporary accumulation of excessive food should be brought to the attention of a vet. Such a swelling may indicate ascites (accumulation of fluids), and it may be the result of a heart, liver or kidney malfunction. The swelling may also derive from an accumulation of tumours or from retention of fluids that the body would normally assimilate. Although it may be temporary, it is rarely a condition that will clear up by itself.

Your cat, probably, will not keep an unhappy condition from you. Its general appearance will worsen, its energy and appetite will wane, and it will no longer look healthy; it may keep to the shadows or disappear.

If the swelling is caused by a heart ailment, then of course your cat will need special care. Be sure to watch its weight and its exercise. The overweight cat loses months and years of its life even if nothing else is the matter. Heart pathology is generally present in the older cat. This is generally a long and slow process, not the kind that leads to a sudden attack. It can usually be caught as a 'murmur' by your vet during a routine examination. The murmur may itself be an indication of something serious developing.

Sometimes there are few warnings, however, and heart congestion or another condition will progress unnoticed. You may hear heavy breathing or see your cat breathing with difficulty because of the accumulation of fluid in the lungs. At this stage the condition has progressed, and the cat may not respond to treatment.

Treatment involves medication to increase circulation, to help the heart and to control water-retention. Such care and medication may prolong the life of a cat with heart disease.

Eye-Disorders

One of the common eye ailments of the older animal is conjunctivitis, although it appears in younger cats as well.

Conjunctivitis is sometimes accompanied by a redness in the white part of the eye, as well as by watering of the eye and sensitivity to light. It may be caused by a number of things, from foreign objects in the air to a toxic, feverish condition. To provide relief, wash out the eye with a medicated eyewash. You may also need an eye-ointment recommended by a vet. If the condition persists, it needs professional care.

Your cat may suddenly become hesitant about jumping to its favourite places, or it may hesitate when it enters a darkened room. If you notice any of these symptoms, examine its eyes. If there is a deep-seated bluish discolouration, it may have a cataract. This is not a common condition, but it is always a possibility in the aging animal. This blue-white discolouration means that the eye has probably been developing a cataract for some time. Professional treatment may postpone loss of sight.

No matter what precautions you take and no matter how devoted your vet is, however, a cat with cataracts is likely to lose its sight. Sometimes a surgical procedure will work, if you and your vet feel it is worthwhile. Such a loss, while understandably painful for you to watch, is not so much a disaster for your cat as you may think. Its other senses—smell, hearing, whiskers—will take it along all its old routes and to all its favourite places. Adjustment occurs almost imperceptibly. Unless you shift to new surroundings, it can live a perfectly normal life.

If you must place a blind cat in different surroundings, be aware of the upset and disorientation that will result. Give it extra consideration, including familiar toys, blankets or dishes; try to maintain some connection with its previous life. Cats adapt very rapidly, almost immediately, in fact, but the blind or partially blind older animal may need a little help from you.

Some Minor Troubles

In addition to these major ailments, there are several minor ones that may develop in the course of events. They may cause discomfort, although in themselves they are not dangerous.

Abscesses are more common in the older cat, particularly abscesses of the anal glands, between the toes, in the teeth or on any part of the skin from an insect-bite or a dog- or cat-bite. Abscesses must be treated by a vet. Even if you recognize one, do not attempt home cures.

For a fuller description of abscesses, as well as of flatulence and oedema, two other ailments the older cat is prone to, see the chapter on ailments.

Lameness is also more common in the old cat, or if not outright lameness, then a tendency to favour one paw over another. The reason may be an infection between the toes. An older cat, particularly one that is considerably overweight, is subject to infections of the feet because of generally lowered resistance, less vitality and less active circulation. This concerns the cat that is allowed to roam free, not the cat confined indoors. The cat will lick, gnaw and rub the infected area. Soak it in warm water or some other solution recommended by your vet. If the condition does not clear up, it may need more extended treatment.

FINAL REMARKS

These are the major and minor ailments most common in the older cat. The chances are excellent, however, that your cat will go through its later years with a minimum of trouble and will give you continued pleasure. A lot depends on the background and nutrition of the younger cat. A cat that inherits several ailments, or is prone to them, and a cat that has not enjoyed a properly balanced diet as a kitten, will obviously be more subject to ailments in its later years.

But these points aside, cats are hardy creatures. If your vet gives your pet a check-up every six months (certainly no more than twelve months apart), you are reasonably sure of protecting it against any serious ailment. And if you do take your cat in for an examination as soon as you suspect something wrong, you will control most ailments in time. These years with your cat may well be your finest, because it is an old friend and settled into the routine of the house. You should want your cat to be at its best, for then your relationship will be at its happiest.

EIGHT

The Breeds: Long-Hairs, Short-Hairs, Foreign

Although most house cats in Britain are not pedigree, the pedigrees are an established part of cat life and history. Of course, as pets and companions, there is no difference between the house cat and the pedigree cat. But for many owners, a pedigree cat gives them the opportunity to choose a colour, coat and personality that suit their own tastes. For example, a person allergic to the long hair of the Persian may prefer a short-haired cat, such as an Abyssinian or a Siamese. Or else an owner may want a particular temperament—even and affectionate as with the Abyssinian or more spirited as with the Siamese. Coat and eye colour (or combinations) may enter into it as well. Both the Persians and the Siamese offer a great variety of colours, either solids or varieties.

Further, an owner may wish to show or breed in a small way, and for that he or she needs a pedigree cat. For the person who just loves cats, the breeds are something lovely to look at, part of nature's abundance of varieties and distinctions. Some of the breeds are themselves straight from nature, but many are the result of careful selection, in which generations of cats have been mated in order to produce a genetic strain of a particular body and head structure, a fixed coat and eye colour, and a general configuration that follows a distinct standard for that breed. The cats that are described in this chapter are, for the most part, the result of the breeders' use of selection to produce a strain of cat that 'breeds true' generation after generation. After four generations of such breeding, a cat is eligible for recognition by one of the cat fanciers' associations, which regulate the breeds.

In the United States, the main division is between long-hairs and short-hairs. The long-hairs are still referred to as Persians, and the short-haired group includes the so-called 'foreign' breeds. Thus, for American classification, all long-hairs except the Angora, Balinese, Birman (not to be confused with the Burmese), Himalayan (or Colourpoint), Maine Coon and Turkish (the Van cat) are considered Persians. This category depends, then, almost completely on the coat length, for within this large group of Persians there are major distinctions of temperament, body configuration, eye colour, coat colour and even the coat itself.

British classification no longer uses 'Persian' to mean long-haired, and there is no attempt to group all such cats. Each recognized breed simply has its own standard. When British cat-fanciers make distinctions, they divide cats into long-hairs and short-hairs for ease of description, not because of any breed grouping. Also, the British tend to classify their cats as those intrinsically British and those that are foreign. At one time, the terms 'Angora' and 'Persian' were used synonymously.

To stick to the long-hairs for the moment: *the best thing for the reader is to forget any larger distinctions, which tend to be meaningless, and to concentrate on a particular breed: its coat, colour, eye colour, body structure, general look and temperament.* What counts is the particular cat, not the class or group to which it belongs. If you like a long-hair, then you can search for one whose colour pleases you. You might want a White, and then you have a choice of eye colour: blue, orange, copper or odd (one blue and one orange). If you like the Tabby—that is, one with black markings, then you have a choice of numerous colour-patterns with the black: blue, brown, cream, red, silver. Or you may choose for temperament: the Balinese, for example, has a temperament similar to that of the Siamese, although it has a longer-haired coat. Thus, there is a long-hair with the Siamese (a short-hair) temperament.

The short-hairs, in which American associations group their own domestic variety along with the so-called 'foreign' breeds, are also full of distinctions, in colour, eyes and body and head configuration. The sole thing they have in common is length of coat, although not all short-hairs are short-haired. The Siamese is the most popular breed in this grouping. The great attractions of the Siamese, in addition to its sleek and beautifully coloured coat, are its lithe appearance, its characteristic lean but strong body, its wedge-shaped head, which tapers to a sweet-looking muzzle, and its oriental-shaped eyes, which slant slightly toward the nose.

Another very popular short-hair is the Abyssinian. This breed resembles those we see in Egyptian art, where the cat was enshrined as an object of worship. The Abyssinian is noted for its 'fresh' look: alert, lithe, jungle-like; yet it is friendly and adapts well within the family. In terms of coat colours, the short-hairs offer a great variety. Within the Siamese alone, there are numerous 'point' colours; by 'points', we mean the muzzle, ears, tail and toes. The points may be blue, chocolate, lilac, red, seal (dark brown), tabby and so on.

But to single out these breeds is not to play down the others. The reader, once again, should see the short-hairs not as a single category but only as a form of classification; the thing that counts is the individual breed and the individual cat.

Whatever their grouping, the breeds have interesting histories, some of which we will pick up as we discuss each type. The origin of all cat species, long- or short-hairs, appears to be a weasel-like animal called the miacis.

From this primeval and quite vicious beast came, in evolutionary stages, the dog, weasel, hyena, lynx and what we know today as the cat.

THE LONG-HAIRS

Angora
History and Origin
The Angora derives from Ankara, Turkey's capital, and at one time was called a 'Persian', meaning that like the Persian it was long-haired. Nevertheless, the types differ, with the Angora being far more slender and lithe than the more massively built Persian. The breed was slow in making its way to the United States because of close Turkish supervision. In fact, only white Angoras were bred and raised. But by the 1960s it began to flourish. It may be seen in the Assessment Classes in Britain.

Characteristics
The Angora is a showman of sorts: affectionate, friendly and avid to learn and perform tricks. It makes a fine family cat.

Colour
The only acceptable colour is white; any mixture disqualifies the cat at shows. The eyes can be blue, amber or odd. (Deafness may be present, a factor in all white-coated cats, especially those blue- or odd-eyed.)

Coat and Body Structure
The coat is less heavy than that of the Persian, of medium length and of silky texture; it may wave, and it tends to become finer as the cat ages. The body is lithe, with a longer trunk than the Persian, giving the impression of sleekness and grace. While the cat may appear dainty, it is actually strongly built, although fine-boned and with tapering silhouette of both head and body.

Balinese
History and Origin
The Balinese was at one time called a 'long-haired Siamese', since it had Siamese qualities with a coat at least 2 inches in length. It was established as a new breed in the USA in 1968, as the Balinese. The Balinese differs from the Colourpoint Himalayan, another breed with which it was confused, by virtue of its similarity to the Siamese body structure, which is lithe, whereas the Colourpoint is of the long-haired type, with a more massive and solidly built body structure. It may be seen in the Assessment Classes in Britain.

Characteristics
Many of the Siamese characteristics are found in the Balinese, but the voice is lower, and the temperament seems more even. It is affectionate and yet an exotic showpiece.

Colour
The body colour—whether white, bluish-white or ivory—should contrast sharply with the points: seal-point, chocolate-point, lilac-point, blue-point and so on. Whatever the body colour, the points should be well defined and without any white. The eyes are deep blue.

Coat and Body Structure
The coat is long and silky, and it requires less grooming than for a long-hair. It sheds relatively little, mats hardly at all and requires little more care than that given to short-hairs. The body, like that of the Angora, is somewhat dainty, but lithe and muscular. The overall silhouette is of slenderness, with potential strength. Both head and body convey a tapering effect.

Bicoloured
History and Origin
Once known as Magpies, Bicoloured cats are those of any two colours, with all kinds of variety permitted: black and white, but also white with blue, orange or cream. The British standard calls for coat and type like those of the long-hair. The Bicolours are a long-recognized variety, and for a time there was an attempt to approximate the intricate patterning of the Dutch rabbit, but this was given up, and the colour-scheme is less formal. The Bicolour is now a standard feature in British shows.

Characteristics
The Bicoloured is a hardy cat, the result of some cross-breeding. It is solid, hardy and long-lived.

Colour
The standard with most registering bodies is a combination of any solid colour and white; no more than two-thirds of the coat should be coloured and no more than half white. The colour areas should be clearly defined and even. The eyes are round, set well apart and deep orange or copper.

Coat and Body Structure
The coat is like that of the long-hairs, and it needs careful and frequent grooming. Its appearance should be of clearly defined colour-patterns, with good contrasts. Texture is silky, like feathering, with frill and tail full. The body, resting on solid and short legs, should be massive, full, giving the appearance of solidity and strength.

Birman
History and Origin
Although Burmese in origin, the Birman, which is long-haired, should not be confused with the Burmese cat, which is short-haired and otherwise quite different. Many legends have grown up about the Birman, including one that made the breed the sacred cat of the Temple of Lao-Tsun. The breed as we know it did not begin to develop in the Western world until after the First

World War; it almost disappeared after the Second World War and was then revived in the 1960s, a period of great activity in cat-breeding.

Characteristics
The Birman is noted for its easy-going personality; it is affectionate, a good family cat, intelligent and loving. It also shows well, since it is not highly strung.

Colour
The standard is the seal, the blue, the chocolate and the lilac, with points, respectively seal, slate, cinnamon and lavender. The eyes should be blue, as deep as possible.

Coat and Body Structure
The coat fur should be silky and long, with the belly hair curled somewhat. The neck should be well ruffed. The body is stocky and strong; the front paws with five toes, the hind four. Overall, the breed conveys the sense of solidity; the head is also full and flattening out above the eyes.

Black
History and Origin
The Black is one of the oldest and most desirable of the long-hairs, although for some time in the nineteenth century it was quite rare. From the first, the difficulty came in trying to obtain the distinctive coat: black, flowing and of sufficient length. To gain that combination, it proved necessary to breed by outcrossing; that is, in order to produce a Black, a black-coated cat was bred with a blue (dam or sire) or with a tortoiseshell, cream and even red and silver Tabbies. In the United States, beginning at the turn of the century, the Black proved very popular.

Characteristics
Even with its luxuriant, flowing appearance, the Black is a gentle and easy-going breed. The males are recommended as studs, and as pets both sexes prove mild and affectionate.

Colour
The coat must be black to the roots, lacking any shading, rustiness or striping or markings. The eyes are orange or copper-coloured, without any green rim.

Coat and Body Structure
The coat is long and flowing and requires regular grooming, or else it will appear 'worn' or off-colour. The body is full, cobby and solid, with a broad head. Despite its size, the Black should look graceful.

Blue (Known in the United States as the Blue Persian)
History and Origin
The Blue or Blue Persian has proved to be a very popular breed and, except

Tortoiseshell-and-White
(Calico), Short-Hair

Norman Johnson

Colourpoint, or Himalayan

Maria N. and Carl Jaspan

Long-Hair, White

Norman Johnson

Long-Hair, Cream

Birman

HOUSE CATS

Typical house cat

Typical
house cat

Bobcat, kittens

Bobcat, adult

WILD CATS

Leopard (Afghanistan■

African lioness and cubs

Siberian tiger

Leopard cat

Puma or cougar or mountain lion,
juvenile, with baby spots

Clouded leopard

Jaguar

Palestine jungle cat

Serval

Snow leopard

Cheetah

Burmese or Siamese jungle cat

Marbled cat

Black leopard
(panther)

Flat-headed cat

Steppe cat, kitten

Caracal

Ocelot

for the Siamese, is the most shown of the pedigrees. The basic breed for the Blue derived from Turkey, probably, and was once referred to as Angora. This breed was of somewhat sleeker and smaller size then the Persian. By means of extensive breeding, self-colours (solid colours) were developed, although the process took a long time. By the latter part of the nineteenth century, at the Crystal Palace show in 1889, the Blue had emerged as a self-colour, without any tabby or white markings. The popularity of the Blue was enhanced by Queen Victoria's ownership of one, and continued ownership by royalty (the 'royal Blue') kept the breed in demand. It became popular in the United States after the turn of the century. In breeding, Blues are necessary to produce the Blue-Cream, by mating with a Cream female. This type of cross-mating is necessary, as the Blue-Cream males are usually sterile.

Characteristics
The Blue has plenty of personality, enjoying attention and, in fact, demanding it. It enjoys being made a fuss of and enters into the life of the family.

Colour
There should be no white markings or shadings; the colouring should be solid and even. The eyes are deep orange and should be large and round, not deep-set.

Coat and Body Structure
The coat should be thick, very long and soft, giving the appearance of a fur frill. It requires no special grooming procedures, however. The body now preferred as a standard follows the other long-hairs: broad head, small ears, massive, cobby body—all giving the sense of fullness but not coarseness or gracelessness.

Blue-Cream
History and Origin
Not until the late 1920s was the Blue-Cream recognized in Britain and not until 1931 in America. The controversy surrounding the recognition of the breed had to do with the colour-patterning, since the Blue-Cream was often referred to as a Blue Tortoiseshell, not as a definite breed. The reddish quality of the Tortoiseshell must be avoided, or else the Blue-Cream is not clearly defined. The typical mating is of a Blue and a Cream to produce the breed, usually female, for males are very rare and are themselves usually sterile.

Characteristics
The Blue-Cream reminds us of a canine pet, in that it attaches itself very companionably to one person, the owner. The breed is friendly and devoted and demands attention from its owner or members of the family. It is also known for its love of activity; it does not sleep all the time.

Colour
British and American standards differ somewhat. In America the colours should be clearly defined, not intermingled, with the body and head of alternating colours and with cream on at least three of the paws. The eyes are a dark orange that shades into copper. In Britain the fur must be the two colours softly intermingled.

Coat and Body Structure
The coat should be dense, of thick texture and yet soft and silky. The body is typically Persian: massive and cobby, the head almost round and quite broad.

Cameo
History and Origin
The Cameo, a pink-coated cat, was often bred by accident, but by the later 1950s it was bred to standard. Gaining the correct shading of coat colour is difficult and is best achieved by crossing a silver and a red. In America a Silver Tabby can be used, since the tabby marking is not a fault, creating a breed called the Cameo Tabby. The general standard is aimed at producing a red-coated cat with a silver undercoating. The shadings here can be very subtle, leading to six basic variations of Shell, Shaded Cameo and Smoke Cameo. All this must be attained without losing the copper eyes or permitting any green shading into the eyes. The cat is seen in Assessment Classes in Britain.

Characteristics
The Cameo, whatever its colour, should be a gentle and companionable cat. In such complicated breeding for purposes of coat colouring, there is always the possibility of producing a bad-tempered litter, but a good breeder will neuter those.

Colour
The colour-standard varies in Britain and America. In both, however, the Cameo should be of a pure colour, unmarked or unstreaked. In the Shell, the undercoat should be off-white (British) to ivory-white (American); the Shaded Cameo, red or cream down the sides to white-cream on the belly (British) and white undercoat (American); the Smoke Cameo, white undercoat in America, with red ticking (bands of colour). The eyes, as noted, must be copper-coloured.

Coat and Body Structure
The coat requires care, although probably no more than that devoted to any other long-hair. But since the breed was developed to gain coat variations, you might be willing to give bathing and combing a little extra time. The body structure is the typical cobby, massive build of the long-hair.

Chinchilla (Shaded Silver)
History and Origin
The earliest version of the present-day Chinchilla resulted from a cross-

breeding between a smoke-coloured and a Silver Tabby, but this early Chinchilla almost certainly had Tabby barring, which is now a fault for the breed. As the standard for the Chinchilla became more defined, the breed became caught between Persian standards of a cobby, massive body and its own more delicate appearance, without the heavy bone structure of the long-hair. Nevertheless, the Chinchilla has thrived and become increasingly popular in America, where it has taken many top awards. The Shaded Silver may be shown in the Assessment Classes in Britain.

Characteristics
Despite its 'in-between' status, the Chinchilla is not delicate; breeding for colour and body structure has not resulted in a weak or temperamental cat. Chinchilla litters are relatively small—usually three, at the most four. It is an easy breed to get along with, even though its 'magical' appearance may make an owner feel it needs special treatment.

Colour
The undercoat must be pure white, but the fur on the points and the back is tipped with black or silver, thus creating the silver effect. The Shaded Silver has shadings on its sides, face, and tail, forming a mantle and creating a darker colour than the Chinchilla. The eyes are blue-green.

Coat and Body Structure
The coat is quite silky in texture, as long as a long-hair's and very thick or dense; the frill is long, the tail bushy. The body structure is not so cobby as that of the long-hair, although the Chinchilla presents a stocky rather than a lithe appearance. In the United States the standard calls for a body as stocky as the Persian's, although the breed is really more delicate in its bone structure.
   NOTE: At birth it is often impossible to distinguish between the Chinchilla and the Shaded Silver, since both types of kittens are born with striping and can go either way. If you wish to register a Chinchilla kitten and it develops into a Shaded, or *vice versa*, then you cannot transfer the cat or show it.

Colourpoint (Himalayan in the United States)
History and Origin
The Colourpoint, or Himalayan, also once known as the Khmer, is the result of intensive and ingenious breeding. The aim was to create a breed with the long-hair type of body and long hair with the distinctive Siamese colouring. Until the 1930s the early types were not clearly patterned, most of them lacking the long-hair silhouette or hair length. The problem was to gain recessive genes from both dam and sire. By selective mating over a period fo time, the Colourpoint was stabilized.

Characteristics
The Colourpoint is much sought after by those who do not want an independent or impersonal cat, for it is very devoted and close to its owners. It is

warm and affectionate and requires attention as well as a display of attachment. The Colourpoint makes a particularly attentive dam.

Colour
There are six colour types accepted: Seal-points with a cream body, Blue-
points with a white body, Chocolate-points with an ivory body, Lilac-points
with a magnolia body, Red-points with an off-white body and Tortie-points
(Tortoiseshell-points) with a cream body. The point-colours should be solid
and well defined. The eyes are bright blue.

Coat and Body Structure
The coat is thick, long, soft to the touch, luxuriant, with a full frill.
Grooming is no different from that for any other long-hair. The body is full,
cobby, with short legs; the head broad and round. The body structure should
not in any way recall the Siamese.

Cream
History and Origin
The Cream (known as the Cream Persian in the United States) was developed in the early 1900s, but the breed did not begin to stabilize until the
1920s. Cream males were mated to Tortie females at first, but this failed to
produce the pale-cream colour of the coat; later, Cream males were mated
to Blues, and this created the standard for the breed. The breeding was
made doubly difficult because of the scarcity of Cream females, the result of
a genetic arrangement.

Characteristics
The Cream, despite its unusual pattern of breeding, has an excellent
temperament. It is affectionate and playful and demands attention from its
owner or family; it enjoys plenty of activity.

Colour
The coat should be pale and uniform cream, without shading or markings.
Eyes are coloured deep copper.

Coat and Body Structure
The coat should be flowing, giving a sense of luxuriance—long, thick and yet
silky in texture; the tail is short and luxuriant. The body is typically long-
hair: massive, cobby, with short and thick legs, the head broad with round
cheeks and a short nose. Very often the cream colour is itself sacrificed so the
breeder can gain the long-hair body type, but the glory of the breed is the
pale cream of the coat.

Maine Coon (Not Recognized in Britain)
History and Origin
The Maine Coon is an extremely popular North-American breed, probably
the result of interbreeding between Angoras brought back by travellers and
local New England cats. The early result of such interbreeding was a

'primitive' form of the Coon going back over a hundred years. But interest in the breed then decreased and was renewed only about twenty-five years ago. Since it can grow to over 30 pounds, the Maine Coon is robust and sturdy, befitting the cold climates in which it thrives. Its name derives from the fact that it was once thought to be part raccoon; with its tabby markings, the Maine Coon was even further associated with the raccoon, but that is biologically impossible. The Coon fits its landscape; with its large-size luxuriant coat and snowshoe feet, it is proudly a Down-Easter.

Characteristics
Despite its size, the Coon is not belligerent. It is an excellent family cat, good with children, intelligent and not noisy.

Colour
The coat may be any colour or combination of colours. The eyes should be complementary to the coat colour, green or otherwise, and should be piercing.

Coat and Body Structure
On the long-hair, the long coat stands out, making the body appear much larger than it is; on the Coon, the coat flows with the contours of the body, lying somewhat flatter but swirling in movement. Stomach feathering contributes to this appearance. Since there is little undercoat, grooming, while necessary, is relatively easy. The coat should be kept so that it falls smoothly and remains fine and heavy. The body is massive, but since it stands high on its legs, the cat appears powerful without seeming bulky. The head is broad, but the nose is much longer than that of the long-hair; the aspect should be of squareness and solidity. Any pointedness of features or an undershot quality to the chin is undesirable.

Peke-Face (Not Recognized in Britain)
History and Origin
This is a separate breed from the Red and Red Tabby Persian only in the structure of its head. The model for the Peke-face is the Pekingese dog, and that means a pushed-in nose structure, with the nose short and seemingly indented between the eyes. The result of the pushed-in look is to produce wrinkles on the muzzle that run from the point where the eye and nose touch to the outside of the mouth. The eyes of the Peke-face are slightly bulbous in appearance, because of the pushed-in nose, and they should be full and piercing.

Out-breeding—mating a Peke with a Red Tabby, for instance—produces the best Peke-face. Because of the 'crowded' face, there may be breathing-difficulties as well as bite-troubles, for correct mouth-closure may be impeded. Some of this depends on the individual cat.

The breed is popular in American cat shows but is not recognized in Britain.

For characteristics, colour, coat and body structure, see the standards for the Red and the Red Tabby.

Red Self (Solid Red)

History and Origin

The Red Self, or Solid Red, was known seventy-five years ago as the Orange, but it was not until much later that breeders attempted to improve the colour. By the 1950s, the Red Self as we know it began to emerge as the result of cross-breeding a Tortie female with a black male, to produce a dark red without faulty markings. The aim of such cross-breeding is to achieve the true red colour without the bars associated with Tabby markings. Part of the problem lies in the scarcity of Red Self females because of genetic difficulties. As a result, like-to-like breeding is still impossible. Torties bred from a Black mated to a Black will produce—besides Torties—a litter of Blacks as well as Red males and females. By further line-breeding, the Red Self can be developed. The kitten, incidentally, may not seem a true breed, as it may be marked at birth.

Characteristics

Typical long-hair temperament. See the Chinchilla, page 195.

Colour

The colour should be deep red, without any markings or barrings. The eyes are deep, intense copper.

Coat and Body Structure

The coat must be long, thick and dense, and silky to the touch. The body is typically cobby, with a broad round head and a flowing tail. Overall, the breed conveys the sense of solidity and strength.

Smoke (Black Smoke: same as the Blue Smoke, if you substitute 'Blue' for 'Black')

History and Origin

The Smoke is a cat of contrasts—it is often referred to that way—because of the alternating black and silver colouring. The ruff is silver, the face black, the ears black with silver tufts; there is a white undercoat and a black topcoat. The Smoke, once known as 'Smokies' or 'Blue Smokies', has had a long lineage, going back over a hundred years, although it was not until the 1890s that it became shown in its own class. Part of the problem in breeding the Smoke is in obtaining the correct colours without sacrificing the long-hair's body structure, since the Smoke, like the Chinchilla, tends to have a less heavy bone structure than the Persian.

Characteristics

Typical Persian. See the Chinchilla.

Colour

The undercoat should be pure white, which preserves the contrast with the black topcoat. The movement of the cat creates the shadings of contrasts. The frill, or ruff (frame for the head), and chest should appear pale silver. Tabby markings are not permitted, and therefore breeding with a Silver

Tabby creates the danger of unwanted markings. Eyes are orange or deep orange-copper. Green is considered a fault.

Coat and Body Structure
The coat is typically long-hair and must be well groomed as the kitten develops. This is true of nearly all long-haired breeds but is especially so for the Smoke because of the complexity and variety of colours.

NOTE: In America, Smokes are recognized as colour-varieties of Exotic Short-hair, the American Short-hair, the Manx and the Rex—that is, a short-haired version of the colour-patterning is recognized.

Tabby
There are five Tabby colour-categories: Blue, Brown, Cream, Red and Silver. Except for the colour-varieties they offer, they will be treated together. (The blue and cream are not recognized in Britain.)

History and Origin
The Brown Tabby is the basic colour-pattern and has been recognized the longest. In America, where it is known as the Brown Tabby Persian, the breed has been registered since the 1890s. In Britain the variety goes back almost a hundred years and was once honoured by the then Prince of Wales, later Edward VII. Like-to-like breeding is difficult to achieve now, and cross-mating is often necessary. The important thing is to maintain the rich sable colour without losing the characteristic type.

Characteristics
This is an affectionate and long-lived breed; it does not fall into the 'independent' stereotype of many cat breeds; on the contrary, it enjoys play and attention. It makes a good family pet.

Colour
The Brown has as its basic colour a rich sable, vibrant and vivid, with distinct black Tabby markings; it has black pencilling on the face, with additional swirls on the cheek and narrow lines on the chest. In the American standard the sides may have classic markings (oval whorls on the side) or mackerel (vertical stripes).

The Blue, not seen in Britain, shows a sharp contrast between the ground colour-pattern of pale bluish ivory and deep-blue markings.

The Cream has as its ground colour a pale cream (including lips and chin) in contrast to the darker markings. This cat is not recognized in Britain.

The Red once known as the Orange, is a deep and intense red, with distinctly defined markings, continued down the chest, legs and tail, with markings of face and neck meeting on the shoulders in a 'butterfly' pattern.

The Silver is rare because of the difficulty of achieving the colour-patterns: intense black markings on a silver ground. Further, at birth, the best specimens tend to be black, whereas the poorest specimens when grown are often well marked as kittens.

The eye colours are as follows: for Brown, hazel or copper; for Blue, intense copper; for Cream, brilliant copper; for Red, deep copper; for Silver, green or hazel.

Coat and Body Structure

The coat for all varieties is long, dense and silky, yet flowing. The body is typically long-hair: cobby with short legs, conveying the sense of massiveness, which increases with the flowing coat.

NOTE: In America the Blue Tabby and Cream Tabby are standard varieties for short-hairs as well: for American Short-hair, Exotic Short-hair, Manx and Rex. These are not acceptable in Britain.

Tortoiseshell (Including Tortoiseshell-and-White, known as Calico in the USA)

History and Origin

The Tortoiseshell (or Tortie) is so called because of its defined patterns of three colours: red, cream and black. When it also has white, it is called, in the United States, a Calico Persian, and in Britain, a Tortie-and-White. The breed probably began by accidental matings between mixed breeds and Black Long-hairs, resulting in tricoloured coats by chance. One of the problems in breeding Torties is that they can produce several litters in succession without producing a Tortie, and therefore the creation of the correctly coloured coat is extremely difficult and uncertain. The Tortie, incidentally, is always female, so that the breeding of like to like is impossible. Any Tabby mating may create markings, and so mating to a Black or Cream male is preferable. The resulting litter will be very mixed, of course. The Tortie-and-White, or Calico Persian, is even more difficult to produce—the breed is only female, like the Tortie. All such matings must be with Bicolours to avoid the loss of the white (Calico) strain.

Characteristics

The Tortie is an alert and active cat, intelligent, a good queen if you choose to mate her and a fine family pet. Careful grooming is necessary here, and any potential owner should be aware of this.

Colour

The standard calls for defined patches of colour—red, cream, and black. These patches or patterns must be distinct and without streaking or brindling. All parts of the cat's body and head, including the ears, must be so patched. For the Calico Persian, the standard calls for a white cat, with distinct patches of black and red, and white underparts. A red or cream blaze (from nose to forehead) is an advantage. The eyes for both Tortie and Calico should be deep orange or copper and round.

Coat and Body Structure

The coat should be long, flowing and luxuriant, with extra length on brush and frill. The body is typically long-hair—full, massive, with short-legs, a broad round head and small but well-tufted ears.

Turkish

History and Origin

The Turkish cat is known as the Van cat in Turkey, having originated in the Lake Van district of south-eastern Turkey. It was formally recognized in Britain in 1969. It has not, as yet, caught on in America. Since the Van is an established breed, it can be mated like to like from Turkish stock.

Characteristics

The Turkish, or Van, is an excellent family cat, active, alert, intelligent; it enjoys attention and affection. Further, it is hardy and durable, able to thrive indoors and outdoors. It eats rather large amounts for its size, and, also unusually, it seems to enjoy water—bathing and even swimming.

Colour

The ground colour is chalk white—a pure white, with no yellowing or traces of any other colour. The face has auburn markings; a white blaze characterizes the face. The eyes are round and amber.

Coat and Body Structure

The Turkish has no undercoat, and its coat is long, soft and silky in texture, with a full brush. Sometimes slight auburn markings appear, but these are not a disqualification in the show ring. The coat is not quite so long as that of the typical long-hair, and because of the lack of undercoat, grooming is not especially demanding. The body is lengthy, less cobby and massive than the long-hair's; the head is wedge-shaped, with large upright ears.

White

The White has three classifications: Blue-eyed, Odd-eyed (one blue and one orange) and Orange- or Copper-eyed.

History and Origin

The Blue-eyed White was descended from the Angora and was one of the first long-hairs registered, although the early type was probably substandard by current evaluations. From this type developed the more popular Orange-eyed White (known in the United States as the Copper-eyed White Persian), recognized in the 1930s as a distinctly separate variety. The Odd-eyed was recognized by American associations in the 1950s and now also has championship status in Britain. Very active in the creation of these Whites is the Blue Persian, whose coat and eye colour show up here. Creams and Blacks are also genetically involved in the production of the White.

Characteristics

Blue-eyed Whites may be deaf. The Odd-eyed may show deafness on the side of the blue eye. The Orange-eyed have escaped this affliction, and so it must be the 'blue eye' strain that causes the deafness rather than the whiteness of the hair. The White is traditionally a sturdy breed, strong and strongly built. It is also an affectionate breed, tending toward backwardness with strangers but then warming up with familiarity. Deafness, incidentally, does not lead to any significant personality differences, although the deaf cat is somewhat more dependent on the owner or family. Occasionally a kitten born deaf will acquire its hearing, and this sudden acquisition is very confusing to the cat at first.

Colour
The coat should be pure white. If shown, the cat needs to be bathed so as to derive the pure white necessary for best results. Markings, shadings or barrings of any kind are faults. The eye colour must be true—deep blue or deep orange, and round and large, piercingly brilliant.

Coat and Body Structure
The coat is long and flowing, luxuriant but never woolly, The cat will have a full frill and brush, conveying the massiveness that is characteristic of the type. The body is cobby, heavily boned and with short legs, round head, eyes well apart, broad muzzle and short nose.

A note on 'Any Other Colour' Among Long-Hairs
There are several pedigree cats for which no standard has yet been established. These breeds cannot participate in championship shows, but they are grouped together and registered separately, being exhibited in Assessment Classes only. Such breeds include, among long-hairs, the Brown, the Blue Chinchilla, the Lilac and the Cameo. These cat breeds, in their placement, are somewhat similar to dogs in the Miscellaneous Class. After some time, when the breeding is true and interest increases, the animal may move up into recognized status and then show at all levels of competition.

These comments are intended only for show cats; as pets, these unrecognized breeds demonstrate no differences from recognized ones or from mixed-breed cats.

THE SHORT-HAIRS

Bicoloured

History and Origin
A Bicolour is a cat with two colours in its coat. At first only four varieties of Bicolour were recognized: black and white, cream and white, orange and white, and blue and white. The markings were designated as very intricate, on the pattern of the Dutch rabbit. Needless to say, the production of both the pattern and the correct colouring was virtually impossible to achieve, and breeders were discouraged. As a consequence, the breed began to decline. With the revised standard in 1971, in Britain, the Bicolour could be any solid colour and white. The patches of colour, however, had to be clear and distinct and make up no more than two-thirds of the coat; white should make up no more than half.

Characteristics

The Bicolour shows no personality difficulties; it is sweet and affectionate and a good family pet as well as a show cat.

Colour

As stated, the standard requires clear patches of colour, evenly distributed, the white no more than half and the patches no more than two-thirds. The face should be patched, with a white blaze running up into the beginning of the ear line. Tabby markings of any kind are a fault, or any variation such as brindling within the patches. Eyes are orange or deep copper, without any green or green rimming.

Coat and Body Structure

The coloured part of the coat as well as the white needs careful grooming, to keep the contrast distinct and clear. The colour should be lustrous, and the white pure. The coat, as for all similar types of short-hairs, must be dense, close, fine in texture and short. The body is muscular but not massive and cobby as in the long-hair. The tail must not be long, with the legs proportional to the body and conveying grace. The forehead is broad, with the eyes set well apart and the ears small and rounded at the top.

Black

History and Origin

This is the Black cat of mystery, a portent of ill luck and even of witchcraft. In legend, this black cat was built on the order of the Siamese, a lithe but muscular type, which slid around corners and hid in dark nooks. The British Black, however, is of a different body structure, more rounded and less slinky. Part of the mysterious nature of the Black was its slightly oriental eyes—leading to inscrutability in the popular imagination—and their deep greenness. Needless to add, the cat that carries these legends is unaware of its long tradition. And the standard does not even permit green eyes—deep copper or orange is now called for.

The real Black, unlike the legendary black cat, goes back to the latter part of the nineteenth century, when standards were begun to be set. But it was not until the 1950s, when so many other breeds were developed in those post-war years, that the Black began to become more fixed in its standard, and several good specimens appeared. Part of the problem was that, in cross-breeding, the body type was developed, but eye colour lagged; green, which is a fault, remained in many otherwise good specimens.

Characteristics

The Black presents no personality problems and should be a good family pet, as well as a fine show cat.

Colour

The standard specifies a jet-black coat, with no white or tinges of any kind. Because of cross-breeding, that pure jet black is difficult to obtain consistently, and yet it is characteristic of the breed. Keeping the colour in first-rate condition requires steady grooming, especially if the Black is to be shown. Brushing and cleaning are necessary; if neglected, the Black may take on a rusty or dirty colour. The eyes should be striking: round and piercing, without any green or green rim, and coloured orange or deep copper.

Coat and Body Structure
The coat is short, dense and of fine quality and lies close to the body. The body is graceful, legs proportional to body, which is itself muscular and lithe in appearance. The Black has a well-developed head without coarseness or massiveness.

Blue-Cream
History and Origin
The Blue-Cream, like so many other cats established in Britain, was produced mainly after the end of the Second World War, in the 1950s. It can be produced by mating like to like, and it is also instrumental in creating Blues and Creams. The best of the breed are, in fact, produced through like-to-like mating, although several other kinds of mating are possible.

Characteristics
The Blue-Cream is a suitable show animal, as well as a pleasant cat, with no personality problems that would interfere with it as a family pet. Grooming is ordinary, but during its shedding, or moulting, season, the owner must be careful to comb out with a fine-tooth comb the cream hairs. They are very fine in texture, and they will create hair-ball problems if the cat swallows them while grooming itself.

Colour
The blue and cream of the coat should be lustrous, without any other colours. In the British standard the two colours are intermingled, not in patches. The North American standard calls for distinctly defined patches of colour, not for intermingling. Both are somewhat difficult to achieve in breeding. The eyes should be copper, deep orange or yellow. A green rim or tinge is a fault.

Coat and Body Structure
The coat should be, as the breed standard indicates, short and fine. The body is muscular but small-scaled. See the Black for the standard. One reason for the smaller scale is that the Blue-Cream is female, and it runs smaller in stature than the male.

Bombay
History and Origin
The Bombay has only recently been accepted for showing in the United States, although it is not yet recognized in Great Britain. The Bombay is a cross between the dense-coated sable-brown Burmese and the American Short-hair. The idea was to produce a breed that was partly indigenously

American intermixed with a 'foreign' strain such as the Burmese. The important element with the Bombay is its coat, a shiny black patent-leather-like covering. In evaluating the Bombay, judges consider the coat and its colour for more than half of the points.

Characteristics
The Bombay is sturdy, active, fearless; it is not a docile pet and must be tended and appreciated if it is to thrive.

Colour
The coat is jet black, patent-leather-like in quality and sheen, with no other colour to the roots. Nose leather and paw pads are also black. The eyes are set well apart and can be from yellow to deep copper.

Coat and Body Structure
The coat is dense, close-lying, of fine texture, short, intense in its sheen. The body is the same as for the Burmese; that is, a wedge-shaped head set on a muscular but lithe and svelte body. Overall, the appearance is one of elegance and grace. The neck is slender, and the legs proportionate to the body, the tail long and without any kink.

British Blue (Also Chartreuse)
History and Origin
The British Blue (in America it is known as the Exotic Short-hair Blue) began to regain real interest in the mid-1950s, when cross-breeding was replaced by mating of like to like. Before the war, British Blues were bred with foreign breeds, and the result was a gradual weakening of type, especially in the bone structure. In France, the 'Blue' is the Chartreuse, so-called because Chartreux monks reputedly bred them. The best results for the production of the Blue seem to come from occasional out-breeding, for example a Blue with a Black, which preserves the bone structure but deepens the colour in some of the latter.

Characteristics
The Blue is a quiet and reflective cat, not given to demonstrations of any kind. If your household is turbulent, the Blue may be unhappy, since it prefers a settled existence. It will sit or lie for hours, although it enjoys some bursts of activity. It has a measure of independence.

Colour
The standard calls for a coat colour of light to medium blue. Definite faults are tabby markings, stripes, blotches, shadings or any white hairs among the blue. Probably the best shade of blue is a deeper one, somewhat between a pale colour and the deeper hues of a plum colour. The eyes should be copper or orange (no green) and should be bright and large.

Coat and Body Structure
The standard, as for all short-hairs, calls for a fine, short, closely lying coat.
The body is standard, as for the Black Short-hair.

Cream
History and Origin
As several commentators on cat breeds have indicated, the Short-haired
Cream has always suffered in comparison with the Long-haired variety,
which has been cited as more luxuriant and feline. In the post-war years of
the 1950s, the Short-hair began to emerge, almost thirty years after it had
first been granted recognition. One reason, besides the popularity of the
Long-hair, for the slow development of the Short-hair Cream was the
difficulty of breeding, since males must almost always carry on the line,
females being very rare in the championship class. This has made like-to-like
breeding very unusual, and the cross-breeding that produces the Cream is
chancy. As a result, the breed has been the victim of genetic difficulties.

Characteristics
The personality of the Cream, like that of most other short-hairs, is well
fitted for family life. For showing, the breed is remarkably easy to maintain,
needing only the daily brushing and freedom from grease that would apply
to all cats, whether shown or not.

Colour
The standard is a rich cream colour that has no stripes, barrings, shadings or
white. The Cream should not tend toward red—what is called a 'hot' colour.
Tabby markings of any kind are a fault. The eyes should be copper or
orange; hazel was once permitted, but no longer.

Coat and Body Structure
The coat follows the standard of fineness, closeness, density and luxuriance.
The body is similar to that of the Black but with a somewhat more delicate
bone structure.

Siamese
The Siamese is almost the prototypical cat—that is, it is the cat in one of its
purest states. Since it demands attention and may even command a household, a potential owner should be certain of himself or herself before
acquiring one. The Siamese, both male and female, is highly sexed and if not
neutered will make unusual demands upon the owner or family. The
Siamese queen in season will call like a frantic child seeking help, and the
unneutered male will spray and make the home smelly and unpleasant (even
more intensely than most other males). The cat demands considerable
affection. It is intelligent, mischievous, greedy, inquisitive and, if ignored or
neglected, destructive through spite. The Siamese usually asks for and
expects to get its own way and must be handled carefully from kittenhood, or
else it will run the household.
     The rewards are equally strong. The Siamese is a decorative item of great

beauty, and it gives in love and attention as much as it receives. It is not, then, a cat to be acquired and then forgotten or ignored. The Siamese is a full experience.

NOTE: There are several varieties of Siamese that differ mainly in their coat colour, but since the breed is so popular, I will take them separately instead of bunching them together. The varieties are: Blue-point, Chocolate-point, Lilac-point, Red-point and Tortie-point, Seal-point, Tabby- and Cream-point. There is also a category called 'Any Other Dilutions' for Siamese with colours besides those recognized as dominant.

General History and Origin of the Siamese

The background of the Siamese is caught up in legend, principally that they were once temple cats of the East, attached to royalty and possessing certain divine powers. The early Siamese may have been rather different from the breed we know now. One was described in the late-eighteenth century, by a German naturalist, as having a body colour of one kind with points coloured black. This kind of development could have occurred only through a mutation, or else the colouring would have been extended beyond the points to the entire body.

In any event, the Siamese entered the first domestic cat exhibition, the Crystal Palace show in 1871, although, once again, we cannot be certain what, if any, standard they fitted. It is very possible that the colouring was Siamese while the body type was cobby or typically British in character. While colour is of great importance in the Siamese, whatever its variety, it is important for the body type to be true also: a lithe, graceful structure, with a wedge-shaped head. Such a combination of colouring and configuration was the result of over half of a century of selective breeding. In the twentieth century, the Siamese has been bred in ever greater numbers, and it has gradually come to be the most popular of the pedigree felines. American standards have generally followed the British, with the Seal-point the best known and the most popular. The Seal-point is, in fact, the model Siamese for most people, and the other varieties often come as a surprise to those unfamiliar with the cat world. All are born white, incidentally, so you cannot tell what breed they will later conform to until the colouring begins to emerge.

One other point: a squint in the Siamese is a fault if you wish to show your cat.

Blue-Point Siamese

History and Origin

After the Seal-point, the Blue-point was the next Siamese recognized. Recognition, however, came gradually, and popularity was not won until the 1930s and 1940s. Right after the Second World War, the Blue-point began to win championships. It entered Britain, however, as early as the 1890s, although that Blue-point may have been quite different from what the standard now calls for.

Characteristics
The Blue-point appears to be one of the most companionable of the Siamese: gentle, affectionate, playful and even-tempered. If not used solely for show, the Blue-point can also make an excellent family pet.

Colour
The ground colour for the Blue-point is a frosty white, which then shades or blends gradually into the blue on the back; the points should be of the same blue colour, a cold blue, somewhat lighter in tone than the back colour. Although it is the colouring that makes the breed distinctive, it is difficult to achieve the right shading, the frosty blue and the glacial white. The American standard calls for a bluish-white body, white on stomach and chest, with points deep blue. The eyes should be a vivid blue.

Coat and Body Structure
The coat must be very short, lie close and have a healthy gloss to it. The texture is fine, not coarse. No special grooming is necessary, although a smoothing down of the coat is necessary after a light brushing. The body for the Blue-point will be basically the same as that for all Siamese varieties: a long, lithe body, proportionately slender legs, with the hind legs slightly longer than the front; the head should be wedge-shaped, the eyes oriental, but without any squint and, as noted, vibrantly blue. The feet are small and dainty, oval in shape, and the tail long and with a taper. The ears are always pricked.

Chocolate-point Siamese
History and Origin
The Chocolate-point is an offshoot of the Seal-point, in that the latter variety carries the genes for the Chocolate-point, although the early ones were probably rather different from those produced now. Despite its appearing many years ago, the Chocolate-point did not gain recognition until 1950 in Britain and a little later in America. Although the breed can be produced by mating like to like, there is considerable difficulty in achieving the delicate blend of type, eye colour and body and point colour. To establish the variety, breeders had to distinguish the Chocolate-point from the Seal-point, and yet many of the former have characteristics of the Seal-point in their colouration.

Characteristics
The Chocolate-point creates no personality problems and can be a fine family pet.

Colour
The body should be ivory, not the glacial white of the Blue-point, with the ivory shading into the milk chocolate of the points. The points should themselves all be of the same colour. Shading of the ivory must be avoided, or else the Chocolate has Seal-point characteristics. Breeders point out that summer heat affects the colouring of the Chocolate and the Seal-point,

dimming their distinctive colours and even creating sunburn. The cats tend to look their best in the colder months, when the coat has a 'frosty' look. The eyes should be a vivid, brilliant blue, clear and piercing.

Coat and Body Structure
The Chocolate-point grooms easily, the coat being fine, close, very short and glossy, never coarse. The body is the same as for all Siamese—for details, see the Blue-point.

Lilac-point Siamese
History and Origin
Lilac-points in some form may have been produced eighty years ago, but the first real attempt to achieve the present standard did not come until 1955, in Britain. Breeding the Lilac-point is a delicate achievement, for the colouring-pattern is extremely difficult to achieve correctly. The glacial white of the body must serve as a contrast with the lilac-grey points, accompanied by a rose-coloured nose and pink pads. The Lilac-point can be bred like to like, although both sire and dam must themselves be strong, or else recessives will appear and upset the delicate balance of colouring.

Characteristics
The Lilac-point, like the Chocolate-point, makes a good family pet and, if shown, requires no special attention besides the routine cleaning, rubbing down and brushing.

Colour
As noted, the body colour should be milk or glacial white, with lilac-grey points. The points should be 'frosty', so that the cat conveys the appearance of a cool, northern animal. The body colour must shade gradually to the tones of the points. The eyes are a bright and deep blue.

Coat and Body Structure
The coat lies close, is fine in texture and has a gloss—this adds to the frosty appearance. The body, like that for all Siamese, calls for a cat of medium size with a lithe, muscular look; a well-proportioned, wedge-shaped face; large ears, wide at the base; plenty of width between the eyes.

Red-Point and Tortie-point Siamese
History and Origin
The Red-point and Tortie-point are considered separate breeds, but they are, nevertheless, very closely connected. The Red-point has a white body shading into apricot. The Tortie-point is always a female and has reds distributed over the darker points. The Tortie-point may have four base colours: Seal, Chocolate, Blue and Lilac; on all, the dark points must have cream or red patches—that is what makes it a Tortie. The Red-point is predictable; bred correctly, all Red-points will look the same. The Tortie-point, however, is unique; no two cats can ever look the same because of the distribution of the red patches. Those who seek a unique cat may be

interested in acquiring a Tortie-point—all the variations of the acceptable colour-patterns fit the standard. Needless to add, breeding it is difficult.

Characteristics

Like the Blue-point, Lilac-point and Chocolate-point, the Red-point and Tortie-point make excellent pets as well as show cats.

Colour

The Red-point has a white body, somewhat frosty in quality, which shades into apricot. The points should be reddish-gold; the legs and feet are also permitted to be apricot. Barring on legs, tail and mask is acceptable. The Tortie-point is, as stated, standard in four shades: Seal, Chocolate, Lilac and Blue. Nose leather and pads must be the same colour as the basic colour. Points must have cream or red patches on their darker areas. The Tortie tricolour of black, light red and dark red must be established, whatever the solid colour that the cat comes in. Eye colour for both is bright blue, deep and vivid.

Coat and Body Structure

The coat conforms to the standard for the Siamese—close, short, fine, not coarse and glossy; the colours should look vibrant and healthy. The body is the same as for the Blue-point.

Seal-Point Siamese

History and Origin

As I mentioned above, the Seal-point is the most popular of the Siamese breeds, the best known and the standard by which most people judge the breed as a whole. The chief characteristic of the Seal-point is, of course, its distinctive body colouring: a creamy light brown or fawn, with dark-brown points that serve as complement or contrast. The Seal-point began to emerge in the latter part of the nineteenth and the early-twentieth century. Within a very few years, the breed was well established and began to win both shows and popular acceptance.

Characteristics

Like the other Siamese, the Seal-point thrives on attention and play. It has a strong personality, which it likes to display, and thus is considered a little temperamental. It is active in play, twisting and vaulting, with a voice that displays a considerable range of emotional life. It can be trained to obey commands and to walk on a leash. The Siamese, like most cats, is inquisitive, only perhaps even more, and it can be destructive of furniture if left to its own devices. It demands and expects good treatment and handling and will respond with hissing or clawing if mistreated.

Colour

The creamy light-brown body, a kind of faded chocolate, is contrasted with the dark points—on mask, ears, tail and legs. The result is a harmony of colours, not a radical clash. The mask tracings should connect with the ears. The eyes are a deep blue.

Coat and Body Structure
The coat follows the Siamese standard: close, fine, very short, never coarse. The body indicates a cat of balanced elements; like the coat colouring, the body conveys a cat in harmony with itself. The body is lithe and lean, with the hind legs slightly higher than the front—conveying a sense of grace. The structure follows that of the Blue-point. The wedge of the face should be clearly defined, giving that 'foreign' look that is the essence of the Siamese.

Tabby-Point (Lynx-Point) Siamese
History and Origin
The Tabby-point goes back to the beginning of the century but did not become well known until fifty years later. In fact, after it gained in popularity, the 'Tabby' designation was thought to be less elegant; and in the United States the designation 'Lynx-point' became standard. Several American associations treat the breed in the Siamese class as the Lynx-point, whereas others place it in a separate breed category called 'the Colourpoint Short-hairs', along with Red-points and Tortie-points. We remind the reader that American associations are not by any means unanimous in their categorization of breeds, there being considerable division among them, while in Britain there is a single governing body. In any event, by the 1960s the Tabby- or Lynx-point was firmly established, being known as Tabby-point in Britain.

Characteristics
The Tabby-point is affectionate, playful and intelligent, although difficult to breed correctly; it makes a delightful pet as well as an interesting showpiece.

Colour
The ground colour of the Tabby-point may be of several types: Seal, Lilac, Tortoiseshell or Red, Blue and Chocolate. The points should conform to the standard for the basic colouring. Besides the colouring, the tabby marking on the legs should be clear, and there should be solid markings on the hind legs. The mask must have distinctive striping. The eyes, set well apart, are a clear blue.

Coat and Body Structure
The coat conforms to the Siamese standard: close, fine, very short. The body is relatively dainty but not weak, conforming to the general Siamese standard. The cat's silhouette is one of elegance and litheness. The head should, of course, be wedge-shaped.

Siamese, any other Dilution
The category 'Any Other Dilution' of Siamese consists of breeds that are a dilution (a variation that results in a weaker hue) of the 'Red Series'; this category is made up of the Tortie-point (in its own category), Cream-point,

Red and Cream Tabby-point and Tortoiseshell Tabby-point, which can have a ground colour of Seal, Chocolate, Blue or Lilac. The various designations here all conform to the Siamese standard of body structure, eye colour, head shape and other characteristics. The personality of these cats is also Siamese—playful, affectionate, intelligent. Many of these breeds are 'look-alikes' with the non-dilute breeds; for example, the Red Tabby-point cannot be distinguished except by genetic tests from the Red-point, nor is it easy to distinguish the Chocolate Tortie Tabby-point from the Chocolate Tortie-point, and so on. Often the distinction is almost invisible to the untrained eye, and many of the signs of colouring become clear only when the cat is fully mature.

They are, as already noted, good pets, perhaps less self-centred than the Seal-point, good as family companions for owner, children or even dogs in the household. With their varied and often exotic colouring, they are conversation-pieces as well as blending in well with household furniture.

NOTE: In the United States a variety known as the Albino Siamese is recognized by some associations; this is a cat with no pigmentation—a white coat, pink skin and pinkish-white eyes. It is not recognized in Britain.

Spotted (A Distinctly British Short-Hair)
History and Origin
The spotted cat, or some version of the present-day Spotted, goes back deep into history, to the Egyptian *Book of the Dead*, in which Ra is portrayed as a spotted cat slaying the serpent representing the dark world. According to this legend, the cat—representing the Good God—kills the serpent, representative of evil; and thus the cat is a legendary saviour, like those knights who slew dragons in medieval romances. About a hundred years ago, the Spotted began to be shown, although this was a less typical breed than now. Shortly afterward, the Spotted became known as the Spotted Tabby, but tabby markings, except on the head, are now a fault in the Spotted. The breed then declined for almost fifty years, and only in the mid-1960s did it begin to reappear.

Characteristics
The Spotted is a pleasing family cat, with no personality problems that would upset an owner or a household.

Colour
The ground colour is not standardized; as a result, any ground colour that blends well with the spots is acceptable. The spots may themselves be of any colour, as long as they also blend in with the ground colour. One may see a ground of red, cream, brown or silver. The eye colour should conform to the coat colour.

Coat and Body Structure
The coat standard stipulates that the spots be clearly defined; they may be of any geometric shape—round, oblong and so on. Stripes except on the face or head are faults. The coat, as for all short-hairs, should be short, close and

finely textured. The body should convey muscularity and litheness, reflecting a cat in good condition. The body should also convey length and depth, with the legs proportional; the head has good breadth between the ears.

Tabby (Brown, Red, Silver)

History and Origin

The Brown Tabby is relatively rare, because the sable ground colour and the patterns of markings are difficult to achieve. For the first forty or fifty years of this century, the Brown commanded little attention, but since the late 1950s interest has increased. The Red Tabby, on the contrary, is fairly rare—perhaps, as Grace Pond indicates, because it is not seen clearly as a distinct breed with its own colour-scheme. Frequently it is confused with ginger or orange-coloured cats and consequently downgraded. Red Tabbies have begun to appear at shows in the last twenty years, however. The Silver Tabby has gained in favour since the end of the Second World War, possibly because the ground silver gives it an aristocratic, lordly appearance.

Characteristics

The Tabby is an easy-going, pleasant and affectionate cat, even from the time it is a kitten. Some feel that the Silver is the most pleasant of all, gentle and affectionate. They all make excellent family pets.

Colour

For the Brown: the ground colour must be a rich sable, extending throughout, without any white or other markings; the markings should be dense and black, separate from the ground. The eyes may be orange, deep yellow or hazel. The Red is a full, rich red, not at all orange; the markings should be an even darker red, also distinct from the ground. The eye colour is copper. The Silver calls for a pure-silver ground, with markings of intense black, quite distinct from the ground. The eyes should be hazel or green. In all the ground colours, no white should appear.

Coat and Body Structure

The coat for all three varieties must show sharp distinctions between ground and markings. The markings must themselves be sharply defined. In the Brown Tabby, the shoulders should have a butterfly marking, the tail and legs ringed. The chest needs two necklaces, with swirls of oyster patterns on the sides. In the Red, three red stripes run down the back, with an oyster pattern on the sides and a butterfly mark on the back of the neck. Markings encircle the neck and ring the tail. The Red also comes in a mackerel-striped variety, with the markings narrow but distinct from the ground colour. The Silver has the same standard for markings, which should be clearly defined and densely black. The butterfly pattern on the back is distinctive. The mackerel-marked version of the Silver, like that of the Red, has narrow but distinct rings. The tails of all the Tabbies are ringed: that is, they have bands of colour running their entire length. The structure of the body is the same as the standard for the Spotted: muscular and lithe.

Tortoiseshell

History and Origin

Some version of the Tortie has been with us for many years, but it is difficult to determine precisely what variety it was. There have been several difficulties in making the breed pure. The colouring itself—the Tortie is a tricolour cat, black, light red and dark red—is not easy to achieve. Further, the Tortie is a female-only variety, with the males usually proving sterile. Still further, the depth of the colouring, not just the colouring, is difficult to attain; it may be either too dark or too light. Since cross-breeding is necessary—usually to a Cream, Red or Black male, the result is chancy.

Characteristics

The Tortoiseshell makes an excellent domestic cat, good with the owner or in a family situation. It is affectionate and gentle, an excellent companion.

Colour

The three colours—black, light red and dark red, recalling the shell colouring of the tortoise—must be clearly defined and distinct from one another. White hairs or tabby markings are a fault. The eye colour may be either orange or copper.

Coat and Body Structure

The Tortie has the same standard as other short-hairs: a fine, close, dense coat. The body is muscular without being massive, legs proportionate, eyes well apart in a broad forehead. Each paw of the Tortie, as well as the tail, must have all three colours.

Tortoiseshell-and-Calico

History and Origin

The name 'Calico' is used in the United States; in Britain it was once known as the Chintz-and-White. The breed probably existed for a long time but in a variety that was somewhat different from what the present standard calls for. The variety resulted from chance matings of different-coloured cats, and it was not until this century that an attempt was made to produce a clearly defined tricolour on a ground of white. The Tortie-and-Calico is a female-only variety, although males do exist, but normally cross-breeding is necessary, usually from Bicolours. The breed has now become quite popular at shows.

Characteristics

The personality is the same as for the Tortoiseshell—that is, gentle, affectionate and companionable.

Colour

The three colours—black, light red and dark red—should be distinctly defined on their grounds of white. There should be no blending or brindling, nor are stripes or tabby markings acceptable. All colour patches should be distinct and clear. The eye colour may be any one of three: hazel, orange or copper. No green is permitted.

Coat and Body Structure
The coat, as for all short-hairs, should be close, dense and fine in texture. The body formation follows that of the Black.

White
History and Origin
The White, both long-haired and short-haired, has a long literary and artistic history, having appeared in fairy tales, in ballets (*Sleeping Beauty*) and, most of all, in paintings. The breed comes with three varieties of eye colour: blue, orange and odd. The continued use of the White in reproductions, advertisements and television has not, however, resulted in overwhelming popularity for the breed. Nevertheless, its standard has remained stable for the last hundred years; that is, it should be a comely but not delicate-looking cat, slender but not dainty. In Britain there is a resurgence of interest, and Whites are entered in many shows. The odd-eyed are also recognized.

Characteristics
The short-haired White has characteristics similar to those of the long-hair. It makes a good pet, as well as a good show cat, and is companionable, although tending toward shyness with strangers. Like the long-hair, the short-hair may be deaf if blue-eyed; the orange-eyed and odd-eyed appear to escape this affliction, although the odd-eyed may be deaf on the side of the blue eye. Remember that all kittens are blue-eyed at birth, and the eye colour develops only after two months. If you acquire a very young kitten, then, you will not know if it might suffer from deafness, and not all blue-eyed Whites are deaf anyway.

Colour
Breeding should produce a pure white coat, without yellow tinges or shadowing. The White may be mated like to like, or to Torties and Tortie-and-Calicos. Mating must be careful, to avoid other colours or markings of any kind. The eyes should be pure of their kind: really a blue blue or a true orange or copper.

Coat and Body Structure
The close and finely textured coat requires some care in grooming if the owner wishes to preserve the pure white. The body follows the standard for the Black. The head should be carefully moulded—broad forehead and fully fashioned cheeks, short pink nose and gently tapered and small ears.

'FOREIGN' BREEDS

There are, in addition to the long-hairs and short-hairs described above, several breeds of great distinction that are chiefly foreign in designation. In using the term 'foreign', I am using it as the British do. 'Foreign', then, designates a cat that may be anything from Russian and Burmese to American. As already stated, it is difficult to deal directly with classifications based on American-recognized breeds because different associations, lacking unanimity, recognize different breeds. I have, therefore, followed the British categorization.

Abyssinian (Ruddy)
History and Origin
The 'Ruddy' designation is American. In Britain, the Abyssinian that is ruddy brown is the standard variety and needs no further naming. The Abyssinian is distinctive for its double or triple ticking, in which each individual hair has two or three distinct bands of colour. As a result, the Abyssinian has an 'agouti' coat pattern, which is normally associated with the wild species of cats, not with domestics. To own such a breed is, then, to own something that recalls the jungle or a more primitive form of life. Indeed, the Abyssinian seems connected, in some form, to the cat worshipped by the Egyptians, whose shape was memorialized in frescoes and bronzes, as well as in statues and other kinds of temple worship. It was once known as 'the cat from the Blue Nile'.

The modern version of the Egyptian Abyssinian (or whatever it was called then) came to Europe in 1868, when a military expedition returned, under Napier, and brought with it a cat from Abyssinia (now called Ethiopia). From that point on the breed was mated with British types, at first haphazardly and then more carefully, to produce the breed as we know it today. The Abyssinian was first recognized in Britain in 1882. The American branch became active by the 1930s, although the breed goes back as far as 1909. Once it became better known, the Abyssinian gained in popularity, and now it ranks third, after the Siamese and the Burmese, in North-American registrations. Since litters are small, demand usually outruns supply.

Characteristics
The Abyssinian, for those uninterested simply in showing, is an ideal pet— friendly, active, playful, intelligent, appealing and companionable. It is a breed with a personality, a curiosity and a warmth that completely destroys the idea of the indifferent or impersonal cat.

Colour
The colour-pattern for the Ruddy variety is a rich golden-brown coat with black or dark-brown ticking. Bars or markings, except for a line down the spine, are a fault. Inside the legs, the colouring may be orange or orange-brown, in harmony with the rest of the coat. White, except on the chin, is also a fault. The eyes, which are almond-shaped, are green, hazel or amber.

Coat and Body Structure
The coat is short and close, creating no grooming problems; stroking will give it a brilliance or sheen. The distinctive aspect of the coat is the ticking,

creating that 'jungle' look that makes the Abyssinian seem like a wildcat. The body stresses litheness and sleekness; the silhouette is of an active and strong cat, not of daintiness. The head is a 'moderate wedge', without flat planes; the tail is fairly long and tapering, the ears pricked and the feet small.

Abyssinian (Red)
History and Origin
The Red is a derivative of the Ruddy, which is the normal colouring for an Abyssinian. The red colouring is recessive, and for it to appear, the recessive gene must be possessed by both sire and dam. The recognition of the variety did not occur until 1963 in both Britain and the United States. Its history is itself no more than twenty years old, although a Red was supposedly seen almost a hundred years ago.

Characteristics
The Red is no different from the Ruddy—an ideal family pet and companion.

Colour
The Red should be a rich copper red on the body, and doubly or trebly ticked with black or dark brown, which serves as a contrast to the body colour. The inside of the legs and the belly area should be apricot to blend in. White markings of any kind are a fault. The nose and leather pads are pink, and the eye colour is the same as for the Ruddy: green, hazel or amber.

Coat and Body Structure
The coat and body are the same as for the Ruddy.

American Short-Hair
History and Origin
The American Short-hair, also known as the Domestic Short-hair, is the oldest known breed in North America. Originally, some version of the Domestic came from Britain, as pets and rodent-killers. The Domestic developed by breeding among themselves, and the result is a tough 'natural' cat, one not at all determined by the selective breeding that characterizes most types. Only in recent years has breeding been more controlled, in order to establish the best qualities of the Domestic. The breed comes in many colour varieties, the most popular being the Silver Tabby and the Red Tabby.

Characteristics
The Domestic makes an excellent pet, as well as a first-rate ratter. It is well recognized for its evenness of temperament and stability and its intelligent and affectionate nature. As a hunter, it is ideal, for it is strong and healthy, with a heavy coat that resists weather changes and difficult underbrush.

Colour
The Domestic is recognized in numerous colour patterns (white, black,

blue, cream, chinchilla, red, shaded silver, black smoke and blue smoke) as well as in five tabby patterns (silver, blue, cream, red and brown), all in either classic or mackerel pattern; also tortoiseshell, calico and blue-cream and even bicolours. The eye colour corresponds to those standards set for the particular coat colour; for example, the white has blue, copper or odd eyes.

Coat and Body Structure
The coat is thick and dense, tough texturally and short. It is not quite the same as that for the British Short-hair. It is a protective coat, growing longer in the winter, although it does not grow too long. Fluffiness or woolliness is a fault. The body of the Domestic conveys the sense of strength, muscularity, activity. The limbs are large without being cobby; the legs should be firm and muscular, the paws fully rounded, the tail strong-looking but tapered, unkinked. The head is full, the muzzle squared off, with a firm chin, not undershot. The ears are set wide apart and somewhat rounded; the eyes, also, should be set well apart. Overall, the Domestic looks like a cat ready for action not for sleep.

American Wire-Hair
History and Origin
The Wire-hair has a strange history, with the mystery that accompanies a mutation in nature rather than something planned. The Wire-hair came into being spontaneously, when the mating of two normally coated house cats in the mid-1960s produced a litter that contained a male with a wiry and tough-feeling coat, rougher than the coat of a Wire-haired Terrier. The appearance of the coat had no precedent, so a breeder attempted to duplicate it, which she did by mating brother and sister (the sister had a normal coat). This produced two more Wire-hairs, and the production of the breed was assured. It began to be shown, and a group in the United States formed, the American Wirehair Cat Society, to maintain the standard of the breed. (A pair had appeared on a bomb-site in Britain and were exhibited at the National Cat Club Show in the pet-section a year or two before this.)

Characteristics
For temperament, see the American Short-hair, which it resembles.

Colour
The colours follow those for the American Short-hair—white, black, cream, blue and tortoiseshell, with corresponding eye colours.

Coat and Body Structure
The coat is unique, being of medium length and very stiff and wiry, with a coarse texture to it. Although it cannot be dense because of its quality, it should not be spare or patchy. Under the chin, chest and abdomen, the hair is less wiry, as is to be expected. The conformation of the body follows the standard for the American Short-hair.

Burmese Blue

History and Origin

The Burmese Blue is an offshoot of the Burmese Brown. The Blue is most probably a dilution of the Brown, and if we work by analogy, we can see that what occurred in modifying the Seal-point Siamese to the Blue-point had also come about with the Burmese, the Blue being a modification of the Brown. As a result of careful breeding, the Blue was established and recognized, in 1960. In the United States, while some of the cat associations have recognized the Blue as a variant of the Brown, the Burmese Cat Fanciers deem the Brown to be the only category of the breed. In Britain the following colours are also recognized: Chocolate, Lilac, Red, Cream, Brown-tortie, Blue-tortie, Chocolate-tortie and Lilac-tortie.

Characteristics

See the Brown for the characteristics they share—hardiness, intelligence and self-reliance.

Colour

The coat of the Blue is almost a soft silver-grey, somewhat paler than the warmer colour of the Russian and British Blue. White hairs are discouraged, although a few are permitted; patches or markings and tabby bars are a fault. The eye colour in Britain should be yellowish green to yellow (not green); in the United States, yellow to gold, a narrower range. The eyes, incidentally, do not shine.

Coat and Body Structure

The coat has a sheen or velvety quality to it, so that the cat appears to glow. The texture is fine, the hair lying close and characteristically short. Compared with the Brown's, the coat of the Blue is not quite so luxuriant, is less fine and lies less close to the body. But these are matters that further breeding could alter. The body follows the standard set for the Brown.

Burmese Brown (Sable)

History and Origin

The Burmese Brown (which preceded the Blue by many years) was a hybrid, the result of mating a Siamese with a dark-coated cat of unknown origin. When such hybrids were bred together, they produced the Burmese. Burmese bred like to like created the breed, which led to recognition in the United States in 1936. The Burmese Cat Club was formed in Britain in 1954. The whole history of the breed is clouded by the fact that hybrids were often shown and sold as pure-bred Burmese, and this hindered the production of the true breed. But by the mid-1950s the problems were ironed out, and the Burmese Brown has proved to be one of the most popular among 'foreign' breeds.

Characteristics

Early species of the Brown found it difficult to adapt to Western climates, and this led to a sickly cat, suffering chiefly from respiratory ailments. But with time the Brown became a hardy breed, strong, adaptable and very pleasant as family pets. You should expect no special problems in raising or keeping them.

Colour
The mature colour is a rich, warm seal brown, with no white patches, although a few white hairs are permissible. Points should be only slightly darker than the body coat, and a sharp contrast is undesirable. Tabby markings may appear on the kittens but not on the mature cat. The eyes should be a deep golden yellow, wide apart, almond-shaped. Green or blue-green is a fault, although many Browns do have chartreuse-yellow eyes.

Coat and Body Structure
The Burmese Brown coat is characteristically glossy, with the sheen of health and well-being. The hair is short, lies close to the body and is fine but not silkily textured. The body of the Burmese is solid, muscular and lithe— not quite so long as the Siamese and not at all cobby. In the United States, the standard calls for a more compact body. The head is wedge-shaped, but not so tapered as the face of the Siamese, slightly rounded on top.

Burmese, Other Colours
There are many different colours of Burmese that, for one reason or another, have not been fully recognized by the cat-fanciers who govern the breeds in North America. In time, these 'Others' will move up into full recognition, although even with the Burmese Blue in America there has been a long wait with the major fancies. The other colours are Cream, Blue-cream, Tortoiseshell, Red, Platinum (so-called in America, Lilac in Britain) and Champagne (the American designation, called Chocolate in Britain). They are recognized and being bred and developed in Britain.

These are similar to all aspects of the Burmese except for the body colour. The coat, characteristically, must be short, lie close to the body, possess a fine texture and have a brilliance that indicates grooming and health. The temperament is the same as for the recognized varieties: active, dauntless and playful. The body type must follow also, even though the coat colour must be achieved.

Egyptian Mau (Oriental Spotted Tabby)
History and Origin
The Egyptian Mau (cat) has a long and honourable background, going back to the Egyptian *Book of the Dead*, a holy document in which the sun-god Ra is represented as a spotted tabby. Since the cat is shown as slaying a serpent (Apepi), we can assume that Ra represented the forces of good, and so the cat entered recorded history as an object of worship, a 'sun-god' and an elemental force of benevolence. Since many tabbies show the scarab mark on their forehead, it was further believed that the Egyptians chose the cat as an object of worship because the scarab was a sign of holiness.

Over the years, examples of the Egyptian surfaced by chance matings, although most were discarded. Once their value was understood, however, they were back-crossed to Siamese so as to preserve type, although coat colour had to be achieved distinct from the Siamese. In America the Egyptian Mau has been developed from two cats from Cairo, by cross-breeding them with domestic and/or foreign stock. The breed has been accepted by several fancies in the United States, although experimentation in breeding is still going on. They are recognized in Britain as the Oriental Spotted Tabby, having been produced by cross-breeding.

Characteristics
Since the Egyptian Mau has most Siamese characteristics, you can expect a playful, active and affectionate temperament. Its voice, however, is less piercing.

Colour
The British standard calls for spotted markings or mackerel-tabby markings on a ground of paler colour. In the United States the mackerel-tabby markings are not permitted, and the scarab mark on the forehead stipulated in Britain is not mentioned in the American standard. In the latter, the light-bronze ground contrasts with dark-brown markings—also the British standard—but adds silver markings against a pale-silver ground. The eye colour should be green, yellow or hazel; oriental in shape for British standard, oval for American.

Coat and Body Structure
The Egyptian Mau coat is soft and glossy, short, with a sheen indicating a healthy, active animal. The body conveys length and muscularity; this is a powerful-looking cat in movement. Massiveness or cobbiness, however, is not permitted. The legs are slender, paws oval and small, the tail long but not kinked.

Exotic Short-hair

History and Origin
The Exotic Short-hair is a hybrid, created by mating a Persian with a short-hair. The coat has the furry texture of the Persian's but is no longer than the Abyssinian's. In breeding, the short-hair that is preferred is the Burmese, since the latter's body type is favoured by American associations. There are, however, several ways of obtaining the Exotic standard, one of them being to mate two short-hairs that both have recessive Persian in their backgrounds. Another is to use any short-hair or the American Short-hair with a Persian. In any event, cats created by these combinations must be shown in the class designated as Exotic Short-hairs, so as to keep them distinct from American Short-hairs and Persians. (The Exotics are not recognized in Britain.)

Characteristics
This is a very pleasant family cat: sturdy, affectionate, playful and even-tempered, with the best personality traits of its forebears. The coat requires only minimal grooming.

Colour
The colours permitted for the Exotic follow those for the Persian: white (with eye colours of blue, copper or odd), black, blue, cream, chinchilla, *et al.*, with eyes corresponding to the particular coat colour.

Coat and Body Structure
The coat is the important thing here, apart from body type, and it should be distinctive: luxuriant, soft in texture and of medium length. A Persian-length coat is undesirable. The body follows the standard for the Persian—a cobby body with a deep chest and large across the shoulders, with a round, massive head and a round face, the eyes set well apart. The aim is to create a body that is large without any loss of gracefulness; there should be a harmony of elements.

Foreign Lilac (Also called Foreign Lavender)
History and Origin
The Foreign Lilac is really a Siamese with a coat of lilac colour or lavender all over—without the point markings peculiar to the Siamese, however. It also has a somewhat more subdued personality than the Siamese, although in its own way it can be demanding. The development of the Lilac preceded both by chance—during the breeding of the Havana Brown (see that breed)—and by design, in the 1950s and 1960s. Now, the Lilac variety seems well established, and the cat appears regularly in large shows.

Characteristics
Lilacs serve well as family pets and as show cats. For the latter they really 'come up', as they enjoy attention. As a pet the Lilac is gentle but insistent on its rights, with a softer voice than the regular Siamese has.

Colour
The British standard calls for a frosty-grey colour with a pinkish tone, without any variations. Overall, the coat looks like antique or faded lavender. Barrings or markings are faults, although the kitten may have tabby markings, which will disappear with maturity. The eyes should be green, not yellow or hazel, and have an oriental shape.

Coat and Body Structure
The coat should be soft, with a sheen and a healthy, well-groomed look. Since the colouring is so delicate, any neglect will show up immediately in the coat. The body of the Lilac is of the Siamese type, long and slender, with a graceful look, slim legs and small paws. The head should be a modified wedge, long and tapering to a finely chiselled muzzle. The tail should be long and without kinks.

Foreign White
History and Origin
The 'Foreign White' is a Siamese with a white coat. Interestingly, it is a breed developed by mating Siamese of different colours, to produce a

dominant white. The other colours remain but are so recessive that they are invisible to the naked eye. The White has been carefully bred to preserve the full Siamese body and head type, and it is among the most perfect of the Siamese kind. The development of the breed is fairly recent, going back to experiments in mating that took place in the 1960s. The aim of all the breeders was to produce a white cat of 'foreign' specifications, avoiding the more typical heavy British body type. Also, the goal was to produce a white cat with blue eyes without the typical deafness associated with that combination. The type seemed well established by 1965, and the designation for the breed became 'Foreign White', after the name 'Chinese White' was dropped in the USA.

Characteristics
The Foreign White is an intelligent, alert cat that has the personality of the Siamese—playful, possessive, self-assertive and generally affectionate.

Colour
The coat must be pure white, with pink nose leather and pads. The white must not contain any other markings or visible colours. The eyes should be piercing blue; any other eye colour is disallowed (also no squint permitted).

Coat and Body Structure
The coat should lie close and be of a fine texture, dense without being coarse. The body is typical of the Siamese: lithe, slender and medium-sized, without any cobbiness; the face is wedge-shaped, with large, pricked ears.

Havana (Also known as Havana Brown)
History and Origin
The Havana or Havana Brown is what is called a 'self-coloured' breed; that is, it is the same colour all over, and in this case a Chocolate Siamese. It is relatively rare, since it is difficult to achieve all its qualities without sacrificing coat colour. The self-coloured Havana is a man-made breed but has a long history, going back to before the turn of the century, but very probably this type was not a true chocolate but a hybrid. The hybrids, in fact, tended to dominate until well into the century, when the standard was not yet firm. Burmese Browns and Siamese hybrids created a breed that looked like the Havana, but coat, eye colour and even body type were erratic. In the 1950s some of the uncertainty went out of breeding the Havana Brown, and the cat as we know it today was established, with official recognition coming in Britain in 1958. The Brown has not caught on in the United States, although it is regularly shown by a small group of breeders. With increasing popularity in Britain however, the breed began to deteriorate in quality because of like-to-like mating, especially with a decline in coat quality; but outcross-breeding began to produce it true to type once again.

Characteristics
The Havana is a cat with a big personality, and any potential owner who wants it as a family pet should be aware of this. The cat is sweet and pleasant,

a delightful companion, but it likes play, mischief and plenty of attention. The Havana is intelligent, learns readily and is hardy, with a particular fondness for outdoor play even in winter. Its qualities make it excellent for show purposes.

Colour
The coat should be a glossy, brilliant chestnut brown, without any white hairs or patches; the health and vibrancy of the coat are important here. The nose leather is also brown, even the whiskers. Only the feet pads can be pink. Black (melanism) in the coat is a fault. The eyes should be green.

Coat and Body Structure
The coat should be short and dense, fine, sound and healthy, and kept that way by firm grooming, which tones the muscles so that the coat benefits. The Brown can digest milk, which apparently benefits its coat. The body follows the Siamese standard, with length and slenderness, lithe muscularity and considerable grace both in repose and in motion. The hind legs are somewhat higher than the front legs, and the tail is long and kinkless. In America the standard calls for oval, not oriental, eyes.

Japanese Bobtail (Not bred in Britain)

History and Origin
The Japanese Bobtail is very much a foreign cat, very popular in Japanese history, with an 'oriental cast' to its face. It is clannish in its tastes and desire for company. The Bobtail can be seen in many areas of Japanese history through prints and paintings, as well as in sculpture, including religious monuments. Like the Akita, a dog that was first bred in Japan, the Bobtail is considered symbolic of good luck, and a gift of the breed is a sign of friendship and benevolence. Although the breed has been well known in Japan for many centuries, the United States was not familiar with it until the late 1960s. (Incidentally, the Bobtail is not bred in Britain.) By 1970 a standard had been set by means of an international association, which included Japan and North America.

Characteristics
The Japanese Bobtail enjoys the company of other Bobtails from its own family, and as a result the dam will not abandon even its grown kittens. It makes a solid family pet, although it is somewhat independent rather than companionable.

Colour
The colours of the Bobtail should fit into a scheme that includes red and white, as well as black—solid tricolours themselves; bicolours of black and white or red and white; tricolours of black, red and white, or tortoiseshell and white; or tortie (black, red and cream). The eyes (round and oval) should be of colours corresponding to the standard for the particular coat.

Coat and Body Structure

For those who desire little shedding in their pets, the Bobtail is a minimal shedder, even though the coat is longer than that of other short-hairs. It should be silky in texture, soft and semi-long—shorter than a long-hair's and longer than a short-hair's. The body is also intermediate between the lithe Siamese and the more cobby British domestic. Of medium size, it should be muscular and strong, without being massive. The hind legs are higher than the front, but they bend slightly, to convey a level appearance. The head has an oriental cast, with slanted eyes, a long nose and cheek-bones that create their own plane. A round or softly curved head is a fault. The tail is short, 2 to 3 inches, and, as the name implies, bobbed. Overall, the breed conveys a sense of litheness and colourful brilliance.

Korat

History and Origin

The history of the Korat is extremely interesting and complicated, since it extends well back into Thai history. The Korat is called the Si-Sawat in Thailand (formerly Siam), a word that means a mingling of grey and light-green colour with good fortune. Thus from the beginning the Korat denoted a particular colour, bringing with it prosperity and good luck. The ancient cat of Siam is memorialized in books, paintings and historical documents. We can even point to a book of drawings in the Bangkok National Museum in which the Korat or a similar cat was depicted, symbolic of beauty and luck. In the first half of the twentieth century the Korat was few and far between, but by the 1960s it showed considerable development, including standards, showing and recognition by some associations. The Korat remains fairly rare.

Characteristics

The Korat is an excellent family pet, intelligent, companionable, affectionate and gentle. It expects and draws attention to itself. Since it is a warm-weather breed, it is prone to upper-respiratory ailments unless suitable care is taken. Prolonged exposure to cold will possibly cause illness and make the coat grow unduly long, which is a fault if shown.

Colour

The single colour scheme of the Korat is silver-blue, from kitten through maturity. The colouring and coat length create a wavelike effect of a shimmering sea—a desirable look for the breed. White of any kind is not acceptable. Pads and nose leather may be either dark blue or lavender. Eyes should be a brilliant green.

Coat and Body Structure

The Korat has no undercoat to speak of. Its hair should be short to medium, not long, lie close to the body and be fine in texture, with a gloss or sheen to it. The coat is extremely important in breeding, the goal being a healthy silvery effect. The body is midway between the lithe Siamese and the cobby British; it is slender but strong and muscular, conveying the sense of power one feels in wild cats. The head is heart-shaped, not angular, with good breadth between the eyes; the chin strong and not undershot. Eyes should be large and brilliant, oriental when closed.

Manx
History and Origin
The Manx gains its name from the Isle of Man in the Irish Sea off the coast of Britain, but its history is wreathed in mystery and ambiguity. Some legends have it that the Manx derived originally from the Far East; this supposition is based on the voice of the Manx, which is reminiscent of the call of the jungle cat in the East. Another legend has it that the breed came to Man from a ship in the Spanish Armada. Whatever the truth or falsity of these stories, the Manx enjoyed wide popularity in Britain in the nineteenth century, and at the turn of the twentieth it became subject to stricter standards, which now hold. Since then, its popularity has been up and down in Great Britain. The chief peculiarity or distinction of the Manx, aside from its personal qualities, is its lack of a tail, which is most likely a mutation. It is truly rounded off at the rump, with a hollow where the tail would normally begin. In America the breed has been popular, principally as a show cat, since the latter part of the nineteenth century. It has been a consistent prize-winner. The Manx is not easy to breed, since the tailless quality is clearly a mutation not a slow evolutionary development, and Manxes bred like to like will not usually reproduce themselves. Further, the litter from like-to-like breeding may carry a genetic defect that leads to dead kittens or early death.

Characteristics
The Manx is a steady cat, intelligent and affectionate, playful and without any difficult personality traits. Besides these qualities, it is, of course, a considerable conversation-piece because it is so different. Even without a tail, incidentally, it is just as agile as other cats.

Colour
Any colour is acceptable: bicolour, tabby, self, white and so on, with eye colour following the standard for the coat.

Coat and Body Structure
The Manx has a distinctive coat, what is called a double coat, consisting of a thick and very soft undercoat, with a long-haired coat, also quite thick, on top. This is like the rabbit's fur. The body is medium-sized, seeming somewhat larger than it is because of the double coat; the hind legs are longer than the forelegs, like the rabbit's. Any semblance of a tail is a fault. The Manx, once again like a rabbit, moves and runs with a hopping gait.

Rex (Cornish)
History and Origin
There are two Rex breeds, the Cornish and the Devon, and while they were once thought to be connected, they are really genetically distinct. The Rex, like the Manx, is a mutation, a change in the normal natural pattern of

genes, leading to a different stage of development from what would usually be expected from a mating of sire and dam. The mutation for the Cornish Rex involves a curly coat, comparable with a rabbit's, especially the Astrex rabbit. The development of the curly-coated Cornish Rex (so-called because it was first discovered in Cornwall and resembled the Rex rabbit) was difficult to accomplish because of the genetic unpredictability. In the 1950s experimentation continued, including a German strain of the breed, developed chiefly in the United States. The Cornish was finally established in Britain and then ran into some trouble because another Rex strain was found, which became known as the Devon Rex. One of the problems in breeding the Cornish Rex derived from crossing it with the British short-hairs, which altered the original, more slender body type. Thus, to preserve the coat mutation, the body type was often sacrificed, but by the late 1960s this problem seemed overcome. The Cornish Rex is now well established.

Characteristics
The Cornish is a healthy breed, pleasant and adaptable as pets. Because of the feed-in of several strains (rather than in-breeding), it is not temperamental and enjoys being around people, taking pleasure in things and wagging its tail. It is, as well, intelligent and affectionate. For its size, incidentally, it has a big appetite.

Colour
All colours are acceptable, with the eyes following the standard for the coat colour. If the Rex has white, it must be a symmetrical white (that is, not haphazardly so), except in the Tortie-and-White.

Coat and Body Structure
The Cornish Rex coat is like a dense, plush rug, short, very thick and luxuriant, with a curl or ripple; it must not have guard hairs. The body must be muscular but not massive—oriental in slenderness rather than cobby or British. The body conveys length, as do the legs and tail. The head is slender, without being dainty, the ears quite large and the eyes oval.

Rex (Devon)
History and Development
Like the Cornish Rex, the Devon Rex is a mutation. The Devon Rex was discovered by chance, a curly-coated kitten found by a woman in Devon, who then sent it on to be mated with a Cornish Rex female. When the mating produced a litter, all the kittens proved to be straight-coated, not curly-coated. This unforeseen result meant that the Cornish and Devon Rex were genetically incompatible. By line-breeding the Devon Rex with its plain-coated litter, more Devons were produced. This was truly a different breed, with a distinct look of its own, the chief characteristic being the huge ears, like the wings of a bat, along with a delicate, pixie-like head and look. The nose was short, almost pug, whereas the Cornish Rex nose is Roman and well defined. In Britain the two breeds were recognized as distinct, and the Devon Rex was standardized by 1967.

Characteristics
The Devon is a hardy cat and becomes an excellent pet, fond of people and eager to be involved in their activities. They get along better with people, in fact, than with other cats. They seem dainty, but they hold up well, although they need warmth when they sleep. The special coat without guard hairs means they lose heat faster than other cats, and as a result they need proportionately more fat in their diet. Another problem may be their very prominent ears, which need periodic cleaning to prevent collections of dirt or infestations of mites.

Colour
All colours except bicolour are acceptable; white is a fault for showing purposes, unless the cat is a Tortie-and-White. The eyes should be in keeping with the standard for the coat colour: green, yellow or chartreuse. The exception, for both Cornish and Devon Rex, is for those with Siamese coat colouring; for them, green, yellow or chartreuse is not permitted.

Coat and Body Structure
The coat is distinctively wavy and curly, short, fine and not coarse, without guard hairs; bareness is a fault, as is a shaggy coat. The body follows the 'foreign' type, with the trunk muscular and hard although slender, the head wedge-shaped, full-cheeked and tapering to a short muzzle. The standard calls litheness mixed with strength, not a delicate look.

Russian Blue
History and Origin
The Russian Blue probably came from Archangel, a port on the Baltic, although its Russian derivation is not certain. At one time, the breed was known as the Spanish, Foreign and even Maltese. When the Russian Blue was introduced in the latter part of the nineteenth century, it was often confused with the domestic British Blue Short-hair, with both being entered at shows in the same class although their body types and head structures were quite different. The Russian Blue has a foreign-style body, slender and with a longer head; the British is characteristically plushier and broader in coat and head. By 1912 the breeds became distinct, with the Russian becoming known as the 'Blue Foreign'. By the end of the Second World War, there was renewed activity in the breeding of the Russian Blue, some of it unfortunate, since it involved cross-breeding to Siamese, among others, and the Blue began to become a hybrid. By the mid-1960s this was rectified, and the standard was revised considerably to accommodate the Russian Blue as a distinct breed, both in Britain and in the United States.

Characteristics
The glory of the Russian Blue is its coat, but the breed is also desirable for other reasons. It is not noisy or demonstrative and is often downright quiet. The cat is hardy, needing no special care or attention. The males are sometimes hostile to other male cats, but the females are even-tempered and personable.

Colour

The standard calls for a clear and unmarked blue, without break, absolutely pure and even, free from any markings or shadings. A medium rather than a pale or dark blue is preferable. In winter expect a silver tipping, whereas in summer the blue may appear somewhat brownish. With correct diet, the coat reverts to form. The skin, incidentally, is also blue. The eyes should be a brilliant piercing green.

Coat and Body Structure

The distinctive coat must be textured and elegant, short, very dense, very fine, standing forth from the skin, with a silky quality to it. The coat is double and thick, so that the breed can stand great variations of weather. The body is graceful and long, with a tapering tail. The head is wedge-shaped, of the foreign type; the eyes almond and not oval, the ears long, wide at the base and pointed.

Sphynx (The Hairless Cat)
(Not bred in Britain)
History and Origin

The Sphynx is known as the Canadian Hairless, so called because its coat has no visible hair, nor are there even whiskers. The Hairless is a mutation that occurred as recently as 1966, when it was born to normal house cats. The hairless kitten was eventually mated with its dam, and this produced further hairless and normal kittens. Mating of the Hairless like to like did not lead to further types of the breed, and only when the Hairless was outcross-bred with American Short-hairs did it reproduce itself. In this way, a line of Hairless cats was reproduced with regularity and with attention to type. Physically, the Hairless is different from the 'normal' kittens in the same litter, having an oblong head shape, with a flatness between the eyes and a central ridge. Both the wedge-shaped head and the round head one might expect are not acceptable. The Hairless, except for its lack of coat, is otherwise a typical cat, and not at all sickly because of its bare condition.

Characteristics

The Sphynx makes an easy, accommodating pet. It needs no special attention because of the hairless condition, although the skin sweats and should be washed off regularly. For those allergic to long or short hair, the Sphynx could be the answer to their needs.

Colour

The Sphynx is acceptable in all colours, uniform over the outer surfaces of the body and shading more lightly on the underparts. All bicolours should have symmetrical patterns. White is acceptable only on the point of the breast and the umbilical area. The eyes should be golden, with no green.

Coat and Body Structure

The skin should be tight, like stretched parchment, and free of wrinkles or folds. The Hairless looks hairless, but it really has either down or longer hair over its body and mask. There is a fine down on the paws, and the face has a short pile, with some length around the ears. The body is on a small scale but muscular, with a barrel-shaped chest; the head is oblong, everything about it square and firm, the eyes somewhat slanted.

Any Other Variety

The British use the term 'Experimental' as a catch-all for varieties that are not yet recognized, many of which are in the process of being developed for future recognition and showing with a particular standard. Since Britain has one governing cat association, this class can be closely supervised and controlled. In the United States, where several cat associations exist and are often in disagreement about standards for a particular breed or over the acceptability of a breed, there is no such category. Instead there exists a way by which new or experimental breeds can be shown as 'Non-Championship Provisional' breeds, although such breeds may be acceptable only to some associations and not to others.

The category, whether British or American, serves as a testing-area for cats of several kinds: those that resulted from chance matings and seem interesting, those scientifically bred for particular ends and those that are variations of established varieties. Once a breed is placed in this provisional category, it remains there until interest is high and the type has produced true for several generations. The association overseeing that breed can then apply for recognition, to the Governing Council of the Cat Fancy in Britain, or to one of seven in the United States, of which the Cat-Fanciers Association and the American Cat-Fanciers Association are by far the largest. Use of the provisional category and the care taken before recognition are the only ways a new breed can be scrutinized, so that we can be certain it breeds true and that no weaknesses are continued on the line. Once standards are imposed, the breed as shown must conform, and this ensures the perpetuation of a healthy line.

Assessment Classes

In Britain until comparatively recently cats and kittens whose coat patterns, colourings and characteristics did not conform with the standard required for any recognized pedigree variety were registered as 'Any Other Colour' or 'Any Other Variety', being entered in classes so called at the shows. It was never very satisfactory to the exhibitors, as the judges had no standards by which the cats could be judged, and the classes were getting bigger and bigger.

After much discussion, and as it was realized that the majority of such cats were the start of new varieties, it was decided that they should be entered in an experimental register, with preliminary standards being worked out for the varieties, but without breed-numbers. Assessment Classes were and are still put on at all Championship shows for such cats. They do not compete with one another but are judged individually by three judges according to the standards exhibited on the pens.

If the judge considers that the cat is close to the standard, a merit card may be awarded, with the number of merit cards awarded counting towards the eventual recognition of the variety. When sufficient merit cards have been given and enough of the particular variety have been bred, it is possible that the Governing Council will grant provisional recognition and a breed-number but not championship status. This, and full recognition, is not given until at least a hundred cats of a specific variety have been produced and are good examples of what is required.

NINE

The Wild Cats

Why, you may ask, do I include a chapter on wild cats in a book on a domesticated animal? The answer is both obvious and not so obvious. First of all, your little house pet is a part of a very important and large family of thirty-eight cats. Second, many of the characteristics—physical as well as temperamental—that you find in your pet are also found in many of the wild varieties. Third, we carry with us a fascination with the wilderness, and the domestic cat derives from that environment. It has adapted to domesticity, but in gait, silhouette and habits it reminds us constantly of those others who have remained outside man's world.

Of the thirty-seven other varieties, the lion, tiger, cougar (puma), cheetah, jaguar and leopard are perhaps the best known in the West. We know many of these from zoos or from television programmes. Yet who are the others? Where do they come from? How do they mate and lead their lives? What are their general as well as specific characteristics? What do they eat—especially those that live in forbidding places? How long does it take each species to be born, how long does it live, how does it die? What are the qualities that bring them together into one family, despite the diversity among them? And why have some captured man's imagination for thousands of years?

To seek some of these answers is to dig among the archaeological and psychological roots not only of animal life but of man's beginnings as well.*

We begin with East Africa, a huge land-mass, far more immense than all of Western Europe combined. It is itself a land of immense heat, considerable desolation and overwhelming mystery. It seems inhospitable to both man and beast. Vast yellow meadow-like fields stretch out as far as the eye can

---

* For many of my observations, I am indebted to the work of C. A. W. Guggisberg, the well-known naturalist.

measure them. But there is water, from rivers, and there is vegetation; and that means the presence of abundant wildlife: zebras, gazelles, wildebeests, impalas. Each animal fits itself into the rhythm of existence: need for food and water, and ever-present danger from the big cats.

The three big cats that endanger other wildlife in this region are the lion, the cheetah and the leopard. They follow a very different pattern from the herds of zebras and wildebeests that inhabit the same grounds.

In the late afternoon, a pride of lions (the only wild cats to travel in family groups) gets up slowly, the first part of a methodical encounter with the grazing animals in the distance. The whole pride—females, adult and young males, and cubs—stand, as though to announce their presence. The lionesses make the first move. They begin a slow trot toward a herd of zebras in the distance. They lower themselves until, except for the tips of their ears, they have vanished in the high grass. The males and cubs follow slowly. There is complete silence, although the zebras by way of some protective system of their own have become alerted. They begin to move slowly, then more rapidly into a trot. Suddenly a lioness's tail stands straight up, and she charges the herd, to drive it in the opposite direction. The zebras, facing a frontal assault, do exactly what is expected of them. They turn and gallop away from the lioness and fall into the oldest of traps, the ambush.

As the zebras move swiftly away from the first lioness, they run directly into the path of the other two or three. The strategy has worked, as it has for thousands of years. The lionesses have placed themselves so as to cut off all chance to retreat. As the zebras crash by, the lionesses launch themselves in a rush of nearly 30 miles an hour, usually bringing down at least one zebra by jumping on its back and breaking its neck. All it takes is one correctly placed smash of a paw. The females have worked together, planned the strategy and made the kill, all without the male.

Off in the distance, perhaps a mile or two away, a lone 'spotted sphinx', as the cheetah has been called, is watching still another herd. She does not move but watches intently over her cubs playing nearby. Suddenly she signals to her cubs in some strange 'birdlike calls'—as much a language as our words of caution—and heads for cover. She has spotted a herd of Thomson's gazelles, her favourite food and a challenge for her hunting ability. The gazelle is the fastest animal on four feet on a sustained run, but the cheetah in short bursts is capable of over 60 miles an hour.

Down she goes into the reeds and rushes lining the river. As she emerges from her cover, the gazelles suspect nothing, because the cheetah has been moving downwind from the herd. Then she does something that no other wild cat does. She does not crouch, and she does not stalk slowly and methodically like all the other cats, but moves forward in a standing position until she is about 100 yards from the gazelles. Then she takes off like a bolt straight for her prey, running it down and choking it to death. She drags the gazelle, which is several times her own weight, back to the cubs. She does this alone, without any back-up aid from either males or other females.

In still another scene, we see through binoculars a peaceful, utterly relaxed spotted cat, most likely asleep, on a large tree branch. But as late afternoon turns into dusk and then into night, its part of the day is beginning. The leopard moves in the dark, and it uses trees as none of the other large cats does. From its perch in the branches, it sees antelope in the distance as they move toward water. The leopard watches patiently, coolly. It is one of the surest of the wild cats, perhaps the most intelligent as well as the most elegant in line and muscular development.

If patience is the sure way to reach heaven, the leopard is bound to ascend, for it will watch for hours, motionless, waiting until the moment is exactly right for the kill. Only the tip of its tail moves ever so slightly. The moment arrives. Using its cover in the high grass, it begins the well-known stalk of the cat, body just brushing the ground, limbs and body harmonious. The popular image of a cat stalking its prey in the jungle is taken from the leopard and its prey—a typical behaviour of wildlife in the human imagination. Every move is economical and cautious.

The closer the leopard approaches to its prey, the more slowly it moves. To the casual eye, it might seem absolutely motionless, suspended in time and space. To the trained eye, an elegant and aesthetically lovely animal is about to make its kill. When it senses that its prey has been distracted and that it is close enough for the kill (perhaps 10 to 25 yards away), it dashes and springs on the antelope's back. It kills swiftly, most often by strangulation and breaking the victim's neck. If the antelope suspects something and begins to run, the leopard must make the catch rapidly, for its great speed can be sustained only in a short chase. In a real run, the antelope will outdistance it.

I have chosen these well-known examples of the great cats of East Africa because they represent three different species of the cat family. Let us look, first, at the lion and the cheetah, which are outsiders in many ways, for they play the game differently from most of the other great cats.

As a family animal, the lion moves in a pride, which is a society and something of a sex-system. A pride may consist of from five to thirty lions, usually four adult males, two to three sub-adults (juveniles) and a few cubs, with females making up the rest. The females will stay together, and the males will mix only with each other. The male, incidentally, is the only cat with a mane. Both males and females have dark tufts at the end of their tails, also something no other cat has.

The cheetah is long-legged, often sits like a dog and cannot retract its nails, which all other cats can do. It is also a courser. That is, rather than stalking its prey, as the other cats do, it openly shows itself and runs down its prey. The cheetah is a unique species, making up the genus *Acinonyx* by itself. Strangely enough, cheetahs have been domesticated and led around, like a large dog, on a chain. The practice was common with ancient Egyptian royalty, and in recent times the Lion of Judah, Haile Selassie of Abyssinia, was often pictured with a cheetah on a chain. It can also be used for hunting, kept hooded until it is released to run down its prey.

When we turn to the leopard, we find a cat that has the silhouette and profile of our house cat, only blown up to twenty-five times the size. It is also a night cat, and comes down to us as a stealthy animal moving by moonlight. The panther is simply a black leopard, and it is probably the panther we think of as the quintessential jungle model for our small black house cat. The leopard is a loner, is nocturnal, uses trees and is unpredictable. The head is roundish and rather short in proportion to the rest of the body, which is lithe, very muscular and powerful. The tail is long, to help with movement in the trees. The claws are sharp enough to shred a man. The teeth are constructed not for crushing or crunching but for tearing and cutting.

Anatomically, we know a great deal about the big cats, but we still know relatively little about them otherwise. I will take them up in order in this chapter and tell you many of the essential facts about them, but what we do not know—that core of mystery—is equal to what we do know. And when we come to the smaller wild cats—a good number of the thirty-eight species, we know even less, for many of them cannot be tracked. They are night animals, or else because of their small size they elude discovery; some move in virtually inaccessible places. Perhaps half of the cat family, eighteen or twenty of those thirty-eight species, are almost completely unknown to mankind and even to most specialists. How many of us have heard of the sand-dune cat, the marble cat, the Chinese Sesat cat and the Andean highland cat?

Part of the problem is logistical and tactical. Since the cats are small— many species are smaller than the average house cat, fast and nocturnal, they cannot be followed into their jungle or mountain habitats. No practical way to study them has been found. When skeletons of the smaller cats have been discovered, it is interesting to note that they do not in any significant way differ from the fossils scientists have dug up dating back more than a million years. The present-day cat is probably very much what its ancient ancestor was.

Possibly, part of the 'mystery' we associate with the cat is connected to these facts: that it is a link with the very deepest aspects of nature, that it is attached to that most mysterious of all creatures, the panther (the black leopard), and that varieties of the feline species have trod all parts of the earth almost since the beginning of time. The self-sufficiency of the house cat, which attracts a particular type of owner, extends out to the smaller varieties of the wild cat and to the great cats themselves. They are a law unto themselves. Balzac's classic story 'A Passion in the Desert' connects a French soldier's experience of a desert panther with 'passion', with both a sexual and a religious experience. The equation is apt, if exaggerated. The sense of awe, however, is religious, for the soldier senses that he is in the presence of something in and yet beyond nature.

Somehow, to know our ancestors is to know something about ourselves. To learn something about the cat's long history and related species is to be astonished at what goes into even nature's smaller creatures. My observation of cat-owners is that their devotion to their pet is fiercer and perhaps more absolute than that of any other kind of owner. For the person who wants to understand more about his or her cat, the following information boils down what we know to the essentials. I will tell you who the other cats are and what they are like—the ways in which they pit their senses against a world that in many instances is pushing them into oblivion.

THIRTY-SEVEN PLUS ONE

There are, as I have said, thirty-seven distinct species of the wild cat and one domestic or house cat, bringing the total to thirty-eight. They are mammals; they are meat-eaters, although if starved they will eat nearly anything. They all belong to the family called *Felidae*.

Within this family, there are three kinds of cats: (1) *Panthera*—all the big cats, such as the tiger, lion, leopard, snow leopard and jaguar; (2) *Acinonyx*—only the cheetah; (3) *Felis*—all the rest of the cats including the house cats.

They are native to all parts of the world with the exception of the West Indies, Iceland, Greenland, the Falkland Islands, Australia, New Zealand, Antarctica, Madagascar and New Guinea.

In another section, I speak of the history of the house cat. But the origin of the entire family remains dim. From paintings or scratchings and fossil-remains, we may assume that ancestors of the cat family existed forty to fifty million years ago, whereas some animal with a distinct resemblance existed ten to fifteen million years ago. The family itself as we know it may go back about five million years. Having evolved to that stage, the cat as we now observe it has distinct affinities with its ancestors of five million years ago. Other mammals hardly even resemble their ancient ancestors, but the cat family has remained constant.

Therefore, to look at any members of this large family is to look not only at the present but at the past, at pre-history, in which everything except what modern science has so far uncovered is mysterious, legendary and mythical.

The arrangement below is according to continent.

EAST AFRICA

Lion

On safaris, some want to see a cheetah, others a leopard, but everyone wants to see the lion in the wild. To be near a lion or just to sense its presence is to enter into a world of immense power and wonder. It is the male which generates this interest, perhaps because of the gigantic mane, or possibly because in the popular imagination *he* is the king of the beasts. No matter that the male is lazy, parasitical, a sponge on the lioness, a ne'er-do-well in most respects—no matter, he is godly and majestic. We believe in legends, and we seek out their living representative, the lion.

Throughout history, emperors, kings and popes have used the lion as a symbol of power. I mentioned Haile Selassie, the Lion of Judah, and there was also Richard the Lion-Hearted, William the Lion, Pope Leo, as well as many others. He may be symbolic of an entire city (the Lion of St Mark for Venice) or of a public library (the two lions outside the New York Public Library); he appears on family crests, as the 'resting lion', or becomes an object of worship. The Cochise Indians carved two sacred lions, side by side, in the New Mexico rocks. In ancient Nineveh, the oldest city in the Assyrian civilization, sculptural slabs of lions suggest worship and protection as though they were gods who could protect man. The Assyrians even pictured their fierce black-bearded kings as huge winged lions with human heads. The Egyptians paid homage to the king of beasts by constructing sphinxes with the bodies of lions and human heads. The sphinx who poses the riddle to Oedipus has the head and breast of a woman, the wings of an eagle and the body of a lion.

Stone lions are seen everywhere as symbolic guards, always representing the power and majesty of the buildings or the gods they are associated with. Lions are connected, for example, with Ishtar, the great war-goddess of ancient Assyria and Babylon. They are also associated with the great mother-goddesses of Greece and Rome. We see them on fortresses and Gothic cathedrals as well.

These representations do not exist only in the West. In ancient India, Buddhist art often depicted a lion between the feet of Buddha, and other gods had the ability to transform themselves into lions whenever they went into battle.

These are just some of the myths. But what about the reality, the lion in everyday life? Unfortunately, our information is sketchy, and far too much comes from unreliable sources such as hunters, editors of picture-books, or television and Hollywood producers. We still have no comprehensive view of this magnificent animal, although we are moving toward one.

The high-powered rifle with its electronic attachments is too much with us these days, and the lion in the wild would have no chance against such a weapon. So natural parks have been established in East Africa—the Nairobi National Park in Kenya, the Masai-Mara in Tanzania and the famous Serengeti in Uganda, for studying lions and other large predators. What, then, do we know about the lion?

He is second in size in the *Panthera* group, the tiger being the biggest of the cats. The head and body length may come to 9 feet, with another 3 for the tail. Males weigh about 300 pounds, females about 75 to 100 pounds less. As we have seen, the male is the only cat with a mane, and both sexes are the only cats that have tufts of hair at the tip of the tail. When the female is in heat, two lions can copulate 100 to 150 times in fifty-five hours, and each copulation lasts about twenty-one seconds. It takes between 105 and 112 days for a cub to be born. Litters run from one to four, but cub mortality is very high, maybe one-third.

The lion is not a great 'jumping cat', but both sexes have been seen to leap 12 feet from a standing-position and up to 25 from a running-start. Like all the cats in the genus *Panthera*, his pupils remain rounded when contracted; he cannot purr, but roars. This is because the connection between the Adam's apple and the skull is made by strong elastic ligaments and not by bones; this makes the sound vibrate and then emerge as a roar. The coat is extremely varied, running from light buff and ochre-tinted silvery grey to yellowish red and dark ochre-brown. The lion's claws are retractable. In the wild, his life-span is a little more than ten years. He is mainly a late-evening hunter and night prowler, but he does attack in the daytime, even at high noon.

The male lion is neither brave, nor regal, nor majestic—this is a human conception of him. As with all animals, his whole being is geared to perpetuating his own kind and to staying alive. He tries to stay out of danger, does not provoke fights and does not take chances. And that is why he has survived, for he goes back to the Great Ice Age in Europe. We have sketches of him in caves appearing much larger than he is today, the great predator of Europe. Gradually, genetic changes and natural selection made him smaller. He left Europe but was still seen in the Balkans about 450 BC—Herodotus, the Greek historian, mentions him. By the time of Christ's birth, he had vanished from all of Europe.

The lion's 'pride' may be as small as six and as large as thirty-five. The territory of a pride can run for up to 20 miles, but the word 'territory' has different meanings for each sex.

The male's sense of territory has to do with females. His territory extends to where they roam, sit, give birth, copulate, care for the young. It has little to do with hunting, although occasionally a few males may team up to bring down a water buffalo. The female is almost always the predator, and to her territory means food. She is responsible for feeding the pride and caring for the cubs.

The favourite get-together for a pride is usually some grassy plain, the savannas, open woodland or brush country, and often under small trees. Lions avoid dense forest areas because of discomfort and the inability to see their prey and stalk them. They are good swimmers and depend primarily on sight and hearing (not smell) to locate their kill.

Two interesting points about the family life of lions. First, if the adult males are weak or defeated by adults from another pride, the cub mortality-rate rises sharply, and a great tension develops between the females. If the males are strong and stable and discourage raids by outsiders, the females get along extremely well, often nurturing each other's cubs. Then the mortality-rate is low.

The second point is just the opposite of what most people believe: that the male eats first, then the female, then the sub-adults, followed by the cubs, in that rigid order. True, the male may take a carcass away from a female and cuff everyone who tries to get near, but in most instances the whole pride goes at it, each trying to get its favourite organ. This gives the cubs the opportunity to enter a competitive world and make use of their cunning and strength to obtain food. Often the male will chase the female away and allow the cubs to eat. If, however, food is scarce, the female will try to devour the carcass and give nothing to the cubs. There is little sense of self-sacrifice when it comes to food.

The male often eats as much as 60 pounds at one sitting and then does not eat again for three or four days. The same is more or less true for the female, although the cubs may eat more regularly if food is available. Young males between thirty months and three years old know they must separate themselves from the pride and establish their own families. The craving to wander beyond their territory and the aggressive behaviour of adult males determine this pattern.

During the day, prides rest, sleep, sometimes play with each other. They enjoy being close. When a young female wanders off and then returns, she greets everyone in a ritualistic fashion by rubbing her cheeks and her head against theirs. In the pride, the males usually stay by themselves, and the females stay by themselves also. Yet closeness and touch are part of their being, intermixed with the need for alertness, boldness and sudden bursts of powerful action.

Leopard

We know very little about the leopard. It lived in Europe and Asia millions of years ago and was then larger than the leopard we know today. We can tell this from skeletons (or bones) found in the Transvaal, Java and China. Leopards vanished rather quickly from Europe and made their homes in Africa and Asia. The ancient Greeks knew them, and Romans imported them from Africa for circuses and the arena. After Rome fell, the leopard showed up in the Byzantine Empire and then in the Courts of medieval Europe. After that, it vanished from Western civilization.

We must now move to Africa to learn something about the leopard, and even there it is an animal of darkness which travels alone. If cats as a whole are mysterious, the leopard is the most mysterious of all. It is extremely difficult to see—it has been called 'the invisible one'—and many hunters, zoologists and ecologists have spent their lives in Africa and Asia without even seeing one. It is also one of the most adaptable of the large cats, ranging from Manchuria to Korea, through China, Burma, India and much of Africa.

Except for the mating-season and the raising of the young, the leopard lives and dies alone. Self-containment is the essence of its existence. It is almost impossible to see two males together, and never two females. When you see more than one, it is always a female followed by her cubs. As in the entire cat family, it is the female who brings up the young.

Aesthetically, leopards are dazzling creatures, and to see them hunt is to observe the cat in all its splendour. The fiercest of the big cats, the leopard stalks its prey in a similar way to the lion and the whole cat family (the cheetah is the only exception) but with much greater patience, stealth and cunning. The leopard usually strangles its prey, unlike the lion, which usually breaks its victim's neck. It usually comes so close to its prey that it does not even need to rush. It is just there, a leap away from its food.

The leopard's appearance even in rest is striking. The tail is longer in proportion to the body than in any of the other big cats; the paws are large and powerful, the claws razor-sharp and retractile; the body is long and slung low. The whole body is so compact and strong that, although the leopard weighs only 80 to 120 pounds, it can carry an animal over 100 pounds straight up a tree trunk. It is a powerful leaper, a good swimmer (but like most cats will avoid water if it can) and a great climber. It can live anywhere, whether on mountains or plains, but it needs cover.

A leopard's colour varies from pale yellow to dull yellow to grey to light brown. The ears are short and black, often tipped with white. Black spots cover its head and chest; underparts are white with black spots; other parts are covered with spots resembling a rose. Black leopards are not unusual but are rather rare in Africa.

The leopard prefers variety in its diet, preferring baboons, pigs, deer, antelope, domestic stock and dogs, which it considers a great delicacy. Leopards get into domestic stock by living just outside a village, where, because they are sly, solitary, elusive and wary, they can get by. The leopard has in somewhat exaggerated form all the qualities we associate with the family of cats, including the house cat.

Generally, what do we know of the leopard's living-habits? It is a loner, nocturnal, with a definite sense of territory. Females will share their territory, but not males. Leopards have a sharp sense of sight and hearing. The young are raised by females, and there is a lot of playing, rubbing and grooming. The cubs are taught to hunt and kill by the mother. Once a leopard learns to kill, it leaves to live by itself.

The leopard likes to spend its time resting in the shade on a hillside, beside a large rock or in the branches of a tree. It moves out at dusk, and when darkness falls you can hear its strange rasping cough. The leopard that emerges is about 5 feet in length, with a tail of about 3 feet and a weight that runs from 80 pounds for females to 120 for males. Its height while on the run is less than 2 feet. Leopard cubs take 90 to 105 days for birth, and they form small litters, usually one to five.

Cheetah

The cheetah is perhaps the most bizarre of all the cats. It has a genus all to itself, *Acinonyx*, and it has characteristics that are not duplicated by the other big cats. Whereas the others must lie to rest, the cheetah can sit or lie like a dog; its claws are not fully retractable, and it purrs with a continuous sound like a house cat. Also, as we said before, it is a courser, not a stalker, although it often does approach its prey on its belly. It does not possess the stealth or the patience of the leopard.

Its head is round and small in proportion to its body, the chest full and deep. The waist is narrow, the legs long and slender. The cheetah is built for speed, not power. It observes its prey, walks slowly toward it and at about 100 yards accelerates to a speed of 45 miles an hour in three seconds, and in another two seconds is running close to 65 miles an hour (a racehorse cannot reach 50). But it cannot sustain that speed for more than a few hundred yards. In most cases, it simply outruns its prey, and it kills by strangulation.

In mood and temperament, the cheetah seems to be a cross between a lion and a leopard but is mainly like the leopard. Most cheetahs are solitary, although some do travel in groups of two, sometimes even five. They greet each other by sniffing and ever so briefly just touching cheeks. There is no rubbing against each other such as one observes in lions and in the house cat. When males and females come together, circles of tension embrace them. If families come together, fierce fighting usually occurs, the males attacking the females and cubs. Togetherness means aggression and combat. When there is companionship, it brings males together with other males.

One hardly ever sees a female and her cubs with other adults, and grown females avoid each other. Because of the cheetah's solitary nature, the cubs must learn to hunt before they are fully grown, for unlike lions they cannot depend on a family for food. The mother makes certain that they learn.

She is a model parent: patient, disciplined as a teacher, affectionate. She lets the cubs hunt by themselves but watches them carefully. Often, she will capture small prey, bring it back to the cubs weak and dazed and then release it so they can learn to kill it. If they fail, she will repeat this over and over until they learn. More than most cats, large or small, the mother cheetah and the cubs enjoy play. They do it to release energy, to learn hunting tactics and, apparently, just for itself.

Cheetahs are weaned very early, about the tenth or eleventh week. When the mother makes a kill, all the cubs are invited to eat. You rarely see the fierce aggression so characteristic of the lion. The female cheetah will not take the carcass away from her cubs to eat herself, as a lioness might do. Males, however, are different. They will take the kill from the female and her cubs. A quality of all cheetahs is their timidity or discretion, or perhaps just wisdom. They will often give their kill to hyenas and to lions.

At a little over a year, cheetahs can run down and kill their prey, and at about fifteen months they are fully grown. Then they do something that is astonishing and enigmatic. One day, one hour, they break with the mother. The break is abrupt and final, absolute.

Lions and leopards do it gradually, and the mother and young will often continue to recognize each other. The cheetah will never even acknowledge its mother, and if they are in the same vicinity they will ignore each other. The young females may stay together for a few days, but then they go their separate ways. Males may stay together for a while. There are no family bonds, and the most striking thing about the inner life of the cheetah is its amazing aloofness. Joy Adamson's name for the cheetah, 'the spotted sphinx' (the name 'cheetah' originated in India and means 'the spotted one'), is precise.

The life of a cheetah in the wild is very often shorter than for the other big cats, about nine to ten years, often only five to seven. In captivity it lives about thirteen years. We must remember that once a cheetah's speed goes, it is not strong enough to survive alone.

The average male weighs about 125 pounds, the female slightly less. From head to back it measures about 6½ feet, with 3 feet for the tail. Shoulder height is 31 inches. The time from conception to birth is between ninety and ninety-five days, with a litter of between three and six cubs. One half of the cubs die in the first few months, usually as the result of hyena or lion raids. A few cheetahs can be found in India and Iran, but almost all of them are now in Africa. They are harmless to man.

Cheetahs were used as the emblem of courage by the Egyptians, who knew how to tame them and use them as hunters. They became the royal pets of two almost mythical emperors, Genghis Khan and Charlemagne. But even when tamed, the cheetah exists for no one; it is a pure consciousness, a pure presence. Repose and the hunt are the essential elements of its being, whatever else man tries to make of it.

The big cats I have talked about so far—the lion, the leopard, to a lesser extent, and the cheetah—lend themselves to some scientific statements. To some degree, they are all known. But as members of the cat family shrink in size, our knowledge decreases. Our information on their life-habits slips into a shadow existence. Many of them are nocturnal and elusive, with great ability to conceal themselves. Since there are few ways to study them in their natural habitat, we find them mysterious and impenetrable.

Caracal

The caracal (from the Turkish '*karakal*', meaning 'black ear'), or the 'desert lynx', as it is often called, is a small version of the leopard. It stalks and pounces like the leopard, but it has some lynx characteristics as well— it is long-legged with narrow, pointed, tufted, triangular ears. Its head and body length come to about 28 inches, its tail to about 9. This is remarkably short for a cat. The male weighs 32 to 36 pounds, the female 25, and its shoulder height is 17 inches. The fur is rather short, dark reddish brown, with the chin, neck and belly mainly white. A thin black line connects each eye to the nose.

Caracals can be found in central India, the Punjab, Afghanistan, Iran, Egypt, Israel, Libya, Algeria and Morocco, but always in bush, tree or mountain country, never in the desert or in the rain forest. The vast majority of the type, however, live in South Africa and Uganda, and a few have been seen in East Africa in the Serengeti National Park.

We know relatively little of their life in the wild because of their solitary nature. They do come together in adult life, but only for brief periods of courtship and mating. The caracal is stern-looking, aloof, self-sufficient, fierce and independent; it moves at night and hunts by day. Its walk is similar to the cheetah's, and so is its speed. The caracal is the fastest cat for its size in the world. To many zoologists it epitomizes the very essence of the cat tribe, and in Swahili it is known as 'little lion' or 'fierce lion'. It is considered untamable.

The caracal preys on lizards, rabbits, birds, chickens, antelopes and goats, and it has even been known to kill eagles. Often, like the leopard, it will drag its kill up a tree and eat it at its pleasure safely out of reach of the other predators.

The female usually gives birth to two or three kittens, sometimes up to five. The embryo takes about seventy days to develop. The mother brings up the kittens, and they stay with her about a year. In captivity, some caracals have lived as long as eighteen years; in the wild, their life-span is about half that.

Serval

Solitary, retiring, fantastically graceful, the serval is much more elegant than the caracal, for it is narrower, with longer, far more slender legs. The compact head has very large round ears with a wide base and a midnight black at the back of each ear surrounding a white spot. The combination of elegance, graceful movement and colour makes it seem ghostly.

The body itself is covered by shadings of yellowish brown or toned-down red with black spots that run into lines or bars. Much of the body and legs is braceleted. The legs are unique in the cat family, in that the front two are longer than the hind ones. The tail is proportionally short, running about one-third of the body length. The serval, apart from the tail, is about 32 inches long and weighs close to 35 pounds. Its shoulder height is 22 inches.

Black servals are not especially rare. Zoologists and naturalists have seen them around Mount Kenya, the Mau Forest and near Kilimanjaro. This cat is not at all so fierce as the caracal—some, in fact, have even been tamed, but it is rarely seen because it moves and hunts in the night. Further, the serval is incredibly swift and agile, so that if you approach, it will take off in long, elastic bounds.

The cat prefers to live in grassland and bush country, in rather dense savannas and small-hill country, but it also likes to be around water, using the high grass and reeds as a cover. It could once be found throughout Africa, but now it lives in western and central Africa, including Senegal, Angola, Uganda and Zambia. It preys on rats, rabbits, small antelopes, lizards and birds, which it loves to stalk in trees. It locates its prey mainly by sound and sight.

The serval has a distinct and shrill cry, which it repeats seven or eight times in succession, but it also can purr and spit and hiss just like the house cat. It can become very dangerous when its food is threatened, or when it is cornered.

The gestation period runs a little more than for the house cat, taking around sixty-nine to seventy-three days; litters are from one to four.

Its greatest enemy is man, especially the tribes in the areas where it hunts. To these tribesmen the serval is valuable for its skin and also as a delectable dish. The skin is fashioned into fur coats called 'karrosses'.

Sand-Dune Cat
When I think of the sand-dune cat, I think of a twilight zone, something between light and dark, for the sand-dune cat moves chiefly at about that time. It remains relatively obscure, having not really been observed in detail. It is sometimes referred to as the *Felis Margarita*, after General Margueritte, who led his men into what came to be known as the French Sahara in the last century and opened it to the world.

We have few hard facts about this strange twilight creature. It is a rather small cat, short-legged, with a big, square-looking head that seems too long for its body. It has firm cheek-whiskers, very broad ears, reddish at the back and tipped black, and set far apart, well down on the side of the head. This suggests extremely acute hearing and makes it possible for the sand-dune cat to flatten itself out so that it becomes almost invisible.

Its body is well adapted to its environment: rocky wastes and deserts. The soles of its paws are covered with thick coarse hair, hiding the pads and enabling it to move quickly over sand that is soft or oven-hot. The paws grip rather than slide. So that it fits into its background, the sand-dune cat has a thick, usually straw-coloured coat. The underpart is white. Each cheek has a bright-brown streak that runs across it to the outer corner of each eye. The lower part of the face is an off-white, and the legs are encased in black bands. The very end of the tail is black.

The head and body together usually average out to between 19 and 20 inches, the tail about 12. Shoulder height is 10 inches.

The sand-dune cat lives in the northern Sahara, eastern Saudi Arabia and western Asia, where it can be seen in such places as Uzbekistan and

Kazakhstan. As I said, it prefers dry land, but not a complete wasteland, for it needs prey. The prey may be rodents, hare, lizards, birds and locusts. It does not need a water-supply, strangely enough, for it gains its liquid needs from the bodies of its victims.

We know nothing about its mating-habits, how it brings up its young or its period of gestation. We do know that the litter is from two to four kittens. That the sand-dune cat has survived to this day, with its mortal enemies— poisonous snakes, vultures and wolves—surrounding it, is one of the miracles of nature.

Black-Footed Cat

The black-footed cat is of great interest because it is the smallest member of the family, and that includes your house cat. The length of the male comes to 17 or 18 inches, the tail about 7 inches; the average weight is only 4 pounds, with females even smaller. Like its relations, it is mainly a night prowler, so that the chances of tracking it are almost nil. It is a cat that is there and not there.

But it has been seen. Here is a description of its incredible fierceness, considering its size, by E. E. Cronje Wilmot, an official in Ngamiland: "This is the smallest of the African wild cats; but what it lacks in size is fully compensated for by its extreme ferocity. Though its weight is only about a quarter of that of a small sheep, this little feline readily attacks those animals. It fastens on the neck and hangs on until the jugular is pierced."

This cat seems to have lodged itself deep in the psyche of the Masarawa Bushmen, for, according to Wilmot, they swear that the black-footed cat can kill a giraffe in the same way: by getting its claws into the jugular. No one has confirmed this, but the power of the cat, however small, arouses the human imagination.

The black-foot's coat is pale, rather tawny or yellow, usually darker on top and paler on the underparts. Three dark rings circle the legs; the body shows bold dark spots, which fuse into stripes in the neck and shoulders, and the face has two horizontal lines. The proportionately short tail is black-tipped, with dark rings. The soles of the paws are black, and that fact accounts for its name. Its roaming is usually confined to the Kalahari Desert and parts of the Transvaal, but it has recently been seen in the Kruger National Park.

It preys on small animals, probably rats and mice, snakes and lizards, maybe birds. Its period of heat, in contrast to the house cat's five or more days, is only five to ten hours. So solitary is the black-foot that mating-time is reduced to the absolute minimum. Gestation itself runs from fifty-nine to sixty-eight days, with litters of one or two. The male vanishes after mating, and the female brings up the kittens and teaches them to hunt and kill. Her method is to bring live mice to the kittens, so that they can practise—but this observation was made of the black-foot in captivity. In the wild, the life of this cat remains a mystery, one of the most mysterious of all in the family and in the entire animal kingdom.

African Wildcat

From what wild species does the house cat derive? Is it in a direct line to the big cats, or to the smaller? First of all, the big cats lie with their front legs out in front; and, second, they do not bury their faeces. The smaller wild cats, however, tuck their front legs under them when they rest, and they cover or hide their faeces. Recent research suggests that the ancient ancestor of the house cat is the African wildcat (*Felis lybica*), sometimes called the cat of Egypt or the Kaffir cat. It was domesticated by the Egyptians about 2500 to 2000 BC.

The African wildcat is somewhat bigger and stronger than most house cats, body and head length coming to 2 feet, with the tail half of that. It stands 14 inches at the shoulder and weighs about 13 pounds (most house cats are 8 to 10 pounds, even less). The African has longer legs, a lean, muscular body, a thin tail tipped black and ringed three times, and round ears rusty at the back.

The coat varies from a pale grey to greyish brown, to dark grey and even silvery grey. The front legs and the upper part of the back legs are ringed with brown circles. Dark lines enclose the eyes, suggesting Nefertiti. More likely, the Nefertiti look came about as an imitation of the cat's eyes, at the time when cats were Egyptian symbols of fertility and happiness.

The African wildcat roams throughout Africa, with the exception of deserts and the great equatorial forest. It does exceptionally well in mountainous terrain. In eastern Africa it keeps to the bush and high grass country; in southern Africa it hugs reed beds. Although it is not so invisible as the black-footed cat, it does not have a high presence; it is mainly a night prowler. Its food consists of rodents, hare, snakes, lizards, insects and birds.

Gestation period for the female is fifty-six to sixty days, just under what is required for the house cat. Litters are small, rarely over two or three. The wildcat is not so fierce and wild that it cannot be brought up in captivity—and many have been.

The African wildcat, domesticated by the Egyptians, first made its appearance in Europe at about the beginning of Christianity. It was generally accepted in Greece, although not widely known; it then moved to the Roman Empire, where it was well accepted by the fourth century. It spread throughout Europe in the next five centuries and reached England in the ninth century, even mating with the local forest wildcats. What is remarkable is how close this cat is to our modern house cat. Try to figure out how a Chihuahua and a Saint Bernard belong to the same species, the canine species; but the cat retains the same look, whether an African wildcat or a present-day Siamese or Persian.

Golden Cat

A strikingly beautiful cat, the golden is one of the most elusive of all. It is almost impossible to capture alive, this 'brother of the leopard', as it has been called. Because of its mysteriousness, it has been associated with much ritual, magic and superstition. Native chiefs in the Cameroons have shown naturalists their royal robes made from skins of the golden, but they have never revealed the areas there the cat lives and hunts. Some Pygmy tribes consider the tail of the golden a symbol or talisman of good fortune—it ensures success in elephant-hunting, but they, too, are silent about the location of the breed.

The golden is more than twice as big as the house cat. It is compact, muscular and extremely strong for its weight, with long legs, large paws, a small head, rounded ears and an average-size tail. The coat colour varies enormously from golden grey to copper-red to greyish brown and dark grey. The cheeks, underparts and inside of the legs are white. Brown-grey spots often cover the body, and the tail is ringed.

The shoulder height is 20 inches, length about 30 and weight in the range of 35 pounds. We know nothing about its family life, if any, or its general behaviour in the wild. Even its mating-season—whether a matter of days or hours—is a mystery.

Central Africa is its main territory: Senegal, Cameroon, Gabon and Kenya. In Uganda it has been seen moving as high as 12,000 feet—somewhat like the snow leopard in Tibet. But it generally prefers tropical forests. It stalks and kills at twilight or even during the deepest part of the night, and it spends the day sleeping or resting in a tree.

This 'small leopard' feeds on chickens, baby antelopes and other small animals. It will often move close to human habitation, although it is only rarely seen.

ASIA

If Africa is the heart of an immense darkness, Asia, the largest of the continents, is also still an enigma shrouded in myth, legend and ritual. Wild cats live in nearly all parts of the continent: the south-west, made up of Afghanistan, Saudi Arabia, Syria, Iraq, Iran, Jordan, Israel, Turkey; the interior, consisting of steppes, forests and deserts—Chinese Turkestan, Russian Turkestan, northern Kansu, Outer and Inner Mongolia, India, parts of Siberia and Tibet, with its towering Himalayas; and eastern and south-eastern Asia, with its Pacific borderlands and the jungles to the south.

Asia has captured the imagination of the Western world, but many of its animals—especially its cats—have not been explored in detail. Except for the tiger and a few others, these cats have remained in a shadowy world, one reason being their inaccessibility. The terrain is immense and includes the highest mountains in the world, huge deserts and some of the densest jungles anywhere. The cats are often astonishingly beautiful, and none more so than the tiger and the snow leopard.

Tiger

There is one animal that best represents both the secret energy and the disquieting silence of Asia, an animal that has half gone over into the world of myth: the tiger.

Like most of the other members of the family, it is a lone hunter, rarely seen, a nocturnal stalker, swift when it has to be and incredibly powerful (it has fought the great bears of Siberia and killed them). Beauty and utility, artistic and technical perfection are all there, as they are in your cat, forming that 'fearful symmetry' that awed William Blake and dozens of other poets and painters. To the Western mind the tiger has become the symbol of cruelty and treachery, words that usually follow ignorance and fear; but to the Eastern eye it is often a symbol of the king and an object of worship. For example, the Koreans think of it as 'King of the Beasts', and to many Indian religious groups it is almost a god.

We do not know much about the tiger's origin. It seems to have sprung out of north-eastern Siberia and then made its way south to Korea, China, Malaysia, India, Sumatra, Java and Indonesia.

It is the largest cat in the family, weighing as much as 500 pounds and measuring about 10 feet, 6½ for the head and body and 3½ for the tail. Its talons, when extended, are 5 inches long and razor-sharp. The tiger is compact yet massive, with a rounded head and small rounded ears and a long, firm body. Its colour varies from reddish orange to reddish ochre. The vertical stripes—which differ for every tiger—can be greyish brown or grey, brown or black. No two tigers are identically marked, and even the two sides of the same tiger may differ from each other. Its muzzle, throat, chest and belly and inside of the limbs are light cream or pure white. Many cats are born black and remain black all their lives (the leopard, for example), but no one has ever seen a black tiger. There are many pure-white tigers, however.

About seventy years ago, close to 45,000 tigers roamed throughout India. After World War II, massacre became a routine event. Large crowds in jeeps and land-rovers drove throughout the land killing every wild animal in sight. The tiger retreated, but poison and insecticides almost finished the job that rifles could not do. By 1964 about three thousand tigers remained in India. Pakistan has no tigers. The Caspian tiger is almost extinct. Indonesia still has a few hundred, as does Russia. The Chinese tiger is about to vanish, but for a somewhat different reason: the Chinese have always regarded the tiger as a source for medication, with virtually every part of its anatomy having medicinal properties. Only in Nepal, where reserves have been established, does the tiger have a chance to live and perpetuate itself. Blake's famous poem 'The Tiger' has an excellent chance of replacing the living presence it describes.

The tiger can live almost anywhere but prefers wet dark forests, savannas, riverbanks, rocky mountain areas and mountain forests. It dislikes the heat of the day and will go anywhere to avoid direct sunlight. It likes water and is an excellent swimmer. The tiger is a great wanderer, with one tiger recorded as having covered 600 miles in twenty-two days. All tigers are territorial. The male will allow females but not males into his territory, which he establishes by spraying.

The tiger feeds on dogs, wolves, lynxes, young elephants, buffaloes and wild pigs, almost always beginning the hunt at dusk and always hunting alone. At one sitting, a tiger may consume anywhere from 45 to 60 pounds of meat.

Mating may occur in any month, with males fighting each other savagely, but rarely to the death, for a female in heat. The weaker one always gives way, to find another mate. Time from conception to birth runs from 95 to 122 days, usually falling within the 103-to-105-day span. Litters average two or three but may go as high as six or as low as one. A tiger cub reaches full maturity at about three years, but continues to grow until five. It can live to about twenty to twenty-five in the wild. Its greatest enemy: man!

Snow Leopard

Snow leopards blend in with their terrain to such an extent that very few have been caught on film, much less studied in their habitat. Their locale is the Himalayas, high plateaus and cloud-piercing mountains swept by snow, ice and wind. The snow leopard lives in surroundings that are almost completely inhospitable to all but a few hardy travellers and explorers. Furthermore, it is elusive, rare and wary of any intrusion on its preserve. The leopard comes to possess the image of Tibet itself; as one writer has suggested, the leopard may not be seen until one is ready, inwardly, 'to see'.

The snow leopard is a little smaller than the African leopard, but its tail is much longer in proportion to its body. It has huge paws, a short-faced 'heraldic head, like a leopard of myth' (as one writer put it), a long, powerful body and extremely powerful back legs, which enable it to make astonishingly long leaps. The head and body come to about 4 feet, and the tail to 2½. The shoulder height averages 23 inches, and the weight from 100 to 135 pounds.

The snow leopard's coat is long and thick, especially around the belly and tail. The colour is light greyish (giving a phantom's appearance), turning to yellow on the flanks and white on the belly. The head is spotted black, as if someone had thrown round black buttons at its face. The whole body is characterized by large rosettes, in which small black spots can be observed.

It usually roams at 5,000 to 6,000 feet, although some have been seen as high as 18,000 feet. The snow leopard is difficult to observe, secretive and solitary, but we do know that central Asia is its territory, especially Tibet, as well as the northern slopes of the Himalayas, Russia, China and Mongolia. Those in captivity are usually from the Tien Shan mountains of Russia.

In summer it lives in open terrain at the timber-line and in wild rocky wildernesses high up on snowfields and glaciers. It has incredible endurance, stamina and determination, climbing as high as the prey it seeks.

In winter it comes down to lower plateaus to get at game and domestic animals. It may even take up life in green country. But, wherever it goes, it always chooses remote habitats that are almost impossible to reach. The male lives out his days alone, except for mating. The female brings up the cubs, who leave her when they are about two. It is she who makes the kill that feeds the cubs. The choice of prey consists of ibex, wild sheep, blue sheep, goat, musk deer, pheasant and red-legged partridge, as well as such domestic animals as sheep, dogs, horses and even cows.

The males are territorial, covering vast stretches of land and marking their area with a pungent scent. Mating usually takes place in winter and spring, the time from conception to birth running about a hundred days, with litters averaging three cubs.

We know nothing about the family life, individual life or social system of the snow leopard.

Asiatic Steppe Wildcat

The Asiatic steppe wildcat, or the Indian desert cat, is about as big as the house cat. It is unattached to any myth, legend or ritual, but it is nocturnal, a loner and difficult to see or study.

It is the colour of light sand or grey, with patterns of transverse stripes that recall the African wildcat; intermixed are round dots of brown, grey or black. The body is compact, measuring 23 inches (with the head), the tail about half that. The weight is about the same as most house cats, 8 to 10 pounds, with some slightly larger. In interior Asia the mating-season runs from January through February, with gestation time about sixty days. Litters vary in size, three or four being normal, two or five not uncommon.

In India, the Asiatic steppe wildcat favours wide, flat, sandy land, while those living in places such as Kazakhstan settle into isolated valleys. They keep themselves well hidden by seeking out high grass near lakes or other bodies of water. In the Tien Shan mountain area in the Soviet Union, the breed favours bush and apple-orchard country and always stays below 6,000 feet. Like all cats, it can adapt perfectly to very different kinds of terrain.

Chinese Desert Cat

It is frustrating to have to report that the life history and habits of the Chinese desert cat are still almost entirely unknown. Roaming the territory between western China and eastern Tibet, this lonely small cat has been observed by natives but never tracked by zoologists. It takes its place among the thirty-eight species by virtue of remnants of its skin and skull that were found almost sixty years ago.

The cat is small, with head and body length coming to 30 inches, the tail 12. The coat is pale yellowish grey, with unvarnished, or clear, flanks. There are brownish streaks across the cheeks, the bands on the outer side of the flanks. The tail has three or four dark circles toward the tail, which is black. The soles are padded with strong tufts but not completely covered as they are in the sand-dune cat. It prefers steppe country and forested mountain areas.

We came to know the little we do about the Chinese desert cat through Prince Henri of Orleans, who headed a scientific expedition to the forbidden city of Lhasa in Tibet. He was forbidden entrance and turned back toward Szechwan. It was there that zoologists from his expedition saw the first two skins of the Chinese desert cat. In 1925 a skull was dug up confirming the existence of this species.

Because of the difficult terrain and the complicated political situation of the region, it is likely that the Chinese desert cat will remain in mystery for another fifty years at least. With its small size and colours that blend into the environment, and its own solitary nature, the species is perhaps the rarest of all thirty-eight.

Temminck's Cat

Temminck's cat (also known as the Asiatic golden cat), named after C J. Temminck, the famous Dutch naturalist, is another mysterious presence. We do know that, physiologically and temperamentally, it is closely linked to the African golden cat. Both, for example, prefer to live in humid forests. Millions of years ago, parts of Africa were much more humid than they are today, and there seems to have been a physical connection between this part of Africa and the wet forest terrain of Asia. It is believed that the African golden cat travelled from Africa to Asia. When Africa became less humid, the cats that were there adapted, and the Asian variety developed in its own environment.

The Asian variety is rather larger than its African counterpart. Its average length is 32 inches, with a very long tail, of 20 inches. The heavy fur coat varies in colour from darkish brown to shiny gold to deep grey. The ears are short and round, black on the back with small grey spots beneath the black. Thinnish white lines, black at the edges, cut across the cheeks and from the corner of each eye to the head. Some cats show no body-markings, whereas others are spotted and marked in a way closely resembling a leopard. A few have been in captivity, and the Basel zoo owns one. But even though some have been captured, we know nothing about its mating and gestation, or its family life, if any. Litters are very small.

Temminck's cat can be found in the foothills of the Himalayas, but it prefers Nepal, Burma, China, Malaysia and Sumatra—the more humid the forest the better. In parts of China it is known as the 'Shilului', the rock cat. Another Chinese name for it is 'yellow leopard', while in Burma it is called 'the fire cat' or 'tiger cat'.

It preys on small and medium-sized mammals—rats, mice, small deer, sheep, goats and even small water buffalo. It is, apparently, very fierce in the wild. Nevertheless, some naturalists have tamed them to become pets.

Bornean Red Cat or Bay Cat
The Bornean red cat is a smaller version of Temminck's cat. We know little about it, and that comes from skins and skeletons. The head is higher and more rounded than on Temminck's cat, and the tooth structure is somewhat different. Some information has come from natives who have seen it and from a very few naturalists who have also observed it. We know nothing about the cat in the wild.

The Bornean cat is native only to Borneo. Its pelt is bright chestnut, less bright on the belly. Faint stripes mark the face. The long tail has a white streak on its lower surface, becoming pure white at the end. The Bornean's head and body average out to 21 inches, the tail almost as long, at 15 inches. We know nothing about mating, gestation or even the number of kittens in the litter.

Some naturalists believe that the species prefers rocky terrain bordering jungles and sometimes marshlands bordering rivers, but others think that it is a dense-forest cat. The Bornean, itself a small cat, preys on small mammals. The chances of our learning more about it in the near future are slim.

Jungle Cat or Reed Cat
The jungle cat, or reed cat, has a very wide distribution, suggesting a great ability to adapt itself to any terrain. Although it is very difficult to obtain a

picture of the jungle cat, the species has been seen in lower Egypt, Israel, Jordan and many other parts of the Middle East, in eastern Transcaucasia and in the southern part of Asia clear across China.

Strong, swift, audacious, cunning, fearless (it has taken a kill literally right under a man's eyes), it is larger than the African wildcat. The jungle cat is 28 inches from head to body, with a tail under a third of that. Shoulder height is 14 inches, and the weight is close to 35 pounds—about four times that of a house cat. The legs are long in proportion to the body, the tail short, the ears black-fringed. The coat is a mixture of yellow and grey, yellow and brown, and dark, dull red. The tail is always tipped black. Naturalists have sometimes seen black jungle cats, but they are extremely rare, and no clear picture exists to back up the field observations.

We do, however, have many paintings of the species. Many ancient Egyptian murals show the jungle cat and suggest that it played an important part in Nile rituals and was trained to hunt.

With the passage of time, the species moved more and more toward the east, finally settling in the interior of Asia as its main habitat and India as its favourite country. It is probably the wild cat most commonly seen in India. It is less nocturnal than most of the family, using the early morning and evening to move around and to hunt. It prefers wooded areas, high grass, reed beds and the interior of sugar-plantations. In Iraq it usually lives in high grass near rivers. It does not shun man; in fact, it moves close to him, often right at the edge of villages.

The jungle cat preys on small animals—rabbits, rats, mice, birds and reptiles, always stalking slowly and patiently (as the paintings show us). The little information we have about its habits is that gestation is usually sixty-six days, about the same as for the house cat, and that its litters run from three to five.

Pallas Cat

The Pallas cat is named after its discoverer, Peter Simon Pallas, the famous German naturalist. For several reasons, this is an unusual species of the family. Of the other thirty-eight species, no one would have any trouble recognizing them as cats. The Pallas, however, seems to have come over from another world.

First of all, it looks like a blown-up flounder, with eyes set high up on the head and almost identical to an owl's. Second, there is the weird head. It is much broader than any other cat's head, with a low forehead and widely separated ears set very low on the head. The round, massive body is supported by squat fat legs. Third, the underparts of the coat are much thicker than in any other cat, a kind of heavy blanket that provides it with the proper insulation when it must lie still for hours on frozen earth. The colour itself varies from pale yellowish grey to a yellowish buff to yellowish brown. Lips, skin and neck are always white. Four bands ring the tail, which is tipped black.

The Pallas is a member of the feline family, but its appearance suggests that it has slipped through the evolutionary net and simply adopted the family as its own. It does not have the grace, beauty or elegance of the other species in the family, but it is indeed a cat and we must see it for what it is. The stranges of all cats, it has the ability—because its eyes are set so high and its ears so low and far back—to peer over rocks without exposing itself. That is one way it survives. And when it hunts in flat country without vegetation for cover, it lies there like a flounder and becomes part of the earth. Under such conditions it is virtually invisible.

The Pallas is about the size of the house cat, head and body coming to 23 inches, tail about 10. The weight rarely exceeds 8 pounds. Gestation runs from sixty-five to sixty-seven days, and the average litter is three to four, occasionally five.

It is usually seen in Central Asia, Tibet and Kashmir and on the steppes of Mongolia. It prefers steppes, deserts, rocky plateaus and treeless mountainsides. It is as though the Pallas cat does not want any cover. It seems absolutely fearless. It is a nocturnal hunter and preys on mice, rats, hare, squirrels, reptiles and birds.

Some zoologists believe that the Pallas may be the ancestor of our modern Angora and Persian, but this is still speculative. The only way to clear the point, as C. A. W. Guggisberg has commented, is through cross-breeding, but this has not as yet occurred.

Marble Cat

Nepal, Sikkim, Assam, Burma, Malaysia, Borneo, Sumatra, Indochina: the words conjure up remoteness, and it is this part of the world that the marble cat has staked out for its territory. Very few zoologists, perhaps no more than a dozen, have seen this elusive cat. We have skins, skulls, descriptions in notebooks and a few drawings—but no photographs. this cat, like most of the small species of the family, has dropped out of civilization.

Structurally, its head is short, rather broad and much rounder than the heads of most other cats. The eyes are set deep and protected by unusually strong bones. It has powerful teeth. Its size is about the same as the house cat (head and body length of 22 inches, tail 15), with small, round ears and a long, thick, furry tail, tipped black. The fur is soft and heavy on the sides and top, with the underparts even thicker and longer. This serves as insulation in the cold climates yet does not seem to impede the cat in its warmer habitats.

It is mainly a night prowler and unlike most other cats prefers to stalk from trees. It goes after birds the same way the house cat does. Its usual prey is rodents, reptiles and squirrels. Its reputation is based on fierceness; it is untamable and does not live long in captivity. As for its life in the wild, we know almost nothing.

Leopard Cat

Fierce, intractable, cunning, an expert at survival, the leopard cat is known throughout south-eastern Asia. Its adaptability is remarkable. It can make a life for itself and its young in both forests and jungles, on low plains and even in high mountains. In winter, however, it tends to move into river valleys.

It roams from Kashmir to India, then on to parts of Nepal, Assam, Burma, Indochina, Tibet and China, where it is seen almost everywhere. It also makes its way to Taiwan and the Philippines.

The name 'leopard cat' has always seemed arbitrary. Although the resemblance to the leopard is there, the spots are arranged in rows along the body and not set in rosettes; the legs also seem long in proportion to the body, and the head is too small. Also, the colour-varieties are endless, from yellow to pale tawny to grey. The underparts are always white. Black streaks run from the head to the lower neck, and a white brush cuts across the face. This cat is a leopard and not a leopard.

Like most other cat species, it is a night prowler, with acute hearing that is sensitive to anything out of the ordinary. It appears to stay in trees a good deal, hunting birds and squirrels. Unlike most other cats, however, it lives close to man, often very short distances from villages. Therefore, chickens, goats and sheep are prey, and the leopard cat does not hesitate to snatch farm animals from under the very nose of their owners. When barnyard stock is unavailable, the species preys on hare, rodents, fish and reptiles.

The period of gestation is only a little more than that of the house cat, from sixty-four to seventy days, and the average litter is small, two, and usually born in May. The size is slightly larger than a house cat, the length coming to about 25 inches, the tail to 11. If you saw this cat in the wild, you would think you were looking at your own domesticated pet who had acquired the spots of the leopard.

Rusty-Spotted Cat

About the size of the black-footed cat of southern Africa (which means smaller than the house cat), the rusty-spotted cat is closely linked to the leopard cat. Both have that small, compact, 'disc-like' head so characteristic of the leopard. Small (under 8 to 10 pounds), with a head and body length of 17 inches, a long tail in proportion (9 inches), the rusty-spotted has small round ears and a short, soft coat. The colour is grey, tinged with brownish red and lined with brown extended blotches. The underparts and the inside of the front and back legs are white, dotted with black spots. White and dark lines cross the face, and four black lines begin at the top of the head and run down to the back of the neck. The tail is a distinct reddish brown, and the soles are black.

The habitat of the rusty-spotted is southern India and Ceylon. In Ceylon it likes to hide itself in the humid forests and stays away from dry terrain. In India it seems to prefer dry grass country and avoids jungles, apparently a complete reversal of the behaviour in Ceylon.

It is a night prowler and preys on birds and small mammals—rodents and hare. Naturalists who have caught them have reported that they are tame, elegant and a delight to observe. But these are reports of a hundred years ago, and we cannot verify their accuracy. No recent reports have been made on the rusty-spotted cat. Although we know the species exists, there have been few attempts to observe it scientifically. We know little to nothing about its mating-habits, the period of gestation or even the size of the litter. Its life in the wild remains a mystery.

Clouded Leopard

The clouded leopard has a name that suits it perfectly, since zoologists cannot agree on its origin. Some see a connection between the clouded leopard and the great cats—tiger, lion, leopard, jaguar. Others firmly believe that it evolved from a small ancient cat—the marble cat, because the smaller cat is an almost exact replica of its larger counterpart. The evidence suggests a compromise. The clouded leopard is unable to roar, and that fact links it with the smaller members of the family. But its pupils, when contracted, have vertical rather than horizontal slits, and that factor connects it with the big cats. It has one other link with one of the large cats now extinct, the sabre-toothed tiger. The upper canines are longer than those of any other members of the feline family, almost tusk-like in their thrust.

The clouded first came to the attention of Western zoologists in the nineteenth century. In Malaya, it was called 'Rimaudahan', 'tree tiger'; in China it was called 'the mint leopard' (its spots resemble mint leaves). It was distinguished from the ordinary leopard, whose roundish spots looked like gold money and led to its being called 'the golden cash leopard'.

The largest Asian member of the purring cats, this 'tree tiger' weighs about as much as a small leopard. A large male can run to 50 pounds, with a head and body length of 38 inches and a tail of up to 30. It is about 20 inches at the shoulder. As you can see, the body is long and low-slung, the legs close to the ground and the tail long enough to curl back to the head. The coat is a rich light brown. Two black bands like railway tracks run across the face, and spots the shape of mint leaves cover the body. The belly is white and covered with large dark spots.

The habitat of the clouded is eastern and south-eastern Asia, and it can be seen also in Nepal and Sikkim and in parts of Burma, Malaysia, Indochina, China and Taiwan. It prefers, apparently, to live in thick, green forests and rarely allows itself to be seen by man. Nevertheless, we do know that its gestation period is about eighty-five to ninety-two days, with litters as low as one and as high as four.

The clouded leopard has been studied in captivity, and from that we know that it spends part of its life in trees, preying on birds. It also hunts on the ground and is much more of a day prowler than most of the species. It is extremely powerful for its size, with vice-like jaws, large strong teeth and a muscular, compact, explosive body. It kills rodents, deer, wild pigs, even monkeys, which it stalks patiently, making its final rush with blinding speed. It knocks its prey over with a single powerful blow and then bites into the neck for the kill.

From zoo studies we know that the mother stays with the cubs constantly for the first four weeks. She then gradually withdraws, and the cubs venture out on their own. At three to six weeks they begin to play with each other, and from six to ten they romp, try to climb trees and follow their mother's directions. At about eleven weeks the mother brings over some live prey to teach the cubs how to kill. She does this repeatedly. She is patient and relaxed, making certain they learn. The clouded seems less highly-strung than the leopard, more caring; but since these observations were all made in captivity, we do not know if its reactions would be the same in the wild. Probably they would not be. The patterns may be similar, but the actual behaviour would differ.

Fishing Cat

The name itself, 'fishing cat', seems to bring together contradictions and conjures up the image of a strange mutation. Here we have a wild cat whose natural habitat is water and whose diet consists mainly of fish, certainly a strange combination for a member of the family.

In fact, the Bengali *mach-bagral*, of which 'fishing cat' is a precise translation, does make its home near rivers and streams so that it can catch fish. One observer, in Ceylon, stated that this fisherman of the family dives into the water and acts 'exactly the same way as a tabby trying to get a goldfish out of a bowl'.

But the fishing cat does not confine itself to water. It also preys on reptiles, frogs, small mammals and birds. Powerful, fearless, it has been known on occasion to attack a whole pack of dogs and send them howling back to their owners. Some local people even believe that it has carried off young babies, but this has never been proved. What we do know from a naturalist who observed it first hand is that it has killed a female leopard twice its size.

The fishing cat is much larger and weighs considerably more than the leopard cat, coming to around 35 pounds. It does not have the elegance, speed or sure-footed quality of the latter. It has a short wide head, short rough hair, often grey, with streaks of brown. Dark lines, as many as eight, run from the top of the head to the back of the neck, and the body has dark-brown spots. The front paws are webbed, with claws that protrude far more than those in other cats. They are like living fishhooks.

Head and body length is about 32 inches, the tail proportionately short at 12. Shoulder height is 15 inches, which means it is low-slung like the leopard. The fishing cat can be found in parts of India, Nepal, Burma, southern China, Taiwan and Sumatra. Although we know relatively little about its mating-season, we do know that gestation lasts between sixty-two and sixty-four days, which is exactly the same as for the house cat. The average litter is quite small, usually no more than two.

Flat-Headed Cat

The next to last of our Asian cats, the flat-headed, has been called a 'very peculiar and exceptional cat'. The description comes from St George Mivart in his fascinating monograph *The Cat*. This is a thoroughly British understatement, for the flat-headed is more than peculiar: it is strange and bizarre, virtually an anomaly. If you take some of the features of the civet, genet, marten, skunk, mink, weasel, badger and, especially, the otter and combine them, you have the flat-headed, or something close to it.

We know what it looks like, but little more. Its skull is broadly flattened and pointed, with the nasal bones forming a ridge. The orbit of the eye is completely encircled by tough bone, and the anterior upper pre-molar has two roots and is longer and better developed than in any other cat. Almost as large as the house cat—which means it weighs about 6 to 8 pounds, the flat-headed has a long low body, short legs and a small, thick tail. Head and body length come to about 22 inches, the tail proportionately short at 7 inches. The pelt is full, smooth, long, dark reddish brown and often tipped silvery white or grey. The belly is white and sometimes covered with large brown spots. Two thick black lines cross the face from cheek to cheek, and a yellow line runs from each eye to the ear.

The flat-headed lives in inaccessible areas of Borneo, Malaysia and Sumatra; it is nocturnal and elusive. It preys on fish, frogs and fowl, usually claiming its territory near riverbanks. This need for fish and water suggests a close link with the fishing cat. We know nothing about its life in the wild, its period of gestation or the size of its litter. Unless a real effort is made to learn something more about this unusual cat, it could well continue to live in shadows for another million years.

Iriomote Cat

The last of the Asian cats, the Iriomote, was discovered only as recently as 1967. Its discovery shook the zoological world—a new species of cat! The discovery itself occurred in Iriomote, a small mountainous island completely covered with rain forest and situated at the southern end of the Ryukyu Island group, 124 miles east of Taiwan.

Although the Iriomote cat was a new species, it did little to change our ideas about the family. But it may tell us something important about evolution. This cat seems closely linked with the leopard cat, and there is nothing unusual about that. However, Yoshimori Imaizumi, of the National Science Museum of Tokyo, suggested that one of the closest kin of the Iriomote is the kodkod cat of South America. How was this possible, since the island east of Taiwan and South America were never linked?

C. A. W. Guggisberg has an explanation that may tell us a good deal about the way evolution works. "Both felines," he says, "are forest-dwellers, and the striking resemblances, which cannot be denied, are much more likely to be due to parallel lines of evolution followed by the two species living under similar ecological conditions than any form of transPacific kinship." It remains speculative, but evolution and ecology seem inexorably connected, and mammals associated for millions of years with the same family and then relegated to different parts of the world may still resemble one another if their habitat and climatic conditions are the same. Terrain, climate and food are destiny.

The Iriomote cat is about the size of the house tabby. The body is long and close to the ground—it measures about 24 inches, with short, sturdy legs and a cut-off tail. The body structure seems perfect for life in wet forest terrain. The coat is dark brown, and there are several lines in the back of the neck that end in front of the shoulders. The ears are round and black on the back. We know nothing about its life in the wild, neither its mating-season nor its period of gestation.

NORTH AND SOUTH AMERICA

Africa and Asia have captured our imagination in ways no other region can quite equal. Yet parts of North and South America, especially the latter, are in several ways as mysterious and haunting as those other continents. While the North may represent civilization and orderliness to some of us, the South still casts a great shadow, dark and unknown in many huge land areas. I am thinking, in particular, of the Amazon Basin, a region as large as all of Western Europe.

At the centre of that world is the mightiest of all cats in the Americas and the third largest in the world—the very real and yet mythical jaguar. This animal has caught the imagination of people as few other cats have.

Jaguar

The jaguar goes back millions of years, to the time when the Great Ice Age gripped the northern earth and when huge carnivores roamed the south. It was then a huge cat, comparable in size to the lions in European cave-drawings. When North and South America were linked, the jaguar slowly made its way down, destroying the larger mammals because of its greater speed and striking force. As its prey grew smaller and the vegetation became denser, the jaguar adapted. It gradually became smaller so that it could hunt and find refuge in the new terrain. When the large animals disappeared altogether, the jaguar remained as it is today.

This jaguar entered into myth, as we shall see. Mythical feelings about it go back thousands of years, to the royal House of Olmec, to statues, vases, pottery and paintings all associated with the royal lineage. This placed it at the centre of much religious worship of the South American Indians.

The jaguar was a symbol of male fertility, and it was connected with the holy men who could prophesy. Often they would dress themselves in its skin and allow their words to be emitted from its mouth. From Aztec times we have many pictures of a jaguar springing forth from a warrior's testicles and in this way embodying procreative powers. Sometimes the jaguar's form is mingled with other life-forms, chiefly birds and serpents, to suggest its all-embodying qualities. Claude Lévi-Strauss, the anthropologist, in a recent study, noted that present-day Indian hunters of the tropical forest still identified with the jaguar, with its power, its hunting abilities, its cunning and stealth.

The name 'jaguar' itself comes from one of the Tupi-Guarani languages spoken in the great central region of South America. The name was originally *yaguara*, which meant, in exaggerated tones, a wild beast that overcomes its victims at a leap. Heavier and stronger than a leopard, which it resembles, but smaller than the tiger and lion, the jaguar conveys compactness. It has a round, firm body and a large powerful chest, all set on extremely strong and compact short legs. The teeth have greater ripping-power than those of any other large cat. The body colour is some variation of yellow with streaking, with the underparts different varieties of white. The rest of the body is marked with spots forming large rosettes. The tail is usually encircled by three black bands and tipped black. Black jaguars, incidentally, are not extremely rare, as most people think, but are difficult to see.

The entire animal conveys power, for it lacks the grace of the leopard. The male's body length often reaches 6 feet, or even more, with the tail coming to almost 2 feet. Shoulder height is 28 inches. The average weight for a jaguar in the north is 160 pounds, but specimens in Brazil have come to 300 pounds and more. Females tend to be much smaller. Although we have little knowledge of its life in the wild, we do know that its gestation period is from 94 to 104 days, and litters run small, from one to four.

Unchallenged by any other animal, the jaguar could roam anywhere, with only man to fear as its enemy. But it prefers to stay within the confines of wet tropical forests, remaining especially close to rivers, streams and even stagnant ponds. It will often pursue its prey by swimming far out into a body of water. Some zoologists think that the jaguar is semi-aquatic, so much does it like to swim and play in water.

It preys on tapirs, alligators, fish, domestic stock, monkeys, birds, sloths, even armadillos and turtles. But its favourite is the capybara, which is the largest living rodent and is found in South America along the banks of rivers and lakes. The capybara has partially webbed feet, which means that it and the jaguar battle it out in the water.

Puma, or Cougar

At about the beginning of the sixteenth century, European explorers of the New World came back with stories about 'lions' prowling along in the vast forests and hill country of West Virginia. The Indians dealing with the New Amsterdam Dutch raised the puma to a living myth by warning the settlers that it was impossible to capture or kill. They said that it had the protection of the gods. The so-called lion the explorers saw was the puma, or cougar, the second largest cat in the Americas after the jaguar. The name 'puma', as C. A. W. Guggisberg tells us, "comes from the Quechua language of Peru", while 'cougar' is probably derived from a Tupi Indian word. The cougar and the puma are the same animal, although many people speak of them as different. In the same way, the panther and leopard are the same animal, with the panther being simply a black leopard.

Physiologically, the puma is different in several important ways from the other big cats. The hardened bones behind the tongue make it incapable of roaring. It purrs and screams like the house cat, only louder. And it licks its coat, also like the house cat, to produce a slick sheen. Its eyes, however, differ from the house cat's: the latter's narrow down to a slit, whereas the puma's always stay round. The puma is rather odd-looking, because of the small, rocket-shaped head and the short round ears. The neck is long and the body muscular, extended and supple. The legs are well-developed and powerfully coiled, the back ones being quite a bit higher than the front ones. The paws are long, and the front claws have tremendous ripping-power. The tail is long and round, with full fur. The coat is usually reddish brown or any combination of reddish brown and some grey.

The head and body come to about 5 feet, the tail to about 3, and the shoulder height to just over 2. The average weight of the male is 150 pounds, but some South American pumas average as much as 250 pounds. Females are much smaller.

Pumas can be found in more places in the Americas than any other wild cat. It is relatively rare in north-eastern Canada and the United States, although reports do come in of sightings in New England, especially Maine. Some can still be observed in the southern Appalachians. They appear to favour the North-west, West and South, most of them settling in the Rocky Mountain area, Texas, New Mexico, California and Washington. There are some in Central America and quite a few in South America, especially Argentina. From this immense variety of terrain, we can see that the puma is one of the most adaptable of the family. It feels equally at home in rocky country, mountains, open high grassland, jungles and tropical rain forests.

'Secretive', 'elusive' and 'wary' are apt words to describe the puma, because it knows how to keep out of sight of its biggest enemy: man. It is a night prowler, almost always alone, and a great wanderer, often covering 25 or more miles in a single night. It is also compulsively territorial, marking its own area with urine and tree-scratchings and carefully avoiding the territory of other pumas.

It is not a choosy eater. A list of its victims includes the entire range of wild and domestic life: deer, mules, cows, sheep, hare, horses, elk, moose, antelope, beavers, porcupines, coyotes, martens, skunks, wild turkeys, birds, fish, lizards and grasshoppers, and in Brazil it even devours ant-eaters. Analysis of its stomach has confirmed all this.

Like all cats, the puma is a silent stalker, using any cover it can find to advantage. Once in position it attacks, but not by a rush; instead, it uses its incredible leaping-powers, often covering 25 feet in a bound. It kills by breaking its victim's neck with one blow from its paw. Incredible as it may sound, a puma can drag a victim up to five times its own weight for several miles.

Pumas have been observed both in the wild and in captivity. Gestation is from ninety to ninety-five days, the litter from one to four. The mother watches them carefully, bringing them food until they are old enough to follow her on the kill. Cubs move out on their own when they are about three. They generally thrive in zoos and can live up to twenty years. In the wild the average life-span is believed to be ten to twelve years.

Ocelot

The ocelot is the third largest cat in the Americas. To the Mexicans it is *tirgillo*, 'little tiger'; to the people of Paraguay it is *chibi-guazu*, 'the large cat'. To us it is simply one of the most beautiful in the world, hunted mercilessly and either killed or captured so that men and women can wear its coat or train it as a pet.

Mainly night prowlers, but often seen in daylight, ocelots very often hunt in pairs and communicate with one another by strange-sounding calls. Compared with the other members of the cat family, they seem placid, even amiable, with little trace of their belligerence and fierceness. Some can be partially domesticated by experts.

They prey on small mammals such as rodents and young deer, as well as reptiles, birds and even domestic fowl. What is unique about the ocelot is the loveliness of its coat, which is short and ranges from dark brownish grey to yellowish brown to clear grey. A bold pattern of black or dark spots or blotches runs along the sides. The head, long legs and feet are always marked with large circular black marks. Two characteristic black stripes mark each cheek, whose upper part is white. The ears are round and black with light straw-coloured spots; the tail is long and circled in black. The underparts are white. The head and body length come to about 3½ feet, sometimes longer, and the tail is 16 or more inches. Shoulder height is 18 inches. Gestation is a little more than for the house cat, seventy days, and litters are small, no more than two.

Generally, the ocelot is a low-level and ground cat, although it is a good climber and may sleep the day away on a branch. The species favours Central and South America and usually does not venture beyond the Mexican border. It can live in almost any habitat, but it prefers dense rain forests, bush country of any kind and marshland. It avoids arid and open country. It dislikes water but is a strong swimmer under necessity.

Margay

The margay looks like an ocelot, but it is not one; it has often been mistaken, also, for an oncilla, but the identification was simply incorrect. Elusive, nocturnal, silent enough to elude the most experienced and persistent hunters, the margay, or 'little ocelot', lives mainly in a habitat that extends from lower Mexico to Argentina.

We know almost nothing about its life in the wild. We do know that it is a tree cat for the most part and preys on birds, lizards and frogs, but it also is a ground hunter, going after small mammals such as rodents, young deer and domestic fowl.

The margay is much smaller than the ocelot, head and body length coming to 25 inches at the most, with females much smaller. The tail is proportionately long, at about 15 inches. The species is thin and narrow in the chest and has long legs for a cat its size.

The coat is short, smooth and light brown, with the underparts, chest and neck white. Dark markings similar to those of the ocelot run chain-like down the back and sides. The backs of both ears are dark with very light spots. The long tail is darkly ringed.

There have been many attempts to 'domesticate' the margay and turn it into a house pet, with mixed results. The species is really wild, and anyone who tries to live with one must put up with constant disarray and torn curtains, sofas and chairs, as well as a good chance of being bitten or clawed.

Geoffroy's Cat

The name sounds like the privileged cat of a French nobleman of the Middle Ages. It is nothing of the kind. Its only connection with France is that it was given its name by Geoffroy Saint-Hilaire, the French zoologist.

This unique cat, the *gato montes*, 'cat of the high hills', as the Argentinians call it, gather together all the traits of the family: silent, elusive, self-reliant and nocturnal. Although smaller than the average house cat, it is tough, muscular and extremely strong. The species has a large head, round ears black at the back with light circular marks, and powerful legs. Its total length is about 2 feet, the tail about 14 inches. Its period of gestation is under that of the house cat, running to sixty days, with very small litters—two is average.

The colour of the coat varies according to the terrain Geoffroy's cat must adapt to. It is generally bright or reddish brown or silvery grey. Numerous black spots cover the body and legs, creating the impression that a painter had arranged them. The same space is left between each spot, as though a certain design or fashion were intended. Some cats have rosettes down the back. Two black bands run across each cheek as if they had been whipped or lashed in. The top of the head has three black lines running to the neck.

The species can be found at the foot of mountains in Bolivia and Argentina, and in Uruguay and Brazil. It is not so adaptable as the puma or ocelot, living mainly in wooded and bush country in foothills. It preys on small mammals, rodents, reptiles and birds.

Although Geoffroy's cat may resemble a house cat, we should not be fooled. Dr Guggisberg tells us that an adult Geoffroy's cat in a zoo "attacked and killed all the female domestic cats which were introduced into the cage for cross-breeding purposes".

Kodkod

I am certain that you have never heard of this species of cat. Before I began my research, I certainly had not. The kodkod is the smallest of the wild cats in America. First discovered by Juan Ignacio Molena, a Chilean librarian, it was given a place in science by the German zoologist Philippi.

The kodkod is not much larger than the black-foot, the smallest feline in the world. Head and body length are about 19 inches, the tail 9 or under— these measurements are for the larger ones. The smaller ones are no more than 16 inches, with a tail of 8 inches. The weight is well under that of the average house cat.

The colour usually varies from dark to yellowish brown, making it look very much like the house cat. It has large black spots over its body and some lines running over the head and down the shoulders. The tail is darkly ringed; the back of the ears is black with tiny light spots. The larger and unmarked of the kodkods live in northern Chile; the smaller, who live in the south, have a bright-brown coat and spots on their legs. Occasionally someone reports having seen a black kodkod.

Although the kodkod is the wild cat of Chile, some have been seen in parts of Argentina. The species lives in thick forests and seeks out its food at night. It is never seen in the day. It preys on small mammals, birds and domestic fowl. We know nothing of its life in the wild, nor anything about its period of gestation or the size of the litter. Except for a few in the scientific community, the kodkod is virtually invisible.

Oncilla

The oncilla, or little spotted cat, looks like a small version of the margay, to which it is closely linked. It lives in thick forest country in Central and South America, chiefly in Colombia, Ecuador, Paraguay, northern Argentina and Brazil. We know nothing about its life in the wild, so that our information must come from those in captivity. Behaviour in captivity is, of course, very different from behaviour in the wild.

The oncilla is a small cat, but its size may vary from one terrain to another. The average is about 22 inches in head and body length, with a tail of about half that. Some, however, have grown no longer than the black-footed, which is about 19 inches and weighs only 7 pounds. The coat is dark or reddish or brown, with black spots of various shapes lining the upper part of the body. The legs are thickly spotted, the belly usually light or white, and the black-tipped tail made up of rings, about eight or nine in all. Black oncillas are not that rare, making up perhaps fifteen per cent of the species.

From the captive cat, we do know that gestation is about seventy-three to seventy-five days, a relatively long period for such a small mammal; the litter is very small, no more than two. Development is very slow for the oncilla—at least in captivity. The average kitten takes about two months to eat firm food. The house cat develops much more rapidly.

The male is fierce and belligerent toward the female and does not mate easily with the domestic house cat. In fact, he often kills any put within reach. When mating does occur, about half the kittens are born dead.

We know very little about this species.

Pampas Cat

Once considered a variation of the kodkod, the Pampas cat—also known as 'the cat that moves through grass'—is now recognized as a distinct species of the family. It is about the same size as a house cat, but it seems stronger and fuller, somehow more solid. The Chilean version is about 23 inches from head to body, with a 12-inch tail; the Argentinian variety runs larger, about 25 to 26 inches, with a tail of 12 inches. Both variations can be found in Ecuador, Peru and Brazil, but mainly in Chile and Argentina.

What makes the Pampas seem so much more solid than the house cat? One thing is its face, which is much broader, with a larger bone structure. This creates the sense of strength and massiveness, even in such a small cat. The ears tend to come to a sharp point, more so than in most other wild cats in the Americas. The back is black, with whitish spots in irregular patterns.

The coat is usually long, thick and white, some variation of white and yellow, or brown. Yellow-brown lines run from the shoulders to the legs, and two thick bars go from the eyes to beneath the throat. The legs and tail are circled by wide brown lines. The appearance of the Chilean Pampas cat seems more vibrant and colourful than its neighbour in Argentina.

In Chile the Pampas can be found throughout the country; in Argentina it prefers high-grass country and thick wet forest regions. It is a night prowler, preying on small mammals, birds and domestic fowl. It is, apparently, fearless, aggressive and untamable. We know nothing about its life in the wild.

Mountain Cat, or Andean Highland Cat

The mountain, or Andean highland, cat is so elusive that it is almost totally unknown to zoologists. I do not know of any zoo that has even one, let alone two for breeding-purposes. A few historical societies and museums have the skins mounted to simulate the real cat. From anatomical evidence we discover that it has a unique skull—apparently two skulls partitioned by a thin membrane.

The species is larger than the average house cat, about 24 inches for head and body length, with a proportionately long tail, 14 inches. Its coat is long and very soft and fine, especially along the back. The colour is light grey, darkish on the back, with straw-coloured, brown or orange markings, irregularly spaced, running across the body. The underparts are white and the tail thick and ringed often, perhaps as many as nine times. In many ways the coat resembles that of the beautiful snow leopard of the Himalayas. This may be no accident, since the South American species lives high up in the Andes Mountains of north-eastern Chile, Peru and northern Argentina. The coat reflects the habitat.

The mountain cat is a night prowler, preying on mammals. We know nothing about its life in the wild, or about its mating-habits and size of litter.

Jaguarundi

The jaguarundi is the one feline species in the Americas that does not resemble a cat. From certain angles, in fact, it looks like a badger, an armonk, a weasel or an otter. And yet it is a cat, connected, as some zoologists feel, with the mountain cat or even the puma.

It is rather small but powerful for its size, with a thin, long body and tail. It stands about 14 inches at the shoulder, with a head and body length of 26 inches and a proportionately long tail at 18 inches. It has a small flattened head and short legs, giving it a low-slung appearance. The ears are small and round. The head conveys compactness and functionalism. The colour of the coat is almost always dark grey or some variation of chestnut red. The young are often born with spots, which they lose as they reach adulthood. While we know relatively little about its life in the wild, we do know that its period of gestation is from 63 to 70 days, a little longer than that of the house cat. The average litter is two or three.

The jaguarundi favours low country, usually living in dense forests and heavy bush. It is found throughout Central and South America. Some are known to have gone as far north as Arizona and Texas.

The species hunts at dawn and dusk as well as at night. With its swiftness and agility, it is an effective day predator—more so than any other cat in this hemisphere. Because of its short legs, it is an excellent stalker, and the body presents a very low silhouette. Its body structure also allows it to move silently through dense bush.

It preys mainly on small mammals, rabbits, young deer, rodents and guinea pigs. One of its peculiarities is that it shares its hunting-terrain with others, something no other cat does.

Bay Lynx or Bobcat

Often called the bobcat or the wildcat, the bay lynx is a solitary northern cat, native to the northern part of the United States and to Canada. It is smaller than the European lynx but extremely wild, ferocious, ungiving and unfriendly.

It is considerably larger than the average house cat, measuring 21 inches at the shoulder, with a head and body length of 33 inches and a tail about half of that. Bay lynxes vary in size, the smaller ones living in the southern parts of the United States and the larger ones around the Canadian border, in the Rockies and in Nova Scotia. Size is determined by climate.

In contrast to the European lynx, the American variety has shades of brown, spotted often in a line with dark or brown blotches. The head is full of black spots. It is also smaller than the European version, with smaller ears and ear tufts that are sparse or even absent. The ears are intensely black at the back, and the tail is black on the upper side.

Besides the regions that it seems to favour—those listed above, the bay lynx or bobcat roams throughout the country, seeming to prefer the middle climate but showing up in brush country, semi-desert areas and even wet forest regions. Although the lynx is solitary, it does move close to man, something the European variety avoids.

In winter the lynx will often hunt under a noon sun. It preys on rabbits, kangaroo rats, gophers, squirrels, birds and rodents of all kinds. Mainly, it does its hunting at night, and it is a stalker.

Mating is extremely rare to observe, but here is a first-hand report:

I was awakened by an uninterrupted series of ferocious hisses, shrill screams, harsh squalls and deep-toned yowls. No alley strays could ever have half-equalled this cat. . . . The female most of the time lay crouched upon the ground, while the big male . . . walked menacingly about her. Sometimes they both sat upright, facing each other. The loud and ludicrous serenade was kept up for almost half an hour, and it ended with a duel climax of discordant, frightening squalls as mating takes place.

Gestation period is fifty days, with an average litter of three. Nursing lasts for three months, and then the kittens are encouraged to follow the mother to learn to kill. The father has long since disappeared. When the kittens are a little more than a year, they move out on their own.

The great enemy of the bay lynx or bobcat is man, with some help from the puma.

EUROPE

There are only two wild cats distinctly associated with Europe. In Scandinavian mythology two giant lynxes draw the chariot of Freya, the great goddess of love and fertility. The name 'lynx' itself derives from the Greek word that means 'one who can see well in dim light' or 'one who can see through walls'. It is the biggest of the European cats.

Lynx

The lynx resembles the American bobcat, but it is larger and has longer legs and more developed and better padded feet. The latter enable it to travel long distances on snow. Even its ear tufts are longer, making it distinctive. The end of the tail is completely circled in black; the side-whiskers are thick, even bushy, and generally white or grey. The upper coat is grizzly grey or brown, featuring dark spots.

The northern lynx stands 27 inches at the shoulder, with a head and body length of 3½ feet, and a short tail, under 10 inches. Southern varieties are smaller by 3 or 4 inches. Gestation time runs to about seventy days, a little more than the house cat, with litters of two or three. The kittens learn how to adapt from the mother, who teaches them to hunt and kill. The main enemies of the lynx are man and the wolf.

Because of its reputation as "undoubtedly a noxious predatory animal", the lynx has been persecuted and hunted in most of Europe, with the lone exception of Britain. Until World War II they were tracked with a vengeance and killed mercilessly, but now there are colonies of lynx in Spain, Portugal, Norway, Sweden, Finland, Poland, Czechoslovakia, Yugoslavia, Greece, Rumania and the Soviet Union. They can even be found in the Siberian woods, in Mongolia, Manchuria and northern China. Without question, the species has a tremendous ability to adapt, reproduce and survive. The lynx does seem to prefer high forest country with thick undergrowth. It preys on snowshoe rabbits, rodents, grouse, ducks, young deer and mountain sheep; its favourite is hare. Like the leopard, it is a silent stalker; when close to its victim, it pounces, or else it jumps on a deer from a branch. The lynx is usually a solitary hunter but has been observed hunting in pairs.

European Wildcat
The last of the species, the forest wildcat, better known as the European wildcat, is a true European. In the eighteenth century the species was known as 'the British tiger'. It was highly destructive of domestic stock—poultry, lambs and kids. As a result, there was a campaign to exterminate the species from Britain and the rest of Europe. The campaign almost succeeded, but by World War I the European wildcat had made a comeback, and by two decades later it was flourishing. It is now a permanent part of the wildlife of upper Scotland and Europe.

The European wildcat is certainly no tiger, but the association of the two is apt. For the European, caught up by the myth of the cat, the wildcat was the closest thing he had to the mythical tiger. In actuality, the species looks something like the average house cat, but is heavier, larger, much stronger and more compact. It suggests potential power. Its legs are longer, its head wider and its heavy bushy tail shorter in relation to its body. The head and body length are about 24 inches, the tail half that or less. The male weighs from 12 to 15 pounds, about double the house cat's weight.

The coat of the European is thick, rich, yellowish grey, with black bands on the flanks. A black stripe often runs down the middle of the back. The throat is cream or often white. This is a very functional-looking cat, with the cut-off tail making it appear extremely compact.

From a distance it seems harmless, not much different from the house cat. But that is an illusion. It avoids civilization and prefers to spend its life in the cold rather than seek shelter in a man-made building. Probably man's odour offends it. If captured, it remains fierce, independent, untamable. Some efforts have been made to bring up European wildcat kittens, but the training is extremely difficult, and they can always revert.

If domestic cats are put in the same cage with the species, the kittens born will tend toward the wild cat appearance and temperament. Gestation time is about sixty-six days, the same as for the house cat, or a little longer; litters are small. The wildcat breeds, however, only once a year, whereas the house cat does so twice or more.

In the wild the European species lives in dense woods and isolated rocky formations, and in the remote forests of Scotland, France, Italy, Germany, Greece, the Soviet Union and the Balkans. It preys on hare, domestic livestock, rodents and birds. In many ways this is the animal your house cat would be if not for domestication. The next time you are at the zoo, take a long look—and do not get too close!

TEN

Travelling, Services, Showing and Some Tips on Grooming

TRAVELLING

Cats generally make good travelling-companions, but you may be taking the kind of holiday in which your cat does not fit. If you are going away for just the weekend, you could consider leaving your cat alone in the flat or house. Provide a clean litter box and plenty of water and food. Your cat will probably not miss you, but if you feel it needs company—and some cats do, ask a neighbour to look in for ten minutes a few times each day and to give fresh food and water as required.

You can, of course, put it in a cattery or one of the so-called 'hotels' designed for both long and short stays. The chief thing in choosing a cattery is to make sure it is clean. Inspect it before you leave your cat. The odour should be fresh, the equipment should look clean, and there should be no droppings or rubbish in evidence. The best place is one recommended by a friend or neighbour, or by a vet you can trust. Make certain all inoculations are up to date before leaving your cat.

If you travel with your cat, whether by car, train, bus or plane, you will need a well-ventilated carrying-box. It should be large enough so that the cat can stand up and stretch out. It is best not to feed it for twelve hours or so before a long-trip. Remember you cannot take your cat with you for a holiday abroad unless you arrange for it to go into quarantine for six months on your return. There it will be given two injections against rabies.

Car

Drive with the cat in a carrying-box or basket, unless other people are along to control it. Never leave a cat locked inside the car in warm weather—80 degrees outside can mean 100 degrees inside the car. Do not feed your cat before a long trip.

Train

Cats can travel by British Rail unaccompanied, but arrangements must be made well in advance. The animal must be in a container that allows room for it to stand up but is not so large that the cat bounces all over the place, possibly injuring itself. If in a basket, which may be draughty, this should be partly covered with brown paper, but leaving ample ventilation. It should be labelled very distinctly with the name of the station of destination and also 'LIVE CAT WITH CARE' and 'TO BE CALLED FOR'.

If a change of train is necessary, check the times carefully and make sure that whoever is picking up the cat from the station knows well beforehand the time of arrival. The cost will of course depend on the weight of the cat and container and the distance to be taken, and can be quite expensive.

Cats may not go to a show unaccompanied but must be taken there by the owner or his/her representative.

When travelling, accompanied cats in containers 18 inches x 18 inches x 18 inches may travel free, but anything larger must be paid for. If the cat is large, this will certainly not be big enough.

Never send or take a cat by rail without first checking that there has been no change in the regulations and that the particular train is actually running.

By Bus and Underground

Cats may be taken on buses and may also travel on the Underground. They may be carried on buses only at the conductor's discretion.

It is always advisable to have the animals in escape-proof containers.

Plane

Every airline will handle a cat as cargo, but each airline has its own regulations and procedures. Well before your trip, call the office of the airline you plan to travel on and find out the procedures. Usually, one animal is permitted in the first-class passenger-compartment on each domestic flight, while all other animals on that flight must go into the baggage-section.

Some Advice

Do not travel with a cat that has recently been ill.
If the weather is warm, make sure water is available.
If you have a nervous cat, ask your vet about sedation.
If you plan to stay anywhere for an extended time, find out if a vet is available.

Foreign Travel

Before taking a cat abroad, check with the consulate of that country about its rules for entering pets. Britain requires a long period of quarantine, six months. All countries will require documents certifying that your cat is free of any contagious disease and has been vaccinated against rabies in the past six months.

Entering the United States and other countries

A cat will need a health-certificate issued by a vet indicating (1) that it is in good health and free from all contagious diseases, and (2) that it has been vaccinated against rabies within six months.

You should check with the Ministry of Agriculture, Hook Rise, South Tolworth, Surbiton, Surrey, as to the requirements for each country. There is no quarantine involved when taking a cat into the United States.

SERVICE INFORMATION

If you have a particular breed of cat, then the club for that breed will have the latest information about it. If you are interested in breeding scientifically, the club for your breed will have relevant information. Scientific breeding can take you into some difficult areas of genetics, and you should approach it gradually if you have no experience. Many breeds cannot be produced by mating like to like but involve far more difficult match-ups. Write to the Secretary, Governing Council of the Cat Fancy, Dovefields, Petworth Road, Witley, Surrey, for lists of clubs and dates of shows. A small charge is made for these.

The British cat periodical *Fur and Feather*, Idle, Bradford, Yorkshire, carries some pages of cat news, clubs and shows, and cat and kitten advertisements.

SHOWING

There are many shows held all over Britain under the auspices of the Governing Council of the Cat Fancy. The shows are organized by various cat clubs, and fall into three categories: championship shows where challenger certificates are awarded to the winners of the adult open classes; sanction shows which are really rehearsals for championship shows, being run on the same lines, but no challenge certificates are given, and exemption shows where the rules are simpler and there are no challenge certificates. The last are ideal for the beginner to learn about showing as the general procedure is much the same.

It is not essential to belong to the club organizing the show to exhibit a cat, but there are advantages in that frequently the fees for members are reduced and special prizes are given for members only.

All pedigree cats, kittens and neuters must be registered with the Governing Council before being entered for a show. Some shows have a special section for pet cats without pedigrees and of no specific variety. Schedules giving details of the classes and judges are usually available about ten weeks before the show, and the entry forms should be completed with full details as on the cats' registration forms, if pedigree, and sent back with correct moneys well before the closing date. Most shows have to return entries, so it is well to be prompt.

The important class is the Open or breed class for which a challenge certificate is given if the judges consider the cats up to the standards required. Three such certificates won at three shows under three different judges entitle the cat to be called a champion. Once a full champion, a cat may enter the Champion of Champion class, and three similar wins means that the cat may be called a Grand Champion. There are similar classes for neuters, but they are referred to as Premiers and Grand Premiers. There are also a number of miscellaneous classes, such as those for breeders, novices, maiden cats and kittens, and so on, and also classes put on by various clubs for their members only. Usually a cat must be entered in at least four classes but not more than twelve.

Some shows have a Best in Show, with a panel of judges choosing the best cat, kitten and neuters, while others have Best of Breed for each variety of cat and kitten.

Your local breed club or cat association will have information on showing. Be sure your cat has received its injection for feline enteritis at least two weeks before you show it, and do not try to enter any cat that is ill or showing signs of developing illness. If not carefully monitored, cat shows can spread feline disease, and in any event a sick cat stands little chance of doing well at a show. The examining vet will probably discover the ailment well before you get into the ring.

In the USA there is no single association that unites all cat standards and policies, as the American Kennel Club does for dogs. Some of the large registries are: Cat Fanciers Association (probably the largest), American Cat Association (the oldest), American Cat Fanciers Association, National Cat Fanciers Association and Independent Cat Federation.

All cat fancies have been connected with the showing of cats, in Britain since 1871 and in the United States since about the turn of the century. The first real American show was in New York in 1895.

One advantage of the American system of registry—as opposed to the British system of centralized control—is the diversity of shows and the more liberal acceptance of new breeds. The difficulty is that a show cat must be registered in the association sanctioning that particular show, and therefore it must live in that area and be registered there. *Cats Magazine* (USA) describes all matters concerning the fancies—records, selection of cats, best cats of colour and breed, and other related information.

SOME TIPS ON GROOMING

1. Start grooming with the kitten—get it accustomed early.
2. Use a wide-toothed metal comb and a fine-toothed flea-comb; you also need a brush with long but not harsh bristles (never use wire bristles as this will tear the hair).
3. Long-hairs need more grooming; do not use the comb too much on short-hairs—it opens the coat.
4. For stains or grease, use a piece of cotton dampened in alcohol; do not go near the eyes.
5. Bay rum rubbed into the coat is good for all cats.
6. Talcum powder is good for white or light-haired coats but must be brushed right out.

7. Bathe the cat only if it is very dirty—and do it in a warm room. Use the sink for a bathtub.

8. Use nail-clippers for the claws. Clip if necessary after veterinary advice.

Glossary

ACA: American Cat Association.

ACFA: American Cat Fanciers Association.

AGOUTI: Coat pattern with bands of brown, yellow and black (in the Abyssinian).

AILUROPHILE: A cat-lover (ailurophobe—a cat-hater).

ALBINO: Lack of pigment colouring: a white coat, pink eyes.

ALMOND-SHAPED: Eye shape in many so-called foreign breeds.

ALTER: To castrate or spay the cat; neuter.

ANGORA: A variety of long-hair found in Turkey; a term once used interchangeably with Persian.

BACK-CROSS: A term used in genetics to indicate the mating of breeds to gain particular characteristics.

BALANCED: Symmetry of the cat's head.

BARRING: Tabby markings; a fault for self-coloured (solid-coloured) cats.

BAT-EARED: Having unusually large ears.

BITE: The conformation of the upper and lower teeth in a closed mouth.

BLAZE: A marking that runs from the forehead to the nose.

BRINDLING: A condition that results when incorrect colouring intermingles with the correct colouring.

BRITISH TYPE: Descriptive of British short-hairs: a cobby body and short, heavy legs.

BRUSH: The full tail of a long-hair.

BUTTERFLY: The distinctive shape of the pattern-marking on the shoulders of Tabbies; also called 'black saddle'.

CCA: Canadian Cat Association.

CCFF: Crown Cat Fanciers Federation (American).

CFA: Cat Fanciers Association (American).

CFF: Cat Fanciers Federation (American).

CALICO: A tortoiseshell-and-white colour-pattern.

CALLING: The distinctive cry of the female in heat.

CASTRATION: Altering or neutering of the male.

CHAMPION: Winner of three or more challenge ribbons.

CHROMOSOME: The structure in the nucleus of the cell that carries the genetic pattern.

CLASSIC: Reference to the most usual pattern of tabby markings; in Britain known as 'marbled'.

COARSE: Harsh rather than soft, said of a cat's coat.

COBBY: A body type that is relatively heavy, low-lying, with short legs; the typical British short-hair.

CONDITION: State of health and fitness.

CPL: Cat's Protection League

CROSS-BRED: The cat that results from the mating of one pure-bred with another.

CRYPTORCHIDISM: A condition in a male cat in which he is missing both testicles in the scrotum; such a male is useless for breeding.

CULL: To pick out from a litter the weak and unhealthy kittens.

DAM: The mother cat.

DILUTION: A colour-variation that produces a weaker hue.

DOCTORING: Altering, castrating.

DOMINANT: The main characteristic that appears in the first generation, inherited from only one of the parents.

DOUBLE COAT: A thick, soft undercoat with a topcoat of long hair; required in the Manx but appearing in several varieties.

EUMELANIN: Black or brown pigmentation.

EXPERIMENTAL: Matings that are made to produce a new variety or strain.

FANCIER: One interested in cats; a cat fancy is an association of those interested in cats or in a particular breed of cat.

FIE: Feline infectious enteritis (also panleukopenia).

FOREIGN: In British terminology the term indicates a distinct body type: long, narrow and svelte, with a narrow head, as in the Siamese.

FRILL: The ruff, the hair around the head that forms a frame to the face.

FUR BALL: Hair ball (which see).

GAIT: The cat's manner of walking.

GCCF: Governing Council of the Cat Fancy.

GENE: The unit that carries hereditary characteristics.

GESTATION: Pregnancy; in cats it lasts about nine weeks.

GHOST MARKINGS: Faint tabby markings on kittens, which then disappear.

GLOVES: White feet, as in the Birman.

GUARD HAIR: The long stiff outer hair protecting the underfur.

HAIR BALL: Same as fur ball, a sausagelike accumulation of hair in the cat's stomach and intestines; it may cause an obstruction that needs surgical remedy.

HAW: The third eyelid, known as the nictitating membrane.

HEAT: The female's season; the oestrum.

HOT: A descriptive term for a colour; it may mean that a colour is excessive—too red, for example.

HYBRID: A cross between two breeds.

ICF: Independent Cat Federation (American)

IN-BREEDING: The breeding of cats closely related to each other.

INFERTILE: Incapable of breeding.

INOCULATION: Vaccination, usually meant against feline infectious enteritis.

JAW PINCH: The pinched effect resulting from an indentation in the jaw.

JOWLS: Overly developed cheeks, usually seen in the older cat.

KINK: A bend in the tail, the result of a malformation.

KITTEN: A cat up to nine months old.

LACTATION: Secretion of milk in the female.

LEVEL BITE: An even bite.

LINE-BREEDING: Mating of close members of the family, as mother and son, or grandfather and daughter, and so on, to produce a particular feature.

LITTER: The kittens that result from a particular pregnancy.

MACKEREL: A pattern of tabby markings that recalls the mackerel.

MALOCCLUSION: Impaired closing of the upper and lower teeth.

MARBLED: British term to indicate the usual pattern of tabby markings.

MASK: The contrast of colours in a cat's face. See SIAMESE.

MONGREL: A cat of mixed background; also called a house cat or a mixed breed.

MONORCHIDISM: A condition in which a male cat is missing one testicle in the scrotum; with both missing, the condition is cryptorchidism.

MUTATION: A genetic term indicating a variation in structure.

MUZZLE: The jaw and nose of the cat.

NCFA: National Cat Fanciers Association (American).

NEUTER: To castrate the male cat or spay the female; also, alter.

NICTITATING MEMBRANE: The haw, or third eyelid.

NOSE LEATHER: The nose skin.

ODD-EYED: A condition in which one eye is orange and the other blue.

ORIENTAL: The shape of the eye in the so-called foreign breeds.

OUTCROSS-BREEDING: The breeding of one kind of cat with another type; the cats are unrelated.

OUT OF COAT: The coat during moulting.

PADS: The leather-like cushions on the soles of the paws.

PARASITE: An organism that lives on the cat.

PARTICOLOUR: A coat with two distinct colours, as in the bicoloured breeds.

PARTURITION: The act of giving birth.

PATCHING: Distinct patches of colouring.

PDSA: People's Dispensary for Sick Animals.

PEDIGREE: The background of the cat, its genealogical table.

PENCILLING: Light markings on the faces of Tabbies.

PERSIANS: Long-hairs.

PHENOTYPE: A set of observable, distinct characteristics.

POINTS: The dark colouring on the extremities of a cat, the head, legs, ears and tail; especially noticeable in the Siamese.

POLYDACTYL: A condition in which the cat has six or more toes on the front feet, five or more on the back.

PREMIER: A champion neutered cat.

PRICKED: Stand-up ears.

PURE-BRED: A cat produced from a sire and dam of the same variety.

QUARANTINE: A period of isolation required by some countries; in the British Isles, for six months.

QUEEN: A female cat used for breeding; a brood queen is a female used exclusively for breeding.

RECESSIVE: A feature passed on in breeding, which may not appear in the first generation.

RECOGNITION: Approval by a governing body of a new variety or breed.

REGISTRATION: Recording of a cat's name, date of birth and pedigree with an appropriate registering body.

RINGS: Bands of colour running in rings down the legs or tail.

RSPCA: Royal Society for Prevention of Cruelty to Animals.

RUFF: Frill, the hair around the neck.

RUMPY: The rear end of the Manx, where the tail would normally be.

SADDLE: Part of the cat's back, resembling a saddle in shape.

SCHEDULE: Details of classes, judges and rules in a cat show.

SCISSOR BITE: A condition that results from the upper teeth overlapping the lower.

SELF: The same colour all over the cat, a solid colour.

SI-REX: The Cornish or Devon Rex with Siamese points (light and dark).

SIRE: The male parent.

SPAYING: The neutering of a female.

SPRAYING: The male cat's urinating, leaving a pungent odour.

SQUINT: A condition in which the eyes look toward the nose; a disqualification now for Siamese.

STANDARD OF POINTS: The characteristics of the variety by which a cat is judged at a show.

STOP: The break between the nose and skull.

STRIATIONS: Stripes.

STRIPES: Markings, as in Tabbies.

STUD: Male cat used for breeding.

STUD BOOK: The record of breeding.

STUMPY: Refers to the tail, usually of the Manx.

TABBY: Reference to the markings of a cat, often stripes, or to the striped cat itself.

TAPERED: A condition of a long slim tail.

THUMB MARK: Markings on the ears of the Tabby-point Siamese.

TICKING: The bands of colour seen on the hair of the Abyssinian.

TIPPING: Colour contrasts at the hair ends.

TRICOLOUR: A coat with three distinct colours.

TYPE: (1) the characteristics of a particular breed; (2) a way of describing the bone structure of a breed—the short nose of the long-hair, for example.

UCF: United Cat Fanciers (American).

UNDERCOAT: The soft hair lying under the outer hair of cats with a double coat.

UNDERSHOT JAW: A condition in which the lower jaw protrudes farther than the upper.

VACCINATION: Inoculation.

WEDGE-SHAPED: The head shape required by the standard for some breeds, as in the Siamese.

WHIP TAIL: A long tapering tail.

WITHERS: The highest point in the shoulders, where the neck joins the body.

WRINKLE: Loose fold of skin on the face of some varieties.

ZOONOSES: Diseases or conditions that can affect both human and cats, such as ringworm and tuberculosis.

Index